BEFORE AUGUSTUS

The Collapse of the Roman Republic

NATALE BARCA

CASEMATE

Philadelphia & Oxford

Published in the United States of America and Great Britain in 2023 by
CASEMATE PUBLISHERS
1950 Lawrence Road, Havertown, PA 19083, USA
and
The Old Music Hall, 106–108 Cowley Road, Oxford OX4 1JE, UK

Hardback Edition: ISBN 978-1-63624-232-3
Digital Edition: ISBN 978-1-63624-233-0

A CIP record for this book is available from the British Library

Printed and bound in the United Kingdom by CPI Group (UK) Ltd, Croydon, CR0 4YY

Typeset in India by Lapiz Digital Services, Chennai.

For a complete list of Casemate titles, please contact:

CASEMATE PUBLISHERS (US)
Telephone (610) 853-9131
Fax (610) 853-9146
Email: casemate@casematepublishers.com
www.casematepublishers.com

CASEMATE PUBLISHERS (UK)
Telephone (0)1226 734350
Email: casemate-uk@casematepublishers.co.uk
www.casematepublishers.co.uk

Front cover: Statue of Augustus from Prima Porta, Vatican Museum, Rome. (Wikimedia Commons)

Contents

Abbreviations

Amm. Marc.	Ammianus Marcellinus, *Rerum Gestarum*
App. *B. Civ*	Appian, *Civil War*
App. *BC*	Appian, *Gallic History (Bella Civilia Gall.)*
Apul. *Apol.*	Apuleius, *Apologia*
Asc. *Mil.*	Asconius, *In defense of Milo*
Avien. *Ora Marit*	Avienus, *Ora Maritima*
Caes. *BAl.*	Caesar, *Alexandrian War*
Caes. *BAfr*	Caesar, *African War*
Dio Cass.	Dio Cassius, *Roman History*
Cic. *Amiciis*	Cicero, *Letters to his Friends*
Cic. *Att.*	Cicero, *Letters to Atticus*
Cic. *Balb.*	Cicero, *In defense of Balbus*
Cic. *Brut.*	Cicero, *Brutus*
Cic. *Cael.*	Cicero, *In defense of Caelius*
Cic. *Cael.*	Cicero, *In defense of Caelio*
Cic. *Deiot.*	Cicero, *For King Deiotarius*
Cic. *Div.*	Cicero, *Concerning Divination*
Cic. *Dom.*	Cicero, *On his House*
Cic. *Har. resp.*	Cicero, *On the Responses of the Haruspices*
Cic. *Leg.*	Cicero, *On the law*
Cic. *Nat. D.*	Cicero, *On the Nature of the Gods*
Cic. *Fam.*	Cicero, *Letters to Relatives*
Cic. *Mil.*	Cicero, *In defense of Milo*
Cic. *Phil.*	Cicero, *Philippics*
Cic. *Pis.*	Cicero, *Against Piso*
Cic. *QFr.*	Cicero, *Letters to his brother Quintus*
Cic. *Red. sen.*	Cicero, *In the Senate after his Return*
Cic. *Rep.*	Cicero, *On the Commonwealth*
Cic. *Sest.*	Cicero, *In defense of Sestius*
Cornutus	Lucius Annaeus Cornutus, *Commentary on Persius*
Diod. Sic.	Diodorus Siculus, *Library of History*
Eutr.	Eutropius, *Abridgment of Roman History*
Flor.	Florus, *Epitome of Roman History*

Gem.	Geminus of Rhodes, *Introduction to the Phenomena*
Hdt.	Herodotus, *Histories*
Hes. *Theog.*	Hesiod, *Theogony*
Hor.	Horace, *Odes and Epodes*
Joseph	Josephus, *Antiquities of Jews*
Liv. *Per.*	Livy, *The Periochae*
Luc.	Lucan, *Pharsalia*
Mela	Pomponius Mela, *De situ orbis*
Mir. ausc.	*De mirabilibus auscultationibus* (author unknown)
Oros.	Orosius, *Histories against the Pagans*
Ov. *Tr.*	Ovid, *Tristia*
Pind. Ol.	*Pindar, Olympian*
Plin.	Pliny the Elder, *Natural History*
Plut. *Ant.*	Plutarch, *Life of Mark Antony*
Plut. *Caes.*	Plutarch, *Life of Caesar*
Plut. *Cat. Min.*	Plutarch, *Life of Cato the Younger*
Plut. *Cic.*	Plutarch, *Life of Cicero*
Plut. *Crass.*	Plutarch, *Life of Crassus*
Plut. *Luc.*	Plutarch, *Life of Lucullus*
Plut. *Pomp.*	Plutarch, *Life of Pompey*
Plut. *Sert.*	Plutarch, *Life of Sertorius*
Pollio	Caius Asinius Pollio, *Histories*
Polyb.	Polybius, *Histories*
Sall.	Sallust, *Bellum Catilinae*
Schol. Bob.	*Scholia Bobiensia*
Sen.	Seneca the Elder, *Controversiae*
Sen. Q. Nat.	Seneca, *Quaestiones naturales*
Stat. *Silv.*	Statius, *Silvae*
Str.	Strabo, *Geography*
Suet. *Iul.*	Suetonius, *Life of Divus Julius*
Suet. *Aug.*	Suetonius, *Life of Augustus*
Suet. *Gram et Rhet.*	Suetonius, *On Famous Men: Grammarians, Rhetoricians*
Suet. Terence	Suetonius, *Life of Terence*
Tac. *Agr.*	Tacitus, *On the life and character of Julius Agricola*
Tac. *Ann.*	Tacitus, *Annals*
Tac. *Germ.*	Tacitus, *Germania*
Val. *Max.*	Valerius Maximus, *Memorable Deeds and Sayings*
Vell. *Pat.*	Velleius Paterculus, *History of Rome*

Glossary

aedile	an elected office of the Roman Republic, based in Rome, responsible for maintenance of public buildings, regulation of public festivals, protection of public peace and originally also for the supply of corn to the city. There were two pairs of aediles, plebeian *aediles* and *curule aediles*, the latter named owing to the fact that they sat on a folding chair called "sella curulis"
aerarium	the public treasury
ager publicus	public land, acquired by Rome by conquest from her enemies or confiscation from rebellious allies
alae	wings
aquilifer	standard-bearer
augurium	augury, divination, prediction, omen, portent
augustus	majestic, venerable, "he who is revered"
bagarre	noisy disturbance or brawl
cavea	cavity or hollow place (the steps for spectators in the theaters and amphitheaters of classical antiquity)
cella	inner chamber
censor	a magistrate in ancient Rome responsible for maintaining the census, supervising public morality, and overseeing certain aspects of the government's finances
civitas libera et immunis	free city, one which doesn't have to pay tax
cognomen	an ancient Roman's third name, or nickname, which later became the family name
coloniae	highest rank of Roman chartered towns. A *colonia*'s inhabitants were Roman citizens who governed themselves

comitia centuriata	"assembly of the people on arms." It met outside the city (in Campus Martius) and decided on war and peace, passed laws, elected consuls, praetors, and censors, and considered appeals of capital convictions. Unlike the older patrician Comitia Curiata, it included plebeians as well as patricians, assigned to classes and *centuriae* (centuries, or groups of 100) by wealth and the equipment they could provide for military duty
comitia tributa	assembly of the people which brought together the tribes, intended as electoral districts; it accordingly met within the city inside the *pomerium* and elected magistrates (plebeian tribunes, plebeian *aediles*, and *quaestors*) who did not exercise *imperium*
Comitium	the original open-air public meeting space of ancient Rome, which had major religious and prophetic significance. The name comes from the Latin word for "assembly"
consilium	according to the case used, either council of advisors or legion staff
consul	consuls, elected in pairs, served jointly for a one-year term, and each had the power to veto the decision of the other. In times of peace, their role was as magistrate, arbitrator, and law promoter. They also commanded the army. The consulship was the second-highest level of the sequential order of public offices held by aspiring politicians in ancient Rome after that of the censor
consul sine collega	consul without a colleague
contio	(plural *contiones,* from the Latin word *convention,* meaning "gathering") public assembly at which magistrates informed the Roman citizens on various topics related to politics
coup d'état	French for "stroke of state." A seizure and removal of a government and its powers; typically, an illegal seizure of power by a constitutional body. It is different from the illegal seizure of power by political faction, politician, cult, rebel group, military, which is sedition
crimen ambitus	crime of political corruption using various means to try to crush ambition, including electoral bribery
crimen vis	crime using force or violence
Curia	primitive subdivision of the Roman people, previous to the Servian reforms
Curia Hostilia	senate house

cura annonae	import and distribution of grain to the residents of Rome
decurion	a member of the council of the Roman colonies and of the "municipia"
dignitas	unique, intangible, and culturally subjective social concept in the ancient Roman mindset; the word does not have a direct translation in English. Some interpretations include "dignity," a derivation from *dignitas*, as well as "prestige," "charisma" and "power from personal respect"
Divus Julius	Divine Julius
deliciae	delight
duumviri	magistracy of two men
ephebe	youth (from 17) who is about to enter full citizenship, especially one undergoing military training
eques	member of a Roman order between the senatorial order and the ordinary citizen. (Plural: *equites*)
eteria	association in which members were bound by an oath, the original Greek word is translated as "pure air"
exequies	funeral rites
fasces	bound bundle of wooden rods, sometimes including an axe, a symbol from Etruscan civilization passed on to ancient Rome, where it symbolized a magistrate's power and jurisdiction
fasces lictoriae	("bundles of the lictors") They symbolised power of life and death (*imperium*) in ancient Rome, beginning with the early Roman kingdom and continuing through the republican and imperial periods. In this case, the Latin word *imperium* has a meaning different than the military command
flamen dialis	high priest of Jupiter
frumentationes	those eligible for the free grain dole
Gallaecia	northwestern part of the Iberian Peninsula, north of the River Douro
Graecostasis	platform in the *Comitium* near the Roman Forum, located to the west of the Tribune of the Orators *(Rostra)*. The name refers to the Greek ambassadors for whom the platform was originally built after the Roman Republic conquered Greece
gladius	short sword

haruspices	person trained to undertake a form of divination involving the inspection of entrails
Hispania Ulterior	the westernmost Roman province situated in the southwest of the Iberian Peninsula; the Romans used the name Hispania for the entirety of what is now mainland Spain and Portugal
homo novus	"new man," the term in ancient Rome for a man who was the first in his family to serve in the Roman Senate (Plural: *homines novi*)
hortus	enclosed garden
imagines (singular *imago*)	portrait, bust
imperator	commander acclaimed as such by the army after winning a decisive battle. This was an essential condition for being authorized by the Senate to celebrate the triumph
imperium	depending upon the case used, either the power to command an army, or the power of life and death
impudicitia	sexual impurity (often of passive homosexuality); immodesty, lewdness
inauguratio	inauguration, the act of officially putting someone into an important position, or the ceremony at which this is done
interrex	provisional ruler
Italia propria	the Italian peninsula that lies south of the imaginary line that connects the mouth of the Magra in Tuscany to the mouth of the Rubicon in Romagna.
ius agendi cum patribus et cum populo	the right to summon the people to the centuriate assembly and to call the Senate
jeunesse dorée	wealthy, stylish, sophisticated young people
lictors	civil servant attending a magistrate who held imperium
magister equitum	master of the cavalry
magnus	the great
maniple	a tactical unit of the Roman legion, represented by two centuries
mos maiorum	"way of the ancestors," the unwritten code from which the ancient Romans derived their social norms
municipia	community incorporated into the Roman state
neōteroi	the "newer" poets, known for breaking away from traditional Latin poetry to write in Greek or the Greek style

oppidum	large, fortified settlement
Optimates	literally meaning "good men," the traditionalist majority in the Senate. Their political opponents were known as the Populares
pantomimus	"imitator of everything," a mime performer in a pantomime
parentes	kindred, relatives
pars	a part of the Roman people (see **Optimates**, **Populares**)
pater patriae	father of the Fatherland
patres	fathers, senators
patricians	the upper class, usually wealthy, as opposed to the plebs. Both classes were hereditary
plebeians (plebs)	the commoners, free Roman citizens who were not patricians, as determined by the census. They range from well-to-do tradesmen (the enriched plebeians) to the very poor
polis	Greek city-state or society, especially when characterized by a sense of community
pomerium	line demarcating an augurally constituted city and considered a sacred boundary
pontifex	"bridge builder," plural **Pontifices**, a member of a council of priests
pontifex maximus	chief high priest of the College of Pontiffs/head of the principal college of priests
porticus	porch, often colonnaded
Populares	Roman political leaders who were on the side of "the people" as indicated by their name. The ultraconservative leaders, in the majority in the Senate, were known as the Optimates
praefectus fabrum	officer in charge of the military camps
praetor	civic magistrate who served under a consul. Among other powers, praetors commanded military forces and acted as judges
praetor pellegrinus	civic magistrate who heard cases between Roman citizens and foreigners, and between foreigners
praetor urbanus	praetor based in the city who, among other things, heard cases between Roman citizens
primus pilus	centurion commander of the first century or cohorts of a legion
princeps	first in time or order

princeps senatus	first member par excellence of the Senate of Rome and a sort of "spokesperson" and "general secretary" of this institution
proconsul	governor or military commander of a province, with the powers of a consul
proscriptus	outlaw, proscribed person, one under a ban
propraetor	magistrate, a former praetor in charge of a province. Like a proconsul, the propraetor was someone who acted as if (pro) he were an official magistrate. He had all the powers of a praetor, but was in fact a former praetor whose term in office was prolonged
publicans	public contractors who erected or maintained public buildings, they supplied armies overseas, or collected sums due to the state such as taxes, tithes and customs
quaestor	public official in ancient Rome. In the Roman Republic, quaestors were elected officials who supervised the state treasury and conducted audits
quaestio perpetua de repetundis	a court that specifically tries defendants of so-called "de repetundis" crimes (bribery, extortion, embezzlement, etc)
quaestio perpetua de maiestate	court for contempt of majesty, intended as the authority and dignity of the State
quindecimviri	members of a college with priestly duties, any member of a group of fifteen officials
res publica	loosely meaning "public affair," it is the root of the word "republic." In ancient Rome, it was the legal system that applied to all Roman citizens, securing their rights and determining their responsibilities, and the form of government of the Roman state, this being the unusual mixture of the monarchy (consuls), oligarchy (Senate), and democracy (assemblies of the people)
rex	king
rex sacrorum	"king of the sacred things", a senatorial priesthood reserved de facto for patricians, who, during the *res publica*, carried out the same functions that had been the prerogative of the kings during the period of the monarchy
senatus consultum	decree of the senate
senatus consultum ultimum	special decree of the Senate of Rome which presupposed a state of national emergency

strategos	military general, frequently functioning as a state officer with wider functions in the Greek states
supplicatio	brief period of public prayer
tetrarch	the most senior political appointment of one of four divisions of a country or province
thermae	facilities for bathing
transitio ad plebem	to transfer oneself from the patrician to the plebeian order
tribune of the plebs	first office of the Roman state to become open to the plebeians, it was, throughout the history of the Republic, the most important check on the power of the Senate and magistrates
tribunicia potestas	(tribunician power) rights granted to Rome's tribune of the plebs—including sacrosanctity, that is, personal inviolability while in office
triplex acies	triple array
triumphator	one celebrating a triumph
triumvirate	a coalition of three men, *triumvirs*, holding power
triumvir monetalis	moneyer during the Roman Republic and the Empire, who oversaw the minting of coins
valla	stockades
vallum	rampart
villa otium	suburban villa often used for study and writing
vulnus	injury

Preface

This book focuses on the political and military history of Rome in the last decades of the Republican Period, in particular from 60 to 27 BC. It sets the characters in the complex social and political system of the time; gives a thorough account of the great historical events; offers detailed portraits of key figures, whether famous or less well-known, and analyses of epic battles. It pays attention not only to the leading and supporting actors of the political process but also to minor characters. Individuals and their relationships with power are placed at the center of the plot in the belief that history is not just made up of great individuals; in fact, there is a close, indissoluble bond between individual persons and the society of which they are a part, which they influence and sometimes mutually define. There is therefore an emphasis on the characters' relationships with family and friends to highlight the ties and frequently competitive interactions between individuals, families, and clans, on which the political process depended. The book is also the result of an effort to decolonize the argument and to view behaviors through the lens of the mentality of the time.

The narrative contained in it forms a continuum, chronologically ordered. It does not aim to be exhaustive, but to provide a broad and evolutionary picture. I refer to what is deducible from archaeological evidence, reported in primary sources, or deducible from the accounts of ancient historians, in which these statements and their connections find their place in their consequentiality.

A characterizing element of this book is the wide use of the "historical present" that is made to represent events and construct the text. The historical present is a verbal form that is used to refer to events that belong to the past yet are presented as contemporary or close to the moment of enunciation, thus obtaining the effect of a perspective approach and an actualization of the events being narrated.

All the dates given in the following pages are BC, "Before Christ," unless otherwise indicated. The names of people mentioned use the forms of their commonly accepted renderings of their Latin or Greek correspondents. Places are written using their current names, or they are written with their ancient name and then, if needs be, with their contemporary name—this is the case, for example, with Dyrrachium in Epirus, the ancient Greek city of Epidamnos, now called Durrës and found in Albania. The literature on the historical period covered in this book is endless. In the "Further

Reading" section, a selection of publications from the last 50 years (1971–2021) is provided, limited to the major actors, supporting cast and extras whose events are discussed in the book and to other characters mentioned in the text.

I would like to thank Casemate Publishers for publishing *Before Augustus*, in particular Ruth Sheppard for the initial vote of confidence and giving her full support, as well as the staff for being supportive in the making of this volume. I am indebted to Anthony Wright for the translation, editing, and proofreading of the text. Grateful thanks go to Rodolfo and Laura Ruocco for their encouragement and cooperation in providing images.

CHAPTER I

Caesar

Family Origins

A clan is a group of families with a common ancestor. In the cast of the *gens Iulia*, the ancestor is Iulus, son of Aeneas, founder of Alba Longa and of the dynasty of Alban kings; family members include Romulus, in turn founder and first king of Rome. Therefore, the Iulii are a clan as illustrious, noble, and ancient as few others can claim to be in Rome, one of those who constitute the *crème de la crème* of Roman society, all patricians, and all descending from the "100 original clans", the first inhabitants of the city founded by Romulus. There are at least five families that make up the *gens Iulia:* Caesar, Iullus, Mento, Libo, and Strabo. The most prominent is the first, and it is this one that we will henceforth be dealing with. Firstly, it must be said that the *cognomen* Caesar should be pronounced "Kaesar." This family is so ancient that its origins are lost in the mists of myth. It trumpets that it descends from the goddess Venus, because Aeneas was the son of Aphrodite, the Greek goddess of love, later assimilated into the Roman pantheon. Over the years, the family has held more religious posts than civic or military ones, the most prestigious of which is the *rex sacrorum*, the priest who, during the *res publica*, carries out the same functions that had been the prerogative of the kings during the period of the monarchy.[1] Before 60 BC, 29 of the Iulii had held the consulship; some of them were members of the Caesar family. We don't know how many exactly, only that a Caesar was consul in 267, another in 157, and a another in 91. We also know that three other Caesars came close to the consulship in their political career: one was praetor in 208, one in 123, and the third in 92. The latter—Caius Julius Caesar the Elder, the father of the more famous Julius Caesar—was also the governor of the Roman province of Asia (either in 91, or in the early 80s). He died suddenly in 85 from a heart attack that struck him down while he was lacing his sandals. He was the brother of Sextus, consul in 91, and had two sisters: Julia Major, who had married Caius Marius, and

---

1   The *rex sacrorum* was probably the highest-ranking priest in the religious hierarchy of the Republic, superordinate to the *pontifex maximus* and the *flamines*

Julia Minor, who was married to Lucius Cornelius Sulla. It is important to highlight these family ties, starting with the bond with Marius.

Caius Marius (157–86) was among the most famous and discussed politicians and military commanders of his era, but he was also a controversial character due to the two sides of his strong-willed personality and his actions both for and against Rome. He was consul seven times (an unmatched feat), celebrated two triumphs (for having won as many wars: the Cimbrian War and the Jugurthine War), reformed the draft and the army, and was hailed by the Senate and the people as the Savior of the Fatherland and the Third Founder of Rome (the first two founders being Romulus and Marcus Furius Camillus[2]). For a quarter of a century, he was one of the major figures of public life in Rome and, for no short period of time, he was First Man in Rome. Even when he was no longer a magistrate, he maintained his ability to influence legislative function, manipulating the tribunes of the plebs aligned to the Populares, a political faction. He continued to do sountil his sixth consulship (100), when one of his protégés, Lucius Appuleius Saturninus, launched a seditious policy that was to cost him his life and compromise Marius politically. Marius only re-emerged from the shadow of his political eclipse in the years from 88 to 86. He returned to public life and was a major player on the political and military scene during the 90s, when his personal conflict with Lucius Cornelius Sulla (139–78)—himself twice a consul (88, 80), winner of the First Mithridatic War (89/88–85), *imperator*, triumphator, and dictator—degenerated into civil war. During that conflict, Marius took Rome after a siege and unleashed terror there before becoming consul for the seventh time (end of 87). He died of illness shortly after, in his bed.

Caius Julius Caesar the Elder married Aurelia Cotta, daughter and granddaughter of consuls, an intelligent, even-tempered woman gifted with great practicality and an independent character. Famous for her beauty, she was universally respected and admired. The couple had three children: one son, Caius, born in 101 or 100, and two daughters, both named Julia, like their aunts (all the women of the *gens Iulia* are called Julia).

The male child born of the marriage of Caius Julius Caesar the Elder and Aurelia Cotta was destined to become very famous as the conqueror of Gaul, five-time consul (59, 48, 46, 45, 44), triumphator, and dictator for life (49–44). From now on, in short, we will call him Julius Caesar, or more simply Caesar.

---

2   According to the legend of the origins of Rome, Romulus, a nephew of Numitor, king of the Latin city of Alba Longa, founded Rome in 753 BC together with Titus Tatius, king of the Sabins, a people different than the Latins, but a neighbor of them. He divided the power with Tatius until the death of the latter. After that, he ruled as the sole king. Remus would be killed by his brother Romulus after the foundation of Rome, but somebody reports this story differently. Marcus Furius Camillus was a military commander and was a dictator for five times. After having resigned from his fourth dictatorship, he did not hesitate to come to the aid of his fellow citizens when, in 390/386, Rome was taken, sacked and forced to pay a ransom by a horde of Gauls led by Brennus. He defeated the Gauls in battle and celebrated the triumph

A Man Who Doesn't Go Unnoticed

In 60, Julius Caesar is a tall 40-year-old, rather thin and wiry but well-proportioned, with sharp, dark eyes and a pale complexion.[3] He has maintained the athletic physique he developed as a boy through physical exercise and sport, and training in wrestling and combat. As a boy he wore his hair short and neatly combed, with locks that fell low over his forehead. Now he tries to cover up his baldness by combing the hair on the sides and the front of his head toward the top. He is in excellent health,[4] takes care of his hygiene and personal appearance, shaves his beard, plucks his eyebrows, keeps his nails well-trimmed, and makes sure his breath isn't unpleasant. Some people make fun of him for this, but he doesn't care.

Caesar dresses in a traditional way, but with elegance and a touch of originality. He is keen on personally choosing the fabric of his clothes. He wears a bordered toga and secures it with a belt, which holds it quite loosely. He makes sure that it is spotless and is always careful to ensure that the folds fall straight. He wears *calcei* (shoe-boots) and sandals of an appropriate size. He is a handsome and dashing man, partly a result of having always played sports (fencing, horse riding, swimming), and he can still display his athletic skills now. He has always been the subject of women's desires, which he reciprocates with gallantry and love. The list of his amorous conquests is long and starts with Servilia Caepio, a descendant of a noble house (founded by Caius Servilius Structus Ahala, consul in 478). Servilia is the wife of Marcus Junius Brutus, a patrician and the descendant of a consul of the same name of 509, one of the founders of the *res publica*. In 85, she gave birth to a son: Marcus. It is rumored that this child isn't the son of Marcus Junius Brutus, but of Caesar. The rumor is not particularly convincing.

Caesar has been educated like all young offspring of the great Roman families, that is, by one or more tutors of good standing, who taught their students in their own homes. One of his grammar teachers was Marcus Antonius Gnipho. Among other things, Caesar studied Latin language and literature, as well as Greek language and literature. To hone his philosophy, oratory, and rhetoric, he went on a study trip to Athens and Rhodes, where he attended lessons given by Apollodorus of Tarsus and Apollonius Molon (Molo of Rhodes). He thus became perfectly bilingual (Latin and Greek, in the form of the Ionic dialect). As for philosophy, he was instinctively inclined to stoicism, the philosophical and spiritual current of a rational and pantheistic imprint, which was founded by Zeno of Citium (336/335–263). It took its name from the *Stoa Poikile* ("Painted Porch"), where Zeno used to present and discuss his ideas with his followers in the Athenian Agora. Stoicism was spread

---

3   Suet., *Iul.*, 45.

4   In 60, the symptoms of the illness (epilepsy?) that Caesar suffered from during the last years of his life had not yet manifested themselves.

in Rome by Caius Blossius of Cumae, who was the tutor, advisor, and friend of Tiberius Sempronius Gracchus, tribune of the plebs in 133.

From an early age, Caesar was drawn toward politics and war, he loved to read, and he familiarized himself with a number of literary works that would become the basis of his military training: *De re militari* by Marcus Porcius Cato the Censor; *On the Cavalry Commander* by Xenophon; the memoirs of Lucius Cornelius Sulla; *De consulatu et de rebus gestis suis* by Lucius Papirius Paetus, a Latin author who was a contemporary of Caesar and a friend of the orator Marcus Tullius Cicero; and various other works by Hellenistic authors, including some technical treatises on the art of besieging and conquering cities and fortifications. Since then, his idol has always been Alexander the Great (356–323), king of Macedon and ruler of Asia and Egypt.

Caesar is very skilled in the art of knowing how to speak in public and shows a particular inclination for writing. He has published a number of orations, the short poem *Laudes Herculis*, and a collection of maxims.[5]

He is captivated by the memories of antiquity, philosophy, and religion in general, but traditional Roman religion in particular. He is a connoisseur of works of art, especially antiques. He has a passion for pearls and gems, primarily because they come from distant lands such as the East. He likes to collect precious cut gems—loose rather than set in rings, for their artistic value—as well as paintings and other works of art. His collection is comparable to other very famous ones such as that of Marcus Aemilius Scaurus—son of the consul of 115 and *princeps senatus*, who died in about 89 and shared his son's name—and that of Cnaeus Pompeius Magnus, which is of great value. It originated in the looting of the treasure of Mithridates VI, king of Pontus, and was dedicated on the Capitoline hill.

Caesar is a vain man, but within limits. He likes to parade around mounted on a fine horse. He gives private banquets that might be talked about throughout the city for their excellent food, tastefully decorated rooms, their "adornments," their dancers, musicians, and actors, and their fine tableware. (Perhaps this praise would be in whispers if a sumptuary law has been broken[6]). However, he is also keen to promote an image of himself as a man with *dignitas*, understood as the expression of a traditional personal commitment to the public good and a measured lifestyle that reflects both his aristocratic heritage and his instinctive propensity for stoicism.

His family did not swim in gold; in fact, in an effort to get the family's budget back in order, his father felt inclined to give the hand of Julia Minor in marriage to

5   Unfortunately, Caesar's early works haven't survived and only their titles are known. We do know, however, that Octavian, after 28 BC—the year he established the large bilingual library on the Palatine—forbade the chief librarian, Pompeius Macer, from circulating them (Suetonius, *Life of Caesar*, 56). The reason for this prohibition should not be sought in the fact that, probably, they were not masterpieces, but rather in the field of politics or morality.

6   The sumptuary laws (*sumptuariae leges*) were intended to limit waste due to excesses of luxury.

Caius Marius, a very rich man. However, Caesar has never lacked funds, especially after he took on the praetorship.

Under the dictatorship of Sulla (82–79), he found himself at loggerheads with the dictator for refusing to divorce his wife Cornelia, daughter of the Marian Lucius Cornelius Cinna, who had been consul from 87–84 and had been declared a public enemy. Because of this Caesar became a fugitive, but was eventually pardoned by Sulla, albeit with much hesitation, following the intercession of Caesar's mother Aurelia, the Vestal Virgins, and other individuals who were very close to the dictator. However, Caesar needed a "change of scene," if only temporarily, so he began his military service in the East. As an officer in the army of Marcus Minucius Thermus, engaged in the siege of Mytilene, a town on Lesbos, he distinguished himself for his bravery and valor. For having saved the life of a Roman citizen in the final assault on the city, he was awarded the *corona civica*, one of the highest honors available in the Roman army.[7] The *corona civica* is a wreath made of oak leaves, the tree sacred to Jupiter. It gives great prestige to the one who has been awarded it, guaranteeing him a series of privileges (for example, a reserved seat in the front row for public shows and events), and greases the wheels of his career as a magistrate, having a major effect on the opinion of the electorate.[8]

Caesar, during the consulship of Cinna, was appointed to the priesthood of Jupiter (*flamen dialis*), the god of the civilized collective, tutelary deity of Rome, and guarantor of its destiny. In 63, he was elected to another highly prestigious religious office, that of *pontifex maximus*, which is conferred for life.[9]

Returning to his homeland from his military service with the reputation of a war hero, Caesar begins a career as a judicial orator and plays a key role in a number of important criminal trials. His eloquence is highly regarded by Cicero, "champion of the Forum." A judicial orator supports prosecution in the courts as a private citizen who is representing the interests of a third party or an entire community, that is, acting in place of the interested party in the exercise of their rights and authority. Caesar is naturally inclined to political oratory and cultivates this inclination with great diligence and success.

Legal Practice

In his exercise of legal advocacy, Caesar makes use of the lessons he learned from his uncle Caius Julius Caesar Strabo Vopiscus and, after the latter's death, from the works that survived him, such as the oration he gave in the trial against Titus

---

7   Suet. *Caes.* 2.2. On the capture of Mytilene: Liv. *Per.* 89.
8   It's possible that one of the privileges, still in force in Sulla's time, consisted of automatic admission to the Senate, as it had during the Second Punic War. On this idea, see A. Goldsworthy, *Caesar: Life of a Colossus* (New Haven, CT: Yale University Press, 2006), 66.
9   The *pontifex maximus* was the highest-ranking of the *pontifices*, the priests who supervised the procedures of religious rites and practices.

Albucius, held in 103. Strabo blamed Albucius for having governed the province of Sardinia and Corsica in 104 in a way that went against the law, for intentionally causing harm to the provincials, and for favoring himself or others. Strabo managed to have Albucius sentenced to exile.

Caesar is in no way inferior to the best of his colleagues. In fact, he even outdoes them. He declaims with a high, piercing voice, gesticulating in an agitated and fervent manner, but is not ungentlemanly. He constructs arguments that are sharp, rich in content, elegant, brilliant, and, in a certain way, extraordinary and magnanimous.[10] He achieves great success due to having proved that he knows how to speak in public while also being well-liked by his fellow citizens for his affability and his courtesy when greeting them and conversing with them.[11]

Legal practice is a good way to put together or reinforce political alliances, find clients, and make oneself known to potential voters. In Rome, it's an obligatory step for all those who aspire to become a politician and hold a civic magistracy. Challenging an established politician whose behavior left something to be desired might be a worthy ideal for an ambitious man trying to make a name for himself, but it also could turn out to be against one's own long-term interests. Moreover, if the lawsuit is directed against rich and powerful men, it could end up being very dangerous. Despite his verbal brilliance, and the worthiness of his argument, Caesar was to experience this in 77, after the trial against a Sullan, Cnaeus Cornelius Dolabella,[12] whom he had accused of having extorted or accepted money and/or other benefits in the exercise of his functions while he was proconsul of Macedonia[13] in Thessalonica.[14]

Cornelia, Caesar's wife, can see the risk to which her husband is exposing himself and fears she will find herself a widow, with a daughter to raise alone. The passage of time does not calm her anxiety but, on the contrary, aggravates it.

At the time of the trial against Dolabella, Caesar was 23 years old. He had accepted the proposal to represent the interests of the provincials in court because this

10   See Plut. *Caes.* 3.2–4, Suet. *Iul.* 55.1–2. Words of praise for Caesar's eloquence can also be found in Cic. *Brut.* 252, 258, and 261. Cicero also speaks very positively of Caesar Strabo: Cic. *Or.* 2.239.
11   Plut. *Caes.* 4.1–4.
12   On the trial of Dolabella: ORF, 386–387; M. C. Alexander, *Trials in the Late Roman Republic, 149 BC to 50 BC* (Toronto: University of Toronto Press, 1990), 71.
13   The Roman province of Macedonia was established after the Third Macedonian War (Revolt of Andriscus, 167) and definitively organized in 146. It is made up of the four regions into which the subjugated Kingdom of Macedon was divided, encompassing Epirus and southern Illyria as well. On the geographical extent of the lands subsumed within the province of Macedonia: C. Letta and S. Segenni, *Roma e le sue province. Dalla prima guerra punica a Diocleziano* (Roma: Carocci, 2015), 164.
14   Thessalonica (Saloniki, Greece) was the most populous city in Macedonia and the capital of the province. Located at the foot of the Kissos massif, with the Axios valley which penetrates into the Balkans behind it, it was at the center of a major road network.

allowed him, at the same time, to go up against a supporter of Sulla, to demonstrate his oratorical ability, and to promote himself. During the debate, he gives some impressive speeches and calls on a group of witnesses from Macedonia to testify. Dolabella is defended by Caius Aurelius Cotta and Quintus Hortensius Hortalus, both influential and esteemed orators. They each make every effort to give their client the best protection so that the jury's decision will not conform with justice but rather with their own overriding interests. Cotta is the primary lawyer, but it is Hortensius who plays the leading role in the trial. The presence of the crowd and the clamor of the Forum requires a vigorous, ardent speaker with efficaciously energetic actions and a resonant voice.[15] From this point of view, Hortensius has better cards to play than Cotta. Despite his brilliant performance, Caesar is beaten by the eloquence of Cotta and Hortensius.[16] As a result, Dolabella is acquitted.

Ultimately a scoundrel at heart, Dolabella takes revenge on his accuser. Caesar feels the full force of the mud-slinging machine operated by Dolabella and his friends—so much so that he needs "a change of scenery" (again), not so much because he fears the revenge of the Sullans, to whom he had made himself vulnerable by taking legal action against one of their most prominent men, but above all because the calumnies being spread about him are harming his honor. To disguise the real reason for his departure, he claims that he is going to Rhodes to attend a course on rhetoric, which would be useful for him to improve his legal activity. Cornelia, who had only recently embraced her husband after his long stay in the East, has to part from him again. All this happened in 74.

The Quaestorship

In 68, Julia Major, widow of Marius and aunt of Caesar, as well as Caesar's wife, Cornelia, pass away within a few days of each other. During the funerals, Caesar gives the eulogy and displays the *imagines* (singular *imago*, portrait busts) of Caius Marius and Caius Marius the Younger in such a way that they are visible to everyone. For the first time in Roman history, a eulogy was given for a woman who had died at a young age. And for the first time since the winter of 82/81, when Sulla had removed them from the Forum, the effigies of Marius and his son are shown in public. The gesture has at once symbolic value, political significance, and an electoral purpose (Caesar is a candidate for the quaestorship for 67). But it is also provocative because it was forbidden to refer to Marius in public; one could only do so under one's breath amongst very loyal friends. What's more, it wouldn't have been possible to predict how the crowd would react; the political climate had changed in 70, and in the wake of the reforms to the Sullan constitution undertaken by the consuls Pompey

---

15   Cic. *Brut.* 317.
16   Val. Max. 8.9.3.

and Crassus the ground was only just settling. In fact, when the busts appear, the few Sullans who are present are indignant. The bulk of the crowd, however, applaud feverishly—indeed, they praise Caesar.

It didn't take long for Caesar to capitalize on this applause. Caesar is elected to the quaestorship for 67 on a wave of popular favor. Shortly after, he is seconded to the propraetor Caius Antistius Vetus, governor of Hispania Ulterior (the westernmost Roman province, situated in the southwest of the Iberian Peninsula),[17] who was headquartered in Corduba (Córdoba), a city in Andalusia. In 206, the Romans had conquered Corduba and made it the capital of Hispania Ulterior. Afterward, Corduba took on typically Roman trappings, and the local society was Romanized.

Caesar remarries before leaving, primarily to give his young daughter Julia a new mother. This would mean she would be able to look after her in his absence and raise and educate her in a better way than he could have himself—Caesar is far from the sort of person who prioritizes staying at home with his family—but also because he is often absent from Rome for long periods and is now leaving it again. Caesar's second wife is called Pompeia, his distant cousin and the granddaughter of Sulla. Most notably, Pompeia is a descendant of Sulla. This is how Caesar mended his rift with the Sullans, sheltering himself from potential political upheaval that might occur during his upcoming absence from Rome.

As quaestor, Caesar frees the province from the financial burdens that had been imposed upon it by the previous governor, Quintus Caecilius Metellus Pius, and carries out frenetic judicial activity, gaining highly formative experience and creating a clientele for himself (something that always brings prestige and, when necessary, money and testimonies). He considers clients as a basis for and a guarantee of lasting power. In fact, his thoughts are already revolving around power, and he is champing at the bit to seize it. One incident in particular is emblematic of the ambition which he harbors. In Gades (Cádiz, Spain), he bursts into tears in front of a statue of Alexander the Great, asking the people around him "Do you think I have not just cause to weep, when I consider that Alexander at my age had conquered so many nations, and I have all this time done nothing that is memorable?"[18]

Caesar sets out to return to Rome at the end of 67, before the expiration of his mandate and the arrival of his successor, to whom he should have personally handed over the reins of his position out of institutional courtesy. Later, when justifying himself before the Senate, he says that he had dreamed about having an incestuous relationship with his mother and that a soothsayer had told him that this indicated the need to return home without delay and that it was a presage of

---

17 The Romans used the name Hispania for the entirety of what is now mainland Spain and Portugal. Therefore, it refers not only to Spain but the whole Iberian Peninsula, contrary to what the assonance of the name might suggest.

18 Plut. *Caes.* 11.5–6.

world domination.[19] In reality, Caesar has learnt that the colonies of Latin law in Gallia Transpadana (that part of northern Italy to the north of the Po) are in a state of unrest, and he wants to ride the wave of these protests.

The Aedileship, the Praetorship, and the Proprietorship

In 65, Caesar as aedile organizes memorable public games which feature hundreds of gladiators. In 62 he is praetor and in 61 rises to propraetor. In the latter capacity, he returns to Hispania Ulterior. By the end of his mandate, he will have succeeded in extending Rome's sovereignty to Gallaecia, the northwestern part of the Iberian Peninsula, north of the River Douro, inhabited by the Callaeci, a mixture of Hispanic peoples who were more or less deeply Celtized.[20]

In pursuit of glory and riches Caesar overloads the provincials with taxes, a portion of which he retains. He leads his own army of 14,000–15,000 men outside his own province and massacres the Lusitani and Vettones to rob them of their possessions. He ravages the mountains where the Lusitani live, sets fire to their homes, seizes their livestock to feed his men, and captures prisoners of war, whom he then sells as slaves. He mistreats and humiliates the survivors of his slaughter. He doesn't care whether the oppression and violence that he himself orders is justified by the circumstances or not. His objectives are to obtain as much gold and silver as possible to pay off his debts and to finance his electoral campaign for the consulship, and to fulfill the requirements that would allow him to request the celebration of a triumph (one of the statutory conditions is having killed at least 5,000 enemies in battle). Caesar is a brilliant person in many ways, but he also has a dark side, ranging from boundless ambition to a total absence of scruples (those who know him in a non-superficial way admire and fear him at the same time); in the future, he will give further evidence that he is an ethically deplorable individual—even by the not high standards of his age.

The old chieftains, lacerated and broken, prostrate themselves before Caesar, who is seated in the curule seat, wearing a breastplate and a red cloak, with two *lictors* at his sides. They implore him to have mercy on them and on their people, humbly asking that they be spared further suffering, that the attacks on them and the rounding-up of prisoners be stopped. Caesar wants, demands, then commands that the Lusitani abandon the mountains and move to new villages built on the plains in order to be better able to control them, and that hostages, all their weapons, and half of all their gold and silver be handed over to him. Only in this way would the vanquished be

19 This episode and that of Gades mentioned just above were reported after the death of Caesar, which occurred in 44. It's likely that these are legends, invented by who knows who, to feed into the myth of the murdered dictator.

20 Ancient Gallaecia corresponded to the present-day regions of Galicia, Asturias, Cantabria, and part of the provinces of León and Zamora, all in Spain, as well as to part of northern Portugal.

able to live in peace, with the additional obligation of supporting Rome in her wars with payments of money, food supplies, and the supply of support troops (*tributum*).

As for the Vettones, who were emigrating north of the River Duero, Caesar accuses them of wanting to escape the authority of Rome, their duties of alliance, and the obligation of paying the *tributum*. Therefore, he goes after them with his cavalry and catches up with them as they start to cross the river on rafts in small groups, where he attacks and exterminates them.

Caesar always wants more: more gold, more silver, and more glory, to be spent in the field of politics. This is why he moves further into Gallaecia, right up to the shores of the Gulf of Ártabro and then further east, along the coast, up to Brigantium (La Coruña). There he kills, ravages, and plunders, leaving a trail of dead behind him and carrying away bountiful spoils of war, including prisoners to be sold as slaves. At the end of the campaign, he is acclaimed as *imperator* by his soldiers.

This gesture is one of the conditions that must be satisfied to receive authorization to celebrate a triumph. It doesn't always happen spontaneously since the celebration of a triumph is the objective of all victorious military commanders and is intertwined with their political ambitions. In fact, it sometimes happens to follow a generous gift being handed to the troops. This is what happened in the year 91 with Julius Caesar's father and in 80 with Pompey. In 61, it happens again with Caesar.

CHAPTER II

Friends and Enemies

All Caesar's Men

The political game is a continuous struggle between the Optimates and Populares, that is, between the ultraconservatives and those who are, or say they are, close to the populace, the most numerous but also the most disadvantaged part of society. The Populares have taken up the baton of the Gracchi, including Caius Marius, his son, Caius Marius the Younger, and Lucius Cornelius Cinna. The contest is tough, often violent, even bloody. It requires courage and determination, as well as strength and prudence. From this there arises a need to forge friendships, understood as alliances, based on mutual trust. Caesar, from the very beginning of his political career, has woven a protective web around himself. Over time, he has managed to surround himself with many friends, whom we can divide between close friends, such as Marcus Licinius Crassus, and people who, in exchange for his gifts and favors, support him and shield him. Many of these other "friends" are former or current magistrates.

The Close Friends

Marcus Licinius Crassus was born in Rome in 115/114. He is the son of the rich and noble Publius Licinius Crassus, consul for 97, who was killed in Rome in 87, together with another of his sons, Lucius, during the days of the Marian terror, perhaps by mistake, perhaps due to a personal vendetta. He has two sons of his own: Marcus and Publius. He is a businessman, real estate speculator, and banker. No other citizen of Rome has the sort of riches that he does. His landed properties alone are estimated to be worth 200 million sesterces! Crassus pities those who cannot afford to maintain their own army, as he can, as poor.[1] He considers that his greatest success in terms of military command was having quashed Spartacus's Revolt (73–71), culminating with the crucifixion of 6,000 prisoners of war along

---

1   Plin., XXIII.134.

the Via Appia. He is a man who has everything, yet he is consumed by ambition. He longs for military glory, to emulate the deeds of Sulla, Lucullus, and Pompey in Asia, to be able to boast of having the title of conqueror, equaling Caesar and Pompey in terms of social prestige, and wishes to go down in history as an immortal hero. Consequently, he is attracted by the idea of undertaking a grand military enterprise. In particular, he wants to wrest Mesopotamia from the Parthian Empire, namely the area between the Syrian border and the city of Babylon.

Crassus is so rich that he is nicknamed "the banker of Rome" and is in the habit of supporting young people who aspire to get into politics, as long as they are particularly gifted, give guarantees to repay the loan on its maturity, and promise to return the favor if they become magistrates. He does so by funding their electoral campaigns, which means pouring out money to bribe everyone who can help candidates win elections, mobilizing his friends to support the candidate, and placing his enormous prestige in the candidate's favor. Since electoral campaigns are expensive, the loan amount is very significant, and therefore the bond that is established between Crassus and those who get into debt with him is very close.

One of the young men of ambition who has found in Crassus the friend who can help them to satisfy their ambitions is Caesar. He is heavily indebted to Crassus, both because his ambitions are unlimited and because his family is not particularly rich, and he tends to live beyond his means. Caesar squanders money and is engulfed in debt, some of which is money borrowed to pay interest on other sums he has borrowed previously. This condition, however, is common among young Roman aristocrats. They spend and spend, and they are all up to their necks in debt, which is partly because the first-born males, designated heirs of the family estate, do not have the estate for as long as their father is alive, and he does not always agree to their requests for money.

There exists a very close bond between Caesar and Crassus, which goes beyond their business relationship. Proof of this was found during Catiline's Conspiracy when Crassus was the only one to defend Caesar at a time when he was risking his life after trying to prevent the seven arrested Catilinarians from being sentenced to death. But let's not get ahead of ourselves.

Lucius Sergius Catilina (108–62) was an aristocrat who fell from grace, a shady, violent, dishonest man gifted with great charisma and consumed by a desire for revenge because, in his view, he had been unjustly prevented from becoming a consul. He managed to create a following of 12,000–20,000 men and women, mostly those who had lived through the days of Sulla and were nostalgic for Marius, both freemen and those of the colonies, who had enlisted not only from the fringes of society amongst the poor, the marginalized, and the oppressed, but also from the ranks of the ruling class who were dissatisfied, up to their necks in debt, or violently inclined. This latter group included a number of magistrates (Caius Antonius Hybrida, among others, perhaps even Caesar and Crassus). His seditious plan aimed at unleashing a social revolution that would lead to the establishment of a dictatorial regime. It involved stoking fires, inciting social unrest, murder, and bloodshed, not just in Rome but also in other parts of Italy and even in Spain and North Africa.

Cicero, a consul at the time, was one of those who was to be killed first. However, the conspiracy failed after it was unmasked and then bloodily suppressed. Many individuals betrayed their fellows, starting with a criminal hooligan by the name of Quintus Curius, who, pressured by his lover, revealed to Cicero the names of the conspirators and all the details of their plan of action in order to receive a reward, which he then didn't get. Some of Curius's revelations were confirmed by Caesar and Crassus, who offered this information voluntarily to distance themselves from suspicions of being involved in the affair. This was followed by Cicero exposing the existence of the conspiracy to the Senate, the arrest of seven conspirators caught *in flagrante delicto*. The Senate, under the watchful eye of Cicero, ordered their execution as an act of political justice, without a trial and without allowing them the right to appeal, recognized by law for every Roman citizen. Caesar attempted—without success—to spare the lives of the arrested Catilinarians, proposing that instead of being sentenced to death they serve life imprisonment, contrary to the argument of Cato and others. Following this, Caesar had to escape being ambushed by a group of senators who were waiting for him outside the Curia. Caius Scribonius Curio helped him to slip away, wrapped in a big cloak.

Catiline was arrested, but he managed to get away from Rome. The affair ended in January 62 in the Pistoia Apennines (near the modern village of Campo Tizzoro), where Catiline and 3,000 followers (those who had remained steadfast beside their leader after all those who had joined the conspiracy in the expectation of carrying out robberies or with a desire for social upheavals had deserted) met the legions of the proconsul Caius Antonius Hybrida, led by Marcus Petreius, at the Battle of Pistoia, and were exterminated. Petreius won an overwhelming victory, with a modest toll to his own forces: around 100 dead. The winners shouted with joy.

The Battle of Pistoia was the tragic end to an unsuccessful "revolution." In theory, Catiline could have won. In the event, he came up against an established power that was more determined to fight than he probably expected, with one major obstacle in particular: Cicero. Moreover, when the hope of being able to plunder or turn society on its head disappeared, he was abandoned by most of his supporters. His had been an ugly life, but it was redeemed by a good death. The fires of revolution were put out before they became an inferno. The praetors—including Quintus Tullius Cicero, brother of Marcus—prevented the flames from being rekindled, intervening across the Italian peninsula.

The Other "Friends"

Caesar's other friends include, among others, Lucius Caesetius Flavus, Lucius Cornelius Lentulus Crus, Lucius Ninnius Quadratus, Caius Herennius, Aelius Ligus, and Marcus Aemilius Scaurus. Let's focus on the latter.

Scaurus is the son of Marcus Aemilius Scaurus and Caecilia Metella Dalmatica. His father was consul in 115 and celebrated a triumph for his victories over the Carni Gauls. He was censor in 109 and *princeps senatus* from 115 until his death in 89. Marcus Aemilius Scaurus (the son) married Mucia Tertia after she had been divorced by Pompey. They had a son, also called Marcus Aemilius Scaurus. Marcus Aemilius Scaurus (the son) married Mucia Tertia after she had been divorced by Pompey and they had a son, who carried on the family names. Scaurus (the latter, son of the consul of 115) served under Pompey as military tribune in the Third Mithridatic War (73–63). He was the first governor of the province of Syria (from 63 to 61), during which time he commanded two legions. In 62 he besieged Petra, capital of the Nabataean Kingdom. In 58, as aedile, he organized lavish games during which a wooden theater with marble columns was temporarily set up.

Caesar's "friends" also include Quintus Fufius Calenus; Publius Vatinius; his maternal uncle Lucius Aurelius Cotta, consul in 65; his cousin Lucius Julius Caesar, consul in 64; his nephew Quintus Pedius; Caius Fabius; Lucius Cornelius Balbus; Caius Oppius; and Mark Antony. It is worth dwelling on some of these individuals, and in the following pages, others will be mentioned too.

Calenus was tribune of the plebs in 61. He spoke in the trial concerning the scandal of the festival of Bona Dea, which we will come to later, as a rebuttal witness.

Publius Vatinius, born in 93, was elected as tribune of the plebs for 59 following crucial support from Caesar. He is a shady figure. In 62 and 61, while he was serving as the commander of a legion in the army of the proconsul Caius Cosconius in Hispania Ulterior, he was accused of theft and embezzlement. Even before this, however, he had made a bad name for himself. In 63 he was quaestor in Puteolis (Puteoli), and one of his duties was supervising port traffic, where the grain imports from Sicily and North Africa were particularly important. Cicero, the consul at the time, was forced to issue a harsh reprimand against him. In fact, he had aroused intense protests from the townsfolk, who were accusing him of abusing his position for personal benefit to the detriment of individuals and of the community as a whole.

Pedius is the son of Marcus Pedius and Julia Major, Caesar's sister, making him Caesar's nephew. He married a Roman noblewoman called Valeria, daughter of Marcus Valerius Messalla Niger and his wife Polla, and sister of the senator Marcus Valerius Messalla Corvinus. He has a son, Quintus Pedius Publicola.

Cotta is Caesar's maternal uncle. He was praetor in 70, consul in 65, and censor in 64. As praetor, he contributed to dismantling the Sullan system of power, of which he himself had been a part as one of Sulla's closest friends. But he remained a

Sullan and an Optimate. Therefore, after being among those who had saved Caesar's life, he opposed him during the early phase of his political career. More recently, however, he has drawn closer to him. He will play an important role in the conquest of independent Gaul and thereafter.

Lucius Julius Caesar is the son of the homonymous consul of 90, and brother of Julia Antonia, the mother of Mark Antony. Therefore, he is a relative (a cousin) of Julius Caesar. He was consul in 64. In the Senate, he supported the proposed death sentence for the arrested supporters of Catiline, even though his brother-in-law Publius Cornelius Lentulus Sura was among them. Later, he was co-opted into the college of augurs.

Fabius was praetor in 58, propraetor of Asia in 57, and tribune of the plebs in 55. He will serve as a legionary commander in the Gallic Wars, reporting to Caesar, from 54 to 49.

Although Balbus and Oppius are absolutely loyal to Caesar, he never mentions them, or only does so in passing. They often serve him in silence and in the shadows. As befits informers, they are inconspicuous figures, but very alert and attentive. Balbus is Hispanic, a member of an ancient and powerful family from Gades (Cádiz in Andalusia, Spain) that claims descent from the god Baal. He was born around 100, so he's the same age as Caesar. He obtained Roman citizenship for excellent services rendered to Cnaeus Pompeius Magnus and Quintus Caecilius Metellus Celer during the Sertorian War, which ended in 72.[2] In 61, he served as chief engineer in Caesar's army (and will do so again in the future). Oppius is an *eque*. Caesar uses him for his relations with other politicians. Oppius, however, is also a friend of Cicero, who makes use of him as an intermediary in his own relations with Caesar. He is the author of various biographies, among which are those of Caesar, Publius Cornelius Scipio Africanus, and Caius Cassius Longinus. In the future, the *Bellum Hispaniense*, an account of Caesar's military campaigns in Spain, will also be attributed to him.

Antony, 23 years old (he was born in 83), is the grandson of Marcus Antonius the Orator on his father's side, one of the most lauded judicial orators of the first quarter of the I century. Antonius the Orator had been consul in 99, censor in 97, and an excellent military commander; in 102, as propraetor of Cilicia, he waged a successful campaign against piracy. He died at the hands of Caius Marius's killers during the days of the Marian terror (late 87–early 86). Antony's father, Marcus Antonius, praetor in 75, had taken on the cognomen Creticus for having fought against the pirates in 74, but his expedition had been a disaster, and he died at a young age in 71, leaving his wife and four children (Antony himself, Lucius, Caius, and Antonia) in debt. Antony's mother, Julia Antonia, is the sister of Lucius Julius Caesar and a second cousin to Caesar. Therefore Antony is a distant relation of the latter on his mother's side. Antony's widowed mother married again, this time to

---

2   Cic. *Balb.*, 56.

Publius Cornelius Lentulus Sura, who later became a follower of Catiline. Lentulus Sura was one of the Catilinarians who were arrested and executed in 63. He didn't adopt Antonius Creticus's orphans, and this resulted in their statutory demotion from senatorial rank to *eques*. Antony is a restless young man with an unruly and lascivious lifestyle. He used to prostitute himself for money and had a homosexual relationship with Caius Scribonius Curio.[3] He is a lover of luxury, a kept man, a heavy drinker, and a spendthrift. He is up to his neck in debt. Before the age of 20 (that is, before 63), he had already run up total debts of around 250 talents, equivalent to 6 million sesterces, an enormous sum. He was the friend, albeit for a short time, of Publius Claudius Pulcher, himself a youth with many excesses and a taste for the good life. He then studied rhetoric in Greece and became a skilled orator with a grandiose Asian style. On his return to Rome, he had every interest in handing himself over to a patron, and he chose to place himself at Caesar's side.

Publius Claudius Pulcher has also recently entered the "magic circle" of Caesar and Crassus. He will play a particularly important role in the political events of his time, and it is therefore worth devoting ample space to him. He will change his name to Clodius for political reasons, which is fully explained in Chapter VII, but we'll start to use it now as it is the name he is best known by.

Clodius

The members of the Pulcher family are well-known among their fellow citizens, not only because they enjoy great social prestige, have a vast following of friends and clients, and are able to get their opinions or proposals approved by the Senate, but also because they have shown that they have fierce, sometimes excessive self-confidence, an unshakable belief in their own abilities, a great desire to express themselves anytime and anywhere, and no little hubris, which makes them proud if warranted, or vain and arrogant if groundless. In addition, they are held to be heartless people. One of them is a great friend of Caesar's.

This is Publius Claudius Pulcher. In 60, he is 32 or 33 years old. He is the son of Appius Claudius Pulcher, who was praetor in 89 and 88, a supporter of Sulla in the First Civil War (83–82), consul in 79, and proconsul of Macedonia in 77, where he fought against the Thracians.[4] He has two brothers and three sisters. He is a young man who is already at the center of a great deal of attention for a series of public wrongdoings and for his alleged incestuous relationship with his sisters.

3   Cic. *Phil.*, II.44–45.
4   The identity of Clodius's mother is not certain. She could have been a Servilia Caepione or a Caecilia Metella, the sister of Metellus Nepos and the second daughter of Quintus Caecilius Metellus Balearicus. Caecilia married Appius Claudius Pulcher, consul in 79. Clodius was born in 93 or 92 as one of their six children—three boys (Appius, Gaius, and Publius) and three girls (all called Claudia).

One of the charges of misconduct leveled against him is having fomented a military revolt in the camp of his brother-in-law, Lucius Licinius Lucullus, during the Third Mithridatic War (74–63), under whom he served as a *capitularius* (recruitment officer). After the Pontic invasion of the Roman province of Asia, Lucullus went on the counter-offensive in Bithynia and Galicia, defeating Tigranes II of Armenia. But his legions didn't want to go deeper into Asia. They wanted him to retreat. Pulcher took advantage of his brother-in-law's momentary absence from the field to instigate the Valerian Legion to turn against him.[5] Lucullus was only able to regain full control over the situation in the summer of 67. In the meantime, he'd had to withstand his enemies taking the initiative against him (Mithridates VI had retaken Pontus, while Tigranes II had devastated Cappadocia).

Pulcher had complained about not having received the honors that he felt were due to him, but it's hard to believe that this was the reason underlying his conduct, or at least not the main one. Another explanation seems more plausible. This is best understood against the wider backdrop of the political games being played between Lucullus, Pompey, Crassus, and the publicans. Pompey was aspiring to take command of the war from Lucullus. Crassus was linked through common interests to the publicans who were operating in Asia Minor, who were unhappy with Lucullus because his interference in local tax affairs had reduced their profits. The publicans also happened to be very powerful. Because they were *equites* they had ties with the rest of this group, which included significant financiers. Furthermore, they had common interests with several senators who had invested capital in their companies.

Pulcher was more on Pompey's side than Lucullus's, but he also had an excellent relationship with Crassus, who was a rival of Pompey and who, despite being younger than him, had been able to demonstrate his greatness. Crassus envied Pompey. He couldn't bear that he'd been so successful on his campaigns, that he'd celebrated a triumph before even becoming a senator, or that he'd been awarded the honorific title of *magnus*, "the great," by law.[6]

Pulcher knew that he would have to face the ire of his brother-in-law and risked prosecution for insubordination, if not for high treason. He deserted and headed to Cilicia, where he knew he would be able to find refuge and protection with another of his brothers-in-law, Quintus Marcius Rex, governor of the province. Therefore, he went to the province's capital of Tarsos (Tarsus, Turkey), a city on the banks of the River Cydnus, around a dozen kilometers from the sea, an agricultural, commercial, and industrial center, and a river port open to maritime trade.

Marcius Rex was the grandson of the consul of 118 (also called Marcius Rex) and a second cousin of Caesar's. He was elected to the consulship for 68 together with Lucius Caecilius Metellus. After serving as consul, he was appointed proconsul of Cilicia for 67. He welcomed Pulcher and entrusted him with significant assignments.

---

5   Plut. *Luc.* 34.1–2.
6   Plut. *Crass.*, 7.1.

One of these assignments was to go to Byzantium to arbitrate a dispute between multiple Greek cities. In carrying it out, Pulcher undertook the task of repatriating several exiles, for which he received a handsome bribe.[7] Byzantium (Constantinopolis, Istanbul) is a city located on the banks of the Bosphorus, the narrow strait that connects the Sea of Marmara to the Black Sea. It was declared *civitas libera et immunis* by Pompey for having sided with Rome in the Third Mithridatic War (83–73). Why some of its citizens had been exiled is unclear. Perhaps it was due to a conflict within the city's ruling class. If so, perhaps the citizens in question were part of an anti-Roman faction and had played an active part in plots hatched against Pompey during the Third Mithridatic War.

At the time, ships sailing in the Aegean Sea and the Eastern Mediterranean were in danger of being boarded and plundered by pirates, an ancient scourge, one that Rome had tried many times to purge with only fleeting success. On his return journey to Tarsos, Pulcher was kidnapped by pirates for the purposes of extortion. He appealed to Ptolemy, King of Cyprus, to pay the ransom for his release. Ptolemy offered two talents (48,000 sesterces),[8] equivalent to the salary of 50 legionaries for a year, too little for Pulcher to obtain his freedom. He took offense at this and began to harbor a deep resentment toward Ptolemy. This was also because, while he was being held against his will, Pulcher "satisfied the lusts even of Cilicians and barbarians."[9] This happened between 67 and 65.

In 64 Pulcher was back in Rome before he was sent to Gallia Narbonensis, the province governed by Lucius Licinius Murena (the father of Fulvia, whom Claudius would later take for his wife, probably in 62; therefore, he is the future father-in-law of Claudius).

Murena was a candidate for the consulship for 63. He entrusted Pulcher with the task of distributing sums of money to the electorate to bribe them. On that occasion too, according to Cicero, Claudius behaved like a criminal, falsifying official documents and committing murder as well as other crimes. Moreover, it seems that he even profited by embezzling funds that had been allocated for corruption.

In 63, Pulcher agreed to take part in the conspiracy of Catiline, but he was estranged from it before it was discovered and later, he helped to uncover it.

In 62, Pulcher was at it again. On the night of 4/5 December, dressed as a woman, he inappropriately entered the house of Caesar, *pontifex maximus* (an appointment he received for life in 63) and praetor in Spain, while a rite in honor of Bona Dea was being celebrated which was reserved exclusively for women. On being discovered, he was thrown out amidst confusion and shouting. It seems that he intended to seduce Caesar's wife Pompeia and he had entered the house with the help of an appropriately

7   Cic. *QFr.*, II.7.2.
8   App. *B. Civ.*, II.23.
9   Cic. *Har. Resp.*, 42.

instructed accomplice. There was uproar as word spread. The incident caused much unrest and a scandal developed, resulting in a judicial process. Pulcher was indicted for impiety. The contentious felony arose from the offended integrity of others, caused by the fact that Pulcher had knowingly and sacrilegiously violated a very strict boundary.

The trial, however, was a scandal in itself because a large amount of money was used to bribe the jurors, and he was acquitted. During the trial, Pulcher had been put into a difficult position by the testimony of Cicero.

Opponents in the Senate

Just as he has many friends both inside and outside the Senate, Caesar also has a lot of political opponents, some of whom are also his personal enemies. The most avid of these is Marcus Porcius Cato (95–46), known as Cato the Younger, or even Cato of Utica,[10] to distinguish him from his more famous ancestor, Marcus Porcius Cato the Elder (234–149), or Cato the Censor, who was consul in 195, a great orator and polemicist, one of the major figures of Latin literature, a traditionalist in his political ideas, and consistent and rigorous by nature.

Cato the Younger (from now on: Cato) is the leader of the extreme right wing of the hyper-conservative Optimates faction in the Senate (from now on: Catonian faction). In 59, he's 36 years old and is a senator. He is a polished and persuasive orator, an intransigent custodian of the *mos maiorum*, an unshakeable opponent of illegality, and the standard bearer *par excellence* of political freedom. He is entirely inward-looking and moves directly ahead on his own path, not caring for the opinions of others and without making exceptions for anyone, not even for his friends. He took a lot from Cato the Censor. Among other things, he has a strong sense of duty toward the state and a taste for simplicity. He is absolutely upstanding and impartial. He believes that both public and private life need to go back to their origins and wants to set an example in this, living a puritanical and austere lifestyle. He is insensitive to material interests and is therefore incorruptible. Moreover, he is indifferent to death threats, which are frequently addressed to him. The poet Marcus Annaeus Lucanus (39–65 AD), in his *De Bello Civili*, also known as the *Pharsalia*, emphasizes Cato's moral integrity and his attachment to the ideal of political freedom.[11]

These qualities of Cato are expounded in his philosophical convictions. The philosophical and spiritual current he adheres to is rational and pantheistic in its

---

10 Cato is commonly known today as Cato of Utica because he died in Utica in North Africa.

11 Positive judgments on Cato of Utica's honesty, moral integrity, firmness of opinion, and courage in defense of legality were frequently made by numerous other authors, including Livy (59 BC–17 AD), Valerius Maximus (1st century BC–1st century AD), Seneca (4 BC–65 AD), Tacitus (c.55/58–c.117/120 AD), Martial (38/41–104 AD), Quintilian (35–96 AD), and Publius Papinius Statius (45–c.96 AD).

imprint, with a strong ethical orientation, and was founded by Zeno of Citium (336/335–263) and took the name Stoicism from the *Stoa Poikile* ("Painted Porch"), where Zeno used to present and discuss his ideas with his followers in the Athenian Agora. Stoicism was diffused in Rome by Caius Blossius of Cumae, who was the tutor, advisor, and friend of Tiberius Sempronius Gracchus, tribune of the plebs in 133.

As a Stoic, Cato aspires to become a wise man and subjects himself to strict discipline. It's said that he doesn't have any vices except for his frequent tendency to hit the bottle, so much so that Caesar branded him *ebrius*, "drunkard." In fact, he's drunk or at least tipsy by the afternoon every day.

In some ways, Cato is an eccentric character: if the Senate meets after lunch, he arrives barefoot wearing only a tunic. He lives outside Rome in a villa in the Alban Hills (modern Monte Porzio Catone, near Frascati in the Castelli Romani), which he used his inheritance to purchase.[12] After the death of Sulla in 86, he joined those who contested the legitimacy of Sulla's dictatorship and called for the restoration of order after the violence and chaos of the previous years. As a conscript, he took part in the repression of Spartacus's Revolt (73–71). Around 71, at the age of 24–25, he married Atilia, daughter of Caius Atilius Serranus, consul in 106 and, from 103 to 100, a bitter political opponent of the tribune of the plebs, Lucius Appuleius Saturninus. A daughter was born from the marriage of Cato and Atilia, named Porcia, who shouldn't be confused with her paternal aunt of the same name.[13]

In 67, Cato was military tribune in Macedonia, where because of his conduct, he obtained "esteem, favor, surpassing honor, and kindness from his soldiers."[14] Once his service was over, he left Macedonia to travel around the East, visiting the provinces and the friends and allies of the Roman people. First, he undertook a long journey, visiting Pergamum, Ephesus, Antioch-on-the-Orontes (then in Syria, today in Turkey), and Pessinus in Galatia.[15] While in Ephesus, he met Pompey. The latter treated him with respect, esteem, and kindness, but also felt uncomfortable in his presence, as if Pompey felt his own style of governing was under scrutiny, so much so that he was happy to let Cato leave.[16] Cato went on to tour Syria, then returned to Ephesus and embarked for Anatolia, where he met Deiotaros, *tetrarch* of Galicia. From Galicia, he traveled on to Phrygia.

---

12 Cato of Utica lived on Monte Porzio Catone until 49, when he departed to join the Pompeian resistance.
13 Porcia, daughter of Cato of Utica (herself not to be confused with the latter's sister of the same name), married Marcus Junius Brutus Caepio, son of Marcus Junius Brutus and Servilia, and future assassin of Caesar.
14 Plut. *Cat. Min.*, 9.4.
15 Plutarch only mentions Syria, while Valerius Maximus omits Syria but adds Epirus (Albania and northwestern Greece), Achaea (Greece), the Cyclades Islands, the coast of Asia Minor, and Cyprus.
16 Plut. *Cat. Min.*, 14.3.

In 66, he supported the request for authorization of Lucius Licinius Lucullus to celebrate a triumph in relation to the military successes achieved in the Third Mithridatic War (74–63). The request had been opposed by Pompey, who was envious of the victory that Lucullus had won at the Battle of Tigranocerta. To prevent it from being granted, Pompey threw mud at the Luculli through Caius Memmius. First, Memmius prosecuted Lucullus's brother, Marcus Terentius Varro Lucullus, for his acts when he was quaestor under Sulla (in 82?), then Lucullus himself, accusing him of having demanded large sums of money to prolong the war.[17]

In 65, Cato was one of the three quaestors of the *aerarium* charged with checking the regularity of the coins issued by the Roman mint, which needed their weight and alloy to be verified. He became a connoisseur of laws and regulations, and he set a great example through the moral rigor, nobility, honesty, and integrity that characterized him.

In 63, he was tribune of the plebs, with the specific intention of counterbalancing the actions of Quintus Caecilius Metellus Nepos, Pompey's lieutenant in the East, to prevent him from obtaining too much power.

The Catilinarian Conspiracy was also in 63. On 5 December, Cato participated in a discussion in the Senate on the punishment to be meted out to the arrested Catalinarians and saw to it that they would be sentenced to death, in contrast to the wishes of Caesar, who had instead supported the option of life imprisonment and the confiscation of their property.[18] It was on this occasion that the enmity between Cato and Caesar was born, which would last until the death of the former in 46 at Utica in North Africa.

Cato's hostility toward Caesar is also fed by the fact that Cato is a half-brother of Servilia Caepio, who, after initially marrying Marcus Junius Brutus (tribune of the plebs in 83) and then Decimus Junius Silanus (praetor in 67), had been Caesar's lover. Cato regularly attacked Caesar both in private and in public, not just for political reasons but also for personal reasons, having never forgiven him for dishonoring Servilia by making her his lover when she was a married woman.

In 62, Cato vehemently opposed the approval of the bill of Quintus Caecilius Metellus Celer that sought to allow Pompey to return to Italy with his troops (that is, without having disbanded the army) to save the city, shaken by the unmasking of the Catilinarian Conspiracy. Cato claimed that this initiative was in fact intended to confer absolute power on Pompey, so he organized a street demonstration on the day of the plebiscite vote. A group of armed men hired by Metellus attacked the demonstrators, but Cato resisted, putting his own life at risk. In doing so, Cato succeeded in bringing the Senate and the Roman people over to his side against

---

17 Plut. *Luc.*, 37.1–2.
18 On Cato's speech in the Senate of 5 December 63: Sall., 52.3–6, 13–15, 24–28, 36.

Metellus and his men, and ensured that the Senate expelled Metellus, who then left for Asia Minor, from where he continued to Syria. Cato was borne aloft in triumph.[19]

The *Caecilii Metelli* are a family of senators and consuls of plebeian descent and equestrian rank, one of the richest and most powerful families in Rome, linked by ties of political friendship or marriage to other noble families who are very rich and powerful themselves. Moreover, they are the stars in the Optimates ranks. For 200 years, they have filled magistracies and military commands at all levels. Their family tree includes six consuls, a *pontifex maximus*, and a Vestal Virgin. Four of them have celebrated a triumph, and five have assumed the role of censor. At present, there are two branches to the Metelli, one of which has its origins in Quintus Caecilius Metellus Macedonicus, while the other descends from Lucius Caecilius Metellus Calvus.

Metellus Celer is the nephew of Lucius Caecilius Metellus Diadematus, himself the son of Metellus Macedonicus. He is an augur and has been tribune (in 72 or 71), aedile (in 67), the legate[20] of Pompey (in 66), and praetor (in 63). In 63, he became the center of attention when, under a pretext, he interrupted the trial of Caius Rabirius, accused of complicity in the murder of the tribune of the plebs Lucius Appuleius Saturninus, which had occurred 37 years previously. In 62, he fought against Catiline and his followers at the Battle of Pistoia and was propraetor of Gallia Cisalpina, demonstrating that he possessed leadership skills and strategic vision.

After 76 he married Claudia (from now on, we will call her Clodia to distinguish her from her two sisters), the sister of Publius Claudius Pulcher, quaestor in 61 and friend of Caesar. In 61, she is still a young woman (she was born in 94), attractive and very seductive, rather cultured and elegant, but also independent, open-minded, and frivolous. She is very rich (she owns some gardens on the Tiber, just outside Rome, and a villa in Baiae in Campania) and she is influential. She adores being courted, and she lives a nonchalant and carefree life. Famed for her beauty, escapades, and depravity, she is one of the most talked-about married women of high social standing in the capital. She loves to dance (some say that she does so more elegantly than befits a respectable woman), she plays the cithara, and she is skilled in public relations and self-promotional activities. She is also versed in other arts that her detractors consider precursors to vice. She is devoid of sexual inhibition. She has had many lovers and, at present, has more than one. Men are entranced by her, and as such, she is greatly admired, longed for, and desired. Even Cicero, in some of his letters to Atticus, writes that he is not insensitive to Clodia's charm.

Clodia is a neighbor of Cicero. Terentia, Cicero's wife, isn't happy about this. She fears Clodia wants to steal her husband away from her and that he, by hamming it up for his audience, is encouraging her. Cicero knows about Terentia's jealousy.

---

19   Plut. *Cat. Min.* 26.5, 28.3, 29.2; Cic. *Sest.*, 62.

20   Each legion had a legate (to be understood here as the legion's commander) and six military tribunes, as well as the cavalry prefects and the prefects of the auxiliary troops.

Therefore, in February 62, when he solicited the mediation of Mucia Tertia and Terentia to put an end to the hostility of Quintus Caecilius Metellus Nepos the Younger toward him, he avoided involving Clodia. (Mucia Tertia and Clodia were both linked to Metellus Nepos, one by blood and the other through her marriage to Metellus Celer).[21]

Metellus Celer and Clodia have a daughter, Caecilia Metella. But theirs is not a happy marriage. It is public knowledge that the couple often fight and argue. The root cause is always the same: Clodia's amorality, her unbridled licentiousness, her sexual excesses caused by lust and vice, and her giving herself to lovers behind her husband's back.

Having returned to Rome from Asia, Pompey attempted to tie himself more closely to Cato, requesting two of his nieces in marriage, one for himself and one for his son, but Cato refused.[22] This pushes Pompey toward Caesar, which will lay the foundations of their mutual understanding that will later be extended to Marcus Licinius Crassus, ultimately resulting in the First Triumvirate.

In 58, the praetors Caius Memmius and Lucius Domitius Ahenobarbus are also political adversaries of Caesar. Caius Memmius (before 90 to 46) is an enriched plebeian, a Pompeian, a highly cultured and intellectual philhellene, and a poet. He is the son of Lucius Memmius, who was *triumvir monetalis* in 109, and the nephew of Caius Memmius, who was the victim of a targeted killing in 100 (the instigator of the assassination was the praetor Caius Servilius Galicia). He married Fausta, daughter of the dictator Sulla, and has a son who has the same name as him. His sister Memmia is the wife of Caius Scribonius Curio.

Lucius Domitius Ahenobarbus is a member of a family of senators and consuls. He is the son of Cnaeus Domitius Ahenobarbus, who was tribune of the plebs in 104, *pontifex maximus* in 103, consul in 96, censor in 92, and died in 88. He is the nephew of the homonymous consul of 94, who ordered a slave to be crucified for having killed a wild boar with a spear because, after the Second Servile War, it was no longer permitted for slaves to bear arms. In 83, Lucius Domitius Ahenobarbus's uncle sided with Sulla and was killed in the Curia Hostilia in Rome, together with other senators, by the praetor Damasippus on the orders of Caius Marius the Younger.

Lucius Domitius Ahenobarbus is married to Porcia, sister of Cato of Utica, with whom he had a son, Lucius. His political ideas correspond with those of Cato: as such, he is a hyper-conservative, an active supporter of the privileges of the aristocracy, and a staunch opponent of the politics that favor the lower-class plebeians advocated by Caesar and Pompey. In 70 he was a witness for the prosecution in the judicial trial of Caius Licinius Verres, propraetor of Sicily from 73 to 71, charged with

21 Cic. *Fam.*, V.2.6.
22 Plut. *Cat. Min.*, 30.2–3.

malfeasance and theft. In 61, as curule aedile, he organized games during which 100 Numidian lions were led into the arena to be hunted.

The *Domitii Ahenobarbi* are a family of Roman *argentarii* (moneychangers), owners of a vast swathe of property in Tuscany which they obtained by way of reimbursement for the loans they gave to the *res publica* during the Second Punic War (218–201). One of their villas is in Domitiana (Porto di Santa Liberata) on the canal of the same name, which connects the western end of the Lagoon of Orbetello to the sea near the northern shore of Argentario (close to the hamlet of Giannella in the commune of Orbetello). It extends over a vast area and consists of a series of buildings that include the residential core, a small bath complex, servants' quarters, a large cistern, fishponds, underground storerooms, and a small port.

CHAPTER III

Caesar Favors a Rapprochement Between Crassus and Pompey

Caesar Asks to Celebrate a Triumph

In 61, Caesar is propraetor for Hispania Ulterior, where he fought victoriously against the Lusitanians and as a result was proclaimed *imperator* by his soldiers. His magistracy is about to expire, but he wants to celebrate a triumph, retain command of his legions, and run for the consulship for 59. These things are incompatible with each another. Candidacy for the consulship and celebrating a triumph is an either/or scenario. Moreover, Caesar won't be able to present himself as a candidate if he is still in possession of *imperium* (military command). Nevertheless, Caesar presents a request to the Senate (he asks for authorization to celebrate his triumph; this act is called a *littera laureata* because it is adorned with a sprig of laurel, the symbol of victory and glory). Predictably, the Catonian faction ensures that the Senate's deliberation of Caesar's request is delayed by obstructing it and burying it amid other items. Caesar has to give up on his idea of parading himself in triumph through the crowds and displaying the spoils from his conquests. But what interests him more is becoming consul.

As a result, he returns to Rome, disbands the army, and presents his candidacy for the consulship for 59. He believes he can win the elections provided he can rely on the support of Crassus and Pompey, who are the richest and most powerful politicians in Rome. In the past they were close friends of Sulla, and they were consular colleagues in 70. During their consulship, however, there was a break in their personal relationship when Crassus could not bear the fact that Pompey had tried to steal the glory of the victory over Spartacus from him, which he had been partially successful in doing. Caesar must pay him back the money (with interest) that he borrowed as a loan to finance his own electoral campaigns and the games he put on while he was aedile. He knows that Crassus is very sensitive about money and glory, but he also knows that Crassus is a partner in and manager of a company of publicans, that this business named too high a price to win the tax collection service contract for the Roman province of Asia at auction, and that, because it's running at a loss, it wants to renegotiate the terms of the tender.

The Roman Alexander

In 59, Pompey is 47 years old (he was born in 106). He descends from a family originally from Picenum (Marche), which owns a large amount of property, including in Umbria, and enjoys vast influence. The family rose to senatorial and consular rank in 141, with the support of the *Cornelii Scipiones*.

His son Cnaeus fought in the Civil War between Marius and Sulla, winning victories in Italy, Sicily, and North Africa. Pompey's career was favored by his special rapport with Sulla and by the volatile nature of the situation at the time. Mainly, however, Pompey's successes are owed to his uncommon organizational and command skills, his strategic genius, and his boundless ambition, so much so that he is now considered the Roman Alexander (referring to Alexander III of Macedon). In recognition of his resounding military victories in Europe, Asia, and Africa, he has been awarded the honorary title of *magnus*, "the great," by law and was able to celebrate the "Triumph of Three Continents."

After the death of Sulla (78), he supported Marcus Aemilius Lepidus in his race for the consulship and then encouraged his *coup d'état*, only to abandon him and march against him at the head of his own personal army on behalf of the Senate. He was victorious in the Sertorian War (82–72), which was fought in Spain. He defeated the pirates of the Mediterranean by virtue of the *lex Gabinia* (67), which had conferred proconsular powers to him (despite the fact he had never been a magistrate and consequently wasn't even a senator) and given him control over all lands within 75 km of the Mediterranean coastline (it's worth remembering that Rome is only about 30 km from the sea). He was tasked with bringing an end to the Third Mithridatic War (73–63) by the *lex Manilia* and did so successfully, scattering the kings of the East, founding cities in his own name, accumulating fabulous spoils of war, reorganizing the political geography of the East, and binding a vast clientele to him (adding them to his clientele in North Africa, Spain, and Gaul). He aided the repression of Spartacus's Revolt (73–71). He was consul in 70, the year in which, in agreement with Crassus, he abolished the Sullan constitution, restoring the *equites* to the jury courts and restoring the powers of the tribunate of the plebs, which Sulla had suppressed. He was opposed by the aristocracy and by the majority of the Senate, led by Optimates, and particularly by the Catonian faction, who feared that he wanted to seize power and physically eliminate his political opponents as Sulla had, thus seeing in him a danger to the *res publica* (though they had to change their minds toward the end of 62 when Pompey returned to Italy from the Mithridatic War and disbanded his army, thereby demonstrating that he didn't want to found his supremacy at the point of a sword).

Even now, however, there's little affinity between Pompey and the Senate, possibly because, since the Pompeii have only belonged to the aristocracy for a short time, they don't have big-name allies (except for the Scipiones, who, however, no longer have the power and visibility they once had) and are closely tied only to the local nobility and large landowners. The most prominent Roman family that has a bond with Pompey is the *Caecilii Metelli*, aristocrats of plebeian extraction but nonetheless very rich and powerful. Pompey divorced his first wife to marry Aemilia Metella and, after her death, married Mucia Tertia, half-sister of Quintus Caecilius Metellus Celer.[1]

Over time, however, the Metelli clashed with Pompey for various reasons. They reproached him for having hindered the Cretan campaign of Quintus Caecilius Metellus Creticus and for having schemed against Lucullus in order to have himself nominated in his place to lead the war effort in the Third Mithridatic War. In 67 and 66, they supported the legal actions against the Pompeians Caius Cornelius and Caius Manilius. Moreover, Metellus Creticus granted the hand of his own daughter to Publius Licinius Crassus despite the fact it was well-known that Pompey and the bride's father—Marcus Licinius Crassus, the "banker of Rome"—were not on good terms.

Pompey is energetically supported by the *equites* group; therefore, his friends usually belong to this circle, which Pompey himself belongs to (among his friends are Marcus Lollius Palicanus, Lucius Afranius, Titus Labienus, and Aulus Gabinius). He is also supported by Cicero, Caesar, and tribunes of the plebs belonging to the Populares faction. Therefore, he can put forward his own candidates for elections for civic magistracies and thereby influence the formulation of laws.

Caesar and the tribunes have already tangibly demonstrated their support for Pompey. Together with Titus Labienus and Quintus Caecilius Metellus Nepos, they had ensured that, by the will of the people gathered in assembly, he could dress as a triumphator or wear a gold crown specifically for certain public ceremonies.[2] Moreover, Caesar, as a judicial orator, supported the charge in a trial in which the indicted was an ex-consul who was hostile toward Pompey.

The Question of the Ratification of the Political Reorganization of the East

Pompey has been waiting for two years for the Senate of Rome to ratify his political reorganization of western Asia and reward his war veterans, allotting each of them a patch of *ager publicus* usable for economic purposes. It is said that the Senate hasn't yet pronounced its decision on these matters because it was irritated by the fact that Pompey took major decisions in the East without involving it (with reference

---

1 Pompey married Mucia Tertia, the third daughter of Quintus Mucius Scaevola Pontifex, consul in 95, and Licinia, herself the daughter of Lucius Licinius Crassus. Mucia Tertia was the half-sister of Quintus Caecilius Metellus Celer and Quintus Caecilius Metellus Nepos, born from Licinia's previous marriage to Quintus Caecilius Metellus Nepos.

2 Vell. Pat., II.40.40; Dio Cass., XXXVII.21.4.

to the institution of the new provinces of Syria and Bithynia and Pontus). But this isn't quite the truth of it. On the one hand, the Optimates, chief among them the Catonian faction, continue to be prejudicially hostile toward Pompey. On the other hand, many senators are reluctant to allow the number of users of *ager publicus* to be enlarged, because this would reduce their room for maneuver (they themselves are the primary users of *ager publicus*).

In 63, to overcome the impasse, Pompey sought to put himself forward as a candidate for the consulship *in absentia*, submitting the request through the tribune of the plebs Quintus Caecilius Metellus Nepos, with Caesar's support. But the Senate vigorously opposed it, declaring a state of emergency, suspending Nepos from his duties, and even threatening to remove him from office. Nepos fled to take refuge with Pompey. To avoid a showdown, the Senate and Pompey reached an agreement whereby Pompey nominated a friend of his, Marcus Pupius Piso Frugi Calpurnianus, his legate from 67 to 62 during the Third Mithridatic War, for the consulship. The elections were postponed to allow him to be in the running, and thus Piso was elected in 62 as consul for 61, together with Marcus Valerius Messalla Corvinus.

During his consulship, Piso proposed and passed the *lex Pupia*, which banned the Senate from meeting on election days, and was at the center of an incident about which Cicero became highly resentful when Piso didn't respect the prescribed order of precedence when requesting opinions during a discussion in the Senate. Afterwards, Piso protected Publius Claudius Pulcher—who had been accused in court of impiety for having violated the mysteries of the Festival of Bona Dea—by not allowing a vote on the *lex Pupia Valeria de incestu Clodii*. Later, Cicero took revenge on Piso by preventing him from being appointed proconsul of Syria.[3]

By the time Piso's year of consulship had passed, Pompey still hadn't obtained ratification for his actions in Asia. Pompey tried to turn the tide on this by having his friend Lucius Afranius elected to the consulship,[4] which was down to the collaboration of Marcus Valerius Messalla Niger, consul in 61, who freely showered money among the tribes during the elections. After the winners had been announced—Afranius was elected in tandem with Quintus Caecilius Metellus Celer—Messalla was indicted for electoral fraud after an action was brought against him by the aedile Lucius Domitius Ahenobarbus. Defended by the great Quintus Hortensius Hortalus, he was acquitted.[5]

Afranius comes from the same part of the world as the Pompeii (Oximum in Picenum). He fought in Pompey's private army during the Sertorian War (82–72)

3   Cic. *Att.*, I.16.8.
4   Plut. *Pomp.*, 44; Cic. *Att.*, I.16.12.
5   Cic. *Att.*, I.16.19.

and during the Third Mithridatic War (66–62).[6] In Spain, he commanded a unit of cavalry at the Battle of Sucro[7] and destroyed the city of Calagurris (Calahorra).[8] In 72 (or 71), he was praetor. Following this, as consul, he kept watch over Gallia Cisalpina. It seems that, in civilian life, his only skill consists of mastering the art of dance.[9] He is worthless as a politician. Cicero despises him. In some of his letters to Atticus, he speaks of him as "a coward, devoid of resoluteness in rebuttals," as "a complete non-entity," and adds that Afranius "behaves in such a way that his consulship is not a consulship but a stigma on our friend [Pompey]."[10] Indeed, Afranius failed to live up to Pompey's expectations, revealing himself to be unable to provide him with help when required.[11] The Senate of Rome and Metellus Celer took advantage of this. The former failed to adopt the measures Pompey expected. The latter reduced Afranius to impotence by vetoing anything he tried to do.

In the past, the opposition to Pompey in the Senate had been led by Quintus Lutatius Catulus Capitolinus, consul in 78, and Quintus Hortensius Hortalus. Then Catulus died (61), after which Hortensius withdrew from public life. It was Lucius Licinius Lucullus who then took charge in the Senate. The political reorganization of Asia, as it had emerged from the Mithridatic War, was finally discussed, but Pompey wanted his actions in this regard to be ratified *en masse*, while Lucullus insisted that they be examined in detail. In the end the latter won, backed by Crassus, Cato, and the Metelli. At that point, Pompey tried to temper the hostility that Cato showed toward him, offering to marry his niece (after divorcing Mucia Tertia). But Cato refused.[12]

A Convergence of Interests

Caesar seeks to get Crassus and Pompey to reconcile with one another and, subsequently, to get all three of them to come to an agreement to guarantee each other mutual support in the achievement of common goals and to take control of political life so that nothing happens in Rome that they do not want to happen. To tie Crassus to himself, he leans on his avarice for riches and his yearning for glory, promising him that, if he is elected to the consulship, he will strive to give

---

6   Plut. *Pomp.*, 34, 36, 39; Dio Cass., XXXVII.5.

7   Plut. *Sert.*, 19.

8   Oros., V.23.14.

9   Dio Cass., XXXVII.49.3.

10   Cic. *Att.*, I.18.5; I.19.4; I.20.5; II.3.1.

11   Dio Cassius confirms this disappointment, as "Afranius, who understood how to dance better than to transact any business, did not assist him at all." Dio Cass., XXXVII.49.3. It seems that Afranius, despite the limitations he exhibited during his consulship, continued his *cursus honorum* in 59 as proconsul for Gallia Cisalpina.

12   Plut. *Pomp.*, 44; Plut. *Cat. Min.*, 30.

him a favorable modification to building contracts and the command of an army to be used for an invasion of the Parthian Empire. He also promises Crassus that he will promote a law to allow the renegotiation of the terms of the contract for Roman Asia. Meanwhile, to tie Pompey to him, he promises him that, if elected, he would work hard to grant him the ratification of his actions in Asia and land to be distributed to his war veterans. In addition, Caesar offers to help Pompey resolve another issue that is close to his heart.

Pompey has fallen in love with Julia, Caesar's daughter, and she is full of admiration for the "First Man in Rome." To facilitate the meeting between Pompey and Julia, Caesar asks his mother, Aurelia, to intercede for him. She acted as a mother to Julia after the death of her own mother, Cornelia, Caesar's first wife.[13] The mutual attraction between Pompey and Julia makes Aurelia's task easier. Julia agrees to break off her engagement to the 26-year-old Quintus Servilius Caepio Brutus to marry Pompey, while Pompey divorces Mucia Tertia, spuriously accusing her of adultery (he had known about his wife's affairs for some time), and, exercising a right recognized by law, holds onto his two sons from the marriage, Cnaeus and Sextus.

Brutus is the son of Marcus Junius Brutus and Servilia Caepio. His father was tribune of the plebs in 83 and founded the colony of Capua in Campania; in 77, as an accomplice of Marcus Aemilius Lepidus during his attempted *coup d'état*, he occupied Gallia Cisalpina with armed troops, but, being besieged in Mutina (Modena) by Pompey, he was forced to surrender and was executed on Pompey's orders. Having been orphaned, Brutus was adopted by a maternal uncle, Quintus Servilius Caepio. At birth, he was called Marcus Junius Brutus. By dint of his adoption, he became Quintus Servilius Caepio Brutus. There is a rumor—the basis for which is unknown—that he is the natural son of Caesar, Servilia's lover.

Pompey and Julia tie the knot between the end of 62 and the start of 61, despite the significant age difference. Pompey is 46 years old while Julia is just 16.

Metellus Celer had always been a follower of Pompey but the latter's repudiation of his sister offends him. He considers it a disgrace that extends to her whole family. As a result, he abandons Pompey and joins the ranks of the Populares. This causes the relationship between Pompey and the Metelli, and between Pompey and the families tied to the Metelli, among whom are the Scaevola family, to be irremediably broken. The result is a political storm, with riots breaking out and a widespread increase in seditious speeches.[14]

---

13 Cornelia died prematurely in 68. Caesar then married again to Pompeia, the granddaughter of Sulla, but divorced her in 62 due to the scandal of the Festival of Bona Dea.

14 Plut. *Pomp.*, 53.

CHAPTER IV

The Triumviral Pact

A Private and Secret Agreement

The agreement between Caesar, Crassus, and Pompey is a private and secret pact. It binds together the parties' strengths, contacts, and ambitions in order that they each obtain whatever they want for as long as they want. It doesn't change either the institutions or the form of government of the state, but it shows that the constitutional organization of the *res publica* is no longer based on law but on relations between the major figures in public life. It is therefore the result of a convergence of interests. It will go down in history as the Triumvirate.

Things go as the Triumvirs planned. Crassus finances the campaign for Caesar's election to the consulship. Pompey sides with Caesar in the election campaign, bringing to bear all the weight of his own immense prestige, guaranteeing him the votes of his war veterans in agreement with Lucius Lucceius, a friend of both his and Cicero. Caesar is elected, and he enters office on 1 January 59.

Shortly after this, Servilia Caepio— someone whom Caesar holds very dear to him—receives a gift of an enormous pearl, worth an exorbitant 6 million sesterces. It is a truly special gift with which Caesar wants not only to privately celebrate his election to the consulship but also to appease Servilia for having induced Julia to break off her engagement to Brutus.

Caesar's consular colleague for 59 is Marcus Calpurnius Bibulus. Although he is of plebeian ancestry, he is supported by the patriciate. He belongs to one of the most ancient familial clans in the capital, the *gens Calpurnia*. Bibulus is a second- or third-rate politician, partly due to his weak personality, but he is the son-in-law of Cato, having married his daughter Porcia, and accompanies him everywhere. He spent a huge amount of money, obtained through donations, to get him the consulship.[1] Porcia was married off to Bibulus at a very young age. She will give him two children, one of whom, Lucius, will emulate his father and his sister in

---

1   Suet. *Iul.*, 19.1.

terms of his sober, rigid, austere way of thinking and behaving. Porcia is tough, uncompromising, and fanatical, bordering on delirious. She is of the same mind as her father and admires him unreservedly and limitlessly.

Bibulus has already been Caesar's colleague on two previous occasions: as aedile (65) and as praetor (62). Each time, he tried unsuccessfully to hinder his career, probably because he was being influenced by Cato.

In Latin, *bibulus* means "drinker." It is a nickname given to a family member who has a habit of drinking, of getting drunk. Over time, it has become part of the family name. Bibulus is also affected by this vice, just as his father-in-law is.

The Death of Metellus Celer

In the meantime, Metellus Celer dies suddenly while preparing to set off for Gallia Narbonensis. This happened "three days after he had been in good health, flourishing in the Curia, in the rostrum, and in the republic; while in the flower of his age, of an excellent constitution, and in the full vigor of manhood, [he] was torn in a most unworthy manner from all good men and from the entire state."[2] He lived in a house that shared a wall with that of Quintus Lutatius Catulus Censorinus, so that the latter heard him snoring on many occasions. While in his death throes, which lasted a couple of days, he invoked Catulus's name several times, beating on the adjoining wall with one hand.

Cicero was present during the last hours of Metellus's life. A doctor certified the cause of death, attributing it to a domestic accident. However, according to hearsay, the cause of death was something else. Metellus was allegedly poisoned by his wife Clodia, who wanted to get rid of him to make more room in her life for her lover at the time, the 28-year-old poet Caius Valerius Catullus (87–54), who was a few years younger than she was. The rumor seems likely. In Rome, it often happens that, in family circles, especially in the "upper" classes, married women are implicated in scandals involving one or more lovers.

Catullus and Clodia

Clodia's new flame is the poet Caius Valerius Catullus, a young scion of a wealthy patrician family who live in Verona, a city nestled on the banks of the Adige where this river descends from the Monti Lesseni and into the Po Valley. The Valerii contributed to the colonial enterprise of 89 that led to the foundation of Verona. Currently, they form part of the minor local nobility.

---

2   Cic. *Cael.*, 59.

They own a fine villa in Sirmione, located at the tip of a peninsula on the southern shore of Lake Garda on the stretch of the Via Gallica that connects Brescia to Verona.[3] This villa is built on a rocky bank and is situated in a wonderful panoramic position, immersed in an atmosphere of irresistible natural splendor. It contains numerous rooms set over multiple floors and is adorned with floor mosaics, bronze objects, fine ceramics, stuccos, and frescoes. The owners use it as a place to spend their holidays and entertain distinguished guests. Caesar stopped there on his journey to the seat of his propraetorship in Corduba (Córdoba), the capital of Hispania Ulterior.

Clodia met Catullus in 63 at his parents' house, where she and her husband were staying as guests. She looked beautiful, and for Catullus, it was love at first sight; meeting Clodia changed the young man's life. Catullus thought only of her and, to follow her and be close to her, he moved to Rome (60). His explanation was that he wanted to finish his studies in the capital, following the tradition of rich provincial patricians. In reality, Clodia had taken possession of the heart and mind of Catullus, so much so that on his arrival in the capital he became her lover.

In Rome, Catullus led a brilliant life and moved within the circles of prominent political and cultural figures, including, among others, Caesar, Pompey, and Cicero, as well as the judicial orator Quintus Hortensius Hortalus, the biographer and historian Cornelius Nepos, and the poet and Epicurean philosopher Titus Lucretius Carus.

Catullus admires Hortensius for the exuberant and ostentatious style he adopts in his legal orations, but he admires him rather less for his poetry. He dedicated to him his own translation of an elegy by Callimachus,[4] *Coma Berenices* ("Berenice's Hair"), which narrates the ascension to heaven, in the form of a constellation, of a lock of hair, given by the queen Berenice as a votive offering for the return of her husband Ptolemy III Evergetes (r. 246–222) from a military campaign in Syria.

Catullus is the author of *Liber*, a collection of 116 *carmina* in the style of Callimachus, divided into three parts, which the author called *nugae* ("trifles," *carmina* 1–60), *carmina docta* (61–68), and *epigrammata* ("epigrams," 69–116). He dedicated it to Cornelius Nepos,[5] with whom he had established a close friendship that—it is said—wasn't free from sexual overtones.

Nepos, 40 years old (he was born in 100), is originally from Hostilia (Ostiglia), a village on the River Po, close to Mantua (Mantua) and on the border of the territory

---

3   The Via Gallica connects the principal towns of the Po Valley. It runs from Gradum (Grado) to Augusta Taurinorum (Turin), passing through Patavium (Padua), Vicetia (Vicenza), Verona, Brixia (Brescia), Bergomum (Bergamo), and Mediolanum (Milan).
4   Callimachus (310–235) was a poet and philologist, the head of the Alexandrian Library, and a court poet in Alexandria in Egypt. He is said to have published 800 books, including some encomiastic poems, which use an innovative style of his own invention following the Homeric tradition of epic poetry.
5   Catull., I.1–3.

of Verona. He too moved to Rome as a young man and there met Cicero and his friends, Atticus and Varro Lucullus among them. He also writes verses in the style of Callimachus but without great results, so he will soon stop writing them, though he will remain in the milieu of the *neōteroi*. In the future he will write prose.

Catullus doesn't actively engage in politics but he cannot avoid following its customs, nor observing and considering how it never cures its diseases which are corruption, personal interests in public activity, and inter-factional fighting. He believes he cannot do otherwise because, in an era of tensions within the *res publica*, isolating oneself from the political reality to seek refuge in the Epicurean *hortus*, as Lucretius does, means estranging oneself from the world of the *polis* and consequently also moving oneself out of the circles of power. He, on the other hand, cares about staying in the limelight, or at least as much as he is required to do to enjoy life, that is, to live and love.

The *Lex Vatinia*

In the first months of 59, when the matter of assigning the consuls their provinces arose, in accordance with the provisions of the *lex Sempronia de provinciis consularibus*, Caesar and his colleague Marcus Calpurnius Bibulus were assigned two very poor regions of southern Italy (*silvae callesque*, "the forests and cattle tracks"). Caesar is outraged and doesn't accept the *fait accompli* but prepares a countermeasure.

In this attempt, he will use a tribune of the plebs from the Populares faction, Publius Vatinius, who, like his new colleagues, entered office on 10 December 60. We have already looked at Vatinius, counting him among Caesar's friends. He was quaestor in 63 and fought in Hispania Ulterior in 62 and 61 as a legionary commander in the army of the proconsul Caius Cosconius. He was investigated for abusing his duties as quaestor for personal enrichment and was severely reprimanded by Cicero, who was consul at the time. Subsequently, he continued to behave dubiously, to the extent that he was charged with theft and embezzlement, and after this incident the fissure that already separated him from Cicero widened. He was elected as tribune of the plebs for 59 with decisive support from Caesar and, as such, is ready and willing to repay him whenever and however he wishes.

Vatinius promotes a plebiscite that seeks to annul the assignment to the *silvae callesque* and, by way of replacement, confer the government of Gallia Cisalpina and Illyricum to Caesar for five years (1 March 59–28 February 54), together with the command of three legions, indemnities in office, and the authority to appoint legionary commanders. Prior to explaining and discussing the plebiscite in public and submitting it to the people gathered in assembly for a vote, Vatinius describes its contents and purposes to the Senate. He explains that the initiative stems from the need to confront an urgent situation caused by the migration/invasion of the Helvetii and the expansionist designs of Ariovistus, which risk upsetting the balance in Gallia Transalpina and will have repercussions extending to Gallia Narbonensis, not to mention the possibility that these barbarians could invade Roman territory, following in the footsteps of the Cimbri, Teutones, and Ambrones; it follows that Caesar's task in Gaul is to be seen as a preventative measure to defend Rome and its transalpine allies. The aim of this move is not so much that political debate is caused by Vatinius's plebiscite but rather, and above all, because it aims to ensure that an extraordinary command is assigned by the Roman people gathered in an assembly, contrary to the law that names the Senate as responsible for deciding on matters relating to state administration, including the conferral of public offices and the appointment of military commanders.[6]

Cato thunders against the initiative, saying that not only does this imply a derogation from the law in force—both as regards the procedure of conferring provinces to consuls and as regards the details of the specific office Vatinius proposes to assign (duration, military forces, and powers granted)—but also because, in his opinion, it threatens the freedom of the *res publica* (creating the risk of seeing a tyrant establishing himself on the Capitoline).[7] He adds that there is no emergency in Gaul, other than the stirring up of trouble that is only desired by those who are interested in starting a war, perhaps for the purpose of retaining their military command.

Cicero, speaking in his turn in the discussion, supports Vatinius, accentuating the threat from the barbarians (though Gaul has been subjugated for the most part, it cannot yet be said to be secure; the Germans are an even more dangerous enemy than the Gauls). But this isn't accurate either: since the establishment of Gallia Narbonensis the Galli Transalpini have no longer constituted a threat to Rome, except for some recent unrest that the governor Caius Pomptinus has taken steps to end. Moreover, Caesar was able to contain Ariovistus without resorting to force and the migration of the Helvetii halted after the death of Orgetorix, who had been leading it.

It escapes no one's attention that all the parties involved—Cato, Vatinius (and, behind him, Caesar), and Cicero—are manipulating the truth, on the one side in building up the portrayal of the emergency, and on the other, in negating its existence. Nonetheless, the majority of the Senate indicates it is in favor of sending the plebiscite on to the relevant popular assembly for a vote. Cato protests loudly. Chaos breaks out, and Cato is thrown out of the building. Afterward, precisely on schedule, the project is described in a *contio* and approved by the *comitia tributa*. The *lex Vatinia de provinciis Caesaris* thus enters into force.

Caesar has had to renounce the honor of his triumph, but he has secured Gallia Cisalpina and Illyricum. A question arises here. Why did he want to be assigned these provinces in particular? His choice wasn't random—as none of his actions

---

6   Suet. *Iul.*, 22.1.
7   Plut. *Cat. Min.*, 33.3.

are (Caesar is a cold, calculating man)—but dovetails with a precise strategic plan. Before explaining the reason, some context is required.

The Romans call central and southern Italy *Italia propria*; more accurately, they use this name for the whole Italian peninsula that lies south of the imaginary line that connects the mouth of the Magra in Tuscany to the mouth of the Rubicon in Romagna. Lucius Cornelius Sulla, dictator from 82 to 79, demarcated this line to prevent *imperium* from being exercised south of the Tuscan-Emilian Apennines. In other words, Sulla fixed two legions in Gallia Cisalpina and demilitarized the entirety of the rest of Italy, placing an impassable barrier between the two that is represented by the course of the Rubicon.

Having said this, the immense strategic importance of Gallia Cisalpina is clear. Whoever controls this region will be able to keep the rest of *Italia propria* in check, Rome included. In short, whoever controls Gallia Cisalpina controls Rome.

But Caesar's strategic vision goes even beyond this. He aims to make Gallia Cisalpina the starting point for a war of conquest across southeastern Europe, one that will lavish wealth and glory on him. This is his motive. Gallia Cisalpina was the scene of the decisive victory of Caius Marius and Quintus Lutatius Catulus over the Cimbri at the Battle of the Raudine Plain (Campi Raudii, also known as the Battle of Vercellae) in 101. Caesar wants to do even more to surpass Marius's greatness. If Marius massacred the barbarians who had invaded Italy, then he would carry the war over the Alps into the lands of the barbarians.

Caesar has also understood that any politician reinforces his position in Rome if he has provincial clients at his back. As such, ever since the start of his political career, he has tried to secure a favorable relationship, if not a "clientele," with those who lived in Gallia Cisalpina. On his return from serving as quaestor in Spain, he supported the claims of the Transpadana populations to grant them Roman citizenship.

CHAPTER V

The Julian Laws of 59

The Measures

The first law in the *Iuliae* series was the one that was approved on the initiative of Lucius Julius Caesar, consul in 90, in the midst of the Social War (91–88) to accelerate the cessation of hostilities. He granted full Roman citizenship to all those Italics who hadn't turned their backs on Rome during the conflict (*lex Iulia de civitate*). In 59, the series is fleshed out with the approval of another six laws, the work of the consul Caesar, a distant cousin of Lucius. The first act seeks to stem the tendency for civic magistrates to abandon themselves to turpitude, whether out of vice or self-interest, rather than carrying out their duties with dignity and honor (*lex Iulia de repetundis*). The second addresses the needs of Cnaeus Pompey Magnus to obtain the ratification of the political reorganization he carried out in Asia after the Third Mithridatic War (73–63) (*lex Iulia de actis Cn. Pompei confirmandis*). The third and fourth authorize the distribution of land to Pompey's war veterans to reward them for their service to the state (*lex Iulia agrarian, lex Iulia agrarian campana*). The fifth allows a company of publicans in which Marcus Licinius Crassus is a stakeholder to renegotiate a contract for a tax collection service (*lex Iulia de publicanis*). The sixth defines the relationship between Rome and Ptolemy XII Auletes, king-pharaoh of Egypt (*lex Iulia de rege alexandrine*).

We want to dwell, in particular, on the laws approved by Caesar that go in favor of Crassus, Pompey, and Ptolemy XII.

In Favor of Crassus

The political reorganization of Asia entailed, among other things, the annexation of Pontus, the Amanus region, and Syria, with the integration of Pontus into the province of Bithynia (renamed Bithynia and Pontus), the integration of the Amanus region into the province of Cilicia, and the establishment of the province of Syria.[1] Caesar sees to it that this systematization is ratified and validated not by the Senate of Rome (which has culpably delayed discussing it) but by the people in assembly. Lucius Licinius Lucullus opposes the bill, but Caesar manages to make him back down. In the end, the proposal is approved.

In Favor of the Publicans

The *lex Iulia de publicanis* reduces the sums that the contractors of tax collection services owe to the public treasury by a third. Caesar thereby achieves multiple results with this initiative: not only does he obtain the gratitude of the publicans, and therefore of the *equites*, and particularly that of Crassus, but he also casts Pompey, a point of reference for *equites* in the political world, in a good light.

In Favor of the Pharaoh of Egypt

In 58, Ptolemy XII Auletes (r. 80–58 and 55–51) fled to Rome, having been forced to leave Egypt due to a popular uprising that broke out in his capital, Alexandria. It had been the Alexandrians who had put him on the throne in 80 as one of the only two remaining heirs of the Ptolemaic Dynasty, the other being his younger brother Ptolemy. Prior to this, his father Ptolemy IX Soter (king, most recently, from 88 to 81) had died, and he had been succeeded by his only indisputably legitimate daughter, Berenice III (also known as Cleopatra Berenice), who reigned from 81 to 80. It seems from this that Ptolemy XII was an illegitimate son. In part due to pressure from the Senate of Rome, Cleopatra Berenice married her stepson and cousin Ptolemy XI Alexander (born in 105, king in 80), who enjoyed Sulla's favor, but she was killed only a few days after the wedding by her new husband, who was then lynched by the vengeful citizens of Alexandria. A will attributed to Ptolemy XI, probably falsified, bequeaths Egypt to the Roman state. It was thus that Ptolemy XII ascended to the throne and, according to dynastic custom, married his sister Cleopatra V Tryphaena shortly afterwards.

In 58, the Alexandrians, always ready to take to the streets, revolted against Ptolemy XII because he had increased taxes to pay off debts he had got himself into

---

1 Syria was conquered by Pompey in 64, seizing it from the hands of the Arabians of Amanus and the Seleucid king Antiochus XIII. In the same year, it was organized into a Roman province. It embraced the area from the Amanus and all the lands between the Mediterranean Sea and the River Euphrates, including Coele-Syria, Phoenicia, Palestine, Edom, and Iturea. In this province, the Roman governor found that his authority was limited by the prerogatives of a whole series of autonomous settlements, by important religious centers, and numerous minor states—Judaea, the Kingdom of Commagene, the Kingdom of Emesa, the Nabataean Kingdom—all independent in name but Roman protectorates *de facto*. Plut. *Pomp.*, 39.2; Dio Cass., 37.7a.

with some Roman financiers. Ptolemy XII, unable to put an end to the riots, left the country. He first went to his brother Ptolemy, king of Cyprus, then to Rome. Currently, he is Pompey's guest in his villa in Alba (Albano Laziale). He accuses his subjects of having expelled him from his own kingdom and distributes money—some of which is his, some of which is borrowed—among the most influential politicians in the Roman state, with a view to being restored to the throne by force if necessary. Among the many senators who go out of their way to convince their colleagues to discuss the subject, the most authoritative is Pompey.

The Julian Law of 59 that relates to Ptolemy XII recognizes him as the sovereign of Egypt (that is, as the legitimate heir of Ptolemy IX) and confers the coveted title of friend and ally of the Roman people on him. It will also constitute the legal and political basis on which Ptolemy XII is able to ask the Romans to intervene militarily in Egypt to restore him to the throne. To obtain this result, Ptolemy XII paid—or promised to pay—6,000 talents to Caesar and to Pompey.[2]

---

2   Suet. *Iul.*, LIV.3.

CHAPTER VI

Cicero

Family Origins

Marius was born in a small house in the territory of Arpinum (Lower Lazio), close to a Temple of Mars and a stone bridge over the Amaseno. Not far from there, the Liri River is joined by the Fibrieno, a small stream with crystalline waters that flows down from a lake. Standing on the banks of that river is a recently renovated *villa rustica*, sizable in scale and in its plots of land. This is the house in which Marcus Tullius Cicero was born in 106 and raised.[1]

The *Tullii Cicerones* are distantly related to the *Marii* of Arpinum, but these families haven't spoken to each other for generations following a quarrel, the cause of which has since been forgotten. In addition to the family seat, they also own a well-established fulling business and trade in olives, grapes, oil, and wine, from which they derive sufficient income to maintain their belonging to the III-*equites* list in the census. The *Tullii Cicerones* are therefore a rather wealthy family of the minor provincial aristocracy.

From a very young age, Marcus was attracted to the art of knowing how to speak in public, and it was recommended he become a judicial orator. Brought to Rome by his father, together with his younger brother Quintus, he was taught by the leading jurists, juriconsults, and judicial orators of the age—Publius Mucius Scaevola Augur, Quintus Mucius Scaevola Pontifex, Lucius Licinius Crassus the Orator—and he spent time in intellectual circles, forming friendships with members of high-ranking families, one of whom—Titus Pomponius Atticus—was destined to remain a friend for life.

Young Friendships

Barely 17, during his military service, Cicero was a fellow soldier alongside Cnaeus Pompeius, the future *magnus*. The Social War (91–89) was raging. Cnaeus was the

---

1   Cicero mentions his birthplace in passing in *leg.,* II.1ff.

son of Cnaeus Pompeius Strabo, the commander of a legionary army that besieged Asculum Picenum (Ascoli Piceno). Marcus was tasked with desk duties in the army's general headquarters. Even then, Pompey, a very young and promising officer, showed an aptitude for command, strategy, war, and carnage. He had a childish air about him, but every so often, his gaze showed flashes of his "dark soul" coming through, that of an evil and unscrupulous person; it wasn't by chance that, much later, he would be labeled *adulescentulus carnifex* ("young butcher"),[2] establishing a parallel between him and his father (himself a malevolent sort, nicknamed "the butcher of Asculum" for the ferocity bordering on savagery with which he treated its citizens after they had surrendered). After the war, Cicero and Pompey returned to the capital. They lived in the same neighborhood—Carinae—and both attended legal teachings given by Publius Mucius Scaevola Augur, a luminary of legal science and highly regarded jurisconsult.

Cicero succeeded in going far in life even though he came from a provincial background and didn't belong to the traditional circles of power. In part, this was possible because social mobility was guaranteed in Rome. In part, it was because Cicero personally possessed wide and in-depth cultural knowledge, built on his study of the literary and political works of Greek authors and a solid anchoring in Roman and Italic traditions. And in part, it was also because he enjoyed the support of the senatorial oligarchy.

His election to the quaestorship for 75 made him a senator, and a *homo novus*. But telling a Roman citizen that he is a *homo novus* doesn't necessarily mean showing him affection or respect. The aristocracy, whose noses are stuck in the air, are predisposed against the *homines novi*. They consider them as social climbers, as *parvenus*.

Cicero climbed all the way to the very top of the ladder of the ordinary magistracies. He was aedile in 69, praetor in 66, and consul in 63. As praetor, he repeatedly backed Pompey in the Senate, such as when he supported the proposal to confer extraordinary powers to him for him to be able to cleanse the Mediterranean of the pirate scourge (67), or when he supported the proposal to entrust him with command in the Third Mithridatic War (74–63), replacing Lucius Licinius Lucullus. In 63, as consul, he exposed, denounced, and repressed the conspiracy of Catiline, which he then spent no little time boasting about.

Cicero was nourished by the ideals and thoughts of the great Romans of the II century, from Marcus Porcius Cato the Censor to Publius Cornelius Scipio Aemilianus Africanus Minor, but he is aware that he also needs to be open to new ideas, particularly those that come from Greece.

Cicero became the judicial orator that he dreamed of being, indeed all that and more, one of the best in his profession. It's commonly believed among his fellow citizens that he is as prepared and expert in law, oratory, and rhetoric as the great

---

2   Val. Max., 6.2.8. Valerius Maximus was a Latin writer who flourished during the reign of Emperor Tiberius (14–37 AD).

Quintus Hortensius Hortalus (114–50), a formidable opponent of his in court and a close friend in private. He started his legal activity no later than 81. In 80, he made a name for himself for his defense of a man charged with parricide in a trial that contributed to the crisis that engulfed and ended the Sullan regime. Between 79 and 77, he journeyed to Athens—where he attended lectures by Antiochus of Ascalon, *scholarch* of the Academy (the school of philosophy founded by Plato)—and Rhodes, where he spent some time at Apollonius Molon's school of oratory and rhetoric. In 70, he supported the accusations of the Sicilians against Caius Licinius Verres, former propraetor of Sicily—and a hardened criminal who specialized in plundering works of art—forcing him to go into exile.

Political Ideas

Cicero is also a first-rate politician whose actions are informed by the political mindset of the Greeks, which he disseminated in Rome and reworked to adapt it to both the specificity of Latin culture and the changes in time and circumstance. He has always tried and is currently committed to consolidating the ruling class and to healing the divisions between the patriciate and the *equites*. At first, he remained neutral between the Optimates and the Populares. His political theory and praxis were based on the principle of class harmony. He argued that segments of society don't differentiate between themselves in terms of classes or groups, but in the functions they exercise, which reflects a diversity of interests that might also conflict with one another, and that it is in the interests of the state that they collaborate with one another to avoid blind conservatism on the one hand and progressivism aimed at collective equalization on the other. After his consulship in 63, driven by circumstances (Catiline's conspiracy had drawn attention to a crisis of moral values that had to be addressed to prevent a political swing toward authoritarianism), he finally made his choice of side that he had been putting off for so long and aligned himself with the Optimates. He began to argue that it was necessary for the different sides of society to unite with each other to fight against a way of understanding politics that only looks to the means of strength and violence as the method for resolving disputes, trying to proselytize not only in Rome but also among the local elites in the colonies and towns of Italy.

At the heart of his thinking is the idea that the Senate of Rome must continue to be the center of political life, the force tasked with managing regulatory power, as it has been in the past. This is, however, the weak point of the construct. The Senate of Rome is no longer a political institution that is separate and independent from the social order. It has fallen into the political game, becoming a sparring partner itself.

Often, however, Cicero's conduct seems opportunistic and ambiguous. In fact, he oscillates between the *eques* Pompey, the *popularis* Caesar, and the *optimas* Cato, depending on the changing circumstances. According to some commentators,

Cicero's political position was that of someone who shuns prejudices and is able to respect even those who don't think the same way as he does. According to others, however, he is someone who simultaneously keeps a foot in two camps that are incompatible with each other and refuses to take a position, keeping them hanging on, in anticipation of possible advantages to be gained from both or to side with the one that proves to be the stronger. But it would be unreasonable to say that Cicero is two-faced, deceitful, or underhanded, someone who acts in the shadows to profit from discordant situations. An explanation for his wavering behavior might be this: he finds it hard to separate himself from his role as a judicial orator, whose work must be to argue their case come what may, no matter how contradictory it might appear.

Real Estate Assets

He was never poor, but he always spent his money parsimoniously, following the example of his mother, a prudent administrator of the family business, and he tried to put it to good use. Over time, he became very rich because he found his provision of legal aid to be a source of donations, legacies, and other gifts.

In this regard, it must be said that in the Roman world judicial orators did not participate in a case to help and defend a party whose members practice an intellectual or liberal profession as their primary source of income (they aren't lawyers in the modern sense of the word) but to assist or favor a friend. This pays off—not immediately, and without the nexus between them being revealed—through the gifting of valuable objects, granting a loan (which is made on the understanding that it won't need to be repaid), freely reallocating assets, or by making a donation or bequest.

As wealth, in an economic sense, is the large availability of goods that have commercial value and can produce revenue such as real estate, equipment, slaves, and money, and measures the financial wellbeing of the possessor, Cicero is rich mainly in properties. He possesses townhouses, estates, and rural villas. These properties are in Rome, elsewhere in Lazio, and in Campania.

Specifically, Cicero owns two residential houses in Rome, a small farm with a manor house in Arpinum, a house in Antium (Anzio), and three out-of-town villas in Formiae, Tusculum, and Pompeii.[3] The farm is in a secluded area, sun-kissed and

---

3   J. Carcopino attributes a minimum of eight rural villas to Cicero, up to a maximum of 11. J. Carcopino, *Les secrets de la correspondance de Cicéron* (Paris, 1947), vol. I, 73ff. Kuzicin calculates that Cicero owned eight rural villas. Some were bought or otherwise acquired before his exile, the others after his return from exile in 58. V. I. Kuziscin, *La grande proprietà agrarian nell'Italia romana* (Roma: Editori Riuniti, 1984), 83ff. After Cicero's return from exile, properties in Anagnia (Anagni) and Astura (Torre Astura), both in Lazio, and Cales (near Capua), Cumae (Cuma), Puteolis (Pozzuoli), and Sinuessa (Mondragone), all in Campania, were all added to his property portfolio.

rich in water. Cicero's least opulent villa is found there.[4] His house in Antium and the villa in Pompeii are recent purchases, made before May 60, perhaps even in 61.[5]

Cicero is a great lover of his villas and is often found in one of them. His favorite is the one in Formiae, a seaside town found on the border between Lazio and Campania, and therefore close to the birthplace of the Cicerones. It's very popular as a seaside holiday resort with both local landowners and Romans from the capital. One of its strengths is the fact that it's easy to get to, as it's located on the Via Appia, the extra-urban road that goes from Rome to Brundisium (Brindisi) via Capua.

---

4   Cic. *QFr.*, 3.1.
5   Cicero speaks about them for the first time in May/June 60: Cic. *Att.*, I.20.1, II.1.1.

CHAPTER VII

Dark Clouds Gather

Clodius: the *Transitio ad Plebem*

Publius Claudius Pulcher is hoping to stand as a candidate for the office of tribune of the plebs for 59. But he is a patrician and cannot do so because the tribunate of the plebs is a magistracy reserved for plebeians. One way to get around the obstacle is to have oneself adopted by a plebeian. But the *transitio ad plebem* is a procedure that is subject to the authorization of the Senate, with whom Pulcher is unpopular due to his history (he fomented a military revolt in Mesopotamia and violated the sanctity of the Festival of Bona Dea).

Caesar has decided to help Pulcher because he plans to make use of him. Where is the benefit in manipulating a tribune of the plebs? It is in the fact that this magistracy has very incisive powers—the power of veto, the power of legislative initiative—and can convene the *comitia tributa* and the *concilia plebis*, which are assemblies that make laws and preside over their application. In Caesar's case, there is a twofold advantage because the tribunate of the plebs is the magistracy that protects the lower-class plebeians, who are the power base of the Populares, the political faction led by Caesar.

Caesar can already avail himself of the collaboration of some tribunes of the plebs, as, during the previous elections for the incoming set of civic magistracies, he channeled people's votes toward candidates belonging to the Populares. One of these is Publius Vatinius, whom we have already discussed. Another is Caius Herennius, the namesake of the person to whom the unknown author of *Rhetorica ad Herennium* dedicated his work, perhaps being a friend or pupil of his (though Herennius is a very common name across Italy).[1] *Rhetorica ad Herennium* is a work on the structure and uses of the art of public speaking. It is the oldest surviving Latin work on rhetoric, published around 90, and it is one of the most important works of its kind ever written.

---

1   F. Cancelli, *La retorica a Gaio Erennio* (Milano: Mondadori, 1992), xx–xxi. *Rhetorica ad Herennium* was a work on the structure and uses of the art of public speaking.

The Tribunate Elections

Herennius presents a plebiscite that aims to obtain authorization for Pulcher's adoption by a plebeian from the people in an assembly, by law, rather than from the Senate. The proposal is discussed in the Senate before being forwarded to the *comitia tributa* for a vote. There is something incendiary about the issue, and Cicero—who returned to Rome on 12 May 60—doesn't fail to point this out: the plebiscite in question is aiming to override the Senate's issuance of authorization, bypassing it completely. In fact, prior to June 60, Cicero speaks in the Senate against Herennius's initiative, delivering a speech that has the effect of burying the matter. Afterwards he decides not to publish his speech, perhaps so as not to completely ruin his relations with Pulcher,[2] but perhaps, and more probably, so as not to set himself against Caesar, who is the one secretly pulling the strings. These relations, let us remind ourselves, became strained in 61 when Cicero testified against Pulcher during the trial following the scandal of the Festival of Bona Dea and only narrowly failed to have him convicted.

However, Pulcher doesn't abandon his endeavor. He tries again in 59, this time with success. He will be adopted by the senator Publius Fonteius, an enriched plebeian who is much younger than he is himself. The *transitio ad plebem* implies an alteration to one's *nomen gentilicium*. In this case, the noble form *Claudius* of the *nomen gentilicium* Pulcher is altered to the plebeian form *Clodius*. Publius Claudius Pulcher thus becomes Publius Clodius Pulcher. From now on, we will call him Clodius for short.

The road is now clear. In the summer of 59, Clodius puts himself forward as a candidate for the tribunate of the plebs for 58 and is elected thanks to the votes of the Populares, which Caesar channels toward him. This event violates the systematized order of civic magistracies, considering that, according to the law, one can only become a tribune of the plebs after having served as quaestor and Clodius has never been quaestor. This point deserves special attention. In the future, Cicero will try to delegitimize Clodius, arguing that his election as tribune of the plebs was illegitimate, with the result that the actions he undertook while in office are invalid.

The Triumvirate has eclipsed the Senate, which no longer seems to be capable of acting autonomously, and taken power away from the popular assemblies. Cicero is critical of all this but believes it to be a temporary phenomenon, so he decides to wait for it to pass. In the meantime, he refuses to become involved in the governmental activity of the Triumvirates. In April (or May) 59, he refuses an invitation to lead an undertaking in Egypt to discover the circumstances that led to Ptolemy XII Auletes being overthrown.[3] His feelings about the current political climate are made abundantly clear in the intense correspondence he exchanges with his close friend Titus Pomponius Atticus.

---

2 Cic. *Att.*, II.1.4–5.
3 Cic. *Att.*, II.5.1, II.16.2.

Cicero: The Letters to Atticus

Pomponius is a rich financier and a very cultured man. He is esteemed and respected by everyone both for his professional competence (he is a financial consultant and a banker) and for his personal virtues—his prudence, and his loyalty and generosity toward his friends, whichever political side they belong to, stand out in this respect—which are partly the fruit of his natural tendencies and partly due to his adherence to Epicureanism. During the civil war between Marius and Sulla he moved to Athens, remaining there for around 20 years, hence his *cognomen*— Atticus—taken from the region in which Athens is found: Attica. From now on, we'll call him Atticus.

In 68, he returns to Rome for good. Occasionally, he leaves it temporarily to inspect his properties, which are scattered around Italy, Hispania Ulterior, and Macedonia. Among his possessions is a fine villa in Buthrotum in Epirus (Butrint in Albania). Whenever he receives a letter from Cicero he responds by return of post, which happens frequently.

In the spring of 59, on the advice of Atticus, Cicero allows himself a holiday outside of Rome. He stays in his house in Antium until 18 April,[4] then he moves to his villa in Formiae, where he stays from 21 April to 6 May.[5] There, he writes, reads, and studies.[6] He works on a commentary in Greek, a commentary in Latin, and a poem. He sketches out a geographical treatise and a collection of historical events in the style of the Greek historian and rhetorician Theopompus of Chios (378/377–320), unfortunately never published. He starts on a work that he will title *Palinode*. He also spends a few days at the *Pompeianum*, a *villa otium* that he bought before May 60 in Stabiae (Castellammare di Stabia), a seaside resort that is highly regarded by rich Romans from the capital.[7]

Burebista

The Dacians are an Indo-European population[8] who live in an area north of the lower course of the Danube, where they are surrounded by the Bastarnae, Celts, and

4   Cic. *Att.*, II.4–9, 12.
5   Cic. *Att.*, II.11, II.14.2.
6   *Ibidem.*
7   Cic. *Att.*, I.20.1, II.8.2, 18.
8   A prehistoric population who spoke proto-Indo-European emigrated, at an unknown time, perhaps in the III millennium, from central-southern Anatolia or from the steppes around the Caspian and Aral Seas, some of whom headed toward Europe, while others moved into Inner Asia. After tracing long and convoluted paths, the migrants settled in Central and Northern Europe, the Iranian plateau, and India. This gave rise to the Celtic, Germanic, Greek, Thracian, Slav, Hittite, Armenian, Tocharian, Persian, and Indian peoples. Today, all these peoples are called Indo-Europeans.

Sarmatians, and from where they are now tending to expand.[9] They are primitive people, surrounded by people who are even more uncivilized. Around 60, the Dacian chief Burebista pushed back the Boii in the west and the Bastarnae in the east and founded a unitary tribal state, of which he made himself king. The capital of Dacia is Sarmizegetusa (near Haţeg in Romania). Sarmizegetusa isn't just a center of political and religious importance, it's also a center for the production of ceramics and working metals such as gold and silver from Transylvania, over which the Dacians have control. The Dacians mainly make their living from agriculture and breeding livestock. They practice apiculture, viticulture, trade with other peoples, and have a monetary economy. The ruling elite have a fairly high standard of living compared to the dominated masses. They live in houses equipped with running water, supplied by terracotta pipes.

Burebista's political activity is inspired or supported as appropriate by his advisers, among whom are various Greeks and a priest of the god Zalmoxis. He aims to extend the sovereignty of the Dacians to all the lands between the Middle Danube and the Black Sea. The cities of the northwestern coast of the Black Sea—Olbia, Tyras, Histria, etc.—which rose from Greek colonies have already been earmarked.

In 59, the consul Caesar argues that the growing power of the Dacians is a threat to the security of Macedonia and plans to quash it, triggering a preventive war. In reality, he plans to invade Dacian lands not so much because he sees an offensive or invasion as inevitable and wants to obtain a strategic advantage before the threat materializes, but primarily because he is in search of glory and riches and wants to receive Rome's gratitude, to elevate himself to the level of Pompey, to pay off his creditors, and to reward his soldiers. Mainly, he is attracted by the gold and silver of Transylvania.

Caesar's immediate goal is to achieve a great military victory. But he is well aware that the Senate will not put the question of going to war against the Dacians to the people in assembly if it's he who asks for it, because the Optimates—who are in the majority in the Senate—are predisposed against any of his initiatives, and not just for political reasons. Cato, the leader of the radical wing within the Optimates camp in the Senate, also opposes Caesar for personal reasons (he is deeply resentful of Caesar for having led his half-sister Servilia to cheat on her husband). In short, if he wants to succeed in his aim, Caesar must get Cato and his friends to soften the tone of their opposition to him just enough to allow him to push his proposal through. This requires that the relations between Caesar and Cato improve significantly.

However, Caesar is tormented about how to do this and chooses to try to get Marcus Calpurnius Bibulus to put him in Cato's good books, as he is his father-in-law.

---

9   Ancient Dacia extended to the east and north of the middle and lower reaches of the Danube, including the Carpathian Mountains, and reached the River Tisza in the west and the River Dniester in the east. It roughly corresponds to present-day Romania and Moldova.

But the relations between Caesar and Bibulus are no better than those between Caesar and Cato. Bibulus was Caesar's colleague as aedile, praetor, and consul and has always tried to hold his career back, but Caesar has always managed to back him into a corner. Recently, Caesar mistreated Bibulus to such an extent that he shut himself up in his house out of shame. There is, however, one person who can act as an intermediary between Caesar, Bibulus, and Cato, a member of the same familial clan as Bibulus. That person is Lucius Calpurnius Piso Caesoninus.[10]

Piso Caesoninus

In 59, Piso is about 46 years old (he was born in 105/101). He is a man with a stern face and a furrowed brow, suggesting the possession of a strong personality based on robust self-esteem. He is descended on his father's side from a family that has held the rank of consul eight times in the past, and on his mother's side from an Insubrian merchant who moved to Rome from Placentia (Piacenza). Piso himself has advanced his career through the magistracies up to the praetorship, which he held in 61, and he aspires to be consul and, looking further ahead, the governor of a province. He's confident about his chances, partly because he is extraordinarily rich and has previously always won when he has put himself forward as a candidate for lesser magistracies, although he is also aware that winning the consulship is a far more difficult task than any other of its kind. He has refined taste in Hellenistic culture and is both a collector of works of art and a follower of Epicurean philosophy. He owns a *villa otium* that is one of the most envied on the Campanian coast.

This is found in Herculaneum and is a large, sumptuous architectural complex on several floors, adorned with murals, mosaic floors, marble and bronze statues, fountains, baths, etc.[11] Among the treasures of that luxury residence, there is a library of literary works from the II to I centuries, comprising at least 650 rolls of papyrus (perhaps more than 1,000). For the most part, these are texts on Epicurean and Stoic philosophy written in Greek. The remaining 60–80 rolls are written in Latin and are on various subjects. The works on Greek philosophy are almost all by Philodemus of Gadara (110–35), an Epicurean philosopher of Palestinian descent who settled permanently in Rome after spending many years in Athens. Philodemus stayed and worked in the villa's library. It is likely that it was he who brought a series of books by Epicurus and other teachers from the Garden to the library, to which he added

---

10   Some of the *Calpurnii Pisones* had the *agnomen* Caesoninus, or Caesonius, while others had the *agnomen* Frugi.

11   This is the famous Villa dei Papiri (Villa of the Papyri) of Herculaneum, which was destroyed, like the whole city and others nearby (Pompeii, Baiae) following the eruption of Vesuvius in 79 AD. On the ownership of the Villa dei Papiri: F. Longo Auricchio, G. Indelli, G. Leone, and G. Del Mastro, *La Villa dei Papiri. Una residenza antica e la sua biblioteca* (Roma: Carocci, 2020), 181–191.

his own writings. Philodemus is also a poet and author of epigrams that deal with carefree love, aimed at arousing unadulterated pleasure for the senses.

Piso lives with his wife, his mother-in-law, and a host of servants in the exclusive residential quarter on the Palatine. His *domus* is situated around 150 meters from Cicero's. Philodemus's erotic epigrams offer an insight into the lascivious lifestyle that those in that house enjoy.

Caesar will support Piso in the race for the consulship for 58, as will Clodius, who is one of Caesar's men. In exchange, Piso will work to ensure that the Catonian faction do not oppose Caesar's plans to wage war on the Dacians sufficiently vigorously to prevent him from doing so. With these terms strictly defined, the pact is sealed by a marriage: Caesar will marry Calpurnia, Piso's daughter.

Calpurnia will be Caesar's fourth wife. His first wife, until 84, was Cossutia.[12] His second, Cornelia Cinna Minore, died in 69. His third was Pompeia, whom he divorced due to the scandal of the Festival of Bona Dea. At the time, Caesar was *pontifex maximus* (appointed for life in 63) and governor of Hispania Ulterior (appointed in 61). He divorced Pompeia due to the reputational damage that the accusations of adultery could cause him.

Piso is elected to the consulship in July 59, in part—perhaps mostly—due to the votes of the Populares, which Caesar channeled toward him. He will take office and begin discharging his duties from 1 January 58, alongside the Pompeian Aulus Gabinius.

Cicero: The Defense of Flaccus

In July 59, Cicero mourns the passing of Diodotus, a Greek Stoic philosopher who died in his home, where he had been a regular guest for years. Diodotus had been his teacher in logic and dialectics[13] during his early youth and was his interlocutor in dialogues on the deepest of subjects. On his death he bequeathed a fair sum of money to his host, some 100,000 sesterces.[14] Cicero is saddened by the loss. He had held Diodotus in the same level of respect as two other Greek philosophers: the Platonic skeptic Philo of Larissa (159/158–84/83) and the Stoic Posidonius of Rhodes (135–51).[15] He always spoke well of him and with evident affection. He will continue to do so in the future, whenever the occasion presents itself.

It is said—though there is no evidence for the many rumors that circulate—that Caesar paid a certain Lucius Vettius to falsely claim that some of Caesar's enemies

---

12 Caesar may not have actually married Cossutia as the two may have separated while they were still engaged. In this case, Calpurnia would be Caesar's third wife rather than his fourth.

13 On Cicero's study of logic and dialectics: Cicero, *Amic.* XIII.6.4; *Acad.*, II.115; *Brutus*, 308–309; *Tusc.*, V.113.

14 Cic. *Att.* II.20.6; *Brutus*, 309.

15 Cic. *Nat. D.*, I.3.

had asked him to assassinate Pompey and that he display their names on the rostrum.[16] But there are others who give a different version of events. According to this account, Cicero and Lucullus sent Vettius to kill Caesar and Pompey because they were unhappy with Caesar's maneuvering to reinforce his political position (with reference to the fact that Caesar was now related to Pompey, having given him his own daughter Julia in marriage despite her already having been promised to Quintus Servilius Caepio Brutus). Thus, Cicero finds himself implicated in a difficult situation, one which is completely alien to him.

The plot was discovered by Bibulus, who informed Pompey about it. Vettius is arrested before he can complete his undertaking and brought before the people in assembly, where he reveals the identities of the instigators: Cicero, Lucullus, and Bibulus. The fact that he also names Bibulus raises doubts about whether he is acting in good faith. This gives rise to the suspicion that Vettius isn't telling the truth regarding Cicero and Lucullus either and that he has been prompted to falsely denounce them through the machinations of their political opponents. Shortly afterward, Vettius is imprisoned, where he dies in suspicious circumstances.[17] This nebulous episode takes place between August and 18 October 59.

In September 59, Cicero has taken on the defense of Lucius Valerius Flaccus, Quintus Minucius Thermus, and Caius Antonius Hybrida, all accused in separate judicial proceedings. Antonius Hybrida, in particular, is accused of *crimen maiestatis*.

Crimen maiestatis is a crime that is provided for and punished under the *lex Appuleia de maiestate* (103 or 102), as modified by the *lex Cornelia de maiestate*, approved under the dictatorship of Sulla (82–79). The first of the cited laws instituted a special tribunal (*quaestio perpetua de maiestate*) to judge cases of *lèse-majesté* against the Roman people, understood as a form of high treason, with a jury composed of *equites*, but did not specify the scope of the crime. The second established that there is high treason in all cases involving acts that (aim to) threaten the institutions of the Republic, and such acts are punishable by death, with the possibility of replacing this sentence to voluntary exile. Among the acts that subvert the institutions of the *res publica* are inciting the army to rebel and undertaking a military campaign without the approval of the Senate and the Roman people, as well as, within a more general scope, a governor leaving his province while still in office, regardless of whether he leaves it with or without troops under his command.

Antonius Hybrida was accused of attacking the *maiestatis* of the Roman people for having supported Catiline prior to removing himself from the conspiracy and leading the army against the conspirators, his former comrades-in-arms, at the Battle of Pistoia in 62. Hybrida has already been indicted once before on another charge following a lawsuit brought by Caesar. He is the son of the deceased Marcus

---

16 Cic. *Att.*, II.24.3; *Sest.*, 132; *Vat.*, 24–26; Plut. *Luc.*, 42.7–8; App., *B. Civ.*, II.12; Suet. *Iul.*, 20.12.
17 Dio Cass., XXXVIII.9.

Antonius, the famed orator, who later took on the *cognomen* Orator to indicate he was the orator *par excellence*. Hybrida was Cicero's colleague in the consulship in 63. In 61, he was governor of Macedonia, where he was responsible for fleecing the local allies near the Black Sea and—in part due to his perfidy—suffered a series of military defeats against the Dardanians in Thrace and against the Scythians and Bastarnae under the walls of Istria, a city on the shores of the Black Sea (near present-day Caranasuf in Romania), conquered by the Romans in 72.

In 59, the accusation against Hybrida is supported by Marcus Caelius Rufus, a promising young judicial orator who has fiery, ironic, scathing eloquence that reflects his high capacity for analysis and a pronounced aptitude for fishing in troubled waters.

A Star is Born

Caelius Rufus is a 23-year-old of extraordinary physical beauty, supreme intelligence, and brilliant temperament. He is an exuberant sort (he's a very good dancer), something of a dandy in his dress sense, a classic exponent of the Roman *jeunesse dorée*, and a common sight in the *dolce vita* of the capital. Caelius's character is that of a disillusioned and cynical man, opportunistic and irreverent, ambitious and corruptible, rarely inclined to excitement. Cicero has seen a person rich in quality in him, who in some ways resembles himself. At first, Rufus submits himself to the political and moral authority of Cicero, his teacher and mentor.

Caelius was born in Interamnia Praetuttiorum (Teramo in Abruzzo) into an equestrian-rank family, but he moved to Rome while he was still very young and was taught the art of law under the auspices of Crassus and Cicero. This apprenticeship, in addition to teaching him "professionally," allowed him to get to know some very important people with some of whom he developed close friendships, such as Caesar.

In 63, he fell under the spell of Catiline and grew estranged from Cicero, but he distanced himself from Catiline's conspiracy before it was uncovered. To put himself above suspicion, he enlisted in the army that the proconsul Quintus Pompeius Rufus was forming to fight against Catiline and his followers. After this, he took part in some military operations in Asia Minor.

On his return to Rome in 61, Caelius takes his first steps in the political world by indicting Antonius Hybrida. Probably, it was Caesar and Pompey who suggested that Caelius indict Hybrida due to being disgusted by his infamy.

Cicero's attitude toward Caesar is reflected in his argument for the defense, which aims to shine an ugly light on Caelius to reduce the credibility of the accusation. Cicero highlights how Caelius is a friend of Caesar, how suspicion of having taken part in the Catilinarian Conspiracy hovers over the latter (in reference to the clemency that he showed in his dealings with the Catilinarian supporters arrested in 63, proposing that their lives be spared, almost as if he were on their side), and how Caesar is responsible, in the view of many citizens, for the violence and the acts contrary to the rules of law that were committed during his consulship.

Eventually, Hybrida is found guilty and is condemned to exile. He will serve his sentence in Greece, specifically in Cephalonia, a mountainous and heavily wooded island in the Ionian Sea, split almost in two by a deep bay.[18]

Thus, Caelius won the case. The student outdid the master. His resounding success makes him a judicial orator who excels in his area of activity and consolidates his social position. Shortly after, Caelius moves house. He goes to live in the most exclusive district of the capital, which is on the Palatine, where many important figures have their residences. His new house is as close to Cicero's as it is to that of Clodia, the sister of Clodius.

---

18   The sentence doesn't prevent him from holding the position of censor in 42.

CHAPTER VIII

Clodius the Tribune

The Threats to Cicero

Clodius is full of resentment toward Cicero. He wants to make him pay for the "offense" that he caused him by testifying against him in the trial following the scandal of the Bona Dea Festival and, more recently, by attempting to block his *transitio ad plebem*.[1] Therefore, he threatens him.

Cicero reports this to Pompey, with whom he is close personal friends, but Pompey is not particularly sensitive to sentimentality, and, in his dealings with Cicero and in the face of the latter's affinity toward him, he refrains from being completely sincere with him. In addition, Pompey has his own ties to Caesar, both in being part of the Triumvirate and in having married off his daughter to him, given that Clodius was elected with crucial support from Caesar and is his man. The only criticism that Cicero makes of Pompey is that of having associated himself with Caesar and Crassus; in his opinion, he stands to lose the most in terms of personal dignity. Pompey reassures Cicero that he has nothing to fear.[2] But his words will be proved wrong by later events.

In the autumn of 59, Clodius starts threatening Cicero again, backed up by his friends. Cicero's vexation returns. In his private conversations, and in his letters to Atticus, he often repeats that he is discontented, that politics no longer interests him, that he feels impotent in the face of its excesses, and that from now on he wants to dedicate himself exclusively to providing legal aid, to the study of classical texts, and to philosophical reflection.

Caesar and Cicero

Unlike Clodius, who wishes ill on Cicero, Caesar instead tries to maintain good relations with him, partly because in some ways he fears him. One way of succeeding in this goal is to demonstrate his friendship to Cicero, both to strengthen his bond

---

1   Cic. *Att.*, I.18.4, I.19.5. The actions that Cicero report here are doubtful.
2   Cic. *Att.*, II.19.4, II.20, II.21.6, II.22, II.23.3, II.24.5.

with him and to move him away from Rome, where dark clouds are gathering over his head. The occasion presents itself in the need to fill the post that has become vacant on the 20-man commission that was established for the implementation of the *lex Iulia agraria* due to the death of Caius Cosconius, who had been praetor in 63, the same year in which Cicero had been consul. At Caesar's invitation, Pompey, Cnaeus Tremellius Scrofa (an authority in the field of agriculture), Marcus Atius Balbus (a relative of both Pompey and Caesar after marrying the latter's sister, Julia Minor, from whose marriage were born Atia Major and Atia Minor), and Caius Octavius Thurinus (a senator of equestrian descent and a rich businessman), among others, already form part of this commission.

Caesar extends an invitation to Cicero to form part of the commission.[3] Cicero politely declines. He doesn't want to disavow his own code of conduct, for which he would deservedly earn the disapproval of honest people, but nor does he wish to expose himself to the ill will of other members of the commission, who do not trust him. He fears that, were he to accept, his personal safety would be in question, and he isn't exactly what one would call "lion-hearted."

In December 59, when he is leaving for Gallia Cisalpina, Caesar proposes to Cicero that he join his personal staff. He could hold the position of legate, that is, a high-ranking advisor, perhaps with a mandate from the Senate, or be given a free traveling pass.[4] In the latter case, he would enjoy the protections that diplomats are entitled to (inviolability, immunity, privileges), but he wouldn't have an obligation to undertake the duties of an ambassador (he could move back and forth from Rome whenever he wanted, without having to give up his position). Cicero is uncertain about whether to accept. He takes his time, turning it over in his mind. In the end, he convinces himself that he doesn't have to fear any threats and, if necessary, he will receive help from the *equites*, who already supported him in his opposition against Catiline. "I don't want to run away; I long to fight," he writes in a letter to Atticus. On 29 December 59, Cicero declines the offer. Then, since Atticus has returned from Epirus, he invites him to dine with him in his town house in Rome.[5]

However, to maintain a cordial relationship with Caesar, he returns the gesture. Since the post of proconsul of Gallia Narbonensis has become vacant due to the sudden and unexpected death of Metellus Celer, Cicero puts Caesar forward as a candidate for this position, justifying his preference convincingly and persuasively. The Senate is convinced Caesar is the man they need, and appoint him to the governorship of Gallia Narbonensis, effective from 1 March 58. Caesar thus adds the proconsulship of Gallia Narbonensis to the proconsulship of Gallia Cisalpina and Illyricum, which he already held.

---

3   Cic. *Att.*, II.19.4.
4   Cic. *Att.*, II.18.3, II.19.5.
5   Cic. *Att.*, II.2.3, II.3.3–4.

The Clodian Laws

Clodius takes office on 10 December 59. He will remain in post for a year, during which he must seek to satisfy the needs of the most disparate circles—the Senate, the *equites*, the lower-class plebeians—while avoiding the veto of the tribune of the plebs loyal to the Senate. He gets off to a searing start. Between December 59 and March 58, Clodius proposes 12 or 13 bills. On the day he enters office, he proposes four.

One aims to introduce the distribution of free grain to the less well-off in the capital and its rural environs, a novelty in the history of Rome, without placing a limit on the number of possible beneficiaries and, to that end, committing 20 percent of the tax revenues due to the state treasury to the enterprise, both for the present year and for each of the years to come (64 million sesterces, an enormous sum). The novelty of the initiative lies in the free nature of the distribution. In the past, grain had only been sold to the public at low prices. The *lex Clodia frumentaria* also tasks the state with paying for the food of the freedmen, modernizing the current situation (previously, these expenses were borne by their patrons). As such, one of its effects will be an increase in the number of slaves being freed.

Clodius's second plebiscite seeks to restore the *collegia* and create new ones. The *collegia* are cultural associations (established for the celebration of regular religious occasions) or trade associations (guilds that bring together artisans, small traders, slaves). Since they had been closely connected to gangs of former Catilinarians, freedmen, and slaves, they had been dissolved by the Senate in the late 60s.[6] Clodius will use them to put pressure on the electorate and constitutional bodies to support his legislative proposals and will draw a number of individuals from them to form a street gang to strike out at his political opponents through the use of hooliganism or violence.

The third plebiscite aims to limit the powers of the censors, who are the principal moral authorities of the state. The proposal stipulates that expulsion from the Senate can no longer be decided by only one censor but with the mutual consent of both.

The fourth plebiscite plans for an increase in the number of days in which it is possible for the popular assemblies to gather, and prevents magistrates from exercising their power to dissolve popular assemblies during the collection of the auspices. From now on, this must be carried out by the convening magistrate himself, in the place where the assembly is taking place and before its work begins.[7]

The Temple of Jupiter Optimus Maximus is situated at the top of the Capitolium (one of the two summits of the Capitoline, the other being called the Arx). On 1 January 58, as in every year, a meeting of the Senate takes place there to inaugurate

---

6   Most probably in 64.
7   The same magistrate who had called the assembly would have presided over it. It was up to the consuls and the praetors to convene the *comitia centuriata* and the *comitia curiata*, and the tribunes of the plebs to convene the *comitia tributa* and the *concilia plebis*.

a new year of activity after the inauguration ceremony for the new consuls. Piso, who has convened the meeting, is now presiding over its proceedings. He performs the ritual sacrifice, a preliminary to any activity by the organs of the state. Once he has ascertained that the auspices aren't bad, he introduces the order of the day and opens the discussion. When giving senators the floor, he calls on Cicero third.[8] Cicero has a start, and a frown quickly crosses his face as he begins to sulk. He is a man with a touchy and meticulous character, and he feels that Piso, by only asking him third, has slighted him and damaged his personal dignity. Therefore, he is upset, resentful, and indignant about the incident; he feels mortally insulted. The incident will deepen the divide that separates him and Piso. There has been bad blood between the two for some time: Cicero considers Piso as one of the people who are most responsible for condemning him to exile. From now on, neither will miss any opportunity to spite each other out of stubborn revenge.

The same day (1 January 58), the senator Caius Octavius Thurinus, Caesar's uncle, dies of an illness aged 42. He leaves his wife Atia Minor and his children—Octavia Major, Caius, and Octavia Minor—mourning his loss. He passes away in the family home of the *Octavii Thurinii*, a villa in Nuvlana (Nola) in Campania.

On 4 January 58, the four plebiscites presented by Clodius on 10 December 59 are submitted to the *comitia tributa* for them to vote on, all together, in an irregular and probably illegitimate way. Three of them are passed without a problem. The fourth—the one that concerns the *collegia*—comes up against the veto of the tribune of the plebs Lucius Ninnius Quadratus. There is a widespread opinion among commentators that Ninnius's move was prompted by his friend Cicero.[9] To get the veto retracted, Clodius assures Cicero that, while he carries out his duties as tribune, he won't do anything to harm him. In other words, saying "if Ninnius doesn't retract the vote, I'll take revenge on you." Cicero catches his drift and intercedes with Ninnius, who will step back from his position. With the block removed, the plebiscite on the *collegia* is approved too and thus becomes a law of the state.

The *lex Clodia frumentaria* competes with Caesar's agrarian law and hinders its implementation, because it disincentivizes the proletarians who live in the city to move to the countryside to work the land, while it incentivizes the peasants of the rural areas to become part of the urban population (both the former and the latter will have food at the state's expense; the former if they remain where they are, and the latter if they relocate to the city). Caesar, the "great elector" of Clodius, is displeased.

---

8   Cic. *Red. sen.*, 17. The regulations of the Senate of Rome stipulate that speeches are given during debates in this college according to a precise order. Cicero was neither the *princeps senatus* nor a consul in office. He was an ex-consul. As such, he had the right to speak, but not the right to be called upon third in order of succession. It should be concluded that Cicero's reaction was down to personal reasons, or rather, his bad personal relationship with Piso.

9   On Cicero's attempt to resist Clodius's four plebiscites of 10 December 59: Cic. *Pis.*, 8–9; Asconius, 15.6–18 ST (=7.9–26 C); Dio Cass., XXXVIII.14.1–3.

Clodius couldn't not have foreseen that it would end like this. Therefore, by promoting and obtaining approval for his grain law, he deliberately took a path that diverged from that of Caesar. However, he has risen in the estimation of the lower-class plebeians. Evidently, this is what he was most interested in.

The system set in place for the provision of grain in the capital is called the *cura annonae*. It is up to its officials to oversee the free distribution of grain to the public at specific events, of which there is a list. Clodius ensures that the man put in charge of the *cura annonae* is one of his freedmen, Sextus Clodius. The aim is clear: to guarantee for himself, through a trusted lackey, control over the distribution of grain, understood as a form of exercising power and as a tool that he can use to create a clientele for himself.

Clodius thinks that he can now rely on his own electoral base and that he therefore no longer needs the support of Caesar. In short, the success of his own legislative initiatives intoxicates Clodius to such an extent that he believes he can make himself independent from Caesar, the leader of the Populares, the political faction to which he belongs.

CHAPTER IX

Cato Is Removed from Rome

An Act of Piracy[1]

Meanwhile, Caesar's attempt to cozy up with Bibulus and Cato through Piso has failed, and Caesar is convinced that the only possible way for his political actions not to be blocked by the Catonian opposition is for Cato to be removed from Rome. In the meantime, however, he has abandoned his plan to attack Burebista because the prerequisite for the action has not been fulfilled. The Dacian ruler, fearing a military invasion by the Romans in the Carpathian–Danubian area, has returned to Transylvania. As a result, the Dacian threat to Macedonia that could have justified the instigation of a preventive war no longer exists, if it ever had in the first place.[2]

To remove Cato from Rome, Caesar chooses to make use of Clodius. Therefore, despite the grain law, the political understanding between Caesar and Clodius remains firm, at least for the moment. To achieve their goal, the two plan to resort to the reliable pretext of conferring high office.[3] Romans frequently act in this way when it comes to freeing a key position in the institutional or bureaucratic apparatus from the person who occupies it by promoting him to a higher, perhaps honorary role if they have no other means by which to remove him. There is a Latin expression that sums up this stratagem clearly and precisely: *promoveatur ut amoveatur* ("let him be promoted to get him out of the way").

Clodius quickly steps into action. In February–March 58, he puts forward two interconnected plebiscites in quick succession. The first regards the Kingdom of Cyprus, governed by Ptolemy (80–58), brother of Ptolemy XII Auletes, ruler of

---

1   Plut. *Cat. Min.*, 34–40. On the Clodian laws relating to Cyprus: G. Rotondi, *Leges publicae populi Romani* (1912), 397

2   We hear Burebista's name again when he attacks the Bastarnae and advances up to the coast of the Black Sea, destroying the ancient Greek city of Olbia.

3   Vell. Pat., 2.45.4.

Egypt. The second aims to secure the appointment of Cato as "high commissioner" of Cyprus.

Clodius's legislative initiative is aimed at finding the financial means necessary to cover the expenses for the free distribution of grain, but it seems that Clodius's desire to take revenge on Ptolemy, whom Clodius holds a grudge against for not having offered a sufficiently large sum to pay his ransom when he had been kidnapped by pirates, is not an altogether unrelated issue.

The bill plans for Ptolemy to be deposed from the throne, for the Kingdom of Cyprus to be abolished, for its territory to be annexed and incorporated into the Roman state, and for its royal treasury to be confiscated and added to the *aerarium* before being sold at auction. If Ptolemy tries to assert his rights by opposing this through armed resistance, he will be wiped out by the legions. What Clodius foreshadows in his bill is therefore armed aggression against an independent and sovereign state to strip it of its wealth and territory. In effect, an act of international piracy. This emerges with even greater clarity if we consider that although the Kingdom of Cyprus isn't formally a friend and ally of the Roman people, it is not its enemy either, nor has it done anything to deserve being subjected to violence—there has been no provocation, no act of war.

Not knowing what else to fabricate to justify his banditry project, Clodius accuses Ptolemy of not having requested political recognition from the Senate of Rome, of having jeopardized the city's food supply by tolerating the presence of pirates' hideouts on his island, and of having dealings—like his brother Ptolemy XII Auletes—with Mithridates VI, king of Pontus, who availed himself of the Cilician pirates in his fight against Rome.

Why on earth should Ptolemy have asked for political recognition from the Senate of Rome? Cyprus isn't a client state of Rome, as Egypt is, for example. As for the charge of the presence of pirate hideouts in Cyprus, this seems to be well-founded, but how important could these be if we consider that the pirates have bases all over the eastern Mediterranean? They can be found in Cilicia, on the Libyan coastline, on Crete, etc. Moreover, Cyprus is a big island: it isn't possible to assiduously monitor its entire coastline, every natural harbor, every bay. As for Mithridates VI, all the states of Western Asia have had relations with the king of Pontus but this doesn't mean that they have all adhered to his foreign policy, much less his policy regarding the pirates. Furthermore, one shouldn't overlook the fact that all the states of the Mediterranean have a hazy policy regarding the pirates. On the one hand, the Romans fight against them, but on the other, they are the main buyers of the slaves that the pirates put on the market and slaves are indispensable to the Roman economy.

The Cyprus bill also includes a passage that doesn't relate to the Roman conquest of the island but the repatriation of a group of citizens of Byzantium who had been condemned to exile. By inserting this into the bill Clodius intended to honor the agreement he made in 69, for which he received (or received the promise of) a bribe.[4] This insertion might be considered inappropriate because the protocol of legislative acts is that they consider homogeneous material, as provided for by the *lex Cecilia Didia*, approved in 98, which prohibits collating provisions concerning disparate matters in a single bill. The logic of its inclusion, however, is the fact that the exiles to be sent back to Byzantium are in Cyprus and that this island, after being conquered by Rome, will be administrated by a Roman magistrate.

The bill also has a corollary, which plans for Cato to be given the office of *pro quaestore pro praetore* (quaestor with the powers of a praetor) to ensure the implementation of the law once it has been approved and entered into force. This office is justified by the fact that the acts of confiscating and transferring Ptolemy's assets to Rome fall within the competence of a quaestor or proquaestor, while the ability to wage war on the sovereign presupposes the attribution of *imperium* (military command), such as a propraetor has, and which also includes the conferral of *ius auspiciorum*, which is the power to consult the gods to establish whether or not they are in favor of the activity to be performed. The officeholder will be physically sacrosanct and, together with the related powers, will receive a series of rights: that of wearing a gold ring as a symbol of recognition and prestige, that of obtaining reimbursements of his travel expenses, and of having a retinue made up both of free men for company and of slaves and freedmen to act as scribes and interpreters. Undertaking the duties of this office will also result in Cato taking care of the repatriation of the Byzantine exiles.[5]

Clodius, in describing his legislative proposal to the Senate, explains that Cato is preferable to any other candidate for the assignment of the office in question, because it involves confiscating huge sums for the *aerarium* and his moral integrity is a guarantee.

To hand the task of ruling on the abolition of the Kingdom of Cyprus and the appointment of Cato to the people gathered in assembly means bypassing the Senate, which is the competent constitutional organ for dealing with both issues of foreign policy and affairs regarding the administration of the state. But it also means damaging the Ptolemies, scorning the agreement that the Triumvirs reached with Ptolemy XII Auletes in 59, according to which both his position on the throne of Egypt and the conferral of the status of friend and ally of Rome were confirmed (to obtain this result, Ptolemy paid a bribe of 140 million sesterces). Of course, "the Ptolemies" doesn't just refer to the Ptolemies of Egypt but also refers to Ptolemy of

4 Dio Cass., XXXVIII.30.5; Str., XIV.6.6; App. *B. Civ.*, II.23. According to Cicero, Clodius had been bribed by the delegates from the Greek cities who came to Rome to plead the case. Cic. *Har. resp.*, 59.

5 According to Plutarch, Clodius modified the *lex Clodia de Catone proquaestore cum imperio praetorio mittendo* through the addition of an amendment concerning the repatriation of the Byzantine exiles to keep Cato away from Rome for longer. Plut. *Cat. Min.*, 34.4.

Cyprus. Despite this, Pompey and Crassus rule in favor of the legislative initiatives of Caesar and Clodius on the Roman conquest of Cyprus and the removal of Cato from Rome.[6] The companies of publicans, the group that carries the most weight among the *equites*, are of the same mind. These businesses support Clodius's initiative because they see the possibility of making new and substantial profits in the annexation of Cyprus to the Roman state (Cyprus is a notoriously rich island).

Cato is aware that Clodius is maneuvering against him. He protests, saying that what the tribune wants to pass off as a favor is in fact a trap and an insult. But Clodius presses on, and between February and March 58, when the law that plans for the annexation of Cyprus and the confiscation of Ptolemy's assets has already been passed, he also obtains approval for its corollary.

A Strenuous Political Climate

In the first months of 58, due to the violence inherent in the politics of the Triumvirs, Rome is under a heavy pall that creates anxiety and stress among the citizens of every class and social group and discourages any attempt at protest. The situation is even worse than the summer of 59, when Cicero had been threatened by Clodius.

Cicero is distressed both by the gravity of the general situation and because he feels he is being targeted. Clodius's hostility toward Cicero, we recall, is because the latter testified against him during the trial after the scandal of the Festival of Bona Dea and then hindered his passage to becoming a plebeian. Eventually, Cicero received assurances from Pompey that Clodius's plan to have himself adopted by Fonteius wasn't directed against him and that therefore he had nothing to fear. Following this, when the Senate was discussing his proposed law on the *collegia*, Clodius reassured Cicero about his intentions toward him.

However, Clodius has no intention of observing the non-aggression pact he made with Cicero. Proof of this comes between 23 February and 1 March 58, when he puts forward a plebiscite that aims to obtain a sentence of exile for former magistrates who have been found guilty of having Roman citizens executed without allowing them their right to appeal against the death penalty. This is a heavy sentence, one that would be applied even in cases in which the allegedly illegal conduct had taken place before the enforcement of the law that provided for it and punished it as a crime. The initiative is part of the long-standing ideological conflict between Populares and Optimates on the rights of Roman citizens versus the state. Clodius uses this to take revenge on Cicero for well-known reasons of personal rancor, but also to issue a warning to all the Optimates. The proposal delights all Catiline's former followers and sympathizers, citizens against the abuse of public powers, and

---

6   This ruling is less surprising when one considers the fact that, as Plutarch states, Caesar and Pompey fear Cato. Plut. *Cat. Min.*, 34.1–3.

all those who believe that the Senate must not interfere in criminal matters to the extent that it replaces the people gathered in assembly. Moreover, it strikes a chord with the past actions of Caesar, who, during the Senate debate of 5 December 63, tried in vain to spare the lives of the seven arrested Catilinarians.

Cicero thus sees, opening wide before him, the horrible prospect of being sanctioned for conduct that, at the time of the events, was not viewed nor was punishable as a crime and which he undertook in an emergency, carrying out a precise mandate from the Senate of Rome, to remove a very great threat to the citizenry. He senses that the same Senate that once hailed him as "Savior of the Republic" is now about to make him the sacrificial lamb to avoid many senators who took part in the meeting of 5 December being indicted (the Senate will be absolved of all guilt if Cicero pays for everyone).

The political climate deteriorates more and more as the days pass between the plebiscite being presented and it being put to a vote, which is planned for 12 March. The tension skyrockets when Cicero is chased down the street by Clodius's gangs, who throw mud and stones at him to publicly ridicule him. Cicero, deeply troubled by the incident, dresses in the clothes of an *eques* and appeals to the people, to the *equites*, and to his "friend" Pompey.

As a result, there follow some public, tumultuous demonstrations of solidarity with Cicero on the Capitoline, with the participation of Roman *equites*, Italics, and senators. The *equites* proclaim that they wish to defend Cicero by any means necessary and will clothe themselves in mourning dress because the state is now without a leader.

Wearing mourning dress is a typical form of protest carried out by the Senate when the state is faced with an emergency. *Vestem mutare* ("to change clothes") means in practice that the senators change out of their normal clothes—the *toga praetexta*, white in color with a red-purple border—and put on the *toga sordida*, which is deep black or blackish gray, like the *toga pulla* or *atra* but darkened with ash or similar. The Romans wear the *toga pulla* as a sign of mourning or loss as well as during certain religious rituals. The *toga sordida*, no longer used for political purposes, is instead worn by the criminally accused, by their families, and by their defenders, starting from the moment of their indictment.

The *equites* call on the consuls to urge the Senate to reject Clodius's legislative proposal. The senators dress in mourning clothes and abandon the Senate's sessions. Clodius denounces the protests. First, he explains that he has coordinated his initiative with the Triumvirs, then he threatens to have the troops camped on the Campus Martius wade in to restore order. The threat is aimed at the supporters of Cicero as a whole, including, therefore, the senators. In short, Clodius allows himself to intimidate the Senate, knowing that Caesar and the consuls are on his side. In fact, Caesar confirms that he is on Clodius's side. As for Pompey and Crassus, they remain silent, but they are with Clodius as well. This is demonstrated by the fact that the consul Gabinius exiled the *eques* Aelius Lamia for having passionately pleaded the cause of Cicero.

Gabinius and his consular colleague Piso mutually agree to ban senators from wearing mourning clothes. This leads to a clear institutional conflict between the consuls, some plebeian magistrates (Clodius and some of his colleagues), and the Triumvirs on the one hand, and the Senate on the other. The affair ends when the protests subside, that is, the cessation of public demonstrations in support of Cicero and any other publicly expressed act designed to show solidarity with him.

Cicero feels he is in imminent danger, and his anxiety deprives him of sleep. He had believed that his privileged relationship with Pompey would have protected him from Clodius's attacks, but he had been mistaken—on the one hand by Clodius's impetuosity and on the other by the hesitation of Pompey, who is seeking to safeguard his own relations with Caesar, who is the protector of Clodius. In the days that follow, Cicero goes to visit Piso to ask him to intercede with Clodius on his behalf, but the consul merely opens his arms in a sign of powerlessness. He then plays another card: he successfully asks his friend Ninnius Quadratus to use his veto on Clodius's bill. Inexplicably, however, the veto is ineffective. Cicero therefore goes to see Pompey at his country house in Alba, but Pompey is nowhere to be found. On the one hand, Pompey is indebted to Cicero, who has always supported him in his political gambits. On the other hand, he doesn't want to challenge Caesar, his son-in-law, friend, and ally, who has previously asked him to drop the reasons for gratitude that bind him to Cicero.[7] But Cicero doesn't give up: he asks Lucullus and other senatorial friends to intercede for him with Pompey by going to visit him, and they duly oblige. Pompey warmly welcomes his colleagues, but, when they explain the reason for their visit to him, he replies that he doesn't want to enter into conflict with a tribune of the plebs over an initiative that the latter has undertaken in the performance of his duties.[8] On 11 March—the eve of the vote on Clodius's bill—Cicero goes back to Piso. The consul recommends that he not persist, that he resigns himself to the inevitable, and that he leaves the city, at least for a time, to spare Rome from a violent crisis, one that could be born from the opposition between Clodius, the Triumvirs, and the consuls on the one hand and the supporters of Cicero on the other. The same day, Cicero consults Cato and other close friends. They also advise him to absent himself from Rome until the waters have calmed again, promising him that they will work on his behalf in the meantime so he can make a glorious return.

In the end, Cicero is convinced and, with the expectation of not having to be away for long, prepares to leave. He says goodbye to his wife Terentia, who will remain in Rome, and then goes up to the Capitolium, one of the two summits of

---

7   Plut. *Cic.,* 31.2–3.
8   Cic. *Pis.,* 76–77.

the Capitoline hill. He goes into the Temple of the Capitoline Triad and dedicates a statuette of Minerva, which he has taken from his own home and is particularly dear to him, to the goddess. Huddled over in prayer before the simulacrum of the goddess, he begs her to preserve moderation and wisdom among the rulers of Rome and by doing so, to save the city, which would otherwise be lost to tyranny. Finally, he leaves Rome, alone and at night, heading for his family home in Arpinum.[9]

He feels safe in the family home of the *Cicerones* on the banks of the Fibrieno and anxiously waits to receive news on the situation's developments. In particular, he is waiting to find out the results of the plans he set in motion with his friends before leaving the capital. Before long, he finds out with relief that the tribune of the plebs Lucius Antistius has reported the illegitimacy or illegality of numerous acts carried out by Caesar during his consulship in 59 to the courts, while the praetors Lucius Domitius Ahenobarbus and Caius Memmius have asked the Senate to annul the Julian Laws of 59. These actions are not so much targeted at Caesar, or rather not him alone, as they are at Clodius. If, in fact, Caesar's actions are annulled, then the *transitio ad plebem* of Clodius will be invalidated, Clodius will forfeit his office as tribune of the plebs, and the Clodian Laws will be overturned.

However, the attempt of Ahenobarbus and Memmius is unsuccessful, on the one hand because Caesar invokes his right as a magistrate to immunity from prosecution, and on the other because Clodius threatens to reduce the debts owed by the publicans to the state by a third, ensuring that the *equites*' support of Cicero—on which the orator and his friends were relying—dwindled.

---

9   Cic. *QFr.*, I.4.4; Cic. *Dom.*, 96; Plut. *Cic.*, 31.6; App. *B. Civ.*, II.15.

CHAPTER X

A Three-Step Strategy

Clodius's Law Concerning Executed Roman Citizens

Clodius has targeted Cicero in the same way that, when hunting, he fixes his gaze and steadily aims his weapon at his target. Beyond his empty reassurances—he says without hesitation that he doesn't have malicious intentions—his purpose is to strike at and take down his prey by implementing a three-step strategy. This happens in 58, when Clodius is tribune of the plebs, duly elected and in office.

The first move consists of presenting a bill that sets the penalty of exile for those who have been found guilty of having a Roman citizen executed without a fair trial, including the *provocatio ad populum*, that is, taking recourse to appealing against the verdict to the people. A fair trial is one that is played out in public, with a cross-examination of each party, on an equal footing, in front of a third-party as an impartial judge; in the event of a death sentence or a sentence to pay a heavy fine, the condemned person may challenge the verdict in front of the people gathered in assembly; the latter can, if it wishes to do so, overturn the judge's sentence. Since Roman criminal law punishes unlawful conduct even if it occurred prior to the entry into force of the law that provides for it and punishes it as a crime, the measure can be applied retroactively.[1] The reference is implicit but it's clear to everyone that Clodius wants to refer to one legal case in particular, that of the seven Roman citizens who had been executed as part of the measures taken against the Catilinarian conspiracy. These measures were adopted by virtue of the state of emergency declared with the *senatus consultum ultimum*[2] of 5 December 63

---

1   The principle of the non-retroactivity of criminal law is that no one can be tried and condemned for actions that weren't considered a crime at the time they were committed. It is summarized in the maxim *nulla poena sine lege* and it is always applicable, unless new laws decriminalize, mitigate, or otherwise correct the previous provisions in favor of the guilty party. Most modern judicial systems are based on the principle of non-retroactivity. The Romans did not recognize it.

2   The *senatus consultum ultimum* is the provision of the Senate that, in the event of serious danger to the *res publica*, it declares an emergency and entrusts the consuls with the use of any means necessary to avoid damage being done to the state.

and implemented with the special powers conferred to the consul Cicero. Capital punishment for the arrested Catilinarians was sanctioned by the death sentences issued by the Senate following a summary judgment, in violation of the right of the accused to benefit from a fair trial and ask for and obtain a second examination of the verdict by the people gathered in assembly. Clodius's plebiscite is put to a vote on 12 March 58 and receives a majority vote. It is thus approved and swiftly comes into force as the *lex Clodia de civibus Romanis interemptis*, "Clodius's law concerning executed Roman citizens." On hearing the news, Cicero becomes greatly agitated—Clodius's strategy is now clear to him and Cicero knows it is aimed against him.

On 13 March 58, the day after the aforementioned law is approved, Clodius makes his second move. He presents a new plebiscite which authorizes Cicero's indictment for having falsified the minutes of the Senate meeting of 5 December 63 by removing the name of his protégé, Faustus Cornelius Sulla, and therein reporting the will of the Senate in a distorted way with a view to ensuring that the sentencing of the seven Catilinarians would be definitive and not open to appeal. The intention behind the new initiative is blatant: Clodius is pursuing the goal of stifling the controversies raised in recent years by the *senatus consultum ultimum* of 5 December 63 by relieving the Senate of all responsibility and placing the blame for what happened on Cicero alone.

While Clodius tightens the noose around Cicero and sees that his second plebiscite also becomes law, Cato leaves for Cyprus. He has been legally tasked with deposing King Ptolemy, confiscating his assets, abolishing the Kingdom of Cyprus, annexing the island to the Roman state, and organizing it into a province. A young man, his 27-year-old half-nephew, will be his assistant. This is Quintus Servilius Caepio Brutus, the son of Marcus Junius Brutus and Servilia Caepio, Cato's half-sister. Caepio Brutus was born in 85 and, after the death of his father, was adopted by his maternal uncle Quintus Servilius Caepio, hence the change of name. It is rumored that he is Caesar's illegitimate son because it is well-known that Servilia cheated on her husband with Caesar. However, the rumor isn't a very convincing one. For one thing, it isn't certain that they were already having an affair at the time of Brutus's conception. In any case, Caepio Brutus is a stellar young man. He has received a high-quality education and refined his skill in rhetoric and philosophy with a period of study in Athens, where he attended lessons given by Antiochus of Ascalon. He has been educated by Cato in the ways of the *mos maiorum* and Stoicism. As such, he is a learned and cultured Roman citizen with traditionalist ideas. He admires the customs of his forefathers and lauds the purest virtues of the Roman people: *libertas, dignitas, res publica*. His behavior appears to be constantly inspired by these principles and values, and he is irreproachable. He was engaged to Julia before her father Caesar gave away her hand in marriage to Pompey Magnus. Caepio Brutus is passionate about poetry and art, and he is (or will be) the author of three moralistic treatises on virtue, patience, and duty, and some historical summaries.

The Law on the Exile of Cicero

In April 58, Clodius makes his final move, a checkmate. He presents a third draft law that aims to get Cicero sentenced to exile due to being found guilty of having transgressed the *lex Clodia de civibus Romanis interemptis*. The logic of the move is this: considering that the *senatus consultum ultimum* of 5 December 63 was falsified and is a distorted reflection of the will of the constitutional body that issued it, and because this flawed legitimacy and culpability for it are attributable to Cicero, it emerges that the latter acted illegally against the arrested Catilinarians, violating their right to benefit from a fair trial and to be able to appeal against their death sentence. The bill includes two final clauses, one of which prohibits the modification, assimilation, or abrogation of the provisions contained in the bill, while the other restricts Cicero's right to appeal.

The people gather in assembly to vote on the plebiscite. Clodius sees to it that the consuls Piso Caesoninus and Gabinius are present at the session. He makes the same request of Pompey and Crassus, but Pompey is nowhere to be seen. The day before the date for which the session has been convened, a gang of armed men set up camp on the Circus Flaminius to ensure that no friend of Cicero can impede the plebiscite's approval.[3] This gang is headed by a free Roman citizen, a certain Fidulius, well-known among his fellow citizens as one of Clodius's henchmen. The session duly takes place, and the plebiscite is approved. The *lex Clodia de exilio Ciceronis* ("Clodius's law on the exile of Cicero") thus enters into force.

The first developments that follow this come in rapid succession: Cicero is expelled from the Senate; his townhouse, located on the Palatine, is confiscated and acquired by the *aerarium*; and his villas in Tusculum and Formiae are set alight and sacked by locals, neighbors, and passers-by.[4] Shortly after, Cicero's house on the Palatine is torn down during a protest that was called by Clodius at which the consuls were also present. The act has a symbolic value. Usually, this occurs to the properties of those who have been found guilty of wanting to make themselves king, and it assumes that, in the case of the seven Catilinarians, Cicero conducted himself like a tyrant.

Due to her husband's conviction, Terentia, Cicero's wife, has been deprived of her privileges, her house, and her marital property, with the risk that she could even

---

3   Cic. *Dom.*, 79.
4   It often happened that houses that were going up in flames were ransacked by opportunistic criminals. The looters were sure to get away with it because there was no law enforcement authority in the city.

lose her dowry as well, since it is debated as to whether Roman law allows this to be confiscated too. She has remained in Rome "to protect the wrecks of the calamity which had fallen on us both."[5] Now, however, she is a "widow" (a husband, when he has been exiled, is considered dead), and so she dresses in mourning clothes. From now on, she will have to look after herself and her two children—Marcus and Tullia—in a context of serious financial hardship, as well as to protect herself and them. When, in the days of the confiscation and destruction of the house on the Palatine, she is insulted and shoved on the street, on the Via Sacra, she decides to take refuge with her half-sister Fabia in the sanctuary of the Vestal Virgins.

Cicero receives the upsetting news while he is in his family's ancestral home in Arpinum. Distraught, he considers with indescribable bitterness that he has undergone the same treatment that has been reserved in the past for enemies of the state and concludes that he is now looked upon as such by his fellow citizens. He contemplates suicide, but he finds some comfort in learning that his friend Atticus is striving to save his villas.[6] As for his townhouse on the Palatine, his chattels, and his slaves, there is unfortunately nothing to be done. They will be auctioned off, supervised by Clodius.

Cicero thinks and thinks, tormenting himself, before finally coming to a decision: he will seek refuge and protection with his friends in Sicily, starting with the island's governor, the praetor Caius Vergilius. He therefore sets off for that province, taking all necessary precautions. In fact, since the extra-urban roads are infested by brigands, the wise thing to do is to travel in groups and armed, or to join senior officials, who travel in convoy and under escort, although they still mutter hexes and hold onto good-luck talismans until they reach their destination.[7]

Cicero on the Road to Exile

Cicero is accompanied on the road to exile by his friend Cnaeus Sallustius and by some of his freedmen, who will see to their safety. Sallustius is a philosopher and a poet. He was born into a family of enriched plebeians who, after his birth, moved to Rome from Amiternum, a Sabine city located in western Samnium (San Vittorino,

---

5   In a letter written to his brother Quintus on 13 June 58 in Thessalonica, Cicero explains the reason why Terentia remained in Rome as follows: *quid, quod mulierem miserrimam, didelissimam coniugem, me prosequi non sum passus, ut esset quae reliquias communis calamitatis, communis liberos tueretur?* ("Need I mention also how I refused to allow my unhappy wife—the truest of helpmates—to accompany me, that there might be someone to protect the wrecks of the calamity which had fallen on us both, and guard our common children?"). Cic. *Q.Fr.,* III.3.3.

6   In the meantime, Atticus's sister Pomponia has married the orator's brother, Quintus Tullius Cicero.

7   The situation persisted during the Principate. The *lex Iulia de vi*, approved during the reign of
Emperor Augustus (27 BC–14 AD), explicitly permitted arms to be carried to defend oneself from being attacked while traveling.

around 11 km north of L'Aquila in Abruzzo). In 58, he is 28 years old. In 63, he had been taken in by Catiline before managing to extricate himself.

While traveling down the Via Appia, Cicero, Sallustius, and their bodyguard take a break in Atina, a town in Lower Lazio that is entirely situated on the top of a hill and is apparently impregnable. There, they are hosted for the night by Cnaeus Plancius in the fine villa he had inherited from his father. Plancius is an *eques* who fought in the North and in Crete. Recently, he was elected to the quaestorship, but he hasn't yet started undertaking his duties: he will take office on 1 January 57. In Atina, Cicero falls asleep at dawn after a sleepless night and has a dream. He sees himself striding along, sad and thoughtful, and then Caius Marius appears, standing before him, dressed as a consul and with the insignia of the office, preceded by his *lictors*. Marius asks Cicero why he is so sad. Cicero explains the situation that has come about after he was sentenced to exile. Marius initially urges him to have hope, then he orders one of his *lictors* to accompany him to the Temple of Honos et Virtus, the temple that he himself had built in Rome to celebrate his victory at the Battle of the Raudine Plain that ended the Cimbrian War (113–101). When he wakes up, Cicero reflects on the dream and feels heartened. He cannot know that he has seen an omen, that is, a portent about the course of future events. Cicero's dream, in fact, contains elements of truth with regard to events that will occur in the future, and which will work in his favor.

Once in Capua, Cicero, Sallustius, and their escort leave the Via Appia and take the Via Popilia, which will take them to Rhegium (Reggio Calabria), a city on the Calabrian shore of the Straits of Messina.

Clodius, who has informants everywhere, follows Cicero's moves from afar and gives him no respite. To prevent him from taking refuge in Sicily, he arranges for the law on Cicero's exile to be modified so that it orders the condemned to put a distance of no less than 400 (or 500) Roman miles (around 740 km) between himself and Rome and punishes anyone who gives him hospitality within this radius with a death sentence and the confiscation of their property. Cicero learns of the news in Bivona, a small place on the outskirts of Valentia in Brutium (Vibo Valentia in Calabria) where he is staying at the estate of Sica, a retired soldier who had been an official under him in 63. At the same time, he receives more bad news. The praetor Vergilius, since he doesn't want to make an enemy of Clodius and suffer the consequences, prohibits Cicero from setting foot in Sicily.

A Change of Plan

Cicero has no choice but to change his travel plans. He chooses to proceed to Macedonia, trusting in the possibility of receiving hospitality in one of his friend Atticus's properties. Therefore, he sets out for Brundisium, the main port of embarkation for Greece on Italian soil. Along the way, he stops at the waypoint of Nares Lucanae (the hamlet of Zuppino in Sicignano degli Alburni, near Salerno), a stopping place for travelers heading for Lucania and Calabria and famous for its grilled pork sausages.

Cicero is still in Nares Lucanae on 8 April, when he writes a letter to Atticus to thank him for having worked to save his villas, to let him know that he wishes to be close to him at this incredibly difficult time, and to ask him for his hospitality in Epirus.[8] After this, he resumes his journey, reaching Thurii (Corigliano-Rossano), a city on the western coast of the Gulf of Taranto. He then continues to Tarentum (Taranto) and Brundisium, reaches Brundisium late on 17 April and stays as the guest of Marcus Laenius Flaccus, a man who places the obligations of friendship above his concern for the consequences to which he is exposed. Flaccus lives in a house in the hills to the north of the port, where he hosts artists, writers, scientists, and poets.[9]

In Brundisium, before leaving for Greece, Cicero thinks of his wife. He is aware of the problems that Terentia will face and admits this in a letter to her: "I don't know how you have got on; whether you are left in possession of anything, or have been, as I fear, entirely plundered."[10] He fears that Terentia, to protect their children and deal with the family's financial situation, will be stripped of her possessions (a huge patrimony, made up of a large property with woods and pastures, a small farm in the *ager publicus*—contested with a certain Mulvius—and other buildings and houses, which all provide an annual income of around 80,000 sesterces), because the expenses to be borne are considerable. Cicero is also worried about the fate of his son Marcus.

In November 58, Terentia plans the sale of the *vicus* but Cicero steps in to dissuade her so as not to damage their son's inheritance, though he is a little resentful for not having been consulted by her in the matter ("In the name of our unhappy fortunes, beware how we put the finishing stroke to the boy's ruin").[11] Terentia succeeds in resolving the issue with the help of some friends, which will be accepted by Cicero through gritted teeth. She thus proves herself to be an independent woman with a rare strength of character, capable of resolving complex problems (she has demonstrated this before by ensuring that their slaves wouldn't be confiscated among the rest of their assets with a false *manumissio*, thereby renouncing them as their property). Added to these problems is the fact that Cicero's brother Quintus's marriage to Pomponia, the sister of Atticus, is on the rocks, as well as the turbulent relationship between Terentia and Quintus due to the latter wanting to take over responsibility for the management of the family assets from his brother and the former preventing him from doing so.

8   Cic. *Att.*, 3.2–3.
9   On the hospitality given to Cicero by Flaccus: Cic. *Fr.*, XIV.4. Another of Flaccus's guests at his house was the poet Quintus Horatius Flaccus (65–8), better known as Horace, possibly a relative of his.
10 Cic. *Amicis*, XIV.4.4.
11 Cic. *Amicis*, XIV.1.

On 29 April, the group embarks for Dyrrachium (Durrës in Albania), the main city of Epirus, a rugged and mountainous region in the Western Balkans (today straddling southern Albania and northwestern Greece), bathed by the Ionian Sea. It's spring, the weather is good, the sea is calm, the journey to be made isn't very long, and the crossing is quick and peaceful. In Dyrrachium, Cicero is welcomed by Plancius, in whose house he stayed in Atina, who is acting as quaestor in Thessalonica under Lucius Calpurnius Piso Caesoninus, proconsul of Macedonia. When he had learned of Cicero's imminent arrival, Plancius rushed to welcome him and put himself at his service. He is dressed in mourning clothes and, when he sees the exile, embraces him, crying and unable to speak from emotion.

Plancius leads his guests to Thessalonica along the Via Egnatia, a 6-meter-wide stone-paved road that crosses the entirety of the Balkan Peninsula—from Illyricum to Macedonia and Thrace (from today's Albania, through North Macedonia and Greece, to European Turkey)—and can be considered as the overseas extension of the Via Appia. The journey is a long one, and the group will only arrive at their destination on 23 May.

Clodius's Real Estate Speculations

In (probably) 62, Clodius married Fulvia,[12] who who doesn't conform to the usual standards for Roman aristocratic women.[13] She does deals without anyone's protection; she uses her own personal political connections to do them; she finances them directly, because she is very rich; and she pursues them determinedly, even if they are illicit. She doesn't hesitate to bribe, if necessary (but she's also capable of using other means). Clodius and Fulvia live in a *domus* on the Palatine, which stands adjacent to the house of Clodia, the tribune's sister, and close to the now-ruined house of Cicero. Clodius bought this house from Marcus Aemilius Scaurus for 14,800,000 sesterces.

Clodius was strengthened politically with the approval of the law on Cicero's exile. The fact that he enjoys the support of both the lower-class plebeians and part of the ruling class makes him feel very confident about himself. As such, he makes the most of this advantageous situation to extract some personal benefit. This is partly because Fulvia, with her energetic character and domineering personality,

---

12   Cicero and other Latin authors—Valerius Maximus, Florus, Velleius Paterculus—not to mention Plutarch, unanimously agree that Fulvia is a woman with an energetic character and a controlling, cruel-hearted, greedy, evil, even merciless personality. In particular, Plutarch writes that she "was a woman who took no thought for spinning or housekeeping, nor would she deign to bear sway over a man of private station, but she wished to rule a ruler and command a commander." Plut. *Ant.*, 10.3.

13   Velleius Paterculus comments that "Fulvia ... had nothing of the woman in her except her sex." Vell. Pat., 2.74.2.

influences him to such an extent that he feels compelled to satisfy all her demands, even the maddest ones. He buys all the properties adjacent to Cicero's house, then conjoins them with his own. By doing so, he ends up with an architectural complex of some 6,150 square meters, five times larger than a normal aristocratic residence. He stops at nothing to reach his goal. Fulvia asks him for the head of their neighbor Quintus Seius Postumus, guilty of not selling her his fine house, and Clodius gives it to her—literally. Clodius asks Seius to sell him his house, which is the one where he is currently residing and has a lovely view. Seius replies disdainfully that Clodius will get his house over his dead body. Clodius insists and threatens Seius that he will build a wall in front of his house's windows, blocking off his view. Seius protests, opposing him as forcefully as he can, but ... he dies after being poisoned. It is commonly believed among commentators that Seius was the victim of a contract killing and that the instigator was Clodius, but there is no evidence to accuse him of the crime. Clodius has hit his target and wastes no time. He has the deceased's house confiscated and buys it at auction, surpassing all other offers with his own.

When Cicero's property (the land and what remains of the buildings) is also set to go under the hammer, Clodius—who is overseeing the auction—purchases it through a straw buyer. He keeps the better part (portico and gymnasium) for himself and gives the lesser part to a family relative who already owns the adjacent lot. In addition, he gives the columns from the gymnasium of Cicero's former home to Piso Caesoninus and plans to erect a small temple in the gymnasium's place, dedicated to the goddess Libertas, as well as four other rooms, three of which will be allocated to the service of the cult and the fourth to connect the others to the rest of the house. Inside the temple, he will place a statue of a woman which was brought to him by his brother Appius from Boeotia.

Clodius then calls on the young Lucius Pinarius Natta to have the sanctity of the site intended to house the small temple declared—a ritual procedure that is the exclusive competence of the *pontifices*—as he is the only *pontifex* who responded to his request. Pinarius Nutta is the stepson of Lucius Licinius Murena, who, in turn, is Clodius's brother-in-law because he is the half-brother of Fulvia.

Clodius also takes possession of the *porticus Catuli*, has it demolished, and, on top of the rubble, now an artificial terrace, erects a garden surrounded by a colonnaded portico, with rooms on one side and a richly paved walkway, 88 meters long and facing to the west on the hillside. By doing so, he gives his house a panoramic view right over the Forum and the Capitoline. All this unification and demolition work, together with the reconstruction of Cicero's old house and the *porticus Catuli*, ends up affecting Clodia's house too, as Clodius builds a wall in its vestibule. Clodia is thus obliged to move her front door to another side of the house.

Clodius Becomes Hostile to Pompey

By now, Clodius is convinced that he can do what he wants, even interfere in a matter that is the exclusive competence of the Senate, such as foreign affairs, and adopt a hostile attitude toward Pompey. He is severely mistaken. Two episodes, pertaining to the relations between the Roman state with Galatia (central Anatolia) and Armenia (in area of the Caucasus), lay the foundations for the upcoming clash between Clodius and Pompey.

The first takes place on 15 April 58. Clodius has proposed and approved a bill that seeks to confer the title of king and friend of the Roman people on Deiotarus, chief *tetrarch* of the Tolistobogii (a Celtic tribe of western Galatia), the only vassal ruler in Anatolia that Rome could trust. In reality, Deiotarus had already received the title of king from Pompey, to whom he is very loyal. And to all intents and purposes he has already been king for a year because the acts undertaken by Pompey relating to the reorganization of the East have been ratified. Pompey made Deiotarus king of all Galatia, while Clodius's law reduces the scope of his territory, establishing that he will reign only over western Galatia from now on and that he will cede eastern Galatia, including the sanctuary of Pessinous (Ballıhisar in Turkey), the center of the cult of Cybele, to his son-in-law Brogitarus, *tetrarch* of the Trocmi (another Celtic tribe of eastern Galatia). To achieve this, Brogitarus paid Clodius a substantial bribe. It is perhaps no coincidence that Clodius proposes the law regarding Deiotarus and has it approved in the same period in which there are celebrations in Rome for the *Megalenses Ludi*, a festival connected with the Roman cult of Cybele (the cult of the Anatolian Great Mother was introduced to the city by the Vestal Virgin Claudia Quinta and is considered the noble "property" of the *Claudii Pulchri*).

The second episode takes place a month later, on 15 May 58. Tigranes the Younger, son of Tigranes II (r. 95–55), king of Armenia, had been handed over to Pompey by Tigranes II to guarantee their agreements will be upheld. He arrived in Rome with Pompey and was placed under the supervision of the praetor Lucius Flavius. Clodius, because he is striving to interfere in the internal affairs of Armenia, tries to ingratiate himself with the prince and future king. With this in mind, he invites him to dine with him and, without saying a word to anyone, helps him to escape from his situation as a hostageand recover his freedom. Clodius then takes him to the Lazio coast and gets him on board a ship. Tigranes sets out for the open sea, heading for Armenia. But he encounters foul weather and stormy seas, and his ship runs aground on a beach near Anzio. There, he is caught by Flavius, who, alarmed by the hostage's escape, had rushed off in pursuit. Flavius and his escort are leading the young man back to Rome when, at the fourth mile of the Via Appia, they are attacked by a gang of Clodius's men, led by Sextus Cloelius. The fight results in a number of casualties, among whom is Marcus Papirius, an *eques* who is very close to Pompey. Tigranes takes advantage of the confusion to escape once again, this time vanishing without a trace.

A situation has thus arisen that is damaging to the general interest of the Roman state and puts Clodius on a collision course with Pompey. Cicero speaks of it in a letter to Atticus and in another to Pompey. Shortly afterwards, Clodius's mob clashes with the militia of the consul Aulus Gabinius, a loyalist to Pompey. Gabinius comes off worst, and his *lictors' fasces* are broken, a gesture that holds strong symbolic value.

Clodius is obligated to reward Gabinius and Piso Caesoninus, whose terms as consul are expiring, for the support that they promised him in order for Cicero to be exiled. Therefore, he proposes a plebiscite that is then approved under which Piso and Gabinius are appointed to the office of proconsul for 57 and puts one in charge of Macedonia and the other in charge of Cilicia. Again, the people gathered in assembly, at Clodius's instigation, have intruded on the Senate's remit in matters of state administration regarding the appointment of promagistrates to the provinces.

Shortly after this, the spark of revolt is lit in Palestine following an uprising by the Jews. Since Gabinius appears as the man who is needed to confront the situation, a new plebiscite, proposed by Clodius, is approved between March and May 58. The move revokes the appointment of Gabinius as governor of Cilicia and instead appoints him as the governor of Syria. Furthermore, it authorizes him to circumvent conscription; he will have the autonomy to make decisions both as regards the recruitment of troops as well asconcerning the appointment of legates and the administration of his very substantial expenses fund (Gabinius obtains all the money that he wants). Moreover, he will also be free to operate in the territories surrounding Syria and in those of free cities.

Pompey finds Clodius's actions to be both provocative and insulting, and he studies ways to block the tribune's ascent to a position of even greater influence in public life. In addition, he wants to regain the upper hand over Caesar, who is winning a lot of victories in Gaul, but without affecting the Triumviral Pact. He reflects on this and considers that if Cicero were to return to Rome from exile, he (Caesar) would then be able to concern himself with finding a solution to the Clodius problem. Therefore, he decides that from this moment on he must actively work, either directly or through intermediaries, toward ensuring Cicero is officially recalled to his homeland.

CHAPTER XI

The Gallic War Explodes

The Germans: A Focus

The Romans' knowledge of Central Europe is limited to what they have learned from Gallic merchants. They imagine it as a harsh, depressing, uncomfortable place to live, a land that is crossed by large rivers, covered by dense forests, and dotted with unhealthy marshes, extending northward from the foot of the northern slopes of the Alps to the shores of a cold, dark sea. They call that country Germania and its inhabitants Germans[1] without distinguishing between one German people and another, as they would do if they had better knowledge. Over time, however, they will discover that the Germans are not a single people but a mass of peoples who are similar to each other in certain ways, yet are also different. Around 98 AD, Publius Cornelius Tacitus—the historian, orator, senator, and main exponent of the historiographic genre of Latin literature—will explain that the Germanic universe is made up of four clusters: Germans of the Rhine, Germans of the Elba, northern Germans, and other Germans.[2]

One of the reasons the Romans only know the Germans superficially is because they speak a language that they don't understand. But the differences are not limited to this. Let's begin with the physical ones. The Romans are individuals with a round head, dark eyes, black or brown hair, which they wear cut short, with a shaved face. They are also of medium to short build: the average size for males is 1.67 m and 1.56 m for females.[3] As Tacitus describes, the Germans are tall (up to 2 meters, sometimes more) with a

---

1   It was the Gauls who called their Central European neighbors Germans. The Romans simply imitated the Gauls. Those directly involved, since they heard themselves being called Germans, got into the habit of calling themselves as such.

2   For descriptions of the Germans, *see* the commentary on the *Gallic Wars* by Caesar, and Tacitus's ethnographic work on the origins, customs, institutions, religious practices, and lands of the German populations between the Rhine and the Danube titled *De origine et situ Germanorum* (On the Origin and Situation of the Germans), more commonly known as the *Germania*.

3   In addition, Romans lived for an average of 27 years. It was rare for someone to pass the age of 49. Infant death under the age of six was moderately common. Women lived longer than men.

long and narrow skull and a solid, robust build. They have "defiant blue" eyes. Their hair is typically white, blond, or auburn, worn long, down to the shoulders; the men have drooping mustaches and long beards and considerable muscular strength. The Romans are astounded when they hear that the Germans can uproot trees and move rocks and earth solely with their arms, that they wear little, even when temperatures are low (some wear nothing but their tattoos), and that they have the habit of rolling around naked in the snow and climbing mountain peaks in the ice. The Germans, moreover, are more resistant than the Romans to pangs of hunger, but they cannot withstand intense, prolonged fatigue, nor can they tolerate either heat or thirst.[4]

The Romans feel profoundly different from the Germans also in terms of their way of reasoning and way of life. In their view, the Germans are unpredictable, as if they reason according to a different form of logic (but this can be said for all the so-called barbarians with whom the Romans deal).

Moreover, unlike the Romans, who identify civilization with a sedentary way of life and agriculture, the Germans know how to be both sedentary and nomadic at the same time. From time to time, they emigrate: all the families, clans, and tribes as one. They travel on foot or on horseback, with pack animals and wagons loaded with food and baggage, and livestock following behind. When they pause for a break, they circle their wagons—hundreds or even thousands of them—into a circle, thus forming a structure that serves to shelter the families and pack animals and to provide protection in the event of an enemy attack. These migrations can last for one or more generations and create a chain reaction of population movements, because one people will forcibly drive another out of their land, who will then try to do the same to another, and so on.

The Germans are among the strongest warriors in Europe, perhaps more so than the Gauls. In battle, the Germans are brave, valiant, as ferocious as wild animals, and determined to win like no other people. They oppose their enemies with the physicality and fervor of their clansmen, and sometimes bring them to their knees. The fighters deployed on the front line have a custom of tying themselves together both to form a solid wall and, if necessary, to prevent themselves from fleeing so as to die together. Furthermore, they are merciless with the vanquished. They cut the heads off the adversaries they have dispatched and affix them to the entrances to their homes. They sacrifice prisoners of war, nailing them to trees or immersing them in boiling oil. They dedicate the remains of their enemies to their gods after having cut them into pieces, throwing them into a sacred pond or spring.

The Germans influence and sometimes even threaten the *res publica*, the most powerful European state of its time. They have resisted and fought against the Romans ever since they first met each other. This gave rise to the struggle between the Romans and the Germans, which is destined to mark a rift in the heart of Europe for centuries.

---

4   Tac. *Germ.*, 4.

The Romans first encountered the Germans during the Cimbrian War (113–101).[5] This conflict arose from the encroachment into Gallia Narbonensis—the Roman territory of Gallia Transalpina (understood as the totality of France, Belgium, Luxembourg, and part of the Netherlands)—of a multitude of migrating men, women, and children constituting entire families, entire peoples. These were the Germanic peoples of the Cimbri and Teutones, the Celto-Germanic tribe of the Ambrones, and the group of Helvetii known as the Tigurini. This movement of populations originated around 120 in Jutland and surrounding areas and, within the span of fewer than 20 years, it had affected half of Europe: from Germania to Noricum, and from the Swiss Plateau to Gallia Transalpina, northeastern Spain, and northern Italy.

By the time it reached the shores of Lake Geneva, the multitude had swelled to 800,000 after being joined by 200,000 Tigurini. Having entered Gallia Transalpina through the Rhône Valley, it roamed around the province for a number of years, defeating various Roman armies in battle (*see*, for example, the victory it won in 107 over the army of the consul Lucius Cassius Longinus at the Battle of Burdigala, or the subsequent one in 105 at the Battle of Arausio), before crossing over into Spain, then returning to Gaul.

Eventually, the horde planned to invade Italy, but it was destroyed by the Romans in two epic battles: the Battle of Aquae Sextiae (Aix-en-Provence, France) in 102 and the Battle of the Raudine Plain (a place of uncertain location in northern Italy) in 101. The Tigurini had been ready to invade Italy through the Eastern Alps, but the news that the Romans had exterminated their allies prompted them to abandon the idea and return to their homes on the Swiss Plateau.

The Cimbrian War had been a real nightmare for the Romans due to the mad, ruthless, frenetic fury of the enemy warriors, who revealed wild, animalistic impulses and violence, typical of an innate disposition for war, ferocious, bestial, inhuman inclinations, and reawakened in them the *metus gallicus*, "the fear of the Gauls," that had thrown them into a panic during the Sack of Rome (390/386) and which left an indelible mark on their collective consciousness. Even now, when the Romans think back to that occasion, they feel a shiver that runs all the way down their spine. Had they not won on the Raudine Plain, even *Italia propria* would have been at their mercy—Rome included.

That conflict, however, opened the Romans up to a previously unknown world, that of the barbarians who live to the north of the Alps and who resemble the Gauls in their features, physical prowess, belligerence, and valor in battle, but who, from the perspective of their level of civilization, are more backward.

---

5   On the Cimbrian War: N. Barca, *Roma contro i Germani. La Guerra Cimbrica 113–101 a.C.*, Gorizia: LEG, 2020.

Gallia: Two Forces Collide

The Germans reappear on the Romans' horizon again in 59, in the northwest of Gallia Narbonensis,[6] simultaneously with a mass migration of the Helvetii. The occasion is preceded by a request for help sent by the Aedui, friends and allies of the Romans, to Caesar, proconsul of Gallia Narbonensis (southern and central France), Gallia Cisalpina (northern Italy), and Illyricum (eastern coast of the Adriatic). The dramatic plea sets off an unstoppable sequence of events that will result in the Gallic Wars (58–50). Caesar will present this conflict as a preventive and defensive war for Gallia Narbonensis, threatened by the Germans of Ariovistus and a multitude of migrants/invaders. Later, however, he will extend that conflict, exploiting the rivalries between the Gallic peoples and ending with the subjugation of Gallia Aquitania, Gallia Celtica, and Gallia Belgica to the dominion of Rome.[7] The conquest will be completed within two years (58–56). What will follow is the suppression of further revolts. Any remaining resistance will end in 52 with the expurgation of Alesia and the capture of Vercingetorix. Gallia Narbonensis and the Gallic territories conquered by Caesar— Aquitania, Celtica, Belgica—will be governed by proconsuls, while the Romanization of Gallia Narbonensis will be accelerated with the foundation of colonies.

The Romans came into contact with the Transalpine Gauls for the first time around the middle of the II century, when the Greek colony of Massilia (Massalia, Marseille), their long-term friend and ally, requested their aid because it was being threatened by the expansion of some Gallic peoples.

The Romans, in supporting the Massiliotes and the Aedui—Transalpine Gauls who became friends and allies of the Romans—defeated the Oxybii and the Deciates of the Var region in battle (154), then the Saluvii, or Salyes (125), followed by the Arverni and Allobroges (121). In 118, they founded the Roman colony of Narbo Martius (Narbona, Narbonne), which soon became the capital of the Roman province of Gallia Narbonensis. At the time, Roman lands in Gallia Transalpina had already been organized into a province called Gallia Bracata; Gallia Narbonensis encompassed a larger amount of territory where Roman dominion had been consolidated, in part through the work of Roman and Italic merchants and businessmen who had settled there. But the region hadn't been completely pacified. Sometimes the Gauls revolted, as happened with the Saluvii (most recently in 77) and the Allobroges (in 62).

---

6   Gallia Narbonensis corresponds to the southern regions of present-day France (Languedoc Roussillon and Provence-Alpes-Côte d'Azur). To the west, it borders Gallia Aquitania, to the north Gallia Celtica, and to the east Italy, from which it was separated by the western Alps.

7   Julius Caesar, in the *Gallic Wars*, divides all that remains of Gallia Transalpina outside of Gallia Narbonensis into three zones: Aquitania, Celtica, and Belgica. Caesar's Aquitania corresponded to the southwest region of modern mainland France. Celtica, roughly, to the rest of mainland France up to the Loire, extending northwest up to the Rhine and the Ardennes. Belgica extended from the Loire in the southwest to the Rhine in the northeast. Today it corresponds to the entirety of Belgium, Luxembourg, and part of the Netherlands.

In the 40 years following the Romans' definitive victory in the Cimbrian War, the general situation in the northwestern part of Gallia Celtica has still been affected by the collective unrest caused by the migration/invasion that caused the conflict to break out. The tribes competed with each other for supremacy, forming variable alliances with one another and with their neighbors. This is particularly the case with the Arverni and their allies. Among the latter, the Sequani are worthy of note. The Aedui live in Nivernais and Burgundy, between the Loire and the Saône rivers. They are considered the brethren[8] and kinsmen of the Romans, so much so that they invented the legend that their capital was founded by descendants of the Trojans.[9] The Arverni live in the Massif Central (Auvergne). The Sequani inhabit the Upper Saône basin (Franche-Comté and part of Burgundy). Recently, the Aedui and their allies have suffered a defeat. They were forced to hand over their most noble citizens to the victors as hostages and pledge not to ask the Romans for help. But they want vengeance and are planning their revenge.

The Germans Occupy Alsace

In 64–63, the Sequani, to strengthen themselves ahead of a revolt by the Aedui and Sequani, enlist 15,000 German mercenaries, made up of Edusii, Harudes, Marcomanni, Nemetes, Suebi, Triboci, and Vangiones,[10] who, under the leadership of Ariovistus, are moving into the lands of the Aedui toward their capital, Bibracte. Ariovistus is a Suebi noble and is fluent in the Gallic language. He has two wives, one from Germania and one from Noricum. The latter is the sister of Voccio, king of Noricum. In 63, the Sequani and the Germans of Ariovistus clash with the Aedui near Magetobriga, a stronghold located in Alsace.[11] The battle ends with the victory of the Sequani and the Germans of Ariovistus. The Aedui "lost all their nobility, all their senate, all their cavalry. And … they were now compelled to give the chief nobles of their state, as hostages to the Sequani, and to bind their state by an oath, that they would neither demand hostages in return, nor supplicate aid from the Roman people, nor refuse to be forever under their sway and empire."[12]

---

8   Cic. *Att.,* 1.19.2.

9   According to the legend of the founding of Rome, Romulus, the founder and first king of Rome, was a descendent of Iulus (Ascanius), son of the Trojan hero Aeneas the Dardanian.

10 The Nemetes, Triboci, and Vangiones live on the near side of the Rhine, in the extreme east of Gallia Celtica (the Vangiones and Nemetes also on the other side in Germania), while the others live in Germania.

11 The exact location of the site is uncertain. It is likely that it is found in Alsace near Sélestat, or on Mont Ardoux, in the commune of Pontailler-sur-Saône/Heuilley-sur-Saône, at the confluence of the Saône and the Ognon.

12 Caes., I.31.6–10.

Ariovistus's Germans, as a reward, are handed some of the lands of the Sequani—Alsace—and settle there permanently. Alsace is the easternmost region of Gallia Transalpina. It is located between the Vosges Massif and the Rhine. More precisely, it borders Germania to the north and east, from which it is separated by the Rhine, with the Swiss Plateau to the south and the hills and mountain pastures of the Vosges to the west, which separates it from the rest of Gallia Transalpina. It is a region of rolling hills and green valleys that offer colorful landscapes in the late spring and summer due to the mild temperatures and long hours of sunshine, while the winter is very harsh and often snowy, with very low temperatures. Over time, the Germans of Alsace are joined by a growing number of other Germans, so much so that their number grows dramatically to 120,000. Most recently, 24,000 Harudes have arrived in Alsace. In order for them to settle, Ariovistus asks the Sequani, forcefully and arrogantly, to cede him other lands, equivalent to a third of the total they possess. The Sequani realize that Ariovistus has become their master, and rebel. They reconcile with the Aedui and, together with them, face the Germans of Alsace. But they are defeated. At this point, the Aedui send a request for help to their Roman "brethren," that is, the governor of Gallia Narbonensis—that is, Caesar.

The Mass Migration of the Helvetii

Meanwhile, a mass of Gallic migrants set off toward the lands of the Santoni, who are found in the southwest of Gallia Transalpina, that is, in Aquitania (central France and part of western France, west of the Auvergne Massif, extending into the upper basin of the Loire and that of the Garonne). It is an enormous mass of people: 372,000 men, women, and children, of whom 299,000 are Aurici, Boii, and Tigurini, and 73,000 are Tulingi, Latobrigi, and Raurici.[13] Of these, 90,000 were able to bear arms. From now on, for the sake of brevity, we will call this collective group of migrants Helvetii, with the awareness that there are not just Helvetii but other Gauls as well. The Tigurini are one of the four tribes into which the Helvetii, the Celtic people who inhabit the Swiss Plateau and southern Germania, are divided. They were based around Lake Murten when their leader, Orgetorix, "by far the most distinguished and wealthy" of the Helvetii,[14] formed a pact of friendship and alliance with Casticus of the Sequani and Dumnorix of the Aedui with the aim of conquering Gallia Celtica. But the pact wasn't respected. Orgetorix was accused of treason, and though he attempted to flee, he met his death. After the death of Orgetorix, the Tigurini continued with the agreed plan of migrating *en masse*. This

---

13 Estimates vary from one another. Some speak of 368,000. It seems likely that there were at least 280,000 migrants. The figure of 378,000 comes from a number of lists, written in Greek, found by the Romans in the enemy camp. Caesar subsequently ordered the number of survivors to be counted. Caes. I.29.

14 Caes., I.2.1.

was nothing new, nor anything out of the ordinary, given that all of Gaul had been populated by migrations of this sort. What raises questions is why the Tigurini decided to leave their lands, given that the issues of hunger or extreme poverty can probably be ruled out. Caesar will explain that the Tigurini felt confined in their territory, which was being encroached on by Germans. The migrants torched their settlements to render them unusable by anyone else and started slowly moving west. Once they reach the shores of Lake Geneva, they must choose which path to take to carry on. They could cross Gallia Narbonensis, or they could strike directly north, between the Rhône and the Jura Mountains. The first route is the easier of the two, but it involves crossing a Roman province. The second is longer and involves crossing the lands of the Aedui. The migrants decide to pass through Gallia Narbonensis. To find out in advance how the Romans will react to this, they send an emissary to Narbo Martius.

Caesar Aids the Aedui

Caesar has set himself the objective of achieving a decisive victory in a major war to demonstrate his worth and his dedication to the state, accumulate substantial spoils of war, and increase his power and prestige to the level of Pompey and Crassus, the most illustrious and powerful men in Rome. To achieve this, he had planned to launch a preventive war against the Dacians of Burebista and had begun preparations for the expedition by gathering the Seventh, Eighth and Ninth Legions, specialist units (3,000 archers, 2,000 Balearic slingers), and contingents of support troops, known in Latin as *auxilia*, in Aquileia, a city-fortress in Eastern Transpadana Gaul, the fulcrum of the defensive system of north-eastern Italy.[15] In this case, the auxilia consist of units of Numidian light infantry (probably javelin throwers) and light cavalry, local infantry units, recruited from loyal tribes (10,000 Aedui),[16] and units of Germanic infantry.[17]

The Aedui's request for help offers Caesar a potentially superior opportunity to achieve his aim. He decides to seize it. Therefore, he changes his plans and hastens his departure. First, he goes to Gallia Cisalpina, where he assumes command of the forces in Aquileia and enlists two new legions: the Eleventh and the Twelfth. In doing this, he bypasses the Senate and the consuls, who are the magistrates responsible

---

15 Caes., I.10.3. Gallia Cisalpina was the Latin name for northern Italy. This physical region is bathed by the Ligurian and Adriatic seas and is separated from Central Europe by the Alps and from the rest of the Italian peninsula by the Apennines. It includes the widest plain in Europe, a very fertile one, now called the Po Valley. Gallia Cisalpina was itself subdivided into Gallia Cispadana and Gallia Transpadana, split by being south of the Po River or north of it.

16 Caes., VIII.10.

17 Caes., VIII.10. It seems likely that the units of Germanic infantry were mercenaries.

for levying and recruiting troops. Then he resumes his journey, leading the army into Gallia Transalpina.

In the Western Alps, every crossing of a pass entails the payment of a toll to the local population who have control over it; likewise, any provision of services must be paid for. The passes of the Cottian Alps (the stretch of the Alps from Monte Viso to Mont Cenis/Moncenisio) are in the hands of Celto-Ligurian populations. These are the Ceutrones, the Graioceli, and the Caturiges, all very primitive peoples who live off robbing travelers and the local populace. Specifically, the Ceutrones live in the upper Val d'Isère, the Graioceli around Mont Cenis, and the Caturiges near Montgenèvre. Rome has formed agreements with the Alpine tribes, but these pacts are frequently not respected.[18] Caesar starts his crossing of the Cottian Alps at Ocelum (near Avigliana, where the Dora flows out onto the plain of the Taurini in the Susa Valley),[19] proceeding along the Via Domitia, the road that connects Augusta Taurinorum (Turin) to Ugernum (Beaucaire), for 480 km, through the Susa Valley and the valleys of the Durance and the Rhône. The Via Domitia is the easiest road to take to cross the Western Alps. Its construction was ordered by Cnaeus Domitius Ahenobarbus between 120 and 118, and it was recently elevated to the status of a military road.

In the high Mons Matrona pass (Montgenèvre Pass) that connects the Susa Valley with the Durance Valley and marks the start of the Via Domitia, local Celto-Ligurians are occupying the high ground and try to block Caesar's passage, despite the very considerable size of his army (probably by rolling large boulders down the slopes, as they had done previously when the Carthaginian leader Hannibal Barca crossed the Alps).[20] Therefore, Caesar must break through by force in order to pass, succeeding in part thanks to the help of Donnus, the ruler of a small kingdom that borders the lands of the Ceutrones, Graioceli, and Caturiges and has its capital in Seguvium (Susa). Donnus supplies Caesar's army at his own expense, offers advice, guides, and pack animals, and subsequently keeps the pass open for the Romans so that it provides them with safe passage. Caesar rewards him with the lands of the neighboring Celto-Ligurian peoples, either in part or in sum.[21] The friendship and alliance with Caesar will allow the Cottians to prosper, thanks in part to the transalpine trade. After some time had elapsed after the death of Caesar, this privileged relationship would be strengthened by Augustus, who would make Cottius, Donnus's son and successor, a Roman citizen and the governor of the Roman province of Alpes Cottiae, which has its capital at Susa.

---

18 M. Ralf-Peter, *Le Alpi nel mondo antico. Da Otzi al Medioevo* (Milano: Bollati Boringhieri, 2018), 64.

19 Ocelum was the extreme western limit of Gallia Cisalpina. Its exact location is unknown.

20 Polyb., III.52.

21 On the crossing of the Cottian Alps: Caes., I.10; G. Oberziner, *Le guerre di Augusto contro le Alpi Cozie e Graie* (Roma: Loescher & C., 1900), 161–162.

Seven days after leaving Ocellum, Caesar arrives in the lands of the Vocontii in Gallia Narbonensis.[22] From there, he moves into the lands of the Allobroges and thence to those of the Segusiani. In the meantime, he has been joined by another two legions, one of which has arrived from Spain, while the other—the Tenth Equestris, also known as Veneria—is brought from its winter quarters in Narbo Martius.

At this point, Caesar has seven legions of Roman citizens, specialist troops, and auxiliary troops available to him for 34,200 infantry (including 10,000 non-combat personnel) and 2,000 cavalry. Of this total, 19,200 are legionaries. Each one of these wears a plumed helmet and a set of armor, *loricata* or *segmentata*, and is equipped with a rectangular shield and armed with two *pila* (singular: *pilum*, javelin) and a short sword with a sharpened point. The 2,000 cavalry are made up of Numidians and Spaniards, subdivided into four *alae* and led by Publius Licinius Crassus, the younger son of the triumvir Crassus, and the same amount of Aedui. As can be seen, Caesar has no legionary cavalry, except for a few messengers. This is because since Caius Marius's reforms to the army and conscription (end of the II century), the legions of Roman citizens have been formed only of heavy infantry.

The Conquest of *Gallia Celtica*

Caesar receives Nammeius and Verucloetius, the migrants' emissaries, on 2 April 58. They inform him of their leaders' intention to head through Gallia Narbonensis. Caesar suggests that he is inclined to grant permission, but he postpones his final decision until 13 April. However, he has already decided not to allow their passage, but he wants to buy time. He fears that the transit of migrants through Roman territory will cause destruction and looting on a vast scale, which will have the knock-on effect of pushing the restless Allobroges to break their alliance with Rome. Caesar also perceives another risk: if the lands on the Swiss Plateau vacated by the Helvetii are then occupied by Germans, the Romans of Gallia Cisalpina will suddenly have some very warlike and fearsome neighbors, and this will put them in danger. Moreover, if the Helvetii reach the Santoni, they could pose a threat to their Gallic allies in the southwest of Gallia Narbonensis.

This is a false and misleading way of looking at the situation, useful for legitimizing an unnecessary war to be used for personal gain. The dangers evoked by Caesar either don't exist or are dramatically overstated. This is proven by the fact that the Helvetian plateau is separated from Gallia Cisalpina by the Alps, while the Santones live 300 km north of Tolosa (Toulouse), and there are at least four other tribes who live between them and the Tolosani. Caesar wants people to believe that he doesn't want the conflict but that it has been imposed by external circumstances and he cannot step back from his obligations, which require him to help allies and prevent

---

22 Caes., I.10.

the community of subjects from being harmed. Furthermore, it is likely the Aedui's appeal isn't aimed at requesting military assistance to repel an invasion but simply to ask for Caesar's vigilance so that the Helvetii's migration through their lands occurs peacefully. Thus, it is a much smaller request.

In fact, no sooner have the Helvetian ambassadors left his presence than Caesar orders his soldiers to destroy the bridge that crosses the Rhône near Genava (Geneva in Switzerland) to make the migrants' crossing more difficult,[23] fortifies the left bank of the river from Lake Geneva to the Jura Mountains in record time, and prepares to repel any attempt to break through the fortifications.

Roman legionaries are, of course, warriors, but also, when the need arises, builders, led by talented engineers and architects. Their discipline, organization, and competence produce outstanding results. A terreplein—5 m high and 28 km long—is built, interspersed with towers and forts, itself protected by a trench.

On 13 April, the ambassadors return to Caesar. They learn that their request has been rejected, and the migrants are warned against entering Roman territory.

For a few weeks thereafter, the migrants try, unsuccessfully, to pass the barrier using boats, rafts, or simply by swimming. Eventually, they give up and change their route. They decide to head further north through the lands of the Sequani and those of the Aedui between the Rhône and the Jura Mountains. The Sequani consent to their passage in exchange for hostages as collateral. The migrants thus enter the lands of the Aedui, and it's there that the problems start. Caesar intervenes. He leaves a few cohorts to guard the fortified stretch of the Rhône, led by Titus Labienus, and leads four legions into the lands of the Aedui, where he will be supplied with food in addition to reinforcements amounting to 2,000 cavalry.

On 6 June, the Tigurini cross the River Saône at its confluence with the Rhône, loaded with baggage, well behind all the other migrants. Caesar sends in three legions to attack them. It is a massacre. The Tigurini are virtually wiped out, with no distinctions drawn between fighters and women, the old, and children. The surviving Tigurini hide in the thick vegetation that covers the riverbank between the land and the water. The extermination of the Tigurini, a defenseless people who were treacherously set upon without any provocation to justify the attack, marks the beginning of the Gallic Wars (58–50), which will lead to the Roman conquest of Gallia Celtica, Belgica, and Aquitania.

The next step is Caesar's attack on the bulk of the migrants. The action is preceded by the construction of a bridge over the Saône, which is completed within a single day by his engineers. When the structure is ready, Caesar leads the army over to the opposite bank.

He tries in vain to negotiate an accord with the migrants that would avoid a confrontation (suggesting he had the intention of coming to an understanding), and

---

23 Caes., I.7–8.

then he follows them. Four thousand soldiers on horseback, under the command of Lucius Aemilius, monitor the imposing column from a distance while they wind their way down the road that leads to Bibracte.

Bibracte is a hillfort, one of the most important of its type in Gallia Transalpina, and is the political, economic, and religious capital of the Aedui (in the future, the Romans will move the capital to Augustodunum). It is situated at the top of Mont Beuvray (821 m) and stands above the drainage basin at the confluence of the Saône, Yonne, Seine, and Loire rivers, where various trans-European routes intertwine. Mont Beuvray is a clump of volcanic rocks cloaked in woodland that forms part of the Morvan Massif (in the commune of Saint-Léger-sous-Beuvray, near Autun in Bourgogne-Franche-Comté). The area is rich in mineral resources.

The 4,000 horsemen keep an eye on the Helvetian column, remaining at a safe distance of 7.5–9 km. Every now and then, the latter close in on the Romans and harry the rearguard. They are around 25 km south of Bibracte and 3 km from the column when they are attacked by 75,000 enraged barbarians. They are unable to resist and are overwhelmed and scatter.

The enemy then approach the bulk of Caesar's army. Caesar marches up to the top of a hill and organizes his legions. The Seventh, Eighth, Ninth, and Tenth Legions and the Aedui auxiliaries are deployed in three defensive lines on the slopes of the hill, about halfway up. The baggage train is gathered higher up inside some hastily dug ditches. The troops' deployment takes place amid trumpet blasts, waving banners, and clouds of dust kicked up by the hobnailed sandals of the soldiers, the hooves of the pack animals, and the wagons carrying the baggage (food, equipment, and other supplies).

The enemy advance to the foot of the hill. They are equipped with a helmet decorated with horsehair, a small breastplate, a round shield, and a long spear. First, they form a few phalanx regiments, then they bring them together to form a single mass of spearmen. The lugubrious sound of a horn signals the start of the battle, and they begin to climb the hill. The Romans welcome the attackers with a dense hail of pila, which opens countless gaps. Those who survive their shield being struck by a pilum find that the javelin has got stuck in it and made it unusable, since it is not easily extracted. Then the Seventh, Eighth, Ninth, and Tenth start to descend the hill, carrying their shields just below their eyes and their *gladius* unsheathed. The Eleventh and Twelfth Legions remain on the hill, guarding the baggage. At this point, the enemy divides: one part remains on the hill, faced by the Tenth, while the remainder withdraws and falls back. The Seventh, Eighth, and Ninth follow the retreating enemy, advancing at a marching pace and in battle formation. Then, 15,000 Boii and Tulingi attack their right flank. Some of the Romans turn and face the attack, while the rest continue the pursuit. The enemy retreat for more than a kilometer, toward the wagons, circled into a circle of wagons. When they reach it, they barricade themselves inside. In the meantime, 132,000 women, old people, and children have evacuated the circle of wagons and set off toward the Vosges. The fighting continues until the evening on the hill and into the night around the wagon circle, and the slaughter is immeasurable. The Helvetii among the wagons resist, but most of them fall in combat. The survivors—a few thousand—turn and flee, but they are followed, chased, hounded, and hunted down relentlessly until they surrender. Among the prisoners are many non-combatants and a few youths from noble families.[24]

At the end of the battle, it's impossible to count the number of dead: there are too many—hundreds of thousands—and are, for the most part, migrants. Their bodies will remain unburied. All the possessions of the vanquished become spoils of war and are divided among the victors. The women, old people, children, and 6,000 warriors who are all fleeing toward the Vosges are followed. In the end, the women, the old people, and the children surrender to their pursuers. The warriors will be rounded up and killed by the Aedui. The prisoners of war will be returned to the Swiss Plateau—except for 20,000 Boii, who will remain in the area as "clients" of the Aedui—though not before being forced to work for the Aedui as reparations for the damage caused by the migration.

Ultimately, the migration of the Helvetii into Gallia Celtica ends with the return of the surviving migrants to their areas of origin, analogously to what happened at the end of the Cimbrian War when the Tigurini, after they learned of the fate of the Cimbrians, Teutones, and Ambrones, were quick to return to the Swiss plateau.

At the same time, Caesar orders the Eleventh Legion and some of the cavalry to go to the lands of the Nantuantes, the Veragri, and the Seduni, situated between the territory of the Allobroges, Lake Geneva, the Rhône, and the Alps.

The War Against Ariovistus

While Caesar was fighting against the Helvetii, Ariovistus had remained out of the conflict. Caesar, after his victory, acknowledged this and, in agreement with the Senate of Rome, granted him the coveted title of king, as well as friend and ally of the Roman people. Now, however, Ariovistus is indicating that he wants to invade the lands of the Aedui and the Sequani, their allies. Caesar hadn't saved the Aedui and the Sequani from the Helvetii only to let them be invaded by Germans, partly because their lands are in Gallia Celtica, which the Romans, by now, consider their own territory. Therefore, when the leaders of the Aedui, after having convened an assembly of the tribes, ask Caesar if they can discuss the issue of how to oppose Ariovistus with him, Caesar summons Ariovistus for a meeting to clear up the issue. Ariovistus responds with insolence and arrogance. In short, he refuses to meet with Caesar. Caesar sends envoys back to Ariovistus and renews his invitation. Ariovistus

---

24 On the Battle of Bibracte: Caes., I.24–28. See also: G. Zecchini, *Le guerre galliche di Roma* (Roma: Carocci, 2009), 96

again responds haughtily and comes across as hostile. In the meantime, he ravages the lands of the Aedui and the Sequani.

Caesar notes that it is going to be impossible to reach a negotiated peace and sets off on a forced march toward Vesontio (Besançon in Bourgogne-Franche-Comté), the administrative center of the Sequani and one of the most strongly fortified settlements in Gallia Transalpina. Vesontio is on a bend on the Doubs River, surrounded by hills, at the point where the Jura Mountains meet the vast arable plains of Franche-Comté. Caesar occupies it, relieves it of its stores of corn and weapons, then prepares to face the Germans.

The merchants of Vesontio recount some terrifying stories, which sow panic in the Roman camp. They describe the Germans as "men of huge stature, of incredible valor and practice in arms that oftentimes they, on encountering them, could not bear even their countenance ..."[25] A feeling of inferiority comes over the Romans, and this disheartens them. The newly appointed officers and those who followed Caesar out of Rome out of "friendship" (i.e. for their career or for reasons connected to their rank) try to slip away, using any pretext to be discharged. Some remain, only because they don't want to be suspected of being cowards, but they can't pretend to have the courage they don't have; sometimes they burst into tears, either alone or with friends, in the privacy of their tents, giving themselves up to their fates. Wills are drawn up all through the camp. Gradually, due to the fear being shown by others, even the war veterans—centurions, prefects, simple soldiers—start to feel doubts as well. Some of them don't say they are afraid of the enemy but of the narrow paths through the thick forests that extend as far as the eye can see, separating them from Ariovistus, and of the possibility that they will run out of provisions. A group of soldiers warn Caesar that, if he orders the army to leave, it is possible no one will move from the camp.[26] Naturally, there are also those who criticize Caesar for his nerve in waging a war against the Germans without having been authorized to do so by the Senate of Rome, and therefore they think about abandoning him so as not to go along with his ambitious and mad plan.

All this endangers the success of the military operations, but Caesar addresses the soldiers, explaining that their fears are unfounded, refuting any possible objections, renewing faith in the Tenth Legion, whose valor he gives as an example to all others, wounds their pride and reassures them, and manages to make the fearful believe again and awaken (or reawaken) their desire to fight.[27] Separately, or more accurately, in a meeting with his senior officers which the centurions attended, Caesar reprimands the officers who expressed concerns regarding the conditions of the roads to be traveled and the supplies, telling them that if anyone should be worrying about such

---

25 Caes., I.39.
26 Caes., I.39.2–7.
27 Caes., I.41.1.

matters, it's him. As for the report that some of the soldiers would disobey his order to advance, he says that it doesn't concern him. Such incidents have occasionally occurred in the past, but only after a defeat or because an overly greedy commander hadn't allocated the army's share of the spoils to them. There is no reason to believe that this could happen to him too, as he has always demonstrated through his integrity and his good fortune (Caesar, like Caius Marius and Lucius Cornelius Sulla before him, has a reputation as being a lucky commander).[28]

In early August 58, Caesar leaves a garrison in Vesontio, crosses the Belfort Gap (on the French-Swiss border), intercepts the enemy, superior in number, who are on the plain between Mulhouse and Cernay, and sets up camp around 35 km from this lowland plain. This time, Ariovistus gets scared and lets Caesar know that he is prepared to meet him so as to try to reach an accord that would avoid a battle.

Caesar and Ariovistus separately reach a knoll halfway between their camps, on the edge of an extensive plain. Each of them has been escorted by 4,000 cavalry. They approach each other with a personal guard of just 10 cavalrymen each. Not trusting his Gallic cavalry, Caesar has them dismount and instead has himself escorted by the infantry of the Tenth Legion, who have mounted the horses instead.

Caesar doesn't have a helmet on and he appears pale and thin compared to his interlocutor, but his eyes are like ice. Ariovistus has powerful limbs, a head of thick blond hair that spills out from under his helmet, and a contemptuous expression. The two speak in Latin (a language that Ariovistus knows well) under a leaden sky. The atmosphere is charged with tension, and tendrils of apprehension take hold. Speaking first, Caesar orders Ariovistus not to allow any more Germans to cross the Rhine, to return his hostages, and to make peace with the Aedui and Sequani. Ariovistus responds equally firmly. He explains that he has not come into Gaul of his own volition but at the request of the Gauls, who had promised him great rewards; that the lands he possesses in Gaul had not been extorted by him but had been granted to him; that the hostages had been handed over to him spontaneously; and that he receives tribute according to a law of war, which victors are accustomed to imposing on the vanquished. It hadn't been he who attacked the Gauls, it had been the Gauls who had attacked him. All the Gauls had taken to the field against him, while he had repelled them and defeated them in a single battle. All this had happened before Caesar and his army had left Gallia Narbonensis and pretended to be their friends when instead they aimed to overwhelm them. If Caesar withdraws, Ariovistus says, turning to his interlocutor, he will continue to be considered as a friend, he will be suitably rewarded, and he will be allowed to wage war on whomever he wants. Otherwise, he will be considered an enemy and killed, which would please many Roman citizens and would win Ariovistus their friendship.[29]

---

28 Caes., I.40.1–15.
29 Caes., I.44.

Ariovistus is still speaking when his escort, made up of impetuous youths, lashes out at Caesar's, throwing stones and missiles at them. Because of this incident, Caesar withdraws from the conference, rejoins his troops at the gallop, and makes preparations while keeping his army on the defensive.

Ariovistus moves his camp closer to that of the Romans (previously they were about 35–36 km apart, but now there is only 9 km between them). The next day, they move to within 3 km. His goal is to cut off the supply lines of the Aedui and Sequani with the Romans. For at least the next five days, Caesar provokes the enemy, putting his troops into battle order outside the camp each morning. To no avail. There are only a few skirmishes, into which Ariovistus throws 6,000 cavalry and as many infantry, who were very mobile.[30]

After interrogating some of his prisoners, Caesar learns that Ariovistus is deliberately delaying the final battle because some Suebi women have read in the random arrangement of twigs they had scattered on a white cloth, and in the whirlpools of a river, that the most propitious moment to engage in battle would be the imminent full moon.

Caesar sets up a second encampment closer to the enemy than the first to house two legions and some of the auxiliary troops (he leaves the other four legions in the bigger camp). The distance between the two armies is thus reduced to 600 paces. Caesar sets up his troops in *triplex acies* while he focuses on setting up camp.

On 18 September, when the sunlit portion of the Moon is entirely visible from Earth, Ariovistus launches an attack with 16,000 men against the smaller Roman encampment which is repelled. The next day, he throws his entire army against the smaller Roman camp. The fighting continues from noon until the evening without either side being able to prevail. The decisive encounter takes place the following day.

Ariovistus arranges his men outside their camp, ordering them up by tribe: first the Harudes, then the Marcomanni, Triboci, Vangiones, Nemetes, and Edusii, and finally the Suebi. The tribes are sheltered by a circle of wagons. On top of the wagons, the women entreat the warriors not to abandon them and their children to the mercy of the Romans and urge them to defeat them.

Caesar places a legate at the head of each legion, deputized by a quaestor, so that the soldiers will have witnesses to their valor[31] (until that moment, Caesar had been the commander-in-chief of the individual units within the army, and of the army as a whole). It is in this scenario that the figure of the legate—understood as a legionary commander, to whom a quaestor who will deal with administrative issues is seconded, and who has military tribunes, prefects, and centurions as subordinate officers—is born.

---

30 Caes., I.48.4–7.
31 Caes., I.52.

Caesar then places himself at the head of the right wing of his formation and advances toward Ariovistus's camp with all six legions, as well as the auxiliary troops, arranged in three ranks. The enemy, set up in dense phalanxes, don't waver and throw their javelins. At the moment of impact—a rock-hard clash—hand-to-hand combat starts. The Romans manage to break up the left wing of the enemy and put them to flight, but they are struggling to resist the pressure of the enemy's right wing. The sending of reinforcements from the third line by the young Publius Licinius Crassus, the cavalry commander, decides the outcome of the battle. The Germans break ranks and flee. The Roman cavalry pursue them as far as the Rhine, many kilometers away, where they catch them as they use any means possible to cross the river, slaying the majority.[32] Only a few fugitives succeed in making it to the opposite bank, mostly by swimming. Ariovistus is saved thanks to his lucky star: just when the danger is greatest, he finds a small boat tied up on the shore.[33]

When the battle is over the plain is littered with corpses and human remains. The losses are counted. The Germans lament the loss of 80,000[34] including two of Ariovistus's wives—one Suebian and the other a Norican—and one of his young daughters. Another of Ariovistus's daughters has been taken prisoner.

Ariovistus will never again disturb the Romans' slumber. The Germans who emigrated to Alsace will largely return to their places of origin. From now on, for the next 400–500 years, the Rhine will form the border of the Roman world in Western Europe; Gallia Transalpina, saved by Caesar from the Germanic terror, will remain subject to Rome and will be Romanized, but it will be able to retain local Celtic elements.

Caesar annexes the lands of the Sequani to Gallia Celtica where he quarters the legions for the winter of 58–57.

The Conquest of Gallia Belgica

Caesar has destroyed the migrating Helvetii in Gallia Narbonensis and has quartered the legions in Gallia Celtica for the winter. At the start of spring 57, the Senones and other Gauls used by Caesar as sources of information let him know that some Celtic and Germanic tribes (from now on, the Belgae) have formed an alliance and are amassing troops, as they fear for their safety (they are afraid that the Romans, having subjugated the Gauls of Celtica, may attack them next). Among the Belgae, the most powerful in valor, prestige, and number are the Bellovaci. They add 60,000 men to the alliance and request and obtain command of operations under the supreme

---

32 Caes., I.52–53.
33 Caes., I.53.
34 In a fragment from his *Gallic History (Bella Civilia Gall.)*, Appian speaks of 80,000 Germans falling in battle. App. *BC*, 4.22.

command of Galba, king of the Suessiones. The Suessiones are a people whose vast swathes of territory include 12 cities. They have made 50,000 men available.

There are also 10,000 Ambiani, 15,000 Atrebates, 19,000 Aduatici, 10,000 Caleti, 7,000 Menapii, 25,000 Morini, and 50,000 Nervii. To all these were also added 10,000 Veliocasses, 10,000 Veromandui, and a further 40,000 Condrusi, Eburones, Caeraesi, and Paemani.[35]

Caesar recruits two legions in Gallia Cisalpina and, at the start of the summer, instructs Quintus Pedius to lead them to Belgica. Then, over 15 days of forced marches, he leads eight legions (Seventh, Eighth, Ninth-*Triumphalis,* Tenth-*Equestris,* Eleventh, Twelfth-*Victrix,* Thirteenth and the Fourteenth), amounting to a total of 42,000 infantry, plus missile troops and auxiliary cavalry, to Belgica as far as Durocortorum (Reims). He accepts the spontaneous surrender of the Remi, who are the Belgae tribe closest to Celtica, on condition that the children of their most senior nobility are handed to him as hostages, and he sees to it that the Aedui, under the leadership of Diviciacus, invade and devastate the lands of the Bellovaci. Then he builds a bridge over the River Aisne, a tributary of the Oise and a sub-tributary of the Seine, leads the army to the opposite shore, and occupies both sides (he garrisons one bank and leaves the legate Quintus Titurius Sabinus on the other with six cohorts).

The Belgae besiege Bibrax, a town of the Remi. This is located 13 kilometers away from the Roman encampment. Caesar intervenes to help the besieged, sending troops from Numidia, Cretan archers, and Balearic slingers. The besiegers ravage the fields surrounding Bibrax and set fire to all the villages and buildings they come across, then they set up camp 3 kilometers from Caesar's own. There are so many of them that their camp extends for more than 13 kilometers.

Caesar strengthens his camp's defenses before deploying six legions, keeping two more in reserve. In turn, the enemy set themselves up on the field. A violent confrontation ensues, which ends with a disorderly retreat by the Belgae. Caesar has the Belgae pursued by the cavalry and three legions, the former commanded by Quintus Pedius and Lucius Aurunculeius Cotta and the latter by Titus Labienus. The Romans massacre the enemy in flight and, as night falls, return to their camp.

The next day, Caesar obtains the capitulation of Noviodunum (Soissons in Hauts-de-France), the principal *oppidum* of the Suessiones. He then moves into the lands of the Bellovaci and accepts the surrender of Bratuspantium (Breteuil-sur-Noye in Oise, between Beauvais and Amiens). Afterward, without a drop of blood being spilled, he also obtains the surrender of the Ambiani, neighbors of the Nervii.

The Nervii have assembled themselves on the banks of the River Sambre (in Flanders, Belgium) alongside the Atrebates and the Veromandui, and they are waiting for the Aduatici. Caesar advances toward them with eight legions, two of which are

---

35 Caes., II.4.

protecting the column and guarding the supplies. He sends the cavalry and specialist units in to engage while he crosses the river himself with the infantry who clash with the enemy, who retreat into the woods where they plan to attack the Romans, who don't dare to go into the depths of the forest. Later, when the legions have set up an entrenched camp, the enemy attack. Caesar is in trouble, but he reacts impulsively and determinedly: he faces the Nervii out in the open and transforms what was nearly a defeat into a victory. The Nervii are exterminated. At the end of the battle, just 500 are still alive. After this, Caesar besieges the main *oppidum* of the Aduatici (Namur in Belgium): he captures it, kills its 4,000 defenders, sacks the settlement, and captures 53,000 men, women, and children, whom he will sell as slaves.

CHAPTER XII

Gang Warfare

Friends Do Their Utmost for Cicero

The 59-year-old Lucius Licinius Lucullus was a great friend of the twice-consul and dictator- for-life Lucius Cornelius Sulla, and after the latter's death, he defended his constitution against attempts to repeal it. He was consul in 74, then was given command of military operations in the Third Mithridatic War (73–63), but only from 73 until 66, when he was no longer supported in his position (and was replaced by Pompey) because he had come to be hated by the very powerful publicans who considered themselves to have been harmed by his fiscal policy. He is an extremely wealthy man, both because he comes from a rich family and because he has accumulated vast riches during his career as a magistrate and from his military command in the East. He lives in a wonderful residence that he owns personally (*Horti Lucullani*), surrounded by gardens and spectacularly set on the slopes of the Pincian Hill, on the edge of Rome. He is also the owner of a great deal of land in Sabinum[1] and Lazio (Tusculum–Tuscolo, Casinum–Cassino), and sumptuous *otium* villas in Neapolis (Naples) and Baiae (Bacoli) in Campania. A skilled orator, impeccable connoisseur of the language and culture of the Greeks, impassioned by literature, and the author of a history of the Social War, he is also keenly interested in philosophy, specifically Platonic philosophy, and has set up a library in his villa in Tusculum that is open to all, starting with Greek scholars. For this reason, he is known as the protector of Greek intellectuals. He is accustomed to offering his guests banquets marked by opulent refinement, which will be named *luculliani* after him. His lifestyle is marked by luxury and defines his position within the ruling class: that of a very refined, influential, and munificent person who still has a place in public life despite no longer being either a magistrate or a military commander.

The 46-year-old younger brother of Lucius Licinius Lucullus is also very rich. He owns houses in Rome, lands in Sabinum, and extra-urban villas in Lazio—in

1   The *Luculli* family originally came from Sabinum, specifically from the area of Reate (Rieti).

Tusculum and Casinum—and in Baiae. His natural parents were Lucius Licinius Lucullus and Caecilia Metella Calva, but he was adopted by Marcus Terentius Varro, and therefore, in compliance with the rules of Roman onomastics, he changed his name from Marcus Licinius Lucullus to Marcus Terentius Varro Lucullus. Like his older brother, he had been educated by the best teachers of his time. Among his teachers, those worthy of note include Lucius Aelius Stilo Praeconinus, the grammarian and antiquarian, and Lucius Accius, poet and philologist. In Athens, where he stayed for the purposes of studying between 84 and 82, he attended lessons given by the Platonic philosopher Antiochus of Ascalon. He is a very cultured person and is especially passionate about etymology and rhetoric. At a philosophical level, he doesn't adhere to any particular school of thought but rather has an eclectic attitude. That is, he takes concepts drawn from different schools or ways of thinking and combines them harmoniously. He combines intense intellectual activity and prolific literary production with his political commitments. In 97, he was a *triumvir capitalis* (helping the praetor in criminal cases, overseeing capital punishment, looking after the prisons). After this, he was a quaestor. He is close to Pompey, on behalf of whom he has held important positions. In 78, he was legate in Illyricum. Between 76 and 72, he was legate and proquaestor in Spain. In 73, he was consul, and, in 72, he was proconsul of Macedonia. During his tenure, he defeated the Bessi in Thrace and advanced as far as the Danube and the west coast of the Black Sea. On his return, he played a role, albeit a minor one, in the repression of Spartacus's Revolt. In 67, he was responsible for naval operations against the pirates in the maritime area between Sicily and Delos. When Pompey had been elected to the consulship for 70, he wrote a treatise on the procedures for convening the Senate and consulting the assembly (*Eisagogikòs*, "Introduction") to advise him in the course of his duties. He is a friend of both Cicero and Atticus, with whom he had been a pupil at the school of Praeconinus, and they are intellectual kindred.

In early May 58, Varro Lucullus—together with Publius Plautius Hypsaeus, previously a praetor and also a friend of Pompey—tries to prompt a discussion in the Senate about an official recall to his homeland for Cicero and the need to accompany the exile's political reintegration with the abrogation of ancillary punishments and any other effects and with the reinstatement of his legal standing, his full rights, his senatorial *dignitas*, and his social reputation. To that end, he argues that the popular assembly that voted through the law condemning Cicero had been misled and that its judgment had been affected by a legislative proposal that was based on non-existent dishonorable and defamatory deeds, or deeds that had been held as such; led astray by a false premise, the assembly had misinterpreted and incorrectly assessed the facts, leading their decision to be unreasonable and unjust. For these reasons, the *lex Ciceronis de exilio* is illegitimate and must be annulled from the legal order.[2] The initiative is nipped in the bud because Clodius reminds the Senate that the *lex Ciceronis de exilio* prohibits the affair from being discussed, the breach of which will have ramifications.

But Pompey is also working on Cicero's behalf. He does so indirectly because he doesn't want to put Clodius into a difficult situation or compromise his own relations with Caesar. On 1 June 58, when the consul Gabinius begins his own "turn" at governing, Pompey asks for his support in the enterprise. He knows he can ask anything of him because Gabinius is completely loyal to him.

Taking up the baton, Gabinius acts through an intermediary. Clodius is away from Rome when the tribune of the plebs Lucius Ninnius Quadratus puts forward a plebiscite that seeks to obtain the same things that Varro Lucullus was asking for. The tribune of the plebs, Aelius Ligus, a friend of Clodius, uses his veto, but Ninnius Quadratus takes no notice and convenes a *contio* to present the project to the people. This triggers numerous disagreements between the Optimates and the Populares, many of which degenerate into bloody brawls.[3]

The majority of the senators are in favor of the exile and they are outraged by the stubborn attitude of the consuls. An original form of protest arises: the Senate suspends its activity, just as if it were to have gone on strike.[4]

Ninnius discusses his own proposal in a *contio* and then puts it on the agenda for a meeting of the *concilium plebis* to be held on 24 June 58. Clodius senses that there is a majority in favor of the plebiscite and that its approval will appear as a verdict in favor of Cicero; he reacts harshly. He forms a gang of people willing to act underhandedly—with elements drawn from his slaves, his followers from the underclass, and his brother Appius's gladiators—and uses it to break up the assembly.

Ninnius protests against Clodius for having created a situation that has prevented him from being able to carry out his duties. Since he is left unsatisfied, he offers Clodius's possessions to the goddess Ceres, following an archaic ritual as meaningful as it is devoid of practical effects.

The elections for the next set of civic magistracies take place routinely in July 58. Publius Cornelius Lentulus Spinther and Quintus Caecilius Metellus Nepos Minor are elected to the consulship. They will take office on 1 January 57. Both descend from patrician families. It isn't the first time that they will have held the same magistracy at the same time as they were colleagues as praetors in 60.

---

2   Cic. *Att.*, III.8.3 ["(…) You bid me thank Varro: I will do so; also Hypsaeus. (…)"]; *Red. sen.* 38; *est.* 71. Judging on laws was also within the purview of the Senate of Rome, which had the power to examine them both on the level of legitimacy as well as that of merit, and thus the power to abrogate them for illegitimacy or inappropriateness.

3   Dio Cass., XXXVIII.30.4. See also Cic., *Red. sen.* 3; *Sest.*, XXI.68.

4   On the consuls' obstruction to the legislative initiatives in favor of Cicero between mid-July and September: Cic. *Att.*, III.15.3, III.19.2, III.20.3; *Dom.*, 69–70; *Red. sen.*, 22.

Spinther was quaestor in 74 and aedile in 63. After his praetorship, he was appointed as governor of Hispania Citerior. He is a friend of Caesar.

Nepos, on the other hand, is close to Pompey, under whom he served as a senior officer during the campaign against the pirates (67) and in the Third Mithridatic War (73–63). In 62, he had been tribune of the plebs. He is the son of Quintus Caecilius Metellus Nepos, who himself was both the son of Quintus Caecilius Metellus Balearicus, censor in 120, and the uncle of Clodius.

Among the newly elected tribunes of the plebs, some are friends of Cicero—Publius Sestius, Titus Annius Milo, Caius Curtius Peducaeanus, Titus Fadius Gallus—while others are friends of Clodius—Aelius Ligur, Quintus Numerius Rufus, Atilius Serranus Gavianus.

It is worth paying particular attention to two of Cicero's friends: Sestius and Milo. Sestius, 33 years old, was quaestor in 63 and fought against Catiline at the Battle of Pistoia. Milo has said that he wants to oppose Clodius's rise to power and has found solid support among his political opponents, Pompey first of all. Milo, 38 years old, was elected to the tribunate of the plebs even though he doesn't belong to the Roman ruling class, neither to the aristocracy, nor to the equestrian nobility. In fact, he was born in Lanuvium (Lanuvio), a small town about 30 km southeast of Rome in the Alban Hills in the area of the Castelli Romani. Lanuvium is the center of the cult of Juno Sospita, a Latin goddess who is usually represented with the pelt of a goat on her head and a spear in her hand, accompanied by a snake.

The Attempt on Pompey's Life

At the same time as the winners of the elections for the magistracies for 57 are being announced, Varro Lucullus makes Clodius aware that Caesar will not oppose the political reintegration of Cicero. Clodius hadn't been expecting such news and is left bewildered. He cannot tolerate Caesar's *volte-face* and cannot stifle his indignation. He convenes a *contio* for 23 July 58, during which Bibulus will reveal that Caesar, during their consulship of 59, never took unfavorable auspices into consideration. This is a serious accusation because it is required of anyone holding a public office that they conform their actions according to the results of the interpretation of divine signals. Taking the floor in the *contio*, Clodius declares that he is joining the Catonian faction in arguing that the actions carried out by Caesar during his consulship were illegitimate and warns that he will oppose any legislative initiative put forward by the Populares from now on. Clodius thus distances himself from Caesar and his friends, repositioning himself alongside their political opponents.

Between the end of September and the start of October 58, the tribune of the plebs Publius Sestius—designate but not yet in office (not until 10 December 58)—goes to Caesar in Gallia Transalpina at the request of Pompey. Sestius informs Caesar that Clodius has taken up a position against him. Caesar replies he isn't worried by this and that he will withdraw his support from Clodius. It is the end of the partnership of Caesar and Clodius, the end of a personal friendship and a political alliance.

Caesar and Sestius plan the presentation of a bill aimed at securing the political rehabilitation of Cicero. After returning to Rome, Sestius ensures that the consuls Spinther and Nepos support the plebiscite born from those plans. On hearing the news, Clodius loses the light of reason and does something heinous: he orders one of his slaves to assassinate Pompey (for having sent Sestius to Caesar and, more generally, for being politically favorable toward Cicero). The plan is for him to be murdered in the Temple of Castor and Pollux, which is the place where the Senate is about to start meeting occasionally as an alternative to its official seat.

The Temple of Castor and Pollux, also known as the Temple of the Dioscuri, overlooks the Roman Forum. It rises from an elevated platform which is accessed by two side stairways, and has six Corinthian columns at its front and 11 down each side. The platform is used as a rostrum during the legislative assemblies that take place in the square in front. The Office of Weights and Measures is found inside the building. Some moneychangers carry out their activities between the columns.

Clodius's slave waits in the space between the *cella* and the columns outside for Pompey to arrive. He is armed with a dagger, which he keeps hidden in the folds of his clothes. But, absent-minded, he carelessly lets the weapon fall to the ground. The clang of iron on the floor draws the attention of those present. Discovered and cornered, the would-be murderer confesses; he names Pompey as the intended victim and Clodius as the one who ordered the hit. Pompey is profoundly shocked by the incident; he shuts himself away in his villa in Alba and remains there for a long time, during which Gabinius hurls insults at Clodius and Clodius offers Gabinius's possessions to Ceres, mimicking the gesture of Ninnius.

Atticus's Friendship

On 28 October 58, all the tribunes of the plebs except those who are friends with Clodius jointly promote a bill aimed at Cicero's political rehabilitation. The plebiscite passes the scrutiny of the Senate without issue. On 3 November 58, it is explained to the people gathered in a *contio*. Clodius, taking the floor, states his opposition to the initiative; in his view, Cicero must remain in exile. Shortly afterward, the tribunes of the plebs Serranus and Rufus, friends of Clodius, use their veto. The law-making process is blocked.[5]

This happens while Cicero is in Thessalonica (Salonica in Greece). He is staying in a house owned by his friend Atticus and is enjoying the protection of the quaestor

---

5   On 28 October, the majority of tribunes proposed a bill to recall Cicero from his exile, but a vote thereupon was blocked. Cic. *Att.,* III.23.1, 4; *Red. sen.,* 8, 29; *Sest.,* 70.

Plancius.[6] The latest news about him floors him completely. Cicero is depressed and no longer recognizes himself. He thinks about the misfortune that has befallen him and the loss of his many riches, not only the material ones but also the immaterial ones, such as his social and political prestige, his vast influence, his rich and varied social life, and the joys of family. He is bitter at the lack of public recognition of his value to the state, at the shame of having been sentenced to exile (a punishment that is considered by the Romans as shameful), at his conviction and his suspicion that he had been wrong to listen to his friends, and at having been badly advised, whether out of envy, deceitfulness, or betrayal. He regrets the haste with which he left Rome, without having attempted to oppose Clodius. He is even resentful toward Atticus, whom he reproaches for not having kept him from leaving but for having stood by in silence. He tells him this in two letters.

Atticus is a person of many wonderful qualities, and he knows how to be a true friend, one whom anyone would like to have. He understands Cicero's state of mind, so he doesn't take offense. He has already made the sum of 250,000 sesterces available to Cicero. He will continue to host him in his properties in Macedonia for free, to keep him up to date with public life in Rome and with developments in the Gallic Wars, writing to him constantly and reporting the political controversies of the day, as well as other news, down to the smallest detail in his letters.

It is in this way that Cicero learns that the political accord between Clodius and Caesar has broken down, because the former has tied himself to the worst enemies of the latter, who in turn has undertaken initiatives that are at odds with those of Clodius.

Atticus isn't Cicero's only source of information while he is in exile. Another is Cicero's neighbor, Clodia, the sister of Clodius and the lover of Catullus.

A Tormented Love

The period between the end of 59 and the end of 58 isn't only a very sad one for Cicero but also for Catullus, albeit for different reasons. The latter heard with great sorrow that his brother had died in the distant Troad and went to visit his parents in Verona with a heavy heart to be close to them and embrace them. While he was in Verona, he learned that Clodia, in his absence, had started a liaison with Marcus Caelius Rufus. Rufus and Clodia had met for the first time when Rufus went to live in the Palatine district. Clodia had made her house one of the most fashionable places for the socialites of Rome's high society to gather, and Rufus began to frequent it. He and Clodia immediately hit it off with one another and began a relationship.

Driven by jealousy, Catullus rushes back to Rome. Clodia returns to him, then starts cheating on him again: if not with Rufus, then with others. Catullus is

---

6   From 23 May to mid-November. On Cicero in Thessalonica: Cic. *Att.*, III.8.1.

blinded by his love for her. Although he is aware of Clodia's continuing infidelities, he tolerates them while feeling depressed and sorry for himself. His love fluctuates between fatal attraction and feelings of revulsion. In one of his poems, he envisages Clodia wandering like a prostitute through the alleys of Rome. In another—number 85, perhaps the most famous poem in his *Liber*—he expresses his own conflicted state of mind, because it is oscillating between two extremes: love and hate.

> *Odi et amo. Quare id faciam, fortasse requiris.*
> *Nescio, sed fieri sentio et excrucior.*
>
> I hate and I love. Wherefore I do this, perhaps you ask.
> I do not know, but I feel it being done and I am tormented.

Catullus is aware that his feelings are paradoxical because he is at the mercy of opposing feelings, provoked by love ("I hate you and love you at the same time"). This is the classic situation that occurs when one of two lovers doesn't return the love of the other as much as the latter expects them to do or when someone who is lovestruck doesn't have their feelings reciprocated by their beloved. The tragedy of Catullus is made even more acute by his perception that his difficulty has arisen independently of his will, and he cannot do anything other than put up with the situation, suffering horribly over it. Toward the end of 58, he is composing verses in which he attributes the hyperbolic figure of 100 lovers to his unfaithful beloved and decides to separate himself from her for good.

Both in order to forget Clodia—and therefore to enjoy himself again—as well as to make some money,[7] Catullus asks—and is allowed—to be able to join the propraetor Caius Memmius, who is about to depart for Nicomedia, the capital of Bithynia and Pontus, because he has just been appointed as governor of this province for 57 and 56 and must travel to the seat of his new office.[8] As well as Catullus, Memmius is joined by another "new poet," Caius Helvius Cinna.

In his *Brutus*—a Platonic dialogue on Roman oratory that he will compose in 46—Cicero will describe Memmius as a highly cultured philhellenic intellectual who, however, is contemptuous about Latin culture, and as a polished orator with a pleasing turn of phrase but who is averse to laborious efforts to improve his eloquence.[9] Indeed, Memmius is a poet. Other than being a friend of Catullus and Cinna, he is also the patron of Titus Lucretius Carus, the poet, Epicurean philosopher, and author of *De rerum natura* ("On the nature of things"), a didactic poem on natural science and philosophy written in six books in dactylic hexameter anddestined to

---

7 It was typical of the mentality of the Roman nobility that they went to the provinces to enrich themselves, taking advantage of the thousands of favorable opportunities when given responsibility for government or administration or to contribute to the performance of such duties.
8 Nicomedia (Izmit in Turkey) was a city situated on the Anatolian coast of the Sea of Marmara.
9 Cic. *Brut.*, 247.

be considered one of the most important works of classical antiquity. The work is dedicated to Memmius, but his name is only mentioned twice therein.[10]

Memmius is hostile toward Caesar. In 58, as praetor, he had attacked his actions as consul in 59, with the support of his colleague Lucius Domitius Ahenobarbus; furthermore, he protested that Publius Vatinius, a friend of Caesar, had broken the *lex Iunia Licinia*, which decrees that draft laws cannot be put before the people gathered in assembly for a vote before three *nundinae* ("market days") have elapsed since its presentation.

In the meantime, Cicero's younger brother, Quintus, has returned to Rome from the province of Asia with a good reputation as an efficient and honest administrator (he governed the province from 61 to 59). He discovers that his house has been rendered unusable by the damage caused by the construction works on Clodius's neighboring building complex, and, while the property is being repaired, he will have to stay elsewhere. It is possibly near the end of 58 when he moves in with his niece Tullia, who suggested that he stay in the house in which she lives with her husband, the quaestor Caius Calpurnius Piso Frugi.[11]

Quintus works tirelessly to build an alliance of forces in support of his brother Marcus. Among other things, he pressures the consuls Piso Caesoninus and Gabinius to support the plebiscite of Ninnius Quadratus, but they appear insensitive to any solicitation on this subject. Indeed, at that time, Gabinius banishes Aelius Lamia from Rome for having expressed solidarity with the exiled Cicero. As can be seen, Gabinius is behaving ambiguously: he officially opposes Cicero being recalled to his homeland but secretly supports Pompey's motions that are aimed at obtaining it.

In 57, probably for the purpose of intimidation, Clodius brings a charge against Quintus Tullius Cicero for having violated the *lex Iulia repetundis*. The case should be discussed before a court presided over by the praetor Appius Claudius Pulcher, Clodius's brother, but it never will be.[12]

Massacre in the Forum

Of the consuls for 57, the one who holds the *fasces* for the first month of their mandates is Lentulus Spinther. Since he knows he can rely on the support of Pompey, eight tribunes of the plebs, and most of the Senate, he highlights how, in

---

10 It is worth considering the hypothesis that the real author of *De rerum natura* is Titus Pomponius Atticus, at least in principle. F. Santangelo, *Roma repubblicana. Una storia in quaranta vite* (Roma: Carocci, 2019), 270–271. On this subject, see also A. Gerlo, "Pseudo Lucretius?" *L'Antiquité Classique* 25 (1956): 41–72; L. Canfora, *Vita di Lucrezio* (Palermo: Sellerio, 1993), 92–94.

11 It seems likely that Quintus Tullius Cicero went to live with Gaius Calpurnius Piso Frugi and his wife Tullia before 5 August 57 when Piso Frugi died.

12 M. C. Alexander, *Trials in the Late Roman Republic, 149 BC to 50 BC* (Toronto: University of Toronto Press, 1990), 128–129, n. 263.

his opinion, it is appropriate for the people gathered in assembly to express their view on the matter of Cicero's political rehabilitation. In practice, he is hoping for a new bill to be presented that will officially allow the exile to return to his homeland. A discussion on the subject follows, during which Clodius, supported by his brother Appius, the consul Metellus Nepos, and the tribunes of the plebs Ligur, Serranus, and Rufus, reiterates his personal opposition to reopening the case. The discussion ends when Serranus uses his veto.[13]

Cicero's friends don't give up. On 23 January 57, on the proposal of the tribune of the plebs Quintus Fabricius, the *comitia tributa* is convened to vote on yet another draft law relating to the case of Cicero.

Clodius feels as though everyone is against him—Pompey, Caesar, the Senate, the consuls, the people in assembly (though Crassus's position isn't clear)—and reacts, this time violently. On the night of 22/23 January 57, his band of criminals, which he has already used as a tool of pressure and intimidation, occupies the Forum. The news spreads rapidly, and during the night numerous followers of Pompey also converge on the Forum. On the morning of 23 January 57, the opposing groups clash in a furious brawl. The fracas, foul and chaotic, is still going on in a noisy exchange of blows when the knives come out. The yells of those who are battling it out mix with cries of pain, the moans of the wounded, the gasps of the dying. Quintus Tullius Cicero gets mixed up in the confusion, but he manages to get away unharmed. Because of the *bagarre*, the assembly is adjourned.[14]

The violence continues between February and July 57, when Clodius and his gang attack the house of Milo but are knocked back, suffering numerous losses (Clodius himself only just saves his own skin). Milo reports the incident to the Urban Praetor and manages to have the perpetrators arrested but not to have them convicted because—after the intervention of the Senate—the defendants are acquitted during the initial investigation and are allowed to go free. After this, Clodius's gang starts threatening Milo again and tries to intimidate Sestius too. Milo and Sestius litigate against Clodius, who is sent to court. However, the trial cannot take place because the consul Nepos, to protect the accused, interrupts all public activities. Milo and Sestius, because they cannot succeed in getting justice from the establishment, decide to take other measures to protect themselves, each equipping themselves with an armed escort formed of gladiators, former soldiers, freedmen, artisans, and shopkeepers. From now on, Clodius's henchmen will have to contend with other groups of armed men determined to get in their way. Thus begins an eventful period in which Sestius's and Milo's gangs attack Clodius's gang non-stop, and vice versa.[15] Many people are killed or injured in the fights that break out in

---

13 Cic. *Amicis*, V.4; *Dom.*, 68; *Pis.*, 34; *Red. pop.*, 11–12; *Red. sen.*, 5, 8–9; *Sest.*, 72–74, 84.
14 Cic. *Sest.* 73–77; Plut. *Cic.*, 33.4; Plut. *Pomp.*, 49.5; Dio Cass., XXXIX.6–7.
15 Dio Cass., XXXIX.8.1.

all corners of the city. In one of these clashes Sestius is hit, loses consciousness, falls to the ground, and is presumed dead, but he will recover. In 56, Cicero, thinking back to the days of 57 in which gang warfare left the streets of the capital running with blood, will record that:

> ... the Tiber was filled with the corpses of the citizens, that the sewers were choked up; that blood was wiped up out of the forum with sponges ... The forum had been taken ... the temple of Castor having been occupied by runaway slaves, as if it had been a fortress! ... Everything was done by the clamor and impetuosity, and violence, and assaults of men desperate through indigence and through their natural audacity ... The magistrates were driven from the temples; others were altogether cut off from all approach to them or to the forum ... The forum was strewed with the corpses of Roman citizens murdered in a nocturnal massacre.[16]

Pressed by the need to put a stop to the violence that had overrun the city's orderly and peaceful existence, Pompey decides to make the Cicero case a question of national importance. Therefore, in the spring of 57, he undertakes a long journey through Italia propria, passing through various *municipia* and *coloniae*, including Capua, where he is the city magistrate, and, with a view to the next *comitia centuriata*, manages to funnel numerous out-of-towners to Rome, who rush to the capital both because they are flattered by the fact that they are considered necessary and because they are tired of the chaos that is paralyzing the state.

---

16 Cic. *Sest.*, 77, 85.

CHAPTER XIII

The Exile's Return

The Turning Point

The city of Buthrotum (Butrint in Albania) is in Epirus and therefore within the Roman province of Macedonia, close to the border with the Roman province of Achaea (Greece). It has been built on the coast, almost opposite the island of Corcyra (Corfu), on the western shore of the Pelodes (today known as Lake Butrint) on a hill that overlooks a small strip of land between this stretch of water and the Vivari Channel, which connects the Pelodes to the sea. The city occupies a strategically important position because it controls access through the Straits of Corfu. It is said to have been founded by Trojan refugees. In any case, it is certainly a very old city.

Atticus takes Cicero to Buthrotum, where he owns a villa that he will put at his friend's disposal.[1] Recently, they met in Dyrrachium in Epirus, the former coming from Rome, the latter from Thessalonica.[2] Cicero has moved in a hurry, well aware that with Piso's arrival he will no longer be safe.

Atticus's residence is situated a short distance from the city,[3] and it is fortified with an imposing perimeter wall and four towers to provide protection against the risk of raids by marauding Illyrian pirates. The property dates back at least to around 230.[4] Atticus bought it and enlarged it. It includes rooms decorated with precious sheets of marble affixed to the walls with special pins, and a small private sanctuary, built near the River Thyamis and shaded by trees.[5] The latter is called

---

1   Cicero is in Dyrrachium between 25 November and the end of the year, perhaps receiving his visit from Atticus in mid-December. Cic. *Att.*, III.25, 26, 27.

2   Cicero leaves Thessalonica for Dyrrachium between mid-November and 25 November: Cic. *Att.*, III.22.4, *Fr.*, XIV.1.7.

3   A recent study has suggested identifying Atticus's rural residence with the monumental complex at Malathrea, a site located in the Pavllë Valley.

4   This dating is based on the fact that a coin issued in 229 in Apollonia, the port of the Greek city of Cyrene in Libya, was discovered in the area.

5   It is likely that a bas-relief depicting a winged and draped Nike (Victoria), carved in Parian marble, and found outside the city, came from the Amaltheum.

the Amaltheum, after the name of the mythical goat Amalthea, to whom Atticus makes offerings and sacrifices.

Meanwhile, in Rome, Quintus Tullius Cicero is dressed in mourning garb. He has never ceased working on his brother's behalf so that he can be readmitted to political life; recently, however, the task has become more arduous due to the inconsistent functioning of the political establishment, which itself is down to the gang warfare currently staining the capital with blood. To prevent the raging turmoil and confusion from paralyzing public life, the consuls, in agreement with the Senate, have issued an edict that considers any attempt to prevent the people from meeting in an assembly as an attack on the security of the state.[6]

On 2 May 57, the Senate of Rome meets in the Temple of Honor and Virtue in the Campus Martius (the religious site, remember, that appeared to Cicero in the prophetic dream he had in Atina). During the meeting, the consul Spinther proposed to his colleagues that they "entrust" Cicero to the governor of Macedonia, Piso Caesoninus. This is an *escamotage* that aimed to reopen the question of Cicero's political reintegration without a tribune of the plebs being able to use his veto. This specific suggestion, in fact, isn't a question of adopting a piece of legislation but rather of expressing an opinion on the security that must be provided by the highest authority of a province to a Roman citizen. After extensive discussions the Senate agrees with the proposal and advocates for Cicero's protection.

This new trajectory slows down in June 57, when the *fasces* are handed to the consul Quintus Caecilius Metellus Nepos Minor, but picks up again the following month, when the *fasces* are returned to Spinther. Clodius tries to obstruct him, leveraging popular discontent to foment unrest.

The Exile Is Officially Recalled to His Homeland

Between 5 and 13 July 57, during the games in honor of Apollo, crowds of plebeians protest first in front of the Curia of Pompey, then in front of the Curia Hostilia, while the Senate is in session. These rallies are motivated by the fact that consumer prices have recently risen, especially those of foodstuffs, which weigh more heavily on the less well-off. The prices of grain and its products are increasing because, due to poor organization, the *annona*—the system supplying the capital with food—isn't working as it should, the public grain warehouses are empty, and the distribution of cereals is at a standstill.

The consul Metellus Nepos has always been hostile towards Cicero, even more than Piso Caesoninus. He was a legate under Pompey Magnus during the war against the pirates (67) and during the Third Mithridatic War (73–63). In 63, he was elected to the tribunate of the plebs for 62 alongside Cato. He publicly accused

---

6   Cic. *Sest.*, 129.

the then consul Cicero of having condemned the arrested Catilinarians to death and prevented him from delivering his end-of-mandate speech by using his veto.

In 57, Nepos is convinced by Spinther, Pompey, and other influential individuals, to change his attitude toward Cicero. This is the turning point in the tumultuous sequence of events revolving around the exile. Shortly after, Nepos and Spinther jointly present a bill and a motion. The draft legislation seeks to abrogate the *lex de exilio Ciceronis*. The motion, to have the Senate appeal to Roman citizens residing in the *coloniae* and *municipia* in Italy to hasten to Rome to vote for the bill.

Large sections of the population enthusiastically welcome the news, expressing their jubilation during theatrical performances or at the circus, both in Rome and elsewhere in Italy. These displays extend through to the middle of May. Pompey and other eminent citizens speak out in favor of the bill. From 6 to 9 July 57, the Senate of Rome meets in the Temple of Jupiter Optimus Maximus to listen to Pompey, who praises Cicero and calls him the savior of the *res publica*. The college meets again on 10 July, this time in the Curia, and discusses the consuls' legislative proposal and, with 417 votes in favor of it and just one against—that of Clodius—authorizes it to be sent on to the *comitia centuriata*. On 4 August 57, the people gathered in assembly vote on the bill and it is passed without issue. The new law, named the *lex Cornelia Caecilia de revocando Cicerone*,[7] repeals the *lex de exilio Ciceronis*, brings Cicero back into the political fold, orders that the exile be officially recalled to his homeland, authorizes the restitution of the possessions that had been confiscated from him, or the payment of compensation in the event of their destruction, and declares anyone who attempts to prevent his repatriation as a public enemy. Many people flocked to Rome to support the initiative and lauded the quaestor Plancius and the many others who supported Cicero during his exile.[8] Clodius's opposition is unceasing and he would like to unleash his mob, but Milo keeps him in check. Cicero's 17-month exile thus finally comes to an end.

A Triumphal Return

Cicero is virtually bursting with happiness from every pore. On 5 August 57, he boards a boat in Dyrrachium and disembarks the next day in Brundisium, joyfully welcomed by many friends and by his daughter Tullia.[9] A week of leisure passes for him to recover from the suffering he has endured, and then, on 11 or 13 August, he continues to Rome.[10] As he gradually proceeds along the Via Appia, he is cheered by joyous crowds. On 4 September, he enters Rome through the Porta Capena,

---

7   Cic. *Dom.*, 71; *Mil.*, 39; *Red. sen.*, 29; *Sest.*, 117–129; Vell. Pat., II.45.3; App. *B. Civ.*, II.59; Dio Cass., XXXIX.8.1–3.
8   Cic. *Div.*, I.59; *Planc.*, 78; *Sest.*, 116; *Schol. Bob.*, 136, 166; Val. Max., I.7.5.
9   Cic. *Att.*, IV.1.4; *Sest.*, 131.
10 Cic. *Att.*, IV.1.4.

where he is welcomed with jubilation. Family members, relatives, friends, clients, magistrates, senators, and ordinary citizens all embrace him. Cicero crosses the city until he reaches the Forum, where he takes the Via Sacra, still followed by a crowd that is loudly and euphorically cheering and championing him. Finally, he climbs the Capitoline.[11] He will temporarily stay in the house of his son-in-law, the now deceased Caius Calpurnius Piso Frugi, currently occupied by his daughter Tullia and his brother Quintus, while he waits to be able to return to his own house.

On 5 September, Cicero gives a speech of thanks in the Senate.[12] Then he gives another to the people who have gathered in a *contio*.[13] On these occasions, he presents his flight from Rome as a voluntary departure, a personal sacrifice, and a heroic action, because—he says—the state departed with him, and this avoided a civil war. He reiterates several times that the salvation of the *res publica* is tied to his own, and he makes it clear that it isn't only he who is convinced of this but also numerous others, above all Pompey. He reaffirms his loyalty and his commitment to the defense of the *res publica*, which, if anything, have only increased. He thanks the gods and all those who worked so hard in various ways to allow him to return home, mentioning them by name: his brother Quintus, as well as Spinther, Nepos, Pompey, Caesar, Plancius. He calls Spinther *parens ac dues*, "parent and god," and says that he has been reborn thanks to him. He thanks the tribune of the plebs for 58, Lucius Ninnius Quadratus, and the tribunes of the plebs for 57, for having given their all for his cause, naming them all one by one: Titus Annius Milo, Publius Sestius, Lucius Ninnius Quadratus, Caius Cestilius, Marcus Cispius, Titus Fadius, Marcus Curtius, Caius Messius, and Quintus Fabricius. He does the same thing with the praetors Lucius Caecilius, Marcus Calidius, Caius Septimius, Quintus Valerius, Publius Crassus, Sextus Quintilius, and Caius Cornutus. He dwells on Milo and Sestius, extolling the former for his ability to identify the enemy within (Clodius) and to act for the good of the fatherland, and justifying the violent means he used against Clodius, while he underlines the zeal demonstrated by Sestius in supporting his cause and calls him *frater*, "brother," both for having made means available to him and for calling on his clients, servants, and freedmen. He praises the absolute fidelity and self-sacrifice shown to him and his family by his son-in-law Caius Calpurnius Piso Frugi, quaestor in 67. In his Cicero's absence, Piso Frugi forewent his attempts to pursue his career as a magistrate in order to be close to his wife and his mother-in-law, working tirelessly for a long time to help Cicero return from exile, and dying prematurely, before his father-in-law's return. Cicero also thanks the people of Italy, who made his return possible by voting in favor of the consuls' proposals, underlining that they rallied and came to Rome from all over Italy just

---

11 Cic. *Att.*, IV.1.5; *Dom.*, 76; *Sest.*, 131; *Pis.*, 52. App. *B. Civ.*, II.16.
12 Cic. *Att.*, IV.1.5; *Planc.*, 74. Dio Cass., XXXIX.9.1.
13 Cic. *Att.*, IV.1.6.

for him, something that has only occurred a few times in the past. He thanks the Roman people gathered in the assembly who approved the draft law that revoked his sentence of exile. He thanks the senators, calling them *parentes* and *patres* for their emotional participation in his misfortune, recalling how they dressed in mourning clothes and sent a delegation to the consuls to ask for his return. He says that he will be forever in their debt. Nor does he fail to mention that, due to the atmosphere of terror and the resultant fear, some senators hadn't adopted a favorable position toward him. He also thanks Piso Caesoninus. This gesture may seem to be aimed at healing their stormy past,[14] but it is a mere formality if not a provocation. Soon after, in fact, Cicero mocks Caesoninus for his scruffy beard, saying that he sees in him a hypocritical representative of ancient Roman morals.

Cicero never mentions Clodius by name during his speeches, at most referring to him as "that tribune of the plebs" or as his "enemy" (his audience knew exactly who he was talking about), probably to make it clear that he isn't even worthy of being named. He doesn't expressly cite Caesar either, but he doesn't fail to point out his ambiguous attitude toward him ("I do not say that he was an enemy of mine, but I do know that he did nothing when he was stated to be my enemy").[15] Instead, he expressly accuses the tribunes of the plebs for 58—Aelius Ligur, Quintus Numerius Rufus, and Atilius Serranus Gavianus—for having hindered initiatives in his favor. He manifests contempt for Gabinius and Piso, accusing them of having exchanged their support for Clodius's plebiscite that had condemned him to exile for their appointments as provincial governors in view of the illicit gains they could derive therefrom. To detoxify the atmosphere, however, he declares in broad terms that he forgives all those who have wronged him.

Cicero's first thought, having returned to Rome, was about politics. Now, however, he must think about his possessions. He is staying in the house of his deceased son-in-law, occupied by his daughter Tullia and his son Quintus, as he waits to be able to return to his own home as soon as possible. Cicero's residence, we recall, had been confiscated and purchased by the Treasury, then ransacked and set ablaze on the orders of Clodius, in the presence of Piso Caesoninus, who had appropriated some of the assets contained therein. Later, it had been auctioned off to a front man for Clodius, who then turned it over to the latter. Clodius had razed the ruins to the ground and built a new architectural complex on the site.

Even his villas in Tusculum (Tuscolo) and Formiae (Formia) had been devastated and sacked by Clodius's mob. Some of Cicero's possessions from the villa in Tusculum ended up in the hands of Gabinius.

---

14 When, in 61, Piso had been consul, he offended Cicero in the Senate by only giving him the floor third. Later, he protected Clodius. Cicero returned this spite by preventing him from taking up office as the governor of Syria, which others had promised to him.

15 Cic. *Red. sen.*, 33.

Cicero manages to regain possession of the area where his house on the Palatine used to be, which is limited to the parts where Clodius built his atrium, the study, and the panoramic promenade. Clodius must therefore also renounce the area previously occupied by the *porticus Catuli*, on which, after having the four-sided portico demolished, he had had the promenade built. This will be demolished, and the four-sided portico will be reconstructed at the state's expense.

The Appointment of Pompey to the *Cura Annonae*

On 6–7 September 57, Clodius took advantage of the persistent, widespread popular discontent to address a captive audience in the Forum and point the finger at Cicero as being responsible for the rise in corn prices.[16] In response, Cicero demonstrates, as if there were any need, that the cause of the phenomenon must be sought elsewhere. During one of his speeches in the Senate, he observes that, since the entry into force of Clodius's *lex frumentaria*, the task of ensuring that Rome receives supplies of grain from the provinces has been carried out by one of Clodius's freedmen. Clodius was certainly well informed on the workings of the *annona*. If he had wanted to, since he was in the right position to do so, he could have exposed the speculators and avoided both the supply crisis and the consequent spiral of inflation. The fact that he hadn't done so meant that the chaos that had caused the shortages wasn't accidental but deliberate. It had had the particular aim of maddening the population in order to then be able to ride the wave of discontent for political ends. In conclusion, Cicero proposes to transfer the *cura annonae*, both by land and sea, to Pompey for the next five years, with all the necessary powers and the ability to avail himself of 15 (de)legates.[17] Of course, Clodius opposes the proposal and suggests entrusting Pompey with another assignment because "nothing ought to have been decreed irregularly to anyone."[18] The Senate chooses to adopt Cicero's proposal and confers the extraordinary office of looking after the *cura annonae* for five years to Pompey, with sweeping powers to intervene wherever necessary, and gives him the ability to make use of an appropriate number of assistants of his choosing. Clodius has lost. Angrily remarking on the Senate's decision, he accuses Pompey of having provoked the crisis with the express purpose of obtaining this

---

16 Cic. *Att.*, IV.1.6; *Dom.*, 6 [14].

17 Cic. *Att.*, IV.1.6. The word *legatus* isn't only applied to legionary commanders. More generally, it befitted any right-hand man of an elected or extraordinary magistrate who had been assigned special duties by them. In 58, legates began to exercise military command in place of a *magistratus cum imperio*, whose trust was placed in them (Caes. I.52). This was done on behalf of the Senate, with some exceptions. Over time, *legati pro praetore* took on a role of increasing importance, eventually assuming permanent command of one or more legions.

18 Cic. *Dom.*, 8 [18] "(…) *quicquam uni extra ordinem decerni* (…)."

position. Cicero, at the end of the meeting, is acclaimed by the people and publicly expresses his gratitude.[19]

He has repaid the debt he owes to Pompey for his hard work in recalling him to his homeland. But the exchange of favors has only just begun. Shortly after, Pompey names Cicero as his *alter ego* for any eventuality related to food supplies. Later, he appoints Quintus Tullius Cicero as his legate for Sardinia.[20] However, there is a risk that Caesar will become jealous of the responsibility conferred to Pompey. To avoid this, Cicero compensates Caesar with something else. In autumn 57, or at the start of 56—in any case, before the pronouncement of the oration *De provinciis consularibus* (56) in favor of the extension of Caesar's proconsulship— which we will need to look at later—he asks for and receives the Senate's declaration of a 15-day *supplicatio* to thank the gods for the victories won by Caesar in Gaul.[21]

The *supplicatio* is a period in which all the temples remain open and the statues of the gods are publicly displayed so that the entire population can offer their thanks and pray. The measure is taken following a great military victory—or a serious defeat. The Senate sets its duration, generally between one and five days. After Pompey's definitive victory over Mithridates VI, king of Pontus, an exceptional 10-day *supplicatio* was decreed.

As we noted earlier, Cicero has obtained the restitution of his house on the Palatine other than the part occupied by the small temple to the goddess Libertas, and the utility rooms that Clodius had built where the gymnasium had been after he had demolished it. Cicero also asks for the restitution of the remaining parts, but it is a delicate matter—the area of his old gymnasium is now consecrated ground—and therefore the Senate, before deciding, asks the College of Pontiffs for its opinion. By 29 September, the Senate has heard this opinion, but it wants to hear from Cicero as well. Cicero maintains that the process of consecrating the ground was conducted irregularly. This is shown by the fact that Clodius did not ask the people gathered in assembly to authorize him to perform the ceremony, as he was required to do, nor did he convene the College of Pontiffs so that it could celebrate the rite. Instead, he had the religious function performed by just one of the members of this college, who was very young and a relative of his to boot. For these reasons, Cicero argues that the act of consecration is invalid due to the violation of the law and must therefore be considered null or annullable.[22] The college, after careful examination and extensive discussions, accepts the invalidity argument and adjudges Clodius's action to have been an individual initiative. This removes the obstacle that was preventing Cicero

19 Cic. *Att.*, IV.1.7.
20 Cic. *Att.*, IV.1.7, IV.2.6; *QFr.*, II.4, VII.5.3; *Scaur.*, 39.
21 Cic. *Balb.*, 61; *Prov. cons.*, 26. On the *supplicatio*: Caes., I.35.4.
22 Cic. *Att.*, IV.2.2.

from regaining possession of the rest of his house. Furthermore, on 1 or 2 October 57, Cicero receives payment of 2 million sesterces from the state as reparations for the damage caused to him by the confiscation of his personal possessions, of which 1,250,000 sesterces are for his residence in the city, 500,000 are for the villa in Tusculum, and 250,000 for the villa in Formiae.[23]

Building works begin. These involve recreating the *porticus Catuli*, demolishing the small temple to Libertas, building a *thermae* in its place and a new four-sided portico above the latter. According to the project's plans, the new four-sided portico will enclose various rooms, including a library, and will have a lawn, a bench, and a few philosophers' statues in the center. Clodius protests, working himself into a frenzy, ranting and raving, and condemns the profanation that, in his opinion, Cicero is preparing to carry out by building on consecrated ground. Since no one is paying him any heed, he orders his henchmen to storm the construction site. On 3 November some of his thugs hurl abuse at the construction workers and throw stones and lit torches into the property, causing serious damage not only to Cicero's house but also to the adjacent property owned by his brother Quintus.[24] In the course of a subsequent attack, the *porticus Catuli*, newly rebuilt, is demolished again. But it isn't over. On 11 November, Cicero is attacked by strangers as he walks down the Via Sacra.[25]

Despite everything, the restoration and rebuilding works are completed. As such, Cicero can go back to living in his own house together with his wife Terentia and their children: his first-born Tullia and the young Marcus. The house is very large and has two floors, everything smells new, and it is fitted out with luxurious amenities. The *porticus Catuli* has also been restored with its original function. Tullia, because she is now a widow, returns to live with her parents.[26] In truth, she had never completely moved away. Her husband—Piso Frugi, whom she had married in 63—was a good man, and as such, he allowed her to spend time with her parents. Despite her grief, Tullia had gone to welcome her father at Brundisium. Terentia had let her go alone. But this isn't the reason why Cicero quarreled with Terentia when he returned to Rome from his exile.[27] The reason is to be found in the family finances: Cicero believes that Philotimus, one of Terentia's freedmen, is a swindler because while he was absent in exile, his wife's wealth, for whom he is the procurator, was looked after, but the management of Cicero's assets, which Terentia looks after, was neglected (her strength of character was also manifested in not asking for advice either from her husband or from her sister-in-law's brother, Atticus).

23 Cic. *Att.*, IV.2.4–5.
24 Cic. *Att.*, IV.3.2; *Fam.*, I.9.3; *Cael.* 89; *Mil.* 87.
25 Cic. *Att.*, IV.3.3.
26 Cic. *Att.*, III.22.1; *Fam.*, XIV.1.4.3, XIV.3. See also Cic. *Sest.*, 131.
27 Cic. *Att.*, IV.1.8, IV.2.7, IV.3.6.

Cicero now has less faith in Terentia than he did when he first left. And he explains why. During his exile, he persistently asked Atticus to sell his clothes, his furniture, and his silverware and to collect some credit. Atticus asked Terentia to use a letter of exchange to pay her husband 12,000 sesterces, the balance of 20,000 sesterces collected by Terentia herself from the Oppii (or the balance of a loan procured by Terentia—the exact details aren't quite clear). But Terentia only sent 10,000 and said that this was the entirety of what remained.

In a letter dated 6 August 47, sent to Atticus, Cicero worriedly asks him: if Terentia acted in such a way when dealing with modest sums, what might she have done in the case of much larger transactions?[28] In short, Cicero suspects Terentia of unlawful business in his absence and of having taken advantage of possibilities offered by the management of the family assets, in which Philotimus was also complicit.

The Political Fading of Clodius

Things are no longer going well for Clodius. He was unable to prevent Cicero's official recall to his homeland or to prevent him from regaining possession of his property. He has had to give up a large part of his real estate portfolio and, together with his wife Fulvia, has had to confine himself in what's left. Moreover, his gang of violent thugs is no longer able to influence public life, institutions, and magistrates as in the past. By now, Pompey is against him and Caesar has abandoned him. All this costs him greatly in terms of image, credibility, popularity, and power.

In the meantime, he has put himself forward as a candidate for the aedileship for 56. What he is seeking, rather than the office itself, is the legal immunity it offers to insure himself against the risk of being found guilty in the trial brought against him by Milo on the charge of having committed or commissioned acts of physical violence against magistrates and senators to prevent the regular and free course of public meetings and, more generally, the functions of the state.

The relevant crime, called *de vi*, is provided for by the *lex Plautia de vi* (80–70) and punishes those found guilty with death, unless the condemned voluntarily offers to go into exile. Clodius is said to have committed the crime against Milo when the latter was tribune of the plebs. At the trial, Clodius is impassioned in his defense of himself and calls on numerous supporters, namely the consul Nepos, his relative; the praetor Appius Claudius Pulcher, his brother; and a tribune of the plebs. Nepos ensures the trial ends in favor of the accused by issuing a decree (the *institium*) that, in emergency situations, suspends the handling of any public affair, including, criminal trials.

More clashes between rival gangs occur in the following months on the streets and in the squares of Rome, so much so that organized violence becomes a key aspect of

---

28 Cic. *Att.*, XI.24.

political life in the city. One of the gangs involved in the fighting is Clodius's gang. The others are those of Milo and Sestius. Fundamentally, by fomenting rioting, the aim is to postpone the date of the magistracy elections for as long as possible given that Clodius is campaigning for the aedileship.

Cicero is eager to settle his score with Clodius. Ever since his return to Rome, he has never lost an opportunity to thunder at him. He portrays him as a reckless, nefarious, thuggish individual. He highlights how his followers are members of the underclass without solid jobs, street-fighting mercenaries, slaves attracted by promises, and gladiators. In December, he tries to thwart Clodius and works with the tribune of the plebs Lucius Racilius—one of those who, during Cicero's exile, worked hard on his behalf—to write the outline of an edict that would postpone the elections.

But the initiative fails.[29] The election takes place on the appointed day and Clodius is elected.

Meanwhile, Caesar has temporarily moved from Gallia Transalpina to northern Italy where he will winter, occupying himself with government affairs relating to Gallia Cisalpina and Illyricum. Caesar, remember, has defeated the Helvetii, conquered independent Gaul, and repelled the Germans beyond the Rhine. Before setting off for northern Italy, he ordered the troops to be quartered for the winter in encampments and fortified posts expressly set up in various places along the Rhine—Xanten, Neuss, Asberg, Bonn, Nijmegen—and on the northern bank of the Loire. The fact that these rivers are excellent ways to penetrate deep into the interior will allow them to be supplied from the sea through the dispatching of ships upstream.

Caesar spends the winter of 57/56 in Aquileia, securing the border of the Carnic and Julian Alps, dealing with some issues concerning the Istrian side of the *colonia* of Aquileia, reinforcing Roman control of Dalmatia (Croatia), and keeping an eye on Burebista, a Dacian leader who has brought several Transdanubian peoples together under his command and is seen as a danger to Macedonia and Lower Illyricum.

---

29 Cic. *QFr.*, II.1.2–3; *Schol. Bob.*, 166.2–4 ST.

CHAPTER XIV

The Lucca Agreement

The Consolidation of the Triumvirate

From the moment he becomes proconsul for both Roman Gaul and Illyricum, Caesar must divide himself between his spheres of competence in northwestern Europe and in Mediterranean Europe. Therefore, as winter 57/56 draws in, he delegates command of the troops in Gaul to Labienus and goes to Gallia Cisalpina (northern Italy), where he will spend the winter busying himself with local government affairs, ready to travel onward to Illyricum (eastern Adriatic coast) as well, if necessary. This occurs after Caesar oversaw where his troops would be quartered in Gaul, which involves them wintering in various fortified locations on the north bank of the Loire and along the Rhine (Xanten, Neuss, Asberg, Bonn, Nijmegen). These troops are the legions who massacred the Helvetii, conquered Aquitania, Belgica, and Celtica, and pushed the Germans back beyond the Rhine. The fact that the Loire and the Rhine are both excellent routes into the interior will allow them to be supplied from the sea.

Caesar is in Rabenna (Ravenna) when he learns that, in Rome, Lucius Domitius Ahenobarbus—one of his fiercest political opponents and a candidate for the consulship for 55—has publicly said that, if elected, he will work to deprive Caesar of his public offices before their natural expiration, as well as the fact that Cicero has aligned himself alongside Ahenobarbus.

We have already spoken about Domitius Ahenobarbus. He is a patrician. He married Porcia, the sister of Cato and aunt of Porcia, wife of Bibulus. In 61, as curule aedile, he supported his brother-in-law's anti-corruption initiatives that were directed at Pompey, who was buying votes for Afranius. In 59, at the instigation of Caesar, he was accused of complicity in the attempted assassination of Pompey by Lucius Vettius, the Catilinarian who, in 63, had let the cat out of the bag on the conspiracy to Cicero. In 58, as praetor, he had unsuccessfully proposed to the Senate to verify the legitimacy of the laws presented and passed by Caesar the previous year. His hyper-conservative ideas place him politically at the extreme right of the Optimates faction in the Senate, headed by Cato (Catonian faction).

Caesar doesn't want to give up his offices either before or after their natural expiration. Therefore, Ahenobarbus's declaration, and especially the support that he has received from Cicero, worries him, as does the state of the mutual relations both between the Triumvirs themselves and between the Triumvirs and the Senate of Rome. There had been a rapprochement between Crassus and Pompey after the discord that marked their consulship of 70. Recently, however, the re-emergence of old differences has divided them again. Now they are avoiding one another, and each of them is seeking to weaken the other. Crassus appears to be behind Clodius's mob. As for the actions undertaken against Clodius's armed gangs by Sestius's and Milo's own gangs, these are in line with the politics of Clodius's adversaries, starting with Pompey. Moreover, after the death of Julia, Pompey has grown more distant from Caesar, primarily because the latter's successes in Gaul are threatening to overshadow his own. Pompey fears losing not just glory and social prestige but also friends and supporters. He would never want to allow them to abandon him and place themselves under the protection and at the service of Caesar.

As for the relations between the Triumvirate and the Senate, they aren't good. The Senate has a dim view of the exponential growth of Caesar's prestige, and it is thus essentially hostile toward him. But, between Crassus and Pompey, it is difficult to say who it prefers. Caesar is convinced that it is appropriate, if not necessary, to reinforce the Triumviral Pact.

Crassus, at Caesar's invitation, goes to him in Rabenna. The two discuss the political situation and the state of their relationship with Pompey. When they learn that Pompey is traveling to Pisae (Pisa), or Labro (Livorno), in Etruria (Tuscany), where he is expected to embark for Olbia, one of the major ports that connects Sardinia to Italy, they set off to meet him.

In September 57, remember, the Senate gave Pompey the task of looking after the grain supply of the capital for the next five years, as well as permission to use irregular powers for this purpose and to avail himself of 15 legates. The closest legate to him is Quintus Tullius Cicero, who is already in Sardinia. Pompey is afraid of getting malaria, but he is going to great lengths to ensure a good wheat harvest. Sardinia is one of the "granary provinces" of Rome and is the first stage of a journey that will also take him to Sicily and North Africa.

On 13 April 45, Caesar, Crassus, and Pompey meet each other in Luca (Lucca in Tuscany), a city about 20 km north of Pisae. Before withdrawing to discuss the matter between themselves behind closed doors, at least 120 senators—second- or third-rate politicians—pay them their respects, having assembled in Luca for the occasion to show that they are on the Triumvirate's side and against Clodius and the Catonian faction. Cicero is absent, holed up in one of his villas. In Luca, the

Triumvirs cement their friendship and the bonds of alliance and mutual support that unite them, and they prefigure their future by mutually committing themselves to ensure that things go according to their plans: Pompey and Crassus will be elected to the consulship for 55, and Caesar will obtain a five-year extension to his proconsulships; after their consulship, Pompey and Crassus will each be appointed to the office of proconsul for 54, with one of them charged with governing Syria and the other with governing the Iberian provinces. Crassus will be able to unleash the war against the Parthians that is so important to him, Domitius Ahenobarbus won't be elected, and Cicero will be made to fall into line. The agreement strengthens the Triumvirs, who confirm themselves as the dominant figures of the *res publica*. They will have control over the major provinces and command about 20 legions in all. Their power is based on three pillars: consular power, military command, and control of certain tribunes of the plebs.

Pompey's Electoral Campaign

The electoral campaigns for the magistracies for 55 have begun, and Pompey talks up a series of building proposals on the Campus Martius with a view both to collecting votes in support of his candidacy for the consulship and to satisfying an old ambition. He aspires to leave a mark on the urban plan and monumental architecture of Rome as various politicians and military commanders have done before him, contributing to the development of the urban décor of the city. There are three major works in particular: a permanent theater, a monumental portico, and a new seat for the Senate. It is worth focusing on the first, both because the construction of a permanent theater is a major novelty for Rome and because the project's plans include innovative architectural ideas.

It's a curious thing, but there are no permanent theaters in Rome, only temporary ones. Performances take place on wooden stages and near a place of worship to maintain the religious character that Roman theater has borrowed from the Greek tradition. The platforms are purposefully set up for individual performances, and, even if they are magnificent, they are dismantled soon afterwards. The citizens have to stand if they really want to watch a theatrical performance.[1] All this depends on the fact that the theaters are considered by the Optimates—the ultraconservatives, who have the majority in the Senate of Rome—as the cause of degeneracy and potential revolts because the shows are full of obscenity and political allusions, and the audience feel legitimated by their strength in numbers to demonstrate through shouting, stamping their feet, and jeering. In 154, an attempt was made to provide the city with a permanent theater, but it failed because of the opposition of the

---

1   Liv. *Per.*, 48.

Senate.[2] Following this, no one dared to challenge the ban on building permanent theaters in Rome, nor was it repealed. It should be clarified that this prohibition only applies to the city of Rome—nothing of the sort applies in the rest of the Roman world.

Pompey has taken the fact that his project of giving the city a permanent theater will spark objections into account, not so much from the common people and the Populares but primarily among the Optimates. To preempt these, he announces that he will create a site for the construction of a Temple of Venus and states that the new building will be accessed via a huge horseshoe-shaped staircase leading up to the temple. The fact that the intended use of the structure that is about to be built is not recreational but cultural renders this statement admissible. From that perspective, it seems irrelevant that the public will sit down on the steps, turning their backs on the temple and facing the wooden stage of a magnificent theater.

Cato's Mission

Meanwhile, in October–November 56, Cato returned from his mission in Cyprus bringing the wealth of King Ptolemy, worth 7,000 talents, to Rome. On his arrival, he received a welcome worthy of a victorious general and the offer of an extraordinary praetorship, which he politely refused. That he stayed aboard his ship, which sailed up the Tiber, until arriving at the place where the treasure would be unloaded and made safe, without pausing to greet all the senators, consuls, and people who thronged the riverbanks, attracted a lot of criticism. He was accused of exaggerated sanctimoniousness and contempt for public office.[3]

Cato recounted his mission to the Senate as follows. Initially, because he didn't have any warships and expected King Ptolemy to offer resistance, he set up a base on Rhodes. Through his ambassador Publius Canidius Crassus,[4] he ordered Ptolemy to renounce his throne and to confer both his rule and the royal treasury to him, guaranteeing him a safe refuge in the Sanctuary of Aphrodite[5] in Paphos.[6] Ptolemy refused to capitulate. But he knew better than anyone that taking on the Roman army would only result in defeat. In the early months of 56, he decided to die like a king and took poison.[7] At that point, the path was clear. Cato seized Ptolemy's

---

2   Liv. *Per.,* 48.

3   Vell. Pat., II.45.5.

4   Plut. *Cat. Min.,* 35. On the identification of Canidius as the person cited by Plutarch in this passage: R. Syme, *La rivoluzione romana* (Torino: Einaudi, 2014), 225.

5   Aphrodite, the Greek goddess of love and beauty, was assimilated into the Roman pantheon with the name Venus.

6   This refers to Palaipaphos, today's Kouklia, around 20 km away from New Paphos. The local sanctuary was the center of the cult of Aphrodite.

7   Plut. *Cat. Min.,* 36; Amm. Marc., XIV.8.15.

riches and annexed Cyprus into the Roman state before adding it to the Roman province of Cilicia.

The young Quintus Servilius Caepio Brutus (formerly Marcus Junius Brutus) returned to Rome with Cato, to whom he had been an assistant during the mission. In Cyprus, he had taken advantage of his own privileged position to act as an intermediary between some Roman bankers and borrowers who took out loans at an interest rate that was significantly higher than the common and legal rate. He exacted usury not only in Cyprus but also in Roman protectorates of southwestern Asia, accumulating significant riches.[8]

On 2 February 56, Cicero gave an oration against Clodius during the trial that the latter had brought against Milo, arousing a lively reaction. The following April, Cicero was in one of his extra-urban villas when he received the news that his residence on the Palatine had been stormed by one of Clodius's gangs but had been effectively defended by Milo and his men. He becomes agitated and worried, and he anxiously returns to Rome.[9] The feud between Cicero and Clodius, therefore, has been rekindled. It will continue over the following months.

In September, Cicero, speaking in the Senate about the response of the haruspices that Clodius had used to accuse him of sacrilege and to force him to give up his house on the Palatine, twisted its meaning around and turned it against Clodius. This time it is he who accuses Clodius of sacrilege, defining him as an enemy of the state. By so doing, he secures full possession of his house.

Toward the end of the year, Cicero has two bronze tablets that were on display to the public on the Capitoline removed, on which records of Clodius's acts as tribune of the plebs were engraved, including the law on Cicero's exile, as well as other tablets relating to Cato's mission in Cyprus.[10] At Clodius's request, the Senate asks Cicero to justify himself. The Orator does so skillfully, reiterating that the process of Clodius's passage to become a plebeian was irregular, and therefore his tribunate of the plebs is illegitimate and all the acts adopted by him in the performance of his duties as tribune are invalid and thus null or annullable. This incident strains relations between Cicero and Cato.

Cato is sweating at the thought that the correctness of his work in Cyprus may be called into question. His problem is born from the fact that it isn't possible to be certain that Ptolemy's assets, at the moment of their confiscation, were worth 7,000 talents and no more, because the inventories that described them in meticulous detail were lost on the return voyage. The freedman who had drawn up the accounts of the king's riches fell overboard with his copy of the documents. The other copy, which had been in Cato's possession, was accidentally burned by sailors when they

---

8   On Brutus's activities in Cilicia: Plut. *Brut.*, 29–32; Cic. *Att.*, V.21.5–13, VI.1.5, VI.2.8–9.
9   Cic. *QFr.*, II.5.4; Dio Cass., XXXIX.20.3.
10   Plut. *Cat. Min.*, 40.1; *Cic.*, 34.1; Dio Cass., XXXIX.21.2–4*.

lit a fire during a stop-off in Corcyra (Corfu). Of course, it is peculiar that Cato hadn't had duplicates of his own copy made before depositing them in two cities in the province, as prescribed by the *lex Iulia de repetundis*.[11] For such a scrupulous person, one would have expected that he would have protected himself against unforeseen events.

But the real political question of the moment is a different one, and it concerns the restoration to the throne of Ptolemy XII Auletes, king-pharaoh of Egypt.

---

11 Unless it is certain that the *lex Iulia de repetundis* was not applicable to Cato, seeing as he didn't go to Cyprus to take up a provincial magistracy but to fulfil a special commission.

CHAPTER XV

The Military Intervention in Egypt

The Dio Incident

In 58, the people of Alexandria rose up against Ptolemy XII Auletes (r. 80–58 and 55–51), king-pharaoh of Egypt, accusing him of being the main person responsible for Roman interference in the internal affairs of the pharaonic state of Ptolemaic Egypt, and forced him to flee the country. Ptolemy XII traveled to Cyprus, where he met Cato the Younger, then went to Rome and asked the Senate to reinstate his rights to the throne. To create a consensus in his favor, he gives expensive gifts to a growing number of senators. From 11 July 57, the throne of Egypt is occupied by Ptolemy XII's daughter, Berenice IV, who enjoys popular support. She sends a diplomatic embassy to Rome to contest the welcome it gave to her father. The delegation is led by Dio, a senior state functionary, Platonic philosopher (he was taught by Antiochus of Ascalon), and the author of a *symposion* that imitated dialogues between Plato and Xenophon. He is currently enjoying the hospitality of various Roman citizens. Dio has been welcomed particularly warmly by Lucius Lucceius, a historian of the Social War and the First Civil War and a friend of Cicero. In 61, Lucceius unsuccessfully competed against Cato for the consulship.

Upon its departure from Egypt, the embassy consisted of 100 members. By the time it set foot in Italy, its size had decreased after a number of mysterious killings. The surviving members, either because they are scared to death or because they have been financially induced not to do so, don't mention the disappearance of their colleagues, and fail to fulfill their duties. The Senate gives them an audience, but they do not show up. Shortly after, Dio also disappears, killed by treachery.

Since it is a rule of thumb that a crime is committed or commissioned by whoever intends to benefit from it, and in this specific case it is Ptolemy XII who stands to gain most, there is widespread suspicion among commentators that it was the former sovereign who is behind the slaughter, who would have used locally recruited hitmen to carry it out. But there is no proof, so the sovereign will not be taken to court.

The Senate examines the issue extensively during its sessions from 13 to 15 January and from 2 to 7 February 56. Some senators are outraged by the inability to see justice done regarding the Dio incident, both due to the lack of proof of Ptolemy XII's involvement and due to the killers' identities remaining unknown. Marcus Favonius, a staunch Catonian, highlights how the Roman state has suffered a double *vulnus:* numerous ambassadors from a friendly and allied state, who were entitled to diplomatic immunity, have been killed while on an official mission to Rome, presumably at the hands of corrupt Roman citizens.[1] The majority of the speakers, however, overlook the Dio incident and give more weight to the need to recover political control of Egypt using any means necessary.

In the end, the Senate decides to adopt Cicero's proposal to appoint Publius Cornelius Lentulus Spinther, consul in 57, to the office of proconsul of Cilicia for 56 and to authorize him to use the legion stationed in the province to restore Ptolemy XII to the throne.

But then something unexpected occurs: a bolt of lightning strikes a statue of Jupiter on Mons Albanus (Monte Cavo in the *comune* of Rocca di Papa in the Castelli Romani, near Rome), where the much-venerated sanctuary of Jupiter Latialis is located. The event is interpreted as a sign from the gods. The Senate asks itself whether or not this means that the proposal to send an armed expedition into Egypt is frowned upon by Jupiter, god of the civilized collective, the tutelary deity of Rome, and the guarantor of their destiny. Therefore, it requests that the *quindecimviri* consult the Sibylline Books.

The Sibylline Books are a collection of prophecies written in Greek, kept in a vault beneath the Temple of Jupiter Optimus Maximus on the Capitoline. The only people who are authorized to interpret their foretellings are the members of the college who hold the books in their safekeeping. Their inspection leads to the discovery of a prophecy that fits the situation perfectly, according to which the Romans will have to provide assistance to the king of Egypt, if he asks for it, given that he is the sovereign of a state that is a friend and ally, but they will have to avoid helping him with a large army on pain of serious consequences.[2]

The response of the *quindecimviri* cannot be divulged to the people unless authorized by the Senate of Rome. But, in this case, this rule is broken. The response is made public by the tribune of the plebs Caius Porcius Cato, who is against military intervention in Egypt, before the Senate could discuss it. Caius Porcius Cato is a second cousin of Cato the Younger. He is an avid anti-Pompeian and a friend of Clodius. In 59, he filed a corruption trial against Aulus Gabinius; on that occasion, while speaking in public, he called Pompey a dictator and ran the risk of being lynched. Elected as tribune of the plebs in 57 for 56, he supported the candidacy

---

1   The affair is narrated in Dio Cass., XXXIX.12–16.
2   Dio Cass., XXXIX.20.1–3, XXXIX.30.4.

of Clodius for the office of aedile and delayed the trial against him until after the election so that the accused could not be sentenced because he would be protected by immunity from prosecution as a magistrate. Moreover, he promoted plebiscites that went against the interests of Lentulus Spinther and Milo, friends of Pompey. He is against military intervention in Egypt.

In light of the new fact, the Senate reconsiders the matter with greater caution. Some senators propose that Spinther restores Ptolemy XII to the throne without the use of arms. Others propose that Ptolemy XII is accompanied to Egypt by Pompey with just two lictors as an escort. But the Catonian faction are opposed to this, fearing that this is exactly what Pompey wants. In their opinion, this would mean acting in a way that is advantageous to him.

The consul Cnaeus Cornelius Lentulus Marcellinus is opposed to the proposal to put Pompey in charge. He is one of those who did his utmost to secure Cicero's political rehabilitation and the restitution of his possessions.

Lentulus Marcellinus was born into a family of the *gens Claudia*, but he was adopted into a family of the *gens Cornelia*. He has been married twice and has two sons. When, in 70, he was still very young, he supported Cicero in the case for the prosecution against Verres. In 61, together with Lucius Cornelius Lentulus Crus, he brought an action against Clodius for having violated the mysteries of Bona Dea. In 59, as praetor, he presided over the trial against Caius Antonius Hybrida, a colleague of Caesar's in 63. As propraetor, he governed Syria for two years (58–57), defending it against Arab attacks. He has always been opposed to both the politics of Cato and the violence of Clodius. Nor is this the first time Lentulus Marcellinus has attacked Pompey. Perhaps Lentulus Marcellinus's continued attacks on Pompey is one of the reasons why the Triumvirs met in Lucca to strengthen their pact.

Not having obtained a majority either for or against military intervention in Egypt, the Senate postpones a decision on the matter until a later date. Therefore, the issue remains unresolved.

Ptolemy XII feels disappointed. He is convinced that he won't receive the help he has asked for. Therefore, he leaves Italy and makes for Ephesus, the capital of the Roman province of Asia, where he will receive refuge and protection in the famous Temple of Artemis (temples are inviolable places of asylum).

Meanwhile, Berenice IV, the daughter of Ptolemy XII and his successor on the throne of Egypt, has married Seleucus VII Philometor (r. 83–69), the second son of Antiochus X Eusebes and Cleopatra Selene. Seleucus VII ruled over the few cities of Syria that had remained loyal to the Seleucids after it was invaded by Tigranes II, king of Armenia. He was a rude man, boorish to the point of being nicknamed *kybiosaktes*, a Greek term used for the foul-smelling work of cutting tuna fish.

Berenice IV was unhappy with her husband because the absence of good manners is seen as a symptom of a lack of logic and common sense and the surest sign of corrupt morals. She couldn't stand him, and, shortly after their nuptials, she had him killed.

Afterward, Berenice IV, not being able to rule alone, married Archelaus, a Cappadocian nobleman and probably an illegitimate son of the deceased Mithridates VI (r. 120–63), king of Pontus, without obtaining authorization from the Senate of Rome. Archelaus is the high priest of *Ma*, an important female deity worshipped in the city of Comana, situated on the Cappadocian coast of the Black Sea. *Ma* was assimilated by the Romans into their goddess Bellona.

The Judicial Misadventures of Caelius

Since the beginning of the year (we're in 56), things haven't been going well for Marcus Caelius Rufus, now 26 years old. Caelius, remember, is a brilliant judicial speaker. He is well-known throughout Rome for having brought trials against very important individuals and for having been highly successful in doing so, such as in the case against Caius Antonius Hybrida, who had been accused of *crimen maiestatis* and who was defended by Cicero, teacher and mentor of Caelius himself.

Recently, Caelius has publicly accused the rich plebeian Lucius Calpurnius Bestia of having acted to manipulate the vote with the intention of falsifying the election (electoral fraud) during his campaign for the aedileship for 57. Bestia had been pronounced as being elected but was indicted soon after. During the trial, Caelius made a mockery of the accused, who, in the end, was adjudged to be guilty and sentenced.

Later, Caelius litigated against Bestia for electoral fraud again, but he had an action brought against him in turn by Lucius Sempronius Atratinus, the adopted son of Bestia, and sent to trial. The charges filed against Caelius pertain to moral, political, electoral, and private issues. Specifically, Caelius is accused of a multitude of amorous misdemeanors (his customs are commonly considered to be very relaxed, if not too relaxed); of having been an accomplice of Catiline in his conspiracy against the state; of having carried out actions designed to falsify the electoral process; of having committed acts of violence against a senator and Alexandrian emissaries; and of having attacked some women who were returning home after a banquet at night.

The defense of the accused will be performed by Cicero. The prosecution will be supported by Marcus Licinius Crassus. As it happens, the "banker of Rome" and the largest real estate speculator in the capital is also a talented judicial speaker.

This criminal trial has significant political implications and resonance. More accurately, it forms part of the political struggle between the circles of power. Caelius is presented by the prosecution as a collaborator of Pompey, who, as we know, has staked his wager on Ptolemy XII. Cato and Clodius are working to weaken Pompey and do not let any opportunity to cast him in a poor light pass them by, both seeing in him, for different reasons, a danger to the *res publica*. Their involvement in the affair is evidenced by the fact that Atratinus's indictment was drawn up by Lucius Plotius Gallus.

Plotius Gallus is the oldest of the Latin rhetoricians and is the first to have opened a school of rhetoric in Rome in which teaching is done in Latin. This school was attended by numerous students before it was closed by the censors of 92, Lucius Licinius Crassus and Domitius Ahenobarbus, who were opposed to the teaching of rhetoric by the Latins. However, it reopened between 88 and 87. Cicero, in a letter to Marcus Titinnius, expresses his regret at not having attended it in his youth.[3]

The trial ends with the acquittal of the accused, and this is considered a plus for Pompey's enemies. But there's no peace for Caelius; shortly after his acquittal, Sempronius Atratinus makes further accusations against him and he is sent to trial again. This time, Caelius is accused of having stolen gold jewelry from Clodia, Clodius's sister, of having tried to use this to remunerate Dio's assassins, and of having tried to poison Clodia to rid himself of an awkward witness. Cicero undertakes the defense of Caelius in this case too, while Atratinus, the prosecution, is, seeing as he is very young (he is only 17 years old), is supported by Lucius Herennius Balbus, a friend of Bestia and of Publius Clodius, an ex-slave of Clodius's who, in the act of his liberation, received Roman citizenship.

Atratinus argues the charge, placing an emphasis on the background of the accused and painting him as an individual who is inherently inclined to violence, socially dangerous, and therefore capable of having perpetrated the alleged offenses. Publius Clodius speaks in turn, followed by Herennius Balbus, who delivers a closing statement that greatly impresses those present and catches the attention of the judges. Herennius depicts Caelius as a depraved young man, capable of all kinds of misdeeds. He says that it was Caelius who was involved in both the attempted murder and then the assassination of Dio while he was a guest of Lucius Lucceius. Herennius's words are confirmed by Clodia's testimony. She reports that, when she had been on excellent terms with Caelius, she received from him and granted a request for a sum of money that, according to him, should have been used for the staging of certain public games. Instead, she later learned that the money had been used to bribe some of Lucceius's slaves to kill Dio. Clodia adds that, after this, Caelius made an agreement with some of Clodia's own slaves to poison their mistress. The slaves, however, informed Clodia of the plot against her, and this allowed her to thwart the attempted murder.

Cicero dismantles the prosecution's charge. He doesn't focus so much on the accusations leveled against the defendant so much as on the plaintiff, or rather, on the person who, in his view, is behind Atratinus and induced him to accuse Caelius. He identifies this person as Clodia. At the outset, he mentions that Caelius left Clodia, who was his lover, after a two-year relationship. Clodia, to take revenge on Caelius, persuaded Atratinus to accuse him of having stolen from her and of trying to poison her. In turn, Atratinus took part in the game to take his own revenge on Caelius,

---

3   Suet. *Gram. et Rhet.*, 2.

who had got Bestia convicted. Cicero traces Caelius's entire life as it unfolded up to the contested facts, giving them a coherent and positive image. He observes that the degenerate behavior ascribed to the accused and traced back by the prosecution to an alleged inclination for erotic escapades is not "juvenile deviance," in which the vices of Roman youth listed by the prosecution (arrogance, wantonness, overindulgence, and propensities for decadence and indebtedness) are reflected, but temporarily yielding to a life of *deliciae*, if not the caprices of an adolescent. Otherwise, Cicero says, Caelius is a fine young man: he has never gone into debt, he has never had a craving for luxury or pleasure, and he is a talented orator, remarking that those who dedicate themselves to this art do not have a debauched lifestyle but rather lead an ascetic life. He also notes that the rumors about Caelius's morality only started to circulate after he had succumbed to the sexual flattery of Clodia, a mature woman who is eager for sex. As such, he depicts Caelius as a naïve teenager who was drawn in and corrupted by a seductress.

Cicero admits that Caelius had been a friend of Catiline, but he denies any involvement in the conspiracy and uses as proof the fact that Caelius wasn't the sort of morally depraved and financially desperate young man who usually turned toward Catiline, himself a malevolent, two-faced individual with a fiendish talent for beguiling youths. As for the accusation of having stolen Clodia's jewelry, Cicero denies that there has even been any theft; Caelius had been lent the jewelry within the context of the intimate relationship that existed at the time between him and Clodia, who falsely denounced him because of having been jilted. By doing so, he reduces the whole matter to the vendetta of an abandoned and rancorous lover, to the perfidy of a woman who wants her former lover to be ruined.

Finally, to remove all credibility from the woman who declares herself to be a victim of the crimes attributed to Caelius, Cicero paints Clodia as a beautiful woman, full of charm, self-confident and very uninhibited, attractive and with a burning gaze, but also lascivious and unfaithful. That is, he attacks her lifestyle, which he defines as the opposite to the life—reserved, modest—that a married woman is expected to lead. Nor does he spare her from the accusation of perversions. He recalls her incestuous relationship with her brother Clodius; he puts forth that it was she who had poisoned her husband Metellus Celer; and he accuses her of having prostituted herself to a bath house employee for the minimum cost of the entrance ticket (a *quadrans*, which is one-quarter of an *as*), and thus hands her the vulgar epithet of *quadrantaria* and which defines her a woman of ill-repute who gives herself away for practically nothing, for a *quadrans*, to be precise. He defines Clodia as a friend to everyone, as someone who offers herself to everyone, and with whom it isn't a sin to entertain oneself; in short, as a common whore. He goes so far as to evoke the spirit of Appius Claudius Caecus, one of Clodia's most famous ancestors, to come forth from the Underworld and reproach his unworthy descendant.

At the end of the trial, Caelius is acquitted, while the image of Clodia, which has already been much discussed, is left destroyed.

The Return of Catullus

Also in 56, Caius Memmius returns to Rome from Bithynia and Pontus, where he has been acting as governor. Catullus and Cinna, who were part of his entourage, also return home. During their homeward voyage, Catullus went to visit his brother's tomb, which is in the Troad (northwestern Anatolia). In Nicomedia, the capital of Bithynia and Pontus, he experienced the refined Graeco-Hellenistic culture which has enriched him from a cultural point of view. However, he laments that he hasn't been able to make as much money as he had been hoping. The only one who has succeeded in this—he says, with a touch of envy—is Memmius. Catullus retires to his family home in Sirmium. He is very attached to the place and draws inspiration from the beauties of its landscape to compose some of his most touching verses.

It isn't long before Catullus returns to Rome, where he reacquaints himself with the atmosphere and his old problems. It is there that, free from his usual troubles of the heart, he composes *carmina* 61 to 68, the *carmina docta*. These compositions are distinguished from his others through their greater length (they use hexameter), their erudite reasoning, and their references to the Hellenistic model. Some of the *carmina docta* speak of a sweet young girl called Lesbia.

Lesbia is a pseudonym. In inventing it from scratch, it seems that Catullus was inspired by Sappho. In reality, Lesbia is Clodia, Catullus's lover.[4] The latter, in his poetry, idolizes her and sings her (often non-existent) virtues. One of the *carmina* dedicated to Lesbia starts with these words: "*Vivamus mea Lesbia, atque amemus ...*" ("Let us live, my Lesbia, and let us love ...").

A Confused Political Situation

The political situation is confused, and the passing of time isn't helping to clear it up. The violence and threats exchanged between the tribunes of the plebs Milo and Clodius are unceasing. The consul Lentulus Marcellinus, having prevented Pompey from being given command of an army to restore Ptolemy XII to the throne, unsuccessfully opposes the consulship candidacies of Pompey and Crassus. The tribune of the plebs Caius Porcius Cato uses his veto on the convocation of popular assemblies to the ballot box on 1 July 56. In effect, he prevents the elections for the

---

4   The identification of Clodia with Lesbia, proposed by the German philologist Ludwig Schwabe in 1862 based on extremely vague indications in Ov. *Tr.*, II.427 and Apul. *Apol.*, 15, is generally accepted today by scholars. See L. Schwabius, *Quaestionum Catullianarum Liber I* (Gissae, 1862). *Contra* T. P. Wiseman, *Catullan Questions* (Leicester: Leicester University Press, 1969).

new sets of magistracies for 55 from being held on the canonical date. The attempt by senators to violate this veto triggers the outbreak of disorder. The Senate declares that the state is experiencing an emergency and its members dress in mourning garb and desert its sessions.

The consul Philippus was propraetor of Syria in 59. Later, he married Atia, daughter of Caius Octavius Thurinus and Julia, thus tying himself to the family of Caesar (Julia, remember, is Caesar's daughter). He thus becomes the adoptive father of Caius Octavius, the future *princeps*, the *augustus*.

In 56, Cicero runs for the censorship for 55, but he is unsuccessful. Publius Servilius Vatia Isauricus (another of those who helped Cicero to return to Rome from his exile) and Marcus Valerius Messalla Niger are elected instead.

In August or September 56—certainly before the celebration of the games of Pompey, which will have to be dealt with later—Piso Caesoninus, Caesar's father-in-law, reports his own activities as proconsul of Macedonia to the Senate, which had gathered again with Crassus presiding over it. In the process, Piso severely attacks Cicero. Cicero responds with a brutal speech, a full-frontal assault, which is intended to be hurtful (the oration *Against Piso*).[5] He accuses Piso of having managed public affairs in Macedonia in a heinous way. He adjudges him to be unworthy of the high offices he has held and of being a Roman citizen. He dubs him an uncultured man and sarcastically remarks that this ought not to be a surprise, seeing as his mother was half Gallic. To ridicule him, he makes a mockery of his physical appearance and of his mannerisms. He takes the pretext of the fact that Piso says that he is an Epicurean to assert that he only follows the more prosaic aspects of Epicureanism, those linked to pleasure. He argues that Piso loves to surround himself with Epicurean philosophers for the sole purpose of involving them in his orgies, which go on for entire nights, between overindulgence in food and drink, drunken singing, and coarse laughter. He also harshly criticizes him for the protection he has afforded to the Epicurean philosopher Philodemus of Gadara, famous for being an author of epigrams with erotic content that deal with carefree love, eliciting pure sensual pleasure. He defines Philodemus as a lewd Hellene, a participant in Piso's revelries.

But Cicero moves his attack against both consuls of 58, and thus also against Gabinius, saying that, during the proconsulship, both of them set their provinces to ruin and asserts that they were assigned to them by passing them off as irregular measures when there was no real emergency that necessitated such a response. Rather, these offices arose out of a private accord, reached with Clodius, under which Gabinius and Piso would receive them in exchange for their acquiescence to, understood as substantial complicity in, Clodius's plan to have Cicero exiled. For his part, Cicero overlooks the fact that, in both provinces, there were hotbeds of tension that could have justified the conferral of irregular offices. Syria was a

---

5   Cic. *Pis.*, 84.

melting pot of populations of different lineages and bordered by potentially hostile peoples: Jews, Arabs, Parthians; while Macedonia had long been a place of indecisive clashes between the Romans and invaders of various provenances, such as Dacians and Thracians.

The Election of Pompey and Crassus to the Consulship for 55

On 9 October 56, the architectural complex gifted by Pompey to the city of Rome is inaugurated. It is in front of the four ancient temples of the Area Sacra (now Largo dei Templi di Torre Argentina) and consists of a theater, a double-colonnaded quadriportico, and a large exedra, which will be used for meetings of the Senate (Curia of Pompey). The theater, glittering with marbles, mosaics, statues, paintings, and gilded friezes, is the first permanent installation of its kind in Rome and is a faithful copy of the theater of Mytilene/Lesbos, only larger and more magnificent. The *cavea*, 150 m in diameter, can seat up to 17,000 spectators. In the center, in the upper part, protrudes the top of the Temple of Venus Victrix, according to the Italic tradition that links theatrical performances to worship.[6] The quadriportico, 185 m long and 135 m wide, is located behind the stage wall of the theater and encloses a densely wooded garden, equipped with fountains and nymphaea, and adorned with numerous statues. The Curia of Pompey is located on the short eastern side of the quadriportico, through which it is accessed. It is a hall 25 m long and 15 m wide, and thus has an area of 400 square meters. A colossal statue (3 m high) fills an apse on one of the long sides of the hall. It portrays Pompey in heroic nudity, with a globe in his left hand, his right arm outstretched, and his body athletically leaning on a semi-column. The seats for the senators are lined along the longer side walls on platforms of staggered levels, while the shorter sides are left free to enable people to walk around.[7]

The inauguration ceremony for the magnificent structure begins five days of celebrations (Pompey's Games), during which performances of Campanian comedies and Greek tragedies will be staged together with shows featuring mimes, athletes, gladiators, processions of soldiers and cavalrymen in splendid parade attire, and hunts involving the killing of hundreds of animals. As usual, a large audience of all classes and social walks of life watch the performances, enchanted. Educated spectators are less impressed. Cicero attends out of a duty of friendship to Pompey, the host, but isn't entertained. While not disdaining pleasure, he prefers that which derives from

---

6   The remains of the Temple of Venus Victrix are visible today in the basement of the Palazzo Pio Righetti (formerly the Palazzo Orsini), a tall building that overlooks the Campo de' Fiori.

7   All that now remains of the Curia of Pompey is a sizeable base in squared tufa, visible behind Temples B and C in Largo di Torre Argentina. The statue of Pompey that was once placed in that hall is currently in the Palazzo Spada, the headquarters of the Italian Council of State, which overlooks the Piazza Capo di Ferro.

a peaceful life and intellectual exercise. In a letter to Atticus, he will write that he was bored and unenthusiastic.

The year 56 passes without it being possible to renew the consulships or the praetorships. Obstacles arise with every new attempt made by the Senate to set a date for the elections. An *interrex* is therefore appointed.

At the end of 56 or in the early days of 55, Clodius takes inspiration from the removal of the tablets from the Capitoline to attack Cato, candidate for the praetorship for 55. Cicero speaks numerous times in the Senate in favor of Cato, speaking against his direct rival, Publius Vatinius, who is being supported by Pompey. By so doing, he tries to heal the fracture that has opened between him and Cato.[8]

We have already talked about Vatinius. He is the "father" of the law of 59 that conferred the proconsulship of the provinces of Gallia Cisalpina and Illyricum to Caesar for five years (*lex Vatinia*). After this, the Senate appointed Caesar to the office of proconsul for Gallia Narbonensis as well for a period of the same duration. Meanwhile, Lucius Vettius accused Cicero and other individuals of plotting to kill Pompey, and Vatinius supported the accusation against Vettius in the ensuing trial. In 58, an action was brought against Vatinius by Caius Licinius Macer Calvus for having transgressed the *lex Licinia et Iunia*, and he was sentenced before the praetor Caius Memmius. He appealed to Clodius, tribune of the plebs, and the trial was interrupted due to violence. In 56, he testified in the trials of both Titus Annius Milo and Publius Sestius. Cicero, who was defending the accused, viciously attacked Vatinius and his political activity in his oration *In Vatinium testem*, attempting to demonstrate his scant credibility—Cicero later boasted to his brother Quintus that he had "cut up Vatinius ... just as I pleased, with the applause of gods and men."[9]

Finally, the long-postponed elections were set for 5 January 55. On the eve of that date, Lucius Domitius Ahenobarbus, since he has been subjected to pressure and threats, withdraws his candidacy for the consulship. Recently, he was attacked by strangers while he was heading to the Forum early one morning in the company of a slave, who was lighting the street with a torch in his hand.

The elections take place on the Campus Martius in the shadow of the Theater of Pompey, whose gigantic bulk looms over the polling stations. The logistical situation influences the voters' choices: the magnificent gift given by Pompey to the city cannot fail to remind the electorate, as they are deciding on their vote, who is in charge of the city and what his ideas, his preferences, his desires are. Another element of pressure on the electorate is represented by the fact that Caesar, to ensure that Pompey and Crassus are elected, has sent many of his soldiers to Rome on leave so that they can attend the elections, under the leadership of his legate Publius Licinius Crassus, son of the consulship candidate Marcus Licinius Crassus.

---

8   Cic. *Fam.*, I.9.19.
9   Cic. *QFr.*, II.4.1.

The senior consul, Philippus, presides over the elections. When the first two centuries have voted and Cato's success is already taking shape, he suspends the vote on a pretext, postponing it to a later date. The postponement allows those who have an active interest to bribe many of the electorate by offering them money. When the vote resumes, Cato's lead evaporates. Pompey and Crassus are elected to the consulship for 55. All the elected officials are the Triumvirs' men. One is Publius Vatinius, a loyalist of Caesar's. He has been elected to the praetorship.

Gabinius Marches on Alexandria

Cicero is an influential man in the Senate. He has many friends, but also many enemies. One is Vatinius. Another is Gabinius, who is Pompey's confidant, though that is not to say he is an agent of his.

We are already familiar with Gabinius. In 87–84, he served as a military tribune in the First Mithridatic War under the orders of Sulla, and he carried out tasks on Sulla's behalf in Greece and Asia Minor. It appears that he has also fought in Hispania and in Cilicia, in the service, respectively, of Pompey (Sertorian War, 82–72) and Publius Servilius Vatia Isauricus (79–74). In 67, as tribune of the plebs, he promoted and approved a bill that sought to hand Pompey exceptional powers to clear the Mediterranean of pirates (*lex Gabinia*). He spoke in support of Pompey being conferred command of the Third Mithridatic War (73–63) in the wake of an oration by Cicero, then he served in this war as Pompey's legate, aiding him in Armenia and in the Caucasus, going as far as the border with the Parthian Empire, and collaborating with him to establish the Roman province of Syria. In 61, as praetor, he organized some memorable games. In 58, as consul, he endorsed Clodius against Cicero.

Gabinius has been proconsul of Syria since 57. According to Cicero, he is a man with a thriftless and dissolute lifestyle. He probably made himself available to govern a province to recover his electoral expenses. To have himself appointed, he pandered to Clodius. But he isn't one of Clodius's men, just as he isn't one of Pompey's. He is an independent and ambitious person who owes his success primarily to his own qualities and his own ability to take advantage of a general situation that is complex, unpredictable, and highly competitive.[10]

As proconsul of Syria, Gabinius has solidified the province's organization, repressed a revolt of the Jews, restored Hyrcanus to the position of High Priest in Jerusalem, introduced significant changes to the government of Judaea, and promoted the reconstruction of numerous cities. But he has also been guilty of abusing his power and systematically taking recourse to corruption. Furthermore, following his instincts, he independently undertakes two legislative initiatives, one of which will have the

10 F. Santangelo, *Roma repubblicana. Una storia in quaranta vite* (Roma: Carocci, 2019), 140–141.

effect of reforming the treatment afforded to ambassadors from provincial cities by the Senate of Rome,[11] and the other that of exempting the Greek city of Delos from all forms of taxation.

Gabinius's initiative in favor of Delos is an attempt to create the conditions for its recovery. Unfortunately, he will not be successful. The destiny of the city is inexorable decline until it is abandoned. What had been the focal point of maritime trade in the Mediterranean, a place of splendid private mansions, public buildings and facilities, temples and gardens, and a meeting place for multitudes, resounding with the calls of pilgrims and the shouts of merchants, will sadly become a silent desert of broken marbles, covered with weeds, and blighted by malaria, a lost corner in the vast sea, a haunt of fugitives and pirates.

In 55, Gabinius intervenes militarily in Egypt to restore Ptolemy XII to the throne, knowing perfectly well he is acting illegally, on the one hand because the Sibylline Books have advised against a military expedition and, on the other, because Roman law forbids provincial governors from conducting military operations outside their province.[12] It is possible he is acting at the request of Pompey, who, in turn, is being pressured by the Roman creditors of Ptolemy XII, one of whom is Caius Rabirius Postumus. More likely, it is because Ptolemy XII promised to give Gabinius 10,000 talents, a mountain of money. Nor should we exclude the possibility he is doing it for both reasons, nor that Ptolemy XII's reward is a contribution to the expenses of the military campaign aiming to reinstate the sovereign on the throne, rather than a dation resulting from an accord (in other words, a bribe, the price of corruption) or from coercion or inducement (the price of extortion).

In any case, Gabinius leads his legions to Egypt (among his cavalry officers is Mark Antony, the future triumvir). Early on, he captures Archelaus, but he sets him free again; it is uncertain whether this is because he fears not being able to claim his reward or because he has been bribed to do so (the possibility that Archelaus managed to escape should not be excluded either). Afterwards, two battles are fought: the first near Alexandria, and the second on the Nile Delta. Archelaus falls in combat. After a campaign that lasted just three months, Ptolemy XII enters Alexandria, escorted by Roman soldiers, and accompanied by Rabirius Postimus, reclaims possession of the Royal Palace, and puts on his crown once again.

In the meantime, Cicero has thundered against the actions of Gabinius before the Senate of Rome, recalling the prophecy of the Sibylline Books. He portrays Gabinius as a man without scruples who doesn't hesitate to abuse his position to gain personal benefit, overriding the rights of both subjects and the publicans who collect the taxes in the province. Crassus offends him, and Cicero takes umbrage and

---

11 Cic. *QFr.*, II.11.3; *Fam.*, I.4.1; *Att.*, I.14.5.
12 Cic. *Fam.* I.1.2, IV.5.6; *QFr.*, II.2.3, II.1–3; App. *B. Civ.*, 2.2.4; Dio Cass., XXXIX.55–59.

responds rakishly. This is, however, a fleeting controversy. In February 55, Cicero will reconcile with Gabinius, with Pompey's mediation.[13]

Having recovered his throne, Ptolemy XII settles the scores with his daughter Berenice IV, the consort of Archelaus of Comana, and all those who supported her. He sentences them to death, and they are executed. He then appoints Rabirius to the office of minister of finance and gives him *carte blanche* to recover the money required to pay the debts that the Egyptian state owes to him and to other Roman citizens, among whom are Caesar and Pompey. Rabirius will recover the debts, burdening his subjects with taxes and using no-nonsense methods if needed (many citizens are killed so that their wealth can be seized), without really concerning himself with the state's finances.

Meanwhile, Gabinius has left Egypt with most of his troops to return to Syria after having learned that it has been devastated by marauders and that Alexander, Aristobulus's brother, had taken up arms against John Hyrcanus II to snatch the title of High Priest of Jerusalem from him. However, Gabinius has left a military garrison—a contingent of Gauls and Germans—in place to protect Ptolemy XII and keep the country under control (from now on, we will use the name "Gabiniani" to refer to these soldiers).

Ptolemy XII will reign for another four years (55–51). After his death, the Gabiniani will remain in Egypt to protect his heirs and successors.[14]

The Assignment of the Provinces

Recently, Cicero has come into possession of a villa in Cumae in Campania, paying for it with his own money. It isn't a luxury residence but it does feature a colonnaded portico and a well-stocked library, rich in philosophical texts, especially Platonic ones. It is there that Cicero will write his *De re publica*, a philosophical treatise in six books. He has toyed with the idea of this treatise ever since his return to Rome from exile. In 55, he is still thinking on it, but he will only begin drafting it in 54 and will publish it in 51. He has already outlined the first two books, which he has discussed with a few friends, including Cnaeus Sallustius, in his villa in Tusculum, where he received their advice to continue in the Aristotelian method. Aristotle (384–322) was one of the most universal, innovative, prolific, and influential minds of all time, taught by Plato, who founded a philosophical school called the Academy, and himself the founder of the Lyceum, a school of Peripatetic philosophy. Between 15 April and 15 May 55, Cicero deeply analyzes Aristotle's thoughts, examining works by him in the library at Faustus Cornelius Sulla's villa in Cumae, close to Cicero's own.[15]

---

13   Cic. *Fam.*, I.9.19.
14   Dio Cass., XLII.3.3, XLII.5.4; Caes., III.4; Val. Max., IV.1.15.
15   Cic. *Att.*, IV.10.1.

Sulla is the son of the late dictator Lucius Cornelius Sulla (138–78) and his fourth wife, Caecilia Metella Dalmatica. He has married Pompeia, who is the daughter of Pompey and his third wife Mucia Tertia. They have three children: Faustus, Lucius Ahenobarbus, and Cornelia. He is an augur and is about to become a *quaestor monetale* (54). His villa in Cumae is the one in which his father, the dictator, spent the last moments of his life after having resigned from all his public offices and retired.

Sulla's library in Cumae is a priceless collection that includes books and documents of inestimable worth called the Library of Aristotle. This collection originates from Athens, where the consul Sulla took possession of it between 86 and 84, appropriating it from Apellicon of Teos, together with a large number of statues, paintings, and precious items, deriving from the sack of Athens. It is a personal library, created by Aristotle for professional purposes (texts useful to a teacher of philosophy, as he was), for personal study (works useful for a scholar's activity), and/or for collecting. In the very last years of his life, Sulla retired to a private life, leaving Rome to live in Cumae in a villa in the country. He died in 78, leaving his son Faustus as the heir to his immense patrimony. The Library of Aristotle was part of this legacy.

In March 55, the tribune of the plebs Caius Trebonius succeeds in having a law approved that appoints the consuls Pompey and Crassus, respectively, to the proconsulship for the Iberian provinces and the proconsulship "for Syria and the neighboring nations," in both cases for a five-year period, with the authority to draw up peace treaties or to declare war at their discretion, availing themselves of all the means and manpower necessary in this regard. The former will be replacing the proconsul Quintus Caecilius Metellus Nepos and will have to deal with a revolt by the Vaccaei, while the other will replace the proconsul Aulus Gabinius and will have to monitor the situation in Egypt at the same time as pursuing his idea of waging a war against the Parthians to win riches and military glory.

Trebonius justifies the conferral of these extraordinary appointments by the fact that, firstly, Hispania Citerior is being troubled by a revolt by the Vaccaei, which risks engulfing the entire province, and, secondly, the ongoing civil war in the Parthian Empire is creating a situation of political instability in the entire region and thus poses a threat to the Roman provinces in Asia.

The plebiscite meets with strong opposition, raised in part by other tribunes of the plebs. They argue that the proposed extraordinary appointments are unjustified. The emergency situations cited in support of the proposed appointments either don't exist or are being exaggerated; in particular, the uprising by the Vaccaei is being utilized as a pretext to confer wider and deeper powers to Pompey than are necessary. Nor is there any unrest on the borders of Syria.

In fact, there had been an emergency situation in Spain for some time. The proconsul Quintus Caecilius Metellus Nepos committed himself to resolving it, but he hasn't yet recorded a decisive victory, meanwhile it is being exploited, if not actively further fueled, to justify the application of extraordinary measures.

In the end, the plebiscite of Trebonius is approved by the people gathered in assembly in an atmosphere of high tension.[16]

The plebiscite's opponents challenged the proposal by refuting the existence of the necessary presuppositions. What happens after Trebonius's plebiscite has become law seems to prove them right. Pompey doesn't take up his office in Spain but obtains the authority to remain in Italy for reasons of state and delegates two *legati pro praetore* to govern in his stead. In this way, he will be able to control strategically important lands from afar at the same time as continuing to exercise his own influence on public life in Rome. His opponents are unable to block the initiative in this case either.

Pompey still has his residence in the city on the Pincian Hill, but, after the departure of Ptolemy XII from Rome, he returns to live in his villa in Albano Laziale, being obliged to remain outside the *pomerium* due to being a magistrate *cum imperio*. The fact that he lives outside of the capital doesn't prevent him from retaining close ties with the political world and its administration. He has numerous friends and clients who represent him wherever he needs them to. Moreover, many senators and magistrates go to visit him to pose questions, obtain his influential opinion, and receive his respected advice.

Cicero, with his oration *De provinciis consularibus*, invites the Senate to prorogue the proconsulships to Caesar; this suggestion will be accepted. In fact, a few days after, Pompey and Crassus promote a project of law which will be approved by the people gathered in assembly and becomes the *lex Pompeia Licinia*. This law confers the government of the Iberian provinces to Pompey and that of Syria to Crassus, and prorogues the proconsulships of Caesar for another five years.

Pompey and Cicero remain in close contact. On 25 or 27 April 55, they meet in Cumae, conversing about politics.[17] On that occasion, Cicero informs Pompey that he would gladly be his legate if he were to govern the Iberian provinces directly (he is currently governing them through trusted men). Then Cicero goes to his house in Antium to sort out his library.[18] At that time (April 55), he suggests to his friend Lucius Lucceius, who agrees, to write a biography about him from his consulship onward.[19]

In 55, at the end of April or in the middle of May, Cicero, through his brother Quintus, who has become a confidant of Pompey, is "advised" not to insist on taking exception to the illegitimacy of Caesar's legislation, such as he recently did regarding the *ager Campanus*.[20] Cicero makes good use of the "advice." On 15 or 16 May 55,

---

16   Plut. *Cat. Min.*, 43.2–8; Plut. *Crass.*, 15.7; Dio Cass., XXXIX.34–36; Liv. *Per.*, CV.

17   Cic. *Att.*, IV.9.1, X.2, XI.1.

18   Cic. *Att.* V.5.3, VIII.2.

19   Cic. *Att.*, IV.6.3; *Fam.*, V.12. The date (April 55) is uncertain. This may instead have taken place in the summer of 56.

20   Cic. *Fam.*, I.9.9–10.

he refrains from participating in the Senate's sessions in which the matter of land distribution in Campania is discussed.[21] Toward the end of May or at the start of June 55, he sings the praises of Caesar in a speech in the Senate. Toward the end of May or in June, he supports Caesar's requests in the Senate. On 2 July, he supports the candidacy for the praetorship of the former tribune of the plebs and member of the Populares, Milo.[22]

21 Cic. *QFr.*, II.6.2.
22 Cic. *Att.*, IV.12.

CHAPTER XVI

The Suppression of the Uprising in Armorica and the Conquest of the Southwest

Preparations for the Clash

Armorica is the geographical area between the Loire and the Seine, bordered to the south and west by the rest of Gallia Celtica and to the north by Gallia Belgica. This region juts out like a wedge into the Atlantic Ocean with Brittany, and into the English Channel with a smaller promontory called the Cotentin Peninsula. Brittany, on its southern side, looks out over the Bay of Biscay from high, rocky cliffs that are incredibly jagged and tormented by the sea. Its northern side, however, faces the Channel with long, wide, sandy beaches.

Armorica is inhabited by various peoples of Celtic extraction: Abricantes, Baiocassi, Cenomani, Coriosolites, Diablintes, Esuvii, Lexovii, Osismii, Redones, Venelli, and Veneti.

The Veneti, Osismii, and Coriosolites live in Brittany, where they settled between the VII and IV centuries, having crossed the sea from Great Britain. As such, they are "cousins" of the Celts of Wales, Cornwall, the Isle of Man, Ireland, and Scotland. Specifically, the Osismii and Coriosolites live in the north, while the Veneti inhabit the regions further south, especially the shores around Quiberon Bay and the Gulf of Morbihan. It is unknown whether the Veneti of Brittany have the same origins as the Adriatic Veneti of Italy and the Vistula Veneti of Germania, but these three peoples all belong to the Indo-European family of languages, so it is possible that the Anatolian people emigrated westward in the Iron Age, first populating the northeast of Italy, then part of Germany, then, after Great Britain, finally settling in Morbihan.

For the most part, the Veneti of Brittany (henceforth, for brevity, the Veneti) are fishermen, sailors, expert shipwrights, master caulkers, and navigator-merchants. They possess numerous large ships, propelled by sails, suitable both for facing the ocean's waves and for navigating shallow waters. These ships have an oak hull, which is particularly rigid and robust, a rather flat bottom, and high gunwales, especially at the bow and the stern. The ships stand upright on the beach when the tide goes out (Brittany is the location of the most significant tidal movements in Europe).[1]

The Veneti use their powerful fleet to trade with their "cousins" from Britannia and to control the harbors that open onto the Bay of Biscay and the English Channel, deriving enormous profits from the imposition of tolls.[2] Another of their economic activities is the production of salt, which takes place on the Guérande Peninsula in the south of Brittany. The salt flakes of Guérande are highly sought after for their violet fragrance.

Publius Licinius Crassus, younger son of the triumvir Marcus Licinius Crassus and commander of the Seventh Legion, had subjugated the Bretons (Veneti, Osismii, Coriosolites) as part of Caesar's wider and unstoppable advance into Gallia Belgica.[3] The peace agreement, in the autumn of 57, is safeguarded by the delivery of hostages. However, the fire of resistance still smolders. In winter 57/56, when the Seventh Legion is quartered in the lands of the Andecavi (between Rennes and Angers in France), Crassus sends some prefects and military tribunes to procure provisions. The Veneti and Coriosolites kidnap four of these officers: Quintus Velanius, Titus Silius, Titus Terrasidius, and Marcus Trebius Gallus.

Shortly after, the Bretons, almost all of the other Gauls of Armorica, as well as two Celtic peoples of Belgica—the Morini and the Menapii—unite and form a league. The Morini and the Menapii inhabit the coastline between the River Aa and the River Lys.[4] The League of Armorica denounces the peace agreement and informs Crassus that it wants to exchange the four hostages with the hostages that were delivered to him in the autumn.[5]

At this time, Caesar is in Illyricum. He immediately understands that the strongest component of the League comprises the Veneti, and this means that to defeat the League, he will have to fight principally at sea. He postpones all military action to the following spring and orders Crassus to build a fleet in the meantime by requesting the provision of ships from the two Armorican tribes who have remained loyal to Rome—the Namnetes and the Pictones—as well as from other Gallic allies.

The Namnetes are centered around the mouth of the Loire, on the northern bank. Their lands border those of the Andecavi to the east, the Ambiliati on the south side of the Loire (Lower Poitou), the Veneti to the northwest, and the Redones to the north. Their main inhabited settlement is Condevicnum, situated at the confluence of the north bank of the Loire with the Erdre. In the III century

---

1 Caes., 3.8–9.
2 Caes., 3.9–10.
3 Caes., 2.34.
4 The Aa is a river in France. It flows through the region of Hauts-de-France and empties into the North Sea, a few kilometers to the northeast of Calais. The Lys is a river in the north of France and Belgium that flows from the west into the Scheldt. The confluence of the two is in Ghent.
5 Caes., 3.8.

AD, it will become known as Portus Namnetus (Nantes). The Pictones, or Picts, live in Upper Poitou (the departments of Vienne and Deux-Sèvres). Their "capital" is Lemonum (Poitiers), a fortified village on a large headland at the confluence of the Clain and Boivre rivers. In 57, they had been subjugated by Caesar who then made an agreement with them, providing them with ships to fight the Veneti and exempting them from the obligation to pay taxes.

As quickly as he can, Crassus will have to build several light galleys known as *liburnae*: ships suitable for navigating the high seas, less resistant to bad weather than enemy ships but more maneuverable and equipped with elevated platforms that would double the height of the hull and thus reach the height of the stern of enemy ships. *Liburnae* are the standard medium-light units of the Roman navy. They are utilized both for combat and reconnaissance.

Firstly, Crassus will have to set up several shipyards on the banks of the Loire and find shipwrights, master carpenters, ship's carpenters, oarsmen, sailors, and helmsmen. Caesar advises him to recruit oarsmen in the south of Gallia Narbonensis and transfer them north with the ships.

While preparing for the spring campaign, Caesar also orders Decimus Junius Brutus Albinus, who is in southern Spain, to bring a fleet of triremes to Brittany. The trireme is among the largest and fastest types of ships in the Roman fleet. Its name comes from the fact that it is propelled by three banks of oars, one on top of the other. It is similar to the *liburna*, only larger (maximum length 39 m, maximum width *c.* 3 m), with a draft of 1.7 m, and has around 20 officers and seamen on board, together with 20–25 marines and 168 oarsmen. It can also be equipped with one or more pieces of artillery (catapults, ballistae).

In due course, Brutus Albinus will be assuming command of the fleet being prepared for the war against the League, understood as command of the ships that emerge from the shipyards of the Loire, the ships supplied by Rome's Gallic allies, and the ships that he himself will have led to Gaul from Spain.

Once he has issued instructions for ships to be built, Decimus Albinus, again on the orders of Caesar, leaves for Aquitania with 12 cohorts and a sizeable number of cavalry to prevent local tribes from reinforcing the League.

Aquitania is a region in the southwest of France, north of Gallia Narbonensis. It spans the land between the mountains of the Pyrenees, the River Garonne, and the Bay of Biscay,[6] and therefore borders Armorica to the north and Gallia Narbonensis to the south. In the future, Pliny the Elder and Ptolemy will frame this region more precisely as being between the Loire to the north and the Cévennes mountains to the east. Aquitania is rich in metals (gold-bearing sands of mountain streams and iron from Périgord in the southeast), produces abundant quantities of oil, wine, and ceramics, and is connected to ports on the Atlantic Ocean because the Garonne is a

---

6   Caes., I.1.

navigable river. Its major center is one such port: Burdigala (Bordeaux). It is situated on the estuary of the Garonne and is the gateway to the European continent for the tin and lead exported from Great Britain.[7]

Finally, Caesar orders his legate Quintus Titurius Sabinus to face the Coriosolites, Lexovii, and Venelli with three legions. He himself will reach Brutus Albinus as soon as possible, with ground troops, to fight the Veneti in their own lands.

The Campaign Against the Veneti

The campaign against the Veneti cannot start at the scheduled time (spring 56) due to a delay in the construction of the *liburnae*. At the start of summer 56, however, Caesar finally has a powerful fleet at his disposal, formed of *liburnae*, triremes, and other ships. Initially, he besieges the cities of the Veneti. The siege operations aren't very successful though, both because the cities rise on promontories joined to the mainland by a low isthmus and become inaccessible at high tide and because, if required, they can be evacuated by sea. There is also the fact that the *liburnae* are often stuck in port due to rough seas. The ships that come to the rescue of the people to evacuate them manage to get to shore due to their size, their large number, and the knowledge that their pilots have of the local tides, currents, shoals, and inlets. As for why the *liburnae* are stuck in ports, this is because these boats were built for navigating the Mediterranean, where the climate is temperate and characterized by dry summers and rainy winters. The climate of Brittany is altogether different. It is of the wet oceanic type and so is characterized by limited temperature variations, abundant rainfall, cool and mild summers, and rainy winters. The weather changes frequently and quickly: a rainy day can change to a sunny one within a few hours. It must be said, however, that in Morbihan, the climate is better than in the rest of the peninsula.

The decisive battle takes place in the second half of the summer of 56, when the ships of Brutus Albinus approach Quiberon Bay and the Veneti surge out to meet them with 220 large, sturdy sailing ships. The fighting takes place offshore, near the western coast, before the eyes of Caesar's legions, who are lined up on the promontory of St. Gildas. It lasts from 10 o'clock in the morning until sunset and will go down in history as the Battle of Morbihan, or the Battle of Quiberon Bay. The Romans have fewer ships than the enemy, but they are more maneuverable and faster. Two or three at a time, they complete revolutions around enemy ships, during which the marines onboard, making use of poles with a very sharp scythe blade attached to the end, try to hook them round the shrouds of the ship alongside, often succeeding in cutting through them. Ships whose halyards, sheets, and stays have been cut through

---

7   C. Letta & S. Segenni, *Roma e le sue province. Dalla prima guerra punica a Diocleziano* (Roma: Carocci, 2015), 124.

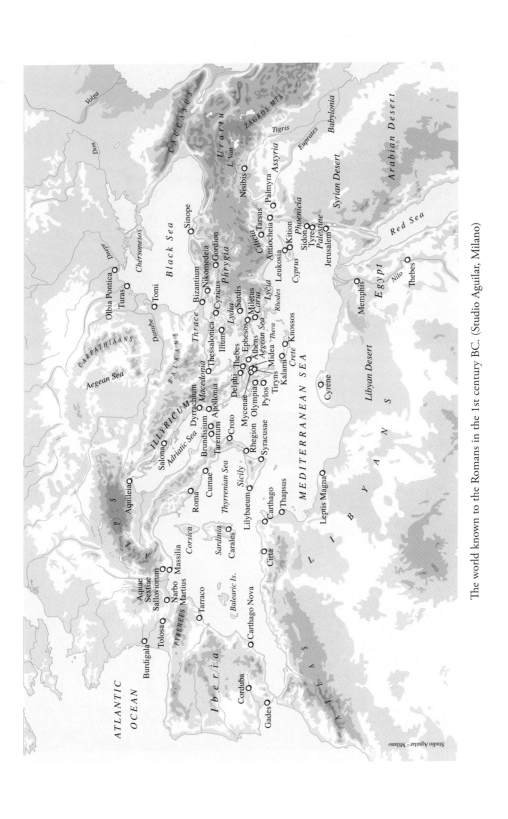

The world known to the Romans in the 1st century BC. (Studio Aguilar, Milano)

Jean-André Rixens, *The Death of Cleopatra,* 1874, oil on canvas, 289 × 198 cm, Toulouse, Musée des Augustins. (Bridgeman Images)

Lawrence Alma-Tadema, *The Meeting of Anthony and Cleopatra,* 1883, oil on panel, 92 × 65 cm, private collection. (Russell Ash Limited / Bridgeman Images)

Presumed portrait of Julius Caesar, 1st century BC, Arles, Musée Départemental Arles Antique. (Bridgeman Images)

Bust of Pompey, 1st century AD, copy of a portrait from the mid-1st century BC, h 26 cm, Copenhagen, Ny Carlsberg Glyptotek. (Bridgeman Images)

George Edward Robertson, *The Funeral Oration of Mark Antony*, c. 1894–1895, oil on canvas, 193 × 134 cm, Hartlepool, Hartlepool Museums and Heritage Service. (Hartlepool Museum Service / Bridgeman Images)

Louis Gauffier, *Cleopatra and Octavian*, 1787–1788, oil on canvas, 112 × 84 cm, Edinburgh, National Galleries of Scotland. (National Galleries of Scotland / Bridgeman Images)

Giovanni Antonio Pellegrini, *Pompey's Head Presented to Caesar*, 1701–1708, oil on canvas, 150 × 162 cm, Caen, Musée des Beaux-Arts. (Bridgeman Images)

Charles Le Brun, *The Death of Cato The Younger*, 1646, oil on canvas, 132 × 99 cm, Arras, Musée des Beaux-Arts. (Bridgeman Images)

Johann Georg Platzer, *Antony and Cleopatra in the Battle of Actium,* 18th century, oil on copper, 80 × 52 cm, London, Apsley House, Wellington Collection. (Historic England / Bridgeman Images)

Jacques Ignatius de Roore, *The Riots in Rome after the Death of Caesar,* 1744, oil on panel, 70 × 55 cm, private collection. (Christie's Images / Bridgeman Images)

Andrea Mantegna, *The Triumphs of Caesar: 6. The Bearers of Corsets*, c. 1484–1492, tempera on canvas, 280 × 271 cm, London, Hampton Court Palace. (Royal Collection / Royal Collection Trust © His Majesty King Charles III 2022 / Bridgeman Images)

William Holmes Sullivan, *"Julius Caesar"*, *Act III, Scene 1, The Assassination*, 1888, oil on canvas, 89 × 58 cm, Stratford-upon-Avon, Warwickshire, Royal Shakespeare Company Collection. (Royal Shakespeare Company / Bridgeman Images)

William Holmes Sullivan, *"Julius Caesar,"* *Act III, Scene 2, The Oration of Mark Antony*, 1888, oil on canvas, 89 × 58 cm, Stratford-upon-Avon, Warwickshire, Royal Shakespeare Company Collection. (Royal Shakespeare Company / Bridgeman Images)

Henri-Paul Motte, *Vercingetorix Surrenders to Caesar,* 1886, oil on canvas, 250 × 172 cm, Le Puy-en-Velay, Musée Crozatier. (Photo Josse / Bridgeman Images)

Joseph Désiré Court, *The Death of Caesar,* 1827, oil on canvas, 42 × 35 cm, Montpellier, Musée Fabre. (Photo Josse / Bridgeman Images)

Pompeo Batoni, *The Death of Mark Antony,* 1763, oil on canvas, 100 × 76 cm, Brest, Musée des Beaux-Arts. (Photo Josse / Bridgeman Images)

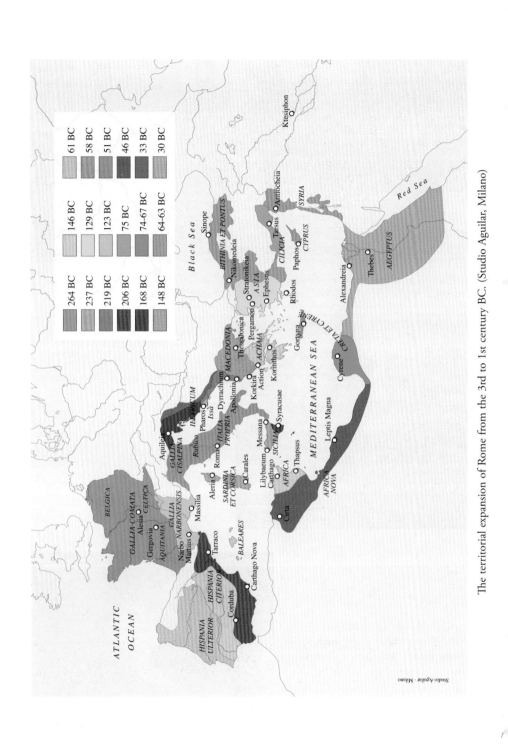

264 BC	146 BC	61 BC
237 BC	129 BC	58 BC
219 BC	123 BC	51 BC
206 BC	75 BC	46 BC
168 BC	74-67 BC	33 BC
148 BC	64-63 BC	30 BC

ATLANTIC OCEAN

Black Sea

Red Sea

MEDITERRANEAN SEA

BELGICA

GALLIA COMATA

CELTICA

Alesia

Gergovia

AQUITANIA

GALLIA NARBONENSIS

Narbo Martius

Massilia

Aquileia

GALLIA CISALPINA

ILLYRICUM

Rubico

Issa

Pharos

Dyrrachium

Apollonia

Korkira

Action

Korinthos

MACEDONIA

Thessalonica

Pergamon

ACHAEA

Stratonikeia

ASIA

Ephesos

Rhodos

BITHNIA ET PONTUS

Sinope

Nikomedeia

Antiocheia

SYRIA

Tarsus

CILICIA

Paphos

CYPRUS

Alexandreia

AEGYPTUS

Thebes

Ktesiphon

ITALIA PROPRIA

Roma

SARDINIA ET CORSICA

Aleria

Carales

Lilybaeum

Messana

SICILIA

Syracusae

Thapsus

Carthago

AFRICA

AFRICA NOVA

Cirta

Leptis Magna

CRETA ET CYRENE

Cyrene

Gortyna

HISPANIA CITERIOR

Tarraco

BALEARES

Carthago Nova

HISPANIA ULTERIOR

Corduba

Studio Aguilar - Milano

The territorial expansion of Rome from the 3rd to 1st century BC. (Studio Aguilar, Milano)

are no longer able to maneuver themselves, leaving them immobilized, and they are rapidly boarded and captured. The other ships of the Veneti turnabout to return to port, but find they cannot move due to a sudden drop in the wind, leaving the seas calm. These too are captured, except for a few that manage to reach the coast.

After the loss of their fleet the cities of the Veneti surrender, while Sabinus keeps the forces of the Venelli, Coriosolites, and Lexovii occupied, preventing them from being able to go to the aid of the Veneti. Therefore, the Romans' victory is absolute, both on land and at sea. Caesar will take revenge on the vanquished, having the nobles killed and selling the prisoners of war and the civilian population to slave traders. He bans the production of salt, and he establishes colonies of Roman veterans in strategic locations (Locmariaquer/Lokmaria-Kaer) and founds the city of Darioritum (the future Vannes/Gwened).

In the meantime, Crassus has conquered Aquitania. In short, by the end of the summer of 56, not only has Caesar routed the Veneti and their allies, regained control of Brittany, and extended the sovereignty of Rome to Normandy, but he has also affirmed the supremacy of Rome in the southwest of Gallia Transalpina.

CHAPTER XVII

The First Landing in Britannia

Caesar Prepares the Invasion

The relations between the two sides of the Channel are very close, both for reasons of trade and because some of the inhabitants of southeast Britannia are blood relatives of certain tribes of Gallia Belgica since these tribes, fleeing from the Romans or the Germans, as the case may be, found refuge and protection in Britannia with other Celts and then mixed with them. Therefore, while most Britons are autochthonous (in the sense that they are Ligurian or Goidelic[1]), some tribes in the southeast of Britannia descend from groups of immigrants, who came from Gallia Belgica from the II century onward. At first, the migrants settled on the Isle of Wight and in Kent (in the southeast of Great Britain, south of the Thames). Later they gradually occupied the entire Thames basin.

This explains why some tribes from southeastern Britannia have the same name as certain tribes from Gallia Belgica and why it isn't unusual for the Continental branch and the Insular branch of a tribe to have the same chieftain. Consider, for example, the cases of the Atrebates and the Parisi. The Atrebates live in part in Gallia Transalpina (Arras, Pas-de-Calais, Hauts-de-France) and in part in Britannia (Berkshire and Surrey, between the forests of Speen and those of Oxfordshire, and extending to Silchester in Hampshire). For their part, the Parisi live in part on the banks of the Seine in the region of Lutetia (Paris) and in part in the southeast of Yorkshire in a marshy region at the mouth of the Humber. It also explains why, respectively, Divitiacus, king of the Suessones, exercised a form of sovereignty over Britannia shortly before the Gallic War;[2] in 57, the leaders of the Bellovaci, who had incited the Gauls of Belgica to rebel against Caesar, fled to Britannia;[3] and in 56, when the Veneti rose up against the Romans, the Britons sent aid to the Gauls of Belgica.[4]

---

1   The Goidelic, or Gaelic, languages are one of the two branches of Insular Celtic languages (the other being Brittonic). These are Irish, Scottish Gaelic, and Manx (Isle of Man).
2   Caes., II.4.7.
3   Caes., II.14.4.
4   Caes., III.9.10.

The Britons in the southeast have founded three powerful states, led by tribal rulers:[5]

the Cantiaci (Cantium, Kent),[6]

the Trinovantes,[7] who occupy the northern side of the Thames estuary (Suffolk, Essex) and have their capital at Camulodunon (Camulodunum, Colchester in Essex), and

the peoples inhabiting an ill-defined region north of the Thames, whose king, at the time of Caesar, is Cassivellaunus.[8]

It is necessary to dwell on Cantium. This is divided between four kings: Cingetorix, Carvilius, Taximagulus, and Segonax.

In the summer of 55, Caesar, a man of boundless ambition, wants to achieve a spectacular success that could impress his fellow citizens even more than the major results he has achieved in northwestern Europe. The conquest of Britannia would be a bold undertaking, one never attempted before. The question is one of conquering a land that lies beyond the English Channel, and therefore beyond the confines of the known world. Moreover, if Caesar succeeds in getting his hands on the riches of Britannia (it is said that, in Britannia, pearls of an unheard-of size are fished and that the Cantiaci control tin deposits and copper mines, which are economically exploitable), he could increase not only his renown but also his personal wealth.

To justify his landing in Britannia, he will say in his *Commentaries* that it was motivated by reasons of security, as Britannia could become the point of departure for secret agents heading for Gallia Belgica with the task of riling up the Gauls in revolt against the Romans or even for an army to support the rebels; moreover, he also only wanted to undertake an initial exploration of unknown lands, not so much because he was impelled to do so by an innate desire for knowledge, but rather to collect first-hand information about the land and its peoples, and thus to be able to verify the degree of difficulty of a future potential conquest. He will forget to mention that the Channel is guarded by warships, making a military intervention of any significance from Britannia improbable. As usual, Caesar exaggerates the danger to depict a non-existent emergency that requires his intervention.

Preliminary Reconnaissance

In 55, the Romans only have vague ideas about Britannia. They only know that it is a large island that stands out on the horizon from Gallia Belgica; that it is rich in tin; that it is surrounded by fog and icy waters; that it remains in the dark for three

---

5   Caes., V.12.1.
6   Caes., V.14.1, V.22.1.
7   Caes., V.20–21.
8   Caes., V.11.8, V.18.1, V.21.2.

months a year; and that it has an "impossible" climate because it frequently rains, and the cold numbs the limbs right to the bone. Who are their sources?[9] The Greek historian Herodotus (484–*c*.425), the unknown author of *The Periplus of Himilco the Navigator*, Pytheas (*c*.389–*c*.310), Diodorus Siculus (90 BC–27 AD), the tales of Roman and Greek merchants who had been to Britannia, though—with rare exceptions—without having ventured into the interior, and the account of Publius Licinius Crassus Dives,[10] who, when he was governing Hispania Ulterior (96–92), went as far as the southern shores of Britannia. This Crassus was the father of the triumvir Marcus Licinius Crassus and the victor in a battle against the Lusitani, following which he celebrated a triumph.[11]

Herodotus speaks of islands situated to the northwest of the known world, from which the Phoenicians of Gades (Cádiz in Spain) obtained their supplies of amber and tin. He called these islands the Kassiterides (Cassiterides), the "Tin Islands" (from *kassiteros*, "tin"), as do other authors after him.[12] He is probably referring to the Isles of Scilly, found off Cornwall, the extreme southwest of the British Isles. At the start of the VI century, an explorer called Midacritus, perhaps having left from *Massalia*, reported tin, it seems, from the Cassiterides.[13] These islands had already been visited by the Phoenicians. It appears as if Midacritus was the first Greek to venture there. Around 520, the Carthaginian admiral Himilco conducted a daring voyage of exploration along the Atlantic coasts of the Iberian Peninsula, Ireland, and Great Britain,[14] later giving an account of it in the homonymous *periplus* (a description of the ports of a certain sea, with useful pointers for navigation and sometimes ethnographic information and on political and religious customs). This was a period of great explorations. In the V century, another Carthaginian, the sailor Hanno, explored the western coast of Africa.

---

9   In Caesar's day, the sources on Britannia didn't yet include Strabo of Amasia (60 BC–21/24 AD), nor Pliny the Elder (23–79 AD), and certainly not Pomponius Mela (d. *c*. 43/44 AD) or Avienius (mid–IV century AD), who would deal with the subject at a later date.

10 Str., III.5.11.

11 It has been ruled out that this could have been the son of Caesar's legionary commander and the conqueror of Aquitania (57–56) who was mentioned earlier regarding the revolt of the tribes of Brittany.

12 Hdt., III.115; Diod. Sic., V.38 [following Posidonius]; Str., 120, 129, 147, 175 [following Posidonius]; Mela, III.47; Plin., IV.119, VII.197.

13 Plin. VII.197.

14 Avien. *Ora Marit.,* 112ff., 380ff., 404ff.; Plin., II.169. In the second half of the IV century AD, Postumius RuPius Festus Avienius, a civic magistrate and Latin scholar, a native of *Volsinii* (Bolsena in Lazio), drew inspiration from *The Periplus of Himilco the Navigator* to write the short poem *Ora Maritima*, of which only part of Book I, 680 verses, survives. *Ora Maritima* describes the ports of Spain and Portugal between Cape Trafalgar and La Coruña, as well as those of the northern coast of Spain, and it includes references to Ireland and Great Britain. Britannia is also mentioned in a Greek *periplus* from the VI century BC, the so-called "Massiliote Periplus," while other information on it is traceable to later sources, or in any case those predating 500.

Around 330, Pytheas, a Greek navigator and geographer, completed a voyage of exploration of Northern Europe, setting out from Massalia, going up the Atlantic coasts of Europe up to Brittany, passing from there to Great Britain and Ireland, perhaps reaching as far as Iceland and the Arctic Circle. He left a written account of all this, titled *On the Ocean*, or perhaps *A Description of Earth*.[15]

Pytheas was the first person from the Mediterranean to speak of the midnight sun, the aurora borealis, and the polar ice and tides, and he was also one of the first foreigners to have explored the Cassiterides. It seems he circumnavigated the islands (possibly only in part) to find the fastest route to the tin country. Tin was then the most precious commodity that the merchants of Massilia imported into Gallia Transalpina. It was extracted on the Isle of Wight and transported from there to Gallia Belgica, where it was loaded onto horses, which would then arrive in Massilia 30 days later.[16]

Pytheas recounts that, having disembarked in Britannia—probably at the promontory of Belerion (Land's End) in Cornwall—he moved along the south coast, up to the headland of Kantion (Kent). After this, having circumnavigated Britannia, he returned to base through the Irish Channel. It is legitimate to doubt that he covered all of Britannia on foot.[17] More likely, he disembarked from his ship at various points.

Pytheas writes in his report of his journey that Britannia is an island shaped like a triangle[18]—its points are the promontories of Kantion, Belerion, and Orkas—and he provides a great deal of information on this land's resources and on the customs of its inhabitants. He says that Cornwall is rich in tin, which is extracted and worked, and he calls the country the *pretannikái nésoi* (the name Britannia derives from this). He also says that the Britons still use light war chariots (this vehicle has fallen into disuse on the Continent by this time, at most being used for ceremonial purposes), that they live in low houses made of earth and brushwood, that they store ears of grain in their rafters, and that their old folk trim the required grain each day by hand.

---

15   This book was judged to be a work of fiction by many later authors. Strabo speaks about it in critical terms in II.4.1–2, reporting the judgment of Polybius. The work of Pytheas is also cited in Gem., VI.9. The intellectuals Eratosthenes, Hipparchus, Posidonius, and Ptolemy divide the extreme north of the globe from everything below the island that Pytheas had called Thule, perhaps Iceland, or possibly Norway or the Faroe Islands. Modern scholars think that Pytheas really did go to Great Britain and, perhaps, Iceland as well.

16   Diod. Sic., V.22, 38.

17   Str., II.4.1.

18   Diod. Sic., V.21.3.

The report of Pytheas's voyage remained famous.[19] Well-known both at the time and in posterity, it can certainly be found in the Library of Alexandria and in the one in Pergamum, as well as in many private libraries. In 55, he is the principal available source on Britannia for those who want to find out more about it.

In addition to literary sources, the Romans also had other information available to them on Britannia derived from the stories reported by various Gallic merchants. In any case, such tales refer to the coasts of Britannia and to their peoples. Normally, foreigners don't go inland due to the dangers to which they would expose themselves.

The Romans would soon come to learn that the inhabitants of the three kingdoms mentioned above are not the only peoples of the southeast of Britannia. To these it is necessary to add the Cenimagni, the Segontiaci, the Ancalites, the Bibroci, and the Cassi.[20]

The following tribes of the south of Britannia can also be added to those mentioned previously: Regnenses (in the region of Chichester, ancient Noviomagus Reginorum), Atrebates, Belgae, Durotriges (New Forest), and Dumnones (Somerset, Devon, Cornwall, and possibly also part of Dorset).

North of the Atrebates are the Dobunni. Wales is inhabited by the Ordovices and the Silures: the former, in the north; the latter, in the south. It is noteworthy that the Silures have a dark complexion and curly hair.[21]

North of the Trinovantes live the Iceni. West of the Iceni live the Coritani (Corieltauvi). Even further west, between Peak Forest and the Irish Sea, are the Cornovii. The middle and the north of Britannia are occupied by Brigantes, a powerful confederacy of tribes reaching from one coast to the other, from the Mersey to the Humber and up to the highlands of Scotland.

The Romans will give the name "Caledonia" to that part of Britannia that extends to the north of the River Forth and the River Clyde (Scotland) from the name that they themselves gave to a local people, the Caledonii. The Caledonii are tall individuals with red hair.[22] These people live in the north of Caledonia. The south of Caledonia, meanwhile, is inhabited by the Selgovae and the Novantae.

The Britons are individuals who are, on average, taller than the Gauls. Their hair is less thick, they are less strong, and, although they are similar to them in culture,

---

19 Pytheas's report of his voyage, widely known in antiquity, has not survived and is today only known through the writings of other authors.

20 All these Britons are cited in Caesar's *Commentaries on the Gallic War* as having sent embassies to offer their surrender. Caes., V.21.1.

21 Tac. *Agr.*, 11.

22 Tacitus erroneously believed that the Caledonii were a people with Germanic origins. Tac. *Agr.*, 11.

they are nevertheless somewhat more unrefined.[23] The men have long hair that falls to their shoulders and a mustache drooping over a big double-pointed beard, and they shave every part of their body except for their head and upper lip. They are in the habit of dying their body blue, including the face, if not always, then at least on special occasions.[24] This caused the Romans to collectively call the inhabitants of Cornwall Picti (Picts). Picti is the Latinization of the ethnic name Pretani, or Priteni. This could derive from the adjective *prettanikè*, "painted one" or "tattooed one," which derives in turn from *pretannikái nésoi*.

In general, the Britons don't sow corn, they live on milk and meat, and they are clad in skins,[25] although they remain semi-naked. As such, they live off hunting and fishing, by gathering plants and shellfish, and by raising livestock. Livestock is their main source of wealth. For religious reasons, they do not eat hare, cockerel, or goose,[26] and therefore they do not breed poultry. They are very numerous, have a thriving trade, and at least seven of the tribes have a monetary economy, adopted rather late (II century). However, they eschew urban life, although there are a few fortified villages that seem to be something more than an *oppidum* in Wales and in Scotland. The civilization of the Britons, thus, is a rural one. Their houses are generally isolated.

Some Britons are considered more civilized than others. The Cantiaci, whose relations with the Gauls of Belgica are continuous and who emigrated to Britannia from the European continent, have a very similar civilization to that of the Gauls of Belgica,[27] which includes having a more developed taste for art. The inhabitants of Cornwall, who have long been in contact with the peoples of the Mediterranean, encountered on the promontory of Belerion where they search for tin, have also adopted some Mediterranean customs.[28]

Moving gradually further inland or further north, however, there are increasingly "primitive" peoples, wild peoples inhabit the midlands and the north. It is reported that some of them practice cannibalism.[29]

The Britons believe themselves to be indigenous[30] and cherish their ancient customs.[31] It seems possible that they practice a cult to the Earth Mother. Their

---

23 These details are found in Str. IV.5.2. There is no doubt that the Romans already knew about the physical appearance of the Britons from hearsay before Caesar disembarked in Britannia.
24 Caes., V.14.2; Mela, III.6.51.
25 Caes., V.14.2.
26 Caes., V.12.6.
27 Caes., V.14.1.
28 Diod. Sic., V.22.1.
29 Diod. Sic., V.32.
30 Diod. Sic., V.21.5; Caes. V.12.1.
31 Diod. Sic., V.21.

pantheon is crowded with gods and goddesses.[32] Their priests are the druids. Druidism was born among the Britons. The ties between Britannia and Gaul are also very close when it comes to religion and ritual. The Transalpine Gauls believe that the doctrine of the druids has been imported to their lands from Britannia, and those who want to study it more deeply go to educate themselves on the other side of the Channel,[33] perhaps with the druids of the Invamori, a Celtic tribe who went to Britannia from Belgica.

Considering that the pre-Celtic or proto-Celtic Britons were peaceful, regarding land as the heritage of the clan, and women as belonging to more than one man,[34] the martial customs of the Britons could be attributed more to the Belgian invaders than to the indigenous peoples.

The Britons have a proud demeanor before foreigners[35] and are hospitable toward those who present themselves in a non-aggressive manner. What is striking is the use that they make of the light two-wheeled chariot,[36] robust and fast, used both as a means of transport and for combat. Each chariot transports multiple warriors, who, as they launch into the attack with a great clamor, shoot their bows in various directions; when they have broken through the enemy lines, they hand the reins to the servant accompanying them,[37] jump to the ground and fight on foot, then climb back up onto the chariot and set off again.[38] It seems to directly echo the style of fighting used in the Trojan War in the duels between Achilles and Hector.

The Britons also possess a strong infantry.[39] Their warriors are armed with swords, spears, bows, and slings, and they fight either naked from the waist up or completely naked, protecting their body with a pelt-covered and painted shield. But Caesar says the sword is too big and too heavy, while the shield is too small.[40] Helmets are reserved for chieftains alone.

So, the Atrebates live partly in Gallia Belgica and partly in Cantium. Caesar subjugated them in 57 and appointed Commius as their king and leader. With his landing in Britannia imminent, he charged Commius with going ahead of him to

32 Inscriptions from the Roman era show us a very large number of local deities, whose names are often associated with that of a Roman god.
33 Caes., VI.13.1 and 11–12.
34 Diod. Sic., V.21.5–6; Caes., V.14.4; Dio Cass., LXXVI.12.
35 Hor. *Carm.*, III.4.33; Tac. *Agr.*, 11.
36 Caesar calls the chariots of the Britons *esseda*. Mela, III.6.52 uses the name *covinni* for particular chariots armed with scythes, and Tacitus uses the same word for the chariots of the Caledonii. Their use is ancient, because Pytheas was already talking about them in the IV century (Diod. Sic., V.21.5, following Timaeus).
37 Tac. *Agr.*, 12.
38 Caes., IV.33, V.15–16.
39 Tac. *Agr.*, 36.
40 Tac. *Agr.*, 12.

Cantium, where he is to report to the local peoples that Caesar is about to arrive and to intimate to them that they should submit to him, with the aim of attracting not only the Atrebates of Britannia but also other Britons to Rome's side to ensure supplies and security when required. He hopes that Commius will find an audience at least among the Atrebates.[41]

The attempt fails: Commius is taken prisoner soon after disembarking in Britannia, when he claims leadership over the Atrebates on the island.[42] The failure of Commius's diplomatic mission doesn't dishearten Caesar, in fact it only encourages him to try again. Since it is difficult to obtain information from Gallic and Britannic prisoners of war and from Gallic merchants, both because they are reluctant to provide it and because, when they do talk, they are in any case inaccurate, Caesar tasks his military tribune Caius Volusenus with conducting reconnaissance of the coastline of Cantium to identify a suitable deep-water port or place to drop anchor. Volusenus spends five days on his mission along the southern coast of Britannia aboard a warship before returning to base with details confirming the coastline, the tides, the meteorological conditions, and the difficulties and risks of navigation. He is unable to report anything on the Britons, their activities, or their resources as he never went ashore and never met any of them. Caesar doesn't appreciate the fact that Volusenus didn't have the nerve to interrogate the local population,[43] but he mistakenly believes that the information that he has collected will be sufficient, and therefore he issues the order to prepare for the disembarkation.

The Landing

On the night of 24/25 August 55, 80 ships set sail from Portus Itius (Gesoriacum, Boulogne-sur-Mer?).[44] Some of them are warships, some of them are transports, seized by the Romans from the Veneti after their victory, and they are all heading for Britannia.

A further 18 ships, these too confiscated from the Veneti, will soon set sail from the nearby Portus Ulterior (possibly Ambleteuse), 13 kilometers to the north. Cavalry, equipment, weapons, baggage, and miscellaneous goods are currently being loaded on board.

It escapes no one's attention that the forces being deployed—two legions (the Seventh and Tenth), about 10,000 men—will appear excessive if the intention is

---

41   Caes., IV.21.7*.

42   Caes., IV.21.18–26.

43   Caes., IV.21.1–5, 26–30.

44   The Romans gave the name Portus Itius to a location on the Strait of Calais between the English Channel (to the west) and the North Sea (to the east) in a region to the south and west of Belgica and to the north of Picardy, which is today called Hauts-de-France and is found in France, but which for a while fell mostly within the Low Countries.

to conduct a simple reconnaissance but insufficient if it is to carry out a full-scale invasion aimed at the conquest and permanent occupation of enemy territory. Indeed, the aim of the expedition is unclear. The hypothesis that this should be considered a quick and sudden raid for the purpose of robbery may not be far from the mark.

The length of the crossing is expected to be 35 km. The night is dark, and the weather forecast doesn't look good. In port, the sea is calm. Offshore, it is marked by regular, long, crestless waves, caused by a wind coming from distant regions afflicted by storms. The sailors know that such waves, of increasing intensity, can precede, and indeed portend, the arrival of bad weather. On the ships, there are some who sleep, but there are also those whose eyes remain open, imagining that they are heading into the darkness of an endless night, their souls torn between the excitement of taking part in an unprecedented expedition and the fear of the unknown.

The tribes of the southeastern coast of Kent—the Cantiaci, the Atrebates, and others—have learned from Commius and from the Gallic merchants who cross the Channel that the Romans are preparing to disembark on the island, and they have readied themselves to repel them. To this end, they have mobilized tens of thousands of infantry and cavalry, supported by war chariots. The scouts scrutinize the sea from the top of the White Cliffs of Dover, which stretch for 13 km and rise to a height of 110 m above the sea. The scouts sight the vanguard of the enemy fleet at 9 o'clock on the morning of 25 August.

The ships that have appeared on the horizon are those that are carrying the legionary infantry. The other ships, with the cavalry, are a considerable distance behind, partly because they started from further away, and because they encountered a strong headwind. As could be predicted, the weather deteriorated after their departure and gradually got worse and worse.

Standing on the deck of the flagship, wrapped up in his purple-red cloak, Caesar scans the coastline which appears to him to be increasingly clear as they draw closer. He sees the fires of the Britons lined up on the clifftops. He realizes that the place that the ships are heading toward isn't suitable for a landing due to the high walls of rock overhanging the sea, and so he decides to look for another one. He orders the fleet to continue along the coast, heading northeast. Finally, he identifies a more suitable landing site on the beaches that run along a coastal plain.[45] He decides to disembark there that afternoon, with the rising tide, without waiting for the cavalry. As such, the boats, having been lightened of their load, will be able to free themselves as the sea level rises and won't be obstacles to those that arrive later. He doesn't know that the 18 ships that are transporting the cavalry were forced back by a strong headwind on the night of 24/25 August and are waiting for the tide to set sail again.

---

45 Perhaps those that extend near to the modern-day towns of Walmer and Deal.

The tide has gone out, so the ships are unable to get close to the coast due to the rocks. However, they have advanced as close to the shore as possible. When, at 3.30 in the afternoon, the legionaries receive the order to disembark, they hesitate to go down into the water. It is as if they have been paralyzed; if the water is deep, they could be pulled under by the weight of their armor, weapons, and equipment. To make matters worse, once they have entered the water, they have to cross 200 m before they can set foot on dry land. During this crossing, they could become the targets of the arrows of the Britons, who, when the ships changed course, moved from Dover to the northeast, never losing sight of them. The moment is dramatic, charged with the greatest of danger. The continuation of the mission depends on this. The entire operation is at risk of failure.

Luckily for Caesar, the *aquilifer* of the Tenth steps forward to set a good example to his comrades. First, he beseeches the gods that what he is about to do will have a happy ending, then he exhorts his comrades to jump down if they don't want the legionary standard to be handed over to the enemy. In any case, he will have done his duty to his homeland and to his commander. With that said, the soldier—who has just given a general's speech, using the classic military virtues of camaraderie, honor, and fidelity as leverage[46]—descends into the water and heads toward the enemy. The sight of him diving in alone and advancing toward the shore, clutching the eagle, instills courage in all the rest, who change their tune and follow him *en masse*, all encouraging one another. Seeing all this unfold, the soldiers in the other ships follow the first, and they advance toward the enemy together.[47]

The Britons try to confine the invaders to the shoreline, firing clouds of arrows and repeatedly charging at them with their cavalry and war chariots. The Romans respond from their ships, launching all sorts of projectiles at them using arrows, slingshots, and catapults and sending men in smaller boats to the areas that need reinforcement. These troops are well-armed, trained, organized, and highly disciplined. They know what to do to push the attackers back. Once on terra firma, the centuries line up in formation, protect themselves with their shields, repel the attacks, and advance compactly. The lack of chivalry takes a toll on the Britons, but what is even more damaging is the psychological aspect. The Britons are so astounded by the order, discipline, and tenacity of the Romans, and by their self-assuredness, that they prefer to retreat. At 7 o'clock that evening, the Romans have a firm foothold on the coastline. The Britons ask for a truce. Caesar grants it on the condition that hostages are delivered to him as a guarantee of their compliance with the agreement. But the unexpected is lurking around the corner.

The 18 ships that are transporting the cavalry for the Romans appear on the horizon on the beach the next day. They are still approaching the coast when, in

---

46 M. Schauer, *La Guerra Gallica* (Gorizia: LEG, 2020), 112.
47 Caes., IV.25.

the afternoon, a strong northeasterly wind suddenly picks up, preventing them from anchoring and pushing them so far offshore that they must turn around and return to the port they set out from.[48] The damage is not insignificant. Caesar is left without his cavalry and baggage, so he cannot go deep into the hinterland and must do without his supplies. Edginess creeps around the tents of the encampment.

The Seventh Legion leaves the camp to go in search of food, but it runs into the enemy, who have set out again with cavalry and war chariots. This restarts the fighting: the Romans are in formation and well-protected, while the Britons are lined up in a Celtic-style phalanx, with support from their cavalry and war chariots. Caesar personally leads a few cohorts to assist the Seventh Legion, which, pressed on all sides and under a hail of arrows, has found itself in grave difficulty. Seeing Caesar arrive, the enemy falters. The Romans regain their courage and, in the end, will sing of their victory.

Over the following days, it rains incessantly. When good weather returns, the Britons renew their assault on the Romans. Caesar sets up his legions in the open field. The fighting resumes, with bloody encounters and many losses among the Britons, who, in the end, are put to flight. The Romans pursue those fleeing and cut many of them down. Moreover, they set all the buildings they find along the way ablaze. Two tribes send Commius back to Caesar and deliver hostages to him, thus indicating their submission to him.[49] The others vanish.

Caesar doesn't have the means to impose peace. The invading force is few in number, has limited autonomy, and is short of food. Furthermore, summer is nearly over, and bad weather is on the way. On 12 September, after only 15 days in Britannia, he orders a withdrawal. He leaves the island without even setting up a garrison, promising himself to return as soon as possible at the head of a more powerful army.[50]

The Power of Propaganda

The results of the campaign are more than modest. Clever propaganda will be used to transform an almost disastrous enterprise into a daring and fearless undertaking, almost epic in its telling. The Senate of Rome receives a bulletin of victory in which Caesar glories in having crossed the ocean and discovered a new world. This is enough to remove the shackles from the imagination, which is then set free to fly over unknown and unlimited horizons. The effect is sensational. The account of the expedition intoxicates a large part of the ruling class and primarily the masses, who celebrate joyfully. The streets and squares of Rome are filled with people celebrating

---

48 Caes., IV.28–29.
49 Caes., IV.27.
50 Caes., IV.34–37.

the success of a titanic enterprise. Cicero is euphoric and even forgets his fear that Caesar wants to make himself dictator. Catullus, who has never been passionate about Caesar—he mentions him in his verses, but only to scorn him—sings his praises, defining his deeds as memorable and heroic. The Senate of Rome sanctions a *supplicatio* of two weeks—an unusual duration—to thank the gods for having delivered a victory to the *res publica* over such a fearsome enemy. Therefore, for 15 days, all the temples will remain open and cult statues will be placed on display so that the faithful can offer ritual sacrifices, offerings, and prayers.

CHAPTER XVIII

A Bridge Over the Rhine

Caesar Crosses the Rhine[1]

The Morini live in Gesoriacum (the Continental coast of the Channel and the North Sea, specifically the area of Boulogne and on the coast up to Bruges) and have their capital at Taruenna (Thérouanne). Their lands border those of the Menapii to the north and those of the Atrebates and the Ambiani to the south. They are sailors and farmers. They collect salt in special salt pans, raise flocks, and cultivate and weave flax. They are fecund, so there are a great many of them. In 57, they promised to participate in the League of Armorica, contributing 25,000 men to it. In 56, they fought against Caesar, eventually surrendering to him, and requesting forgiveness for their previous actions. Shortly after, however, they attacked a detachment of Romans returning from Britannia, hoping for a rich booty, and Labienus had to subjugate them once again. They will rebel again in 52, uniting themselves with other peoples in revolt and sending 5,000 men to the aid of Vercingetorix at Alesia. They will rebel yet again in 29.

In 55, having already quartered his legions in the lands of the Belgae, Caesar cuts the Morini to pieces. He torches their villages, devastates their fields, and destroys their crops.

Commius, tribal ruler of the Atrebates, has remained loyal to Caesar (and he will remain so even during the anti-Roman revolts of 54 and 53, which will be dealt with later). For this reason, after having restored order in Gallia Belgica, Caesar respects the independence of the Atrebates and exempts them from paying taxes. In addition, he gives Commius control over the Morini.[2]

In the meantime, to escape pressure from the Suebi, 430,000 Usipii and Tencteri—Germanic tribes—have abandoned their lands, situated to the north of the Main (possibly the valleys of the Lahn and the Sieg) between the lands of the

1   Plut. *Caes.*, 22–23.
2   Caes., VII.76.1.

Chatti and those of the Sugambri, and wandered for three years, swarming into the lands of the Menapii situated at the confluence of the Rhine with the Meuse, on both banks of the former.

Frightened by the arrival of such a large number of people, the Menapii abandon their fields, farmhouses, and villages on the far side of the river and line up on the opposite bank to prevent the migrants from passing through into Gaul. Caesar intervenes. He offers the migrants an opportunity to negotiate an agreement. They send him an embassy, but, during the talks, they treacherously attack him with 800 cavalry and rout 5,000 mounted Roman soldiers. Then they send other ambassadors. Caesar puts them in chains and attacks the horde. There are no words to describe what happens next, such is the horror. The legions massacre men, women, and children. It is an unprecedented slaughter—400,000 victims—and even hearing about the appalling, lurid event in passing is enough to take your breath away. When the news of the hecatomb reaches Rome Cato will tremble with indignation and will not hesitate to propose to the Senate that Caesar should be handed over to the Germans to punish him for not having respected diplomatic immunity, consequently exposing Rome to the wrath of the gods.

The survivors of the immense massacre took refuge across the Rhine in the lands of the Sugambri. Caesar orders the Sugambri to hand them over to him, but they respond that he has no jurisdiction over them because the river demarcates the border. Therefore, they do not comply.

Later, the Ubii request help from the Romans, with whom they are allied, to defend them against the Suebi. Caesar builds a bridge over the Rhine (at Neuwied, 15 km downstream of Koblenz and south of Bonn) and leads his legions into Germania, both because he wants to discourage the Suebi from crossing the Rhine themselves and because he wants to be the first Roman to cross the Rhine at the head of an army.

The bridge is built in just 10 days, thanks to the great effort and skill of the engineers, at a point where the river is particularly wide and deep; the rapidity of the water requires a very solid structure. It is just less than 500 m long and reaches from one side of the river to the other with 56 bays, each of which are 8 m long. It was constructed by placing a thick deck on enormous girders, themselves placed on huge trestles that were made to sink deep into the riverbed, achieved by utilizing an ingenious mechanism operated by dozens of men. This machine (the forerunner of modern piledriving) lifts a heavy mallet to a great height and then lets it drop onto the pole that is driven into the riverbed, driving it further and further down.

To ensure the bridge was not only solid but also elastic, rope bindings were used instead of nails in the construction. Other poles were sunk obliquely into the river downstream to increase the resistance of the bridge to the current, while some palisades were erected further upstream to prevent any trees or boats from colliding with the structure and damaging it. The bridge is so wide that it allows two wagons to cross side by side (therefore being at least 4 meters across). It is perfect in every detail, it is functional, exact, consistent in its dimensions, and complete in its structure. It is as beautiful as if it had been built by a divine hand. It is, nonetheless, a temporary work, destined to be demolished as soon as it's no longer needed.

The genius of the construction and the discipline of the legions who, after crossing the bridge, keep coming at a marching pace are both things that leave a big impression on the Sugambri, who hide in the woods. The Romans are reluctant to go deep into the forests of Germania, thinking that they will find monsters there and, in any case, believing that they will never get out of them again, so vast do they seem to their eyes. Therefore, they don't go into the forests but instead burn the abandoned crops and villages.

After staying for 18 days on Germanic soil, the Romans return to the western bank of the Rhine, dismantle the bridge, and return to Gaul.

Meanwhile, in Rome …

During this campaign, both Caesar's mother and daughter die in Rome, the former of old age, the latter in childbirth. Julia was the wife of Pompey and the mother of a young girl, Atia. Both she and the child she bore passed away during the birth.[3] She was only 22 years old. During the marriage, which lasted six years, she had been a sweet and loving wife, and she had managed to influence her husband, working with him and fulfilling his expectations. The loss of both his close relatives is a very hard blow for Caesar. However, he represses his emotions. It isn't in his nature to show either what he thinks or what he feels. He has always been this way. No one has ever seen him lose his self-control. Nobody ever knows what thoughts are running around inside his head, if his heart is beating faster, if his temples are throbbing more than usual, if he really is as calm as he appears, or if he is in a cold sweat.

Pompey, however, has a more open nature. Everyone can see that he cannot make his peace with the loss of his adoring wife. Even Marcus Junius Brutus (Quintus Servilius Caepio Brutus), the man to whom Julia had been promised before being given by her father in marriage to Pompey, will mourn the death of the woman he has never ceased to love.

Meanwhile, Cicero spends the final months of 55 in his villa in Tusculum (Tuscolo), where rather than dedicating himself to preparing legal cases, he is writing above all about philosophy. He is working on *De oratore*, a dialogue in three books,

---

3   Plut. *Caes.*, 23.

in which the profile of the ideal orator is outlined and is imagined as the moral guide of the state. When, in the middle of November, he has completed it, he will dedicate it to his brother Quintus and send it to Atticus to have it published, that is, copied and distributed.[4] Cicero is also working on *De temporibus meis*,[5] a poem in three cantos that speaks of the author's vicissitudes, with particular emphasis on the period between the conspiracy of Catiline and his return from exile.[6] This work seems to have been a rehash of *De consolatu suo*, which he wrote in 60 prior to his exile but never published (however, this version will never be published either).[7]

---

4   Cic. *Att.,* IV.13.2*.
5   Cic. *Fam.,* I.9.23.
6   The existence of this work is deducible from the orator's correspondence and from allusions made to it by other authors.
7   Cited in Cic. *Att.,* I.19.10. The identification of *De temporibus meis* with *De consolatu suo* is based on Cic. *Fam.* I.9.23.

CHAPTER XIX

The Second Landing in Britannia

The Operation Against the Pirusti

Southeastern Britannia, on the northern side of the Thames estuary (East Anglia: the counties of Essex and Suffolk, and part of Cambridgeshire), is a region that is partly flat and marshy, partly slightly hilly. It is a fertile land, suitable for agriculture and horticulture. The Trinovantes—commonly regarded as the most powerful tribe in Britannia—live there. Their capital is the fortified village of Braughing and, later, Camulodunum (Colchester in Essex). It was there that Imanuentius ruled until Cassivellaunus, the king of the Catuvellauni, killed him and replaced him as tribal leader. Mandubracius, the son and legitimate heir of Imanuentius, was forced to flee. He crossed the sea and landed in Gallia Belgica, where he found refuge and protection.

In 54, Caesar receives him at Portus Itius, where he had quartered the legions ahead of the winter. Mandubracius requests his aid to recover his throne. Caesar finds that Mandubracius is giving him a good reason to return to Britannia and doesn't hesitate to seize the opportunity. He promises his personal support to Mandubracius and orders his legions to prepare to cross the Channel in the spring. At the same time, the same legions will have to build as many ships as possible. Caesar's plan is based on the possibility of having 600 new transport ships available in spring 53, together with 200 other transport ships that had been used the previous year, plus 28 warships, which he intends to use to transport five legions (a total of 30,000 men) and 2,000 cavalrymen, as well as horses, heavy weaponry, various materials, and baggage, to the other side of the Channel. The ships to be built will have to have a lower freeboard than is used in the Mediterranean Sea, taking the tides into account as well as the fact that the coastal waves are smaller in the Channel. Furthermore, their hulls will have to be wider than usual to transport a greater load, including the horses and pack animals. In addition, these ships will have to be able to be propelled by both sails and oars.

Caesar, let us remind ourselves, is not only proconsul of Gallia Narbonensis for five years but also of Gallia Cisalpina and Illyricum. In the winter of 54/53, while he is staying in Aquileia, he learns that the Pirusti have attacked Narona, the largest Roman stronghold in Illyricum and their launchpad for further military operations into the interior.

The Pirusti are an Illyrian people who live on the shores of the Sinus Rhizonicus (Boka Kotorska/Bay of Kotor in Montenegro), a series of four interconnected inlets on the coast of Epirus forming one of the best natural harbors in the Mediterranean, perfectly sheltered from the sea and easily defended against enemies. Narona is located far to the north of the Sinus Rhizonicus in the interior of Dalmatia. Caesar swoops on Narona, orders the local population to collaborate in setting up an expedition against the Pirusti, and indicates the place the military forces are to focus on. The Pirusti, scared by Caesar's determination, let him know that they accept responsibility for their actions, that they are ready to pay compensation for the damage caused, and that they will put themselves before an arbiter to calculate the reparations owed. Caesar refrains from punishing them, granting them peace, but obliges them to hand over hostages to guarantee that the agreement will be observed.

With the arrival of spring, Caesar returns to Portus Itius. He takes note of a delay in the construction of the ships: they will not be ready for use before July. The landing in Britannia must therefore be postponed until the height of summer.

The Treveri do not take part in the assemblies of the Gauls' representatives and do not obey the orders of the Roman authorities. They are a Celto-Germanic people. They live in the northeast of Belgica on both banks of the Moselle, bordering the lands of other Celtic tribes—Aduatici, Vangiones, Nemetes, Mediomatrici, Remi—and of the Germanic tribe of the Ubii. They possess a large number of infantry and the best cavalry in Gaul. Among the tribe, two chieftains are competing for power: the pro-Roman Cingetorix and the anti-Roman Indutiomarus.[1] The Romans suspect that Indutiomarus fought against the Transrhenane Germans and thus provoked them to cross the river.[2]

Caesar enters the lands of the Treveri with four legions and 800 cavalry and summons Cingetorix and Indutiomarus. Cingetorix is quick to forge ties of friendship and alliance with the Romans in the name of himself and his people, and he assures Caesar that he will fulfill his obligations. Indutiomarus, however, prepares for war against Cingetorix and the Romans. But his plan will not come to fruition. He is abandoned by many of his people and must submit himself to the Romans. One of the hostages that he will have to deliver as a guarantee is his son.[3]

1   Caes., V.3–4, V.56–57, V.8.
2   Caes., V.1–2.
3   Caes., V.1–4.

The Return to Britannia[4]

In early July 53, 800 transport ships and 28 warships are preparing to untie their moorings at Portus Itius. They are loaded up with soldiers: around 30,000 legionaries, including infantrymen (Roman citizens), Eastern archers and Balearic slingers, and 2,000 Gallic cavalry. Caesar has delegated command of three legions and 2,000 cavalry to his deputy Titus Labienus, who has the assignment of garrisoning the port—to which the army leaving for Britannia will return—to ensure grain is stockpiled in case the campaign lasts longer than expected or he cannot supply himself with food on the ground, and to monitor the Gauls of Belgica, lest they rebel in Caesar's absence.

On 6 July 53, at midnight, with the arrival of high tide, Caesar orders the immense fleet to set sail. His expedition has been appropriately publicized and will be followed with great emotion by the Senate and the Roman people. Waiting with bated breath and their mind wandering amid countless fantasies, any Roman not on board one of the ships crossing the Channel that night will feel as if they are alongside the embarking legionaries in spirit.

The wind is blowing lightly as the ships depart but it drops during the crossing so that they have to row, fighting against the currents to hold their course. The invasion force reaches its destination around noon the following day at the end of a 30-mile journey.

The ships drop anchor off the beach between Deal and Sandwich, which clings to a gentle and open coastline, the same one where Caesar had disembarked the previous year. The landing meets no resistance. A camp is set up somewhere near the coast not far from the shore, and the ships are moored at anchor offshore. Caesar hands the task of defending the camp and the boats to Quintus Atrius, who is in charge of 10 cohorts (one legion) and 300 cavalry. Some cavalry patrols explore the environs and capture prisoners, who will inform their captors that a sizeable Britannic army had gathered on the coast, awaiting the arrival of the Romans, but then withdrew inland, where it remains in hiding.

Toward midnight, Caesar moves inland with the bulk of his army and intercepts the enemy at a ford in the River Stour, about 20 kilometers from the encampment on the coast. At dawn on 8 July, there is a first small clash, at the end of which the Romans are victorious. The surviving enemies scatter and will find refuge in a place protected by embankments and ditches at Bigbury, about a mile-and-a-half from the ford.

The legionaries of the Seventh have no issue with taking that fort, at the cost of only a few losses. The surviving defenders flee, and, on 9 July, Caesar dispatches his cavalry to pursue them. Just then, news reaches him that, during the night, a strong easterly wind has caused chaos among the ships at anchor. Neither the anchors nor

---

4   *Ibidem.*

the hawsers were able to take the strain, and the ships, out of control, either collided with one another, causing serious damage, or were hurled toward the beach, where they ran aground. At least 40 vessels have been lost; the crews hadn't been able to do anything to avoid the disaster.

It is interesting to note that all this happened in the same place and for the same reasons as the analogous disaster of the year before, as if nothing had been learned from the experience. It must also be said that not far away there is a place a great deal more suitable for ships to wait at anchor: Richborough. A more adequate exploration would have discovered this. It is reasonable to ask why this wasn't done.

The cavalry pulls back, the army returns to the coast, and the fleet is pulled ashore and protected within the encampment. While the ships that had not been irretrievably damaged were repaired, Labienus was asked to supply a further 60 ships. All this happens within the space of 10 days.

On 19 July, Caesar leads the army inland again in search of enemies to fight. In the meantime, the Britons of Kent have set aside their mutual hatred and have forged an alliance, giving overall command to Cassivellaunus. Another battle, larger than the previous one, takes place at the ford across the Stour. Again, the Romans are victorious.

Cassivellaunus, being pursued, is on the run toward the Thames. He takes refuge in the woods and, from the depths of the forests, launches short-range attacks against the Romans with an equally short-lived intensity. Although the legions are a practically invincible weapon in pitched battles, they aren't suitable for countering guerilla warfare. But they must make a virtue of necessity. The enemy attacks and withdraws, using "hit and run" tactics, suddenly appearing and then vanishing again just as quickly, like phantoms. The Romans, in response, conduct thorough searches of the countryside, making the most of the opportunity to raid the food supplies and livestock they find, setting the rest ablaze.

Before long, the united front of the Britons falls apart. Some tribes send ambassadors to Caesar with offers of peace and useful information on the location of Cassivellaunus's secret haven. This hideout is strategically placed between a forest and a swamp on the hill of Wheathampstead, not far from the Roman camp. At the end of July or the beginning of August, the Romans attack the fort and capture it, forcing Cassivellaunus and his family to flee. Caesar pursues the fugitives, forces them to surrender, and restores Mandubracius as king of the Trinovantes. Cassivellaunus will have to return what he has stolen, deliver hostages, and undertake not to harass the Trinovantes in the future.

Caesar also obtains the submission of other tribes, those that sued for peace: the Cenimagni, the Segontiaci, the Ancalites, the Bibroci, and the Cassi. To achieve this, he uses Commius again. Caesar, we recall, had used Commius before in preparation for his first expedition to Britannia in 55. At this point, Caesar decides to return to the Continent. As such, he retreats. But there is an insufficient number of ships available (Labienus has only sent a few). The transport must therefore be undertaken in several shuttles, dividing the troops into groups. By the end of the summer, Caesar has brought the army back to Belgica.[5]

The second expedition to Britannia hasn't led to the occupation of the island either, not even of a small part. Furthermore, it isn't clear how Caesar can punish Cassivellaunus if he doesn't comply with the pacts, beyond being able to retaliate against the hostages. Thus, Caesar's success is more illusory than anything else. Again, however, his propaganda has the effect of reinforcing the aura of greatness that surrounds him in the eyes of his fellow citizens, some of whom, holding him in as high esteem as Pompey, have nicknamed him *magnus*.

The Death of Catullus, Rabirius, Gabinius; Memmius in Court

In 54, Catullus passed away, aged only about 30. He had retired to the family villa in Sirmium on Lake Garda after having spent one last period in Rome, during which he had definitively broken off his relations with Clodia. Exhausted by some form of disease (tuberculosis?) and by the torment caused by his misfortune in love, he died alone, disappointed, and embittered.

At the same time, Caius Rabirius Postumus, a notable financier and leading actor on the Roman political scene, has returned to Rome from Egypt. Still trembling with fear (the inhabitants of Alexandria revolted against him and forced him to flee hastily), he has only just set foot in the city again when he is indicted on the charges of violence and malfeasance. Cicero will deliver an oration in defense of Rabirius (*Pro C. Rabirio Postumo*),[6] but he isn't able to prevent the accused from being judged to be guilty and condemned to exile.[7]

In the case of Gabinius, he has just returned to Rome from Syria when, in September 54, he is indicted for high treason after an action is brought against him by Lucius Cornelius Lentulus (Cruscellio?), under pressure from the publicans. The charge is *crimen maiestatis*, "having infringed the *dignitas* of the Roman people."

Gabinius's trial unfolds before the *quaestio perpetua de maiestate*, presided over by the praetor Caius Alfius Flavius, a friend of Caesar's, and in front of a jury of

---

5 Caes., V.11, V.15, V.21–23.

6 This must be distinguished from the oration *Pro C. Rabirio perduellionis reo oratio ad quirites*, pronounced by Cicero in 63 in defense of the senator Gaius Rabirius, the father of Gaius Rabirius Postumus, who had been accused of *perduellio* (high treason) for complicity in the killing of the tribune of the plebs Lucius Appuleius Saturninus in 100.

7 Rabirius was officially recalled from exile during Caesar's dictatorship.

70 members, including Lucius Aelius Lamia, Caius Porcius Cato, and Cnaeus Domitius Calvinus.

Lamia is the one who was exiled by Gabinius because he had expressed solidarity with Cicero, who had been sentenced to exile.

Caius Porcius Cato is probably the son of the homonymous consul of 114 and the grandson of Marcus Porcius Cato Licinianus, in which case he would also be a great-grandson of Cato the Censor and second cousin of Cato of Utica. He is a dogged anti-Pompeian. In 59, he had attempted to charge Gabinius with corruption, but without success (the praetors had made sure that they could not be reached for the deposition of the case); speaking then from the Rostra, he had accused Pompey, Gabinius's protector, of being a *de facto* dictator, as a result of which he risked losing his life. In 56, he was tribune of the plebs. In this capacity, he busied himself as follows: he sought to ensure that Clodius could be elected as aedile before a trial against him could commence so he could be shielded with immunity from prosecution; he proposed bills against the interests of Publius Cornelius Lentulus Spinther and Titus Annius Milo, friends of Pompey; and he influenced the Senate in their response to the request of Ptolemy XII Auletes to be restored to the throne of Egypt with the aid of a Roman military intervention, inappropriately divulging a prophecy from the Sibylline Books. In 55, he was praetor.

Cnaeus Domitius Calvinus had been tribune of the plebs in 59 and praetor in 56. In 59, together with his colleagues Quintus Ancarius and Caius Fannius, and with support from the consul Bibulus as well as Cato, he vetoed the agrarian law proposal that Caesar was about to submit to the people gathered in assembly, inciting a hostile reaction from the crowd (a brawl broke out that set the tribunes and Cato to flight; the next day, Bibulus was showered with feces). In 56, Calvinus was praetor and presided over the trial of Bestia, who had been accused of corruption and was defended by Cicero. He probably also presided over the trial of Caelius.

Gabinius, in defending himself against the charge of *crimen maiestatis*, claims that he intervened to put an end to the pirate incursions that Archelaus, the consort of Berenice IV, was carrying out along the coasts of Syria. Cicero is called to testify as a witness because, shortly after Gabinius's return to Rome, he heavily criticized him in the Senate, and Gabinius had been brutal in his retort. Pompey doesn't add his own voice to that of the prosecution, but nor does he abstain from testifying about what he knows of him. What he says isn't in favor of the accused; rather, he speaks out to save himself (the trial has a political dimension that not only involves Gabinius but Pompey as well).[8] This would prove that Pompey and Gabinius are joined by ties of friendship and common interests but also that they are free to make their own choices.[9] In the end, Gabinius is found not guilty, with 38 votes

8   F. Santangelo, *Roma repubblicana. Una storia in quaranta vite* (Roma: Carocci, 2019), 244.
9   F. Santangelo, *Roma repubblicana. Una storia in quaranta vite* (Roma: Carocci, 2019), 239–246.

in favor and 32 against,[10] perhaps to prevent a guilty verdict from casting a poor reflection on Pompey.[11]

Shortly afterwards, in October 54, Gabinius is tried again, this time for violating the *lex Iulia de repetundis* (for having accepted the dation from Ptolemy XII), following a complaint brought by the tribune of the plebs Caius Memmius and by Lucius Cornelius Lentulus (Cruscellio?), Tiberius Claudius Nero, and Caius Ateius Capito. Presiding over the trial is the praetor Marcus Porcius Cato, son of the homonymous tribune of the plebs, himself the son of Marcus Porcius Cato Salonianus, and therefore the great-grandson of Cato the Censor and Salonia. In this case, Cicero doesn't limit himself to testifying against Gabinius but supports the accusation against him. The accused is found guilty, even though some citizens of Alexandria have testified in his favor. He will be sentenced to exile and its accessory punishments.[12]

As a result of the turmoil that has erupted in the city—due to havoc being wreaked by the armed gangs of Clodius, Sestius, and Milo, and due to the highly confused and tense situation that has arisen therefrom—the next set of elections for the civic magistracies for 53 are postponed. The candidates for the consulship in this round of elections are Caius Memmius, Cnaeus Domitius Calvinus, Marcus Valerius Messalla Rufus, and Marcus Aemilius Scaurus.

It is worth focusing our attention on Memmius. He had been propraetor of Bithynia and Pontus in 57. In 55, he repudiated his wife Fausta, daughter of the dictator Sulla, accusing her of infidelity (Fausta will later get married again, this time to Milo). He and Domitius Calvinus are supported by Caesar. During the electoral campaign, they get the consuls Appius Claudius Pulcher (the brother of Clodius) and Lucius Domitius Ahenobarbus to use their influence to have them elected. They have promised that, in the event they are elected, they will pay 10 million sesterces to the century that votes for them first, with another 4,000 (or 40,000, it isn't clear) sesterces to the consuls to bribe three augurs and two former consuls. In exchange for the bribe, the consuls will have to falsely certify that certain acts have been adopted that are indispensable for them to obtain the governorship of a proconsular province, once their term as consul is over. A *lex curiata* and a senatorial decree are mentioned.

10   Cic. *Att.*, IV.18.1; *QFr.* II.12.2, III.1.15, 24, III.2.3, III.3.3, III.4.1–3, III.7.1; App. *B. Civ.*, 2.24; Dio Cass., XXXIX.55.2–5, XXXIX.62.3; *Schol. Bob.*, 168; T. Stangl, *Pseudoasconiana. Textgestaltung und Sprache der anonymen Scholien zu Ciceros vier ersten Verrinen auf Grand der erstmals verwerteten ältesten Handschriften* (Paderborn, 1909); M. C. Alexander, *Trials in the Late Roman Republic, 149 BC to 50 BC* (Toronto: Toronto University Press, 1990), 145 n. 296.

11   On the trial *de maiestate* of Gabinius: M. C. Alexander, *Trials in the Late Roman Republic, 149 BC to 50 BC* (Toronto: Toronto University Press, 1990), 145, n. 296.

12   On the trial *de repetundis* of Gabinius: M. C. Alexander, *Trials in the Late Roman Republic, 149 BC to 50 BC* (Toronto: Toronto University Press, 1990), 148, n. 303.

The agreement puts such a large amount of money into circulation that the interest rates on loans doubles. It should remain a secret, but Memmius lets the Senate know about it. Why he does so is unclear. Perhaps he argued with the consuls. Perhaps he is hoping to make a good impression, emerging as a man of integrity. Perhaps he wants to ensure the elections are further postponed so that Caesar can return to Rome and support his candidacy.

Cato, who is praetor in 54, proposes to the Senate that the four candidates for the consulship for 53 be privately tried on charges of electoral fraud, but not everyone agrees, and the dissenters appeal to the tribunes of the plebs. On 9 August, the Senate postpones the elections yet again and officially proposes a private trial. The tribune of the plebs Aulus Terentius Varro Murena, however, uses his veto. The four candidates will be tried in public. A tribune of the plebs who is a relative of Memmius accuses Domitius. Quintus Acutius accuses Memmius. Quintus Pompeius accuses Messalla. Lucius Julius Caesar accuses Scaurus.

Domitius and Messalla are declared elected. Memmius and Scaurus are prosecuted. Memmius, to obtain immunity (he will not be charged if he unmasks a corrupter), accuses Quintus Caecilius Metellus Scipio Nasica—to no avail. Metellus Scipio is the father-in-law of Pompey, who isn't interested in convicting a relative. At this point, there is nothing left for Memmius other than to leave Rome in voluntary exile, and so he will travel to Athens. But we haven't heard the last of him.[13]

---

13 In 50, the fact that Gaius Scribonius Curio, the son of Memmius's sister, is tribune of the plebs leads Memmius to hope for a return to Rome, but, due to the increasing tension in the political environment (because of the combined maneuvers of the Senate and Pompey aimed at ensuring Caesar is stripped of his proconsular offices to render him vulnerable to legal prosecution), the question takes a back seat. Memmius dies sometime before 46.

CHAPTER XX

A Crisis Explodes on the Banks of the Rhine

The Revolt of the Belgae

Caesar has 10 legions across Gaul. Recently, he has recruited two new ones in Gallia Cisalpina—the Fourteenth (to replace the Thirteenth) and the Fifteenth—and has received another—the Sixteenth—from Pompey, who has "loaned" it to him for the good of the state and as a pledge of friendship. In view of the onset of winter 54/53, he spreads them across Belgica (present-day northern France, Belgium, and southern Netherlands, up to the Rhine).

He sends the legion of Caius Fabius to the Morini; that of Quintus Tullius Cicero to the Nervii; that of Lucius Roscius Fabatus to the Esuvii; that of Titus Labienus to the Remi; and those of Quintus Titurius Sabinus and his deputy Lucius Aurunculeius Cotta, together with five additional cohorts, to the Eburones. He also stations the three legions commanded by the quaestor Marcus Licinius Crassus and by the legates Lucius Munatius Plancus and Caius Trebonius in Belgica. These legions are deployed across the land in such a way that there are no more than 160 kilometers between one and the next, except for Roscius's legion, which is wintering in a calm and secure region.

Caesar should be leaving for Italy to take care of affairs in Gallia Cisalpina and Illyricum, minister to the wide network of contacts and clients he has in these regions, and to recruit additional troops. But he prefers to delay his departure until it has been confirmed that all the legions have settled in the places assigned to them in fortified encampments.

When he learns that all the legions have stationed themselves in their winter quarters, he receives further news. Tasgetius, tribal ruler of the Carnutes—a Gallic people who live in Gallia Celtica, north of the middle course of the Loire, and who have their capital at Cenabum (Orléans)—has become the victim of a conspiracy hatched by his political opponents, with the support of the people. To avoid the Carnutes breaking away from their alliance with the Romans, he orders Munatius Plancus to move his legion into their lands, to spend the winter there, and to arrest the conspirators and their supporters and send them to him.

A fortnight later, the Eburones rebel against Roman rule. The Eburones are a Germanic people who live north of the Ardennes—specifically between the Meuse and the Rhine, as well as in all likelihood between the Scheldt and the Meuse, including all or the majority of the Campine lowlands. They are led in part by Ambiorix and in part by Catuvolcus, and they offer human sacrifices to their divinities. Their capital is Atuatuca, a fortified settlement probably situated on the River Jeker, between the Meuse and the Rhine (near Tongeren in Belgium, northwest of Liège).

The Eburones of Ambiorix attack the Fourteenth Legion, commanded by Titurius Sabinus and Aurunculeius Cotta. They overwhelm some legionaries who are preparing firewood and besiege the encampment with enormous numbers, but they are repelled. However, they remain around the camp. Ambiorix offers Sabinus an escape route. If he withdraws, he will be able to do so without being harmed and can safely reach Cicero's camp or that of Labienus, the former about 80 kilometers away, the latter a little more. To convince him, he tells him that he isn't acting alone but together with all the other Gauls of Belgica, who have formed an alliance to revolt against the Romans and have planned to besiege all of Caesar's winter camps on the same day so that no legion is able to come to the aid of another. Cotta and many military tribunes and higher-ranking centurions advise Sabinus not to trust him. It would be better—they say—not to take initiatives without first having received orders from Caesar and to remain in the camp, where they can withstand the siege and wait for reinforcements, who will swiftly join them as soon as the news of what is happening in Atuatuca spreads. Sabinus thinks otherwise, fearing that Caesar may already have left for Italy. Unknowingly, he is about to lead his men into disaster.

The Romans leave the camp in a column. During the march toward the closest fort, when they find themselves in a wide valley, they are attacked by the Eburones from the rear. The Eburones, roaring cries of victory, launch an assault, disrupting the Roman ranks. The fighting is rough and bloody. Just when the Romans are about to be overpowered, Sabinus offers—and is granted—their surrender. But as he is negotiating terms with Ambiorix, he is betrayed and killed.

The fighting resumes. Cotta, previously wounded by a slingshot that caught him full in the face, falls in battle, as do most of his men. The few survivors of the carnage manage to take refuge in the encampment they had left, but they are relentlessly attacked until nightfall; in the darkness, no longer hoping for salvation, they decide to commit suicide *en masse*, except for someone who, by taking an unsafe route through the woods, is able to reach Labienus and inform him of what has occurred.

Emboldened by the victory, Ambiorix leads his men to the Atuatuci with the cavalry in front and the infantry following at a running pace. He incites them to rebel. The next day, he moves into the lands of the Nervii and prompts them to rebel as well. Then he does the same with the Ceutrones, the Grudii, the Levaci, the Pleumoxii, and the Geiduni.[1] Moreover, the Treveri have also risen in revolt.

Caesar had wanted to place Cingetorix on the throne of the Treveri both to reward him for his loyalty and because it was important that these people be led by a man in whom he could place his trust. But Cingetorix's supremacy was contested by Indutiomarus, who had indeed submitted, but who continued to harbor a deep resentment. Indutiomarus overthrew Cingetorix and declared him a public enemy. Cingetorix could therefore be killed by any member of his tribe as if he were any other enemy. However, he was able to take flight with his relatives, and they took refuge with Labienus.

Indutiomarus gathers the Treveri in assembly and announces that he will lead them to the Senones and the Carnutes to join with them and their neighbors—the Nervii and the Atuatuci—to form a united front against the Romans and lead a grand uprising by all the Gauls. To reach them, he says, they will pass through the lands of the Remi, allies of the Romans, and devastate them.

Labienus calls cavalry troops from all corners to him, and they manage to join him even though Indutiomarus is roaming around his encampment with a mass of cavalry and targeting them with projectiles. At an opportune moment, Labienus orders a sortie. His cavalry moves out *en masse* at the gallop from two gates and charge at the Treveri, followed by the cohorts, who set off at a running pace. The attempt to break the encirclement is successful. Many of the fleeing enemies are chased and cut down. Afterwards, a battle takes place near the River Semois, about 20 km east of the Meuse. The Treveri are overwhelmed and surrender. Indutiomarus is killed while he is wading across the river to try to save himself. His head will be delivered to Labienus, who will show it triumphantly to his soldiers while they are celebrating the victory.

Cingetorix is reinstated as the leader of the Treveri. Indutiomarus's relatives saved themselves by fleeing. They have not given up, however. They gather allies both among the Gauls and among the Germans on both sides of the Rhine and conduct a mutual exchange of hostages and guarantees. The entirety of Gallia Belgica is oppressed by an atmosphere of high anxiety. The tension explodes when Caesar, at the head of four legions, attacks the Nervii at the River Sambre.

Victories Over the Belgae Tribes and the Destruction of the Eburones: The Expedition Beyond the Rhine.

The Nervii are the most powerful and warlike people in Belgica. They are of Germanic origin and have lived in the Scheldt basin since 100. Their culture recalls the far

---

1   Caes., V.26–37.

more ancient culture of the Spartans. Previously, in 57, as part of the Belgae alliance, the Nervii had resisted the Roman conquest.

In 54, they attack the Fourteenth Legion, commanded by Quintus Tullius Cicero. Two cohorts from the legion, focused on searching for construction timber, are ambushed and annihilated by a large squadron of cavalry. Cicero is then besieged by a force of 60,000, comprising Eburones, Nervii, and Atuatuci and their friends and allies, but he faces the situation with expertise, solicitude and self-sacrifice, despite the fact that he isn't in good health. He and his men reinforce the fortifications in record time and hold out against attacks for a week, obstinately refusing to surrender. On the seventh day, although they are subjected to a deluge of white-hot clay slingshots and incendiary arrows, and with fires breaking out in all corners of the camp, they repel the enemy, who had climbed the ramparts with mobile towers, mantlets and ladders, inflicting heavy losses. In that situation, the courage and fighting spirit of the centurions Titus Pullo and Lucius Vorenus shine forth, without it being possible to say which of the two exceeded the other in valor and bravery.

Finally, Cicero manages to get a request for help through to Caesar, 100 kilometers distant, through the servant of a Nervian deserter named Vertico. Caesar gathers his forces and sets off with two legions (including the Tenth) and 2,000 cavalry. While he is on the march, he finds a way to alert Cicero to his imminent arrival. The 60,000 Gauls, informed by their scouts that Caesar is approaching, lift the siege of the Fourteenth's camp and head toward him. Cicero is able to warn Caesar that the enemy has moved away from him and is now moving toward Caesar. Caesar entrenches himself and is besieged, but he breaks through the enemy lines with an overwhelming sortie. He slaughters the enemy, setting the survivors to flight, and captures prisoners whom he will sell as slaves. The few who manage to avoid capture will join the Eburones of Ambiorix.

Caesar thus reaches Cicero,[2] after which he marches against the Carnutes and the Senones, who lay down their arms and beg him for forgiveness. One of the prisoners taken is Acco, leader and military chieftain of the Senones.

In the summer of 53, Caesar calls an assembly of representatives of the Gauls at Dorucortorum (Reims in France), but delegates from the Eburones and the Atuatuci are not present. During the gathering, he accuses Acco of having fomented a revolt among his people and has him publicly flogged to death and beheaded as a warning not to challenge the might of Rome. Then he forces the Atuatuci to surrender, obligating them to deliver hostages, and commandeers a large amount of their livestock and ravages their fields. He then moves into the lands of the Menapii with five legions, burns numerous villages, ravages their fields, raids their livestock, and takes many prisoners. The Gallic Menapii live around the Rhine estuary and southward along the Scheldt, as far as the Ardennes. They border the Morini to

---

2   Caes., V.38–53.

the west, the Nervii to the southeast, the Eburones to the northeast and east, and the Sugambri and Batavi (as well as the mouth of the Scheldt) to the north. Their primary stronghold is the *oppidum* of Cassel, near Thérouanne. They obtain peace on the condition that they deliver hostages and deny asylum to the Eburones.

Caesar orders Labienus to patrol the lands of the Menapii as far as the sea with three legions. Then he decides to settle the score with the Eburones. He commands Caius Trebonius to plunder their lands with three legions. He will lead the remaining legions to the confluence of the Scheldt with the Meuse, where Ambiorix has reportedly been sighted. Trebonius attacks the Eburones with full force. Those who are attacked, terrified and in a state of panic, disperse into the forests, into the swamps, and onto the chain of small islands off the coast. The elderly Catuvolcus curses Ambiorix for having involved him in the revolt and commits suicide. Even the Segni and the Condrusi, neighbors of the Eburones, begin to panic. They implore Caesar not to consider them as enemies. Caesar gives them assurances, but he also demands that they hand over the Eburones who have taken refuge among them. To find the Eburones in the remote places where they have gone into hiding, Caesar would have to venture into wild territory, full of dangers, which would endanger the army. He prefers that others do this for him. He sends emissaries to all the Gauls of Belgica and to the Sugambri of Germania and receives their cooperation based on promises of considerable booty. For the Eburones, it is the end. A multitude hunts them down, flushes them out, and massacres them, while 2,000 mounted Sugambri cross the Rhine on a Roman bridge and raid their livestock.

Thus Caesar exterminates the Eburones, burning and plundering their villages, hamlets, and isolated farms, slaughtering some livestock, and seizing herds of cattle and harvests. But Ambiorix is still at large; free and elusive, he constantly moves from one hiding place to another with the few men who have remained loyal to him.

While waiting for the end game with Ambiorix, Caesar has a magnificent new bridge erected over the Rhine[3] and inaugurates it by leading the legions to the opposite bank into the region of Germany east of Belgica, just beyond the river. His objective is twofold: to aid the Ubii, allies of the Romans, who are being threatened by the Suebi, and to avenge the massacre of Sabinus and his men. The Suebi retreat into the impenetrable forests and marshes, and Caesar gives up on pursuing them and instead returns to the Gallic side of the Rhine. This time he doesn't have the bridge dismantled but keeps it in place. In fact, he has a fort and a four-story tower erected in Gallic territory to defend the crossing.[4]

---

3   In a location understood to be between Urmitz and Weißenthurm, a little over 2 km upriver from the place where he had the previous bridge built and, subsequently, dismantled.

4   Caes., VI.29.

Caesar deploys the army across Gallia Celtica. Two legions will keep watch over the lands bordering those of the Treveri, two over the lands of the Lingones, and the remaining six garrison Agendicum (Sens), among the Senones.

In the meantime, news of the death of Crassus reaches him. The triumvir was killed in combat in Mesopotamia, together with his son Quintus and most of his army, after invading the Parthian Empire and having been defeated at the Battle of Carrhae. This news elicits a series of mixed feelings and considerations. Crassus, "the banker of Rome," had lent Caesar money on numerous occasions and was a friend who had defended him in the Senate, risking his life by doing so. He was one of the most prominent elements of the Populares faction of the Roman people. He was the provider of equilibrium within the Triumvirate.

Caesar spends the rest of summer 53 suppressing revolts in the northeast of Belgica, along the Rhine, and in the neighboring regions, and he also enlists troops on the Swiss Plateau to fill the gaps and provide reinforcements. Then he assigns the quarters for his troops for the winter, delegates their command to his lieutenant Labienus,[5] and heads for Italy, where he will spend the winter.

The Revolt of Vercingetorix

In the winter of 53/52, Europe is shivering from the cold and seems to be in a state of hibernation. In Gaul, the general situation seems to be calm, but this is only on the surface. The peace imposed by force of arms on Celtica and Belgica is fragile and is about to be shattered. Various Gallic peoples have agreed among themselves to rise up against the Romans, considering them as bloodthirsty invaders who sow violence, terror, and death, kill women, children, babies, and fetuses in the womb, abuse the elderly, the weak, and those who cannot defend themselves, and sacrifice girls on the altar of the troops' pleasure.

The sudden outbreak of the revolt catches Labienus off-guard. The inhabitants of Cenabum (Orléans), seat of the Carnutes, slaughter Roman merchants, including an *eques* who had been given the task by Caesar of supplying him with grain. Similar incidents occur in other major settlements.

The leader of the rebels is an Arvernian noble called Vercingetorix, the son of Celtillus and a heroic warrior. He had been expelled from his city, Gergovia, the capital of the Arverni (situated on a high plateau, near modern Clermont-Ferrand), but he had returned and become king of his people. Caesar will write in his *Commentaries on the Gallic Wars* (which we will examine more closely in due course) that Vercingetorix had learned about warfare from the Romans and that he had rebelled because Caesar had denied him the crown of the Arverni. Leading the rebellion was not out of love

---

5   Labienus had full command of all the legions when Caesar wasn't in Gaul.

for his homeland but due to personal resentment. However, what Caesar writes to explain and justify himself mustn't be taken at face value.

Vercingetorix quickly becomes the leader of the leaders of all of Gaul—Belgica, Celtica, Aquitania—or at least of all those who refuse to submit to the dominion of Rome. When he attacks the Romans' Gallic allies through his lieutenant Lucterius, starting with the Remi and the Bituriges, they call for aid from the Aedui, who pass the request on to Labienus. Labienus doesn't intervene—perhaps due to an error of judgment—but sends a dispatch rider to Caesar to inform him of what has occurred. The courier charged with delivering the message is a member of the cavalry unit set up by Caesar to relay information in double-quick time (*dispositi equites*). He sets off, wrapped up in his cloak with a saddlebag over his shoulder, and rides at a full gallop, day and night, never dismounting except to rest for a few hours wherever he must, change his mount at a relay point, or to let the animal drink at a river, under a bridge. He travels at speed over mountains and through valleys, across the immense Padan Plain, covered with snow, racing for more than 1,200 km until he finally reaches Aquileia.

It is February 52. Caesar cannot fail to help his allies, otherwise they will abandon him. Therefore, he does not hesitate to act. He quickly arrives in Gallia Transalpina and retakes command of the army. First, he reorganizes his forces, mustering those in the area and conscripting new soldiers, and he reinforces the garrisons on the Rhine. Then he sends Labienus with four (or five) legions to fight against the Senones and the Parisi, while he gathers troops between the Rhône and a mountainous region southeast of the Massif Central (Cévennes). Finally, two days after his arrival in Narbo, he leaves Decimus Junius Brutus Albinus with the task of engaging the Arverni; he will quickly take himself off to Vienne, where he will enlist 400 Germanic horsemen, then to the Lingones, whom he will ask for more reinforcements. The Alverni are not expecting to be attacked because the passes of the Cévennes, which separate Gallia Narbonensis from their lands, are blocked off by snow, but this is what happens. Labienus bursts into Auvergne with his legions, killing and wreaking devastation, while Vercingetorix heads toward Gorgobina (La Guerche), a city of the Boii, who are dependants of the Aedui.

The Battle of Avaricum

Caesar leaves two legions and the baggage train at Agendicum and marches with eight legions (around 30,000 men) and 8,000 auxiliaries for Gorgobina. He receives the surrender of the Senones at Vellaunodunum (Montargis, situated between Sens and Orléans) and sends two legions to Cenabum. These troops occupy, sack, and burn the settlement. The inhabitants of the burning city try to reach the opposite bank of the Loire, but they are caught on a bridge by the legionaries and are slaughtered.

In turn, Caesar takes Noviodunum (perhaps Neuvy-sur-Barangeon, northwest of Bourges), a city of the Bituriges, following a siege, after having repelled Vercingetorix who had tried to come to the aid of the besieged. Next, he besieges Avaricum (Bourges), a mighty stronghold situated on high ground rising above a river and a swamp, accessible via only a single, arduous road. Vercingetorix sets all the villages around Avaricum ablaze and remains at the Romans' backs to prevent them from receiving additional food and supplies. Meanwhile, Caesar has set up fortifications and is waiting for the right moment to launch the final assault. Avaricum is stormed and captured amid immense bloodshed. Of the 40,000 men, women, and children inside the city, only 800 manage to escape and reach Vercingetorix.

In the meantime, the Nitiobroges have also rebelled, as have (sensationally!) the Aedui, who have killed any Italics they found among them. Caesar wants to attack the Aedui, but the army won't follow him, so instead he has to agree to pursue Vercingetorix, who has barricaded himself in Gergovia. Therefore, the Romans besiege Gergovia. Vercingetorix resists. Caesar loses 700 men and retreats.

He returns to Noviodunum, where he had left the public money, food reserves, and baggage, but he finds nothing there because the Aedui have sacked and burned the city. As a result, he goes to Agendicum and rejoins Labienus, who, in the meantime, had attacked Lutetia (Paris), the main center of the Parisi defended effectively by Camulogenus, their king and chieftain, (who will fall in battle in 51 in an engagement near the city, on the ground that now makes up the Plain of Vaugirard). Caesar and Labienus thus return to Caesar's encampment.

The Battle of Alesia

Caesar has 40,000 legionaries and 10,000 auxiliaries with him. In the summer of 52, the rebels attack him, but he repels them and follows them as far as Alesia (Chaux-des-Crotenay in Jura, Franche-Comté, 40 km northwest of Dijon), where Vercingetorix has barricaded himself inside with 80,000 men. Caesar besieges Vercingetorix's encampment, set up to the east of the settlement, protected by a ditch and a dry stone wall. His intention is to starve the defenders into surrender. Contemporaneously, he fortifies his own encampment, which he has set up nearby. To this end, he builds a double line of trenches and embankments 16 km long with 23 redoubts. The circumvallation serves to besiege Alesia, while the contravallation protects his back.

Vercingetorix, in fact, is awaiting reinforcements (he has sent men trusted among their respective peoples to muster all able-bodied men). Since provisions are running low, Vercingetorix purges all the elderly, the women and children, who aren't able to contribute to the defense of the city, making them leave. Caesar refuses to take in the refugees, and they die of starvation between the defensive and offensive lines of fortifications.

Vercingetorix receives the expected reinforcements, an imposing army—250,000 infantry and 8,000 cavalry—led by Commius, the tribal ruler of the Atrebates, the same man Caesar had placed as chieftain of the Trinovantes and who had then betrayed him, unmindful of the favors received. Caesar repels three successive attacks launched by the Gauls on his encampment. In the end, he succeeds in having his cavalry outflank the relief army. This force is defeated and scatters amid an immense massacre. Alesia capitulates in the final months of 52.

On the day of the surrender, Vercingetorix puts on his finest armor and leaves the fortified encampment alone on a ceremonially harnessed horse. Proceeding at a walking pace, he enters the Roman camp, where Caesar, seated on a dais in the center of the camp, is awaiting him. He circles around him before dismounting and stripping himself of his weapons, then waits in silence before the victor. Caesar will keep him locked up in a cage for months, throwing food to him as if he were an animal, while he will sell his other prisoners of war as slaves, except for the Arverni and Aedui, who had surrendered. Then he will have Vercingetorix transferred to Rome and have him locked away in the deepest and innermost part of the *carcer*—a horrible and notorious prison, dug into the tufa in a slope of the Capitoline—in anticipation of displaying him among his spoils of war during the celebration of his own Gallic triumph.

The fall of Alesia signals the end of the revolt of the Gauls of Gallia Transalpina and completes the Roman conquest of Aquitania, Celtica, and Belgica that began in 58. From now on, all of Gallia Transalpina will be subjugated to Roman rule and colonized. Caesar will organize it into three provinces: Aquitania in the southwest, between the Pyrenees and the Loire; Lugdunensis in the center, up to the Seine and the Marne; and Belgica, furthest north, up to the Rhine.

The War in Retrospect

The Gallic Wars lasted a decade. Caesar pursued it with callousness, amid slaughter and destruction, fighting against more than 4 million enemies, subjugating 400 tribes and more than 800 cities (between those that rebelled and those that were subjugated for the first time), and annexing vast swathes of territory in Northwestern and Central Europe (corresponding to present-day France, Belgium, Luxembourg, and parts of Switzerland, the Netherlands, and Germany) and placing them under Roman sovereignty. The conflict hadn't been a preventive and defensive action, as Caesar endeavors to present it, nor a war waged as a defense against an existing threat or unrighteous threat (that is, from a concrete, imminent, and persistent danger), nor even was it an unjustifiably aggressive act of asserting one's own rights or those of others. It had been, instead, a war of conquest, waged out of a desire for glory and riches. Certainly, it is among the greatest undertakings in Roman history, but it is also one of the most costly for the vanquished. This becomes starkly apparent when considering that the Romans killed 1 million people,[6] perhaps 1,192,000,[7] and enslaved another million. 2 million people, compared to the total population of 8 million, means 25 percent, or one in four, were killed or enslaved.

In terms of loss of life, the cost of the defeat is so high that it could reasonably be argued that the Romans committed genocide against the Gallic, Helvetian, and Germanic populations affected by the war—not to mention the families destroyed, the communities dismembered, the riches plundered, and the suffering endured. All this explains why, among the more perceptive Romans, some will bluntly consider Caesar's conclusive victory in Gallia Transalpina as "an outrage committed upon mankind."[8]

Moreover, this isn't the first time that the Romans had methodically destroyed an ethnic group, sparing only its culture. Just remember the fate of the Boii, victims of slaughter and brutality during the Roman conquest of northern Italy (III–II century).

---

6   Plut. *Caes.*, 15.5 [(…) For although it was not full ten years that he waged war in Gaul, he took by storm more than eight hundred cities, subdued three hundred nations, and fought pitched battles at different times with three million men, of whom he slew one million in hand-to-hand fighting and took as many more prisoner. (…)]; Plut. *Pomp.*, 67.6 [(…) taking a hundred times ten thousand prisoners, and slaying as many, after routing them on the battle-field.]; App. *BC*, fragment 20a.

7   Plin., 7.25. However, the estimates vary. Vell. Pat., II.60.5, II.47.1, speaks of 400,000 dead and a greater number of prisoners. Plut. *Cat. Min.*, 51.1 Plutarch speaks of 300,000 Germans being slain, while App. *BC* 1.12 speaks of 400,000 dead just in the campaign against the Usipetes and Teutones, conducted in 55.

8   Plin., 7.25. See also L. Canfora, *Giulio Cesare. Il dittatore democratic* (Roma-Bari: Laterza, 1999), 135–139.

CHAPTER XXI

The End of the Triumvirate

An Excellent Murder

For several years, Clodius has been one of the central protagonists of public life. In 58, as tribune of the plebs, he embarked on a particularly intense legislative project that weakened the Senate and strengthened the public assemblies. Later, the fact that he wasn't successful in preventing the Senate from politically rehabilitating Cicero—by officially recalling him to his homeland, reinstating him with his senatorial *dignitas* and compensating him for the damage done—caused him to lose prestige. In the meantime, he formed a mob, which he used to intimidate the Senate, magistrates, popular assemblies, and individual Roman citizens. In 56, he was elected to the aedileship in an atmosphere of fear and intimidation. His administration of public duties and, above all, the organization of public games, made him more popular than ever before. In 53, he ran as a candidate for the praetorship for 52, unveiling a "revolutionary"[1] program and running his entire electoral campaign under the banner of attacks on his competitor Titus Milo. The latter was unpopular with Pompey, but he was supported by Cato and Cicero,[2] who wanted to use him against Clodius.

A few days before the elections for the magistracies for 52, Clodius is killed. The motives for the murder are hatred and vendetta. Milo is behind it. The ones doing the dirty work are some of Milo's hirelings, headed by Marcus Saufeius.[3] The scene

---

1 One of the legislative initiatives put forward by Clodius regarded the further distribution of freedmen through the tribes, as they were then limited to the four urban tribes (the aim was to have them registered with the 31 rural tribes as well). *See* Cic. Mil., 33, 87. It seems that another regarded the modality of the manumission of slaves. *See* Cic. Mil., 33, 89.
2 Cic. *Mil.*, 25.
3 The incident of Clodius's murder is told in different ways by different authors so the exact course of events isn't certain. One version is the Ciceronian one, as recounted in his oration *In defense of Milo*. This dramatizes the homonymous speech given by Cicero during Milo's trial on 8 April 52. It is commonly believed by scholars that it isn't a very reliable version. Another very thorough version is provided by the commentary of Quintus Asconius Pedianus (9 BC–76 AD) on the Ciceronian *In defense of Milo*. See A. C. Q. Clark, *Asconii Pediani Orationum Ciceronis quinque enarratio* (Oxford: Oxford University Press, 1907).

of the crime is the stretch of the Via Appia between Aricia and Bovillae, nearer to the latter, close to the *sacrarium* (shrine) of Bona Dea, profaned by Clodius in recent years, and a trattoria with adjoining rooms.

Bovillae (district of Frattocchie in the commune of Marino) is on the crossroads of the Via delle Transumanze with the Via Appia. It is the first residential area encountered after leaving Rome by the Via Appia. Some lands in the area were bought by Caius Julius Caesar III, Caesar's grandfather, with the money that he obtained from Quintus Lutatius Catulus, to whom he had given up his son Quintus for adoption. He hoped to draw enough income from the transaction to allow his other two male children—Lucius and Caius—to embark on a career through the magistracies.

Aricia (Ariccia) is the second civilian town on the Via Appia after Bovillae, less than 30 km to the south of Rome. Its urban layout sprawls over both the plain at the foot of a hill and on its sides and summit. Clodius had gone there to visit the local senate and took the opportunity to carry out an inspection of his farms in Bovillae. In the early morning of 18 January 52, he sets off again for Rome together with his friends Publius Pomponius and Caius Causinius Schola, as well as about 30 of his slaves, all armed with swords, who acted as his escort. The group are traveling on horseback. The Pomponius in question is a member of the familial clan to which Titus Pomponius Atticus, the close friend of Cicero, also belongs (the *gens Pomponia* is made up of half-a-dozen families: Rufus, Matho, Veientanus, Bononiensis, Molo, Musa). Schola gave false testimony in favor of Clodius during the Bona Dea scandal trial of 61, at which Clodius was accused of sacrilege.

Clodius and his companions haven't yet left the lands of Bovillae when they come across another group of travelers who are heading in the opposite direction. These travelers are Milo, his wife and a friend, some servants, and a few youths who are little more than adolescents, all traveling on a wagon, in addition to their escort formed of numerous slaves, including gladiators. Two members of the escort are called Eudamus and Birria. The group are making for Lanuvium (Lanuvio). Milo had appeared in the Senate in Rome early that morning, before leaving for Lanuvium to participate in the ceremony for the appointment of the new priest of Juno Sospita, scheduled for the following day.

When the two groups pass each other, Clodius and Milo give each other a contemptuous look, but they remain silent and continue on their way. Fighting talk is, however, exchanged between the escorts. Some of them come to blows, and uproar breaks out. Clodius turns around, yelling and making threats. Birria, without giving him the time to defend himself, thrusts his sword into his shoulder. Clodius collapses, bleeding profusely. His companions carry him in their arms to the nearby inn. Clodius's fate is decided in a few minutes. Milo has a golden opportunity to get rid of his hated enemy for good, and he judges that it will be easier for him to wriggle out of the accusation of killing Clodius than it would be to avoid his retaliation, were he to survive his injury.[4] He orders Saufeius to drag Clodius out of the inn and kill him. He obeys. Clodius is dispatched, together with part of his escort, while the survivors flee. Milo and his men hurry away from the scene of the crime. The bloody bodies of the victims are left abandoned on the roadway.

Shortly afterwards, the old senator Sextus Tedius passes by, returning to Rome from the countryside. He travels on a litter, also under escort. The scene that appears before him is spine-chilling. Numerous lacerated bodies are lying on the cobblestones in the shade of the line of trees that follows the road. One of them is Clodius, perfectly recognizable. It is somewhat ironic that he has been dumped on the road that one of his ancestors, the censor Appius Claudius Pulcher, had built in 312. Tedius has Clodius's corpse placed on his own litter and orders the litter-bearers and his escort to take it to Rome. He will go back on foot, alone, probably to keep himself away from the chaos that will inevitably break out in Rome as soon as Clodius's body arrives in the city.

In fact, the news of the bloodshed strikes Rome like a bolt of lightning, followed by an explosion of thunder. It sparks a chain of events that will leave a mark on the history of the city. Plebeians and slaves converge in droves on Clodius's house on the Palatine, where his body is lying in the atrium, while Fulvia, his widow, cries and grieves over him, showing the bloody corpse to the crowd and stoking its rage. The throng that gathers in front of the building's entrance grows as the hours go by. Everyone wants to go in to honor the deceased, pass by him in a reverent manner, and offer their condolences to the family. The crowd is such that, at Fulvia's request, some friends, clients, and slaves squeeze together in front of the door, forming a chain with their arms and setting their feet in the ground, to stop more people from coming in. Some among the crowd stand on tiptoe to try to see through the blocked doorway, but they can't see anything due to the confused dance of lights and shadows. The gathering continues to grow in silence, filled with an atmosphere anticipation. A vigil is kept over the body all night (18/19 January 52).

The following morning, an even bigger crowd, led by Sextus Cloelius, forms a cortège and follows the bloody body of the victim, who, laid in an open casket, is carried on the shoulders of the mourners down to the square in the Forum, which is crammed with people.

Cloelius, we recall, has been one of Clodius's closest collaborators. In 58, he embarked on an initiative that was to procure widespread support both for him and for Clodius. With the backing of the then consul Piso Caesoninus, the *ludi Compitalicii*, banned by a law from 64, were celebrated. A few days later, Clodius promoted and obtained approval for a plebiscite that sought the legalization of the

---

4   Dio Cass., XL.48.2.

collegia, which had been outlawed by the Senate, and to increase the number of those eligible for the free grain dole (*frumentationes*). Cloelius was later tasked with presiding over the *frumentationes* by Clodius. Cloelius held onto this office until September 57, when it was passed on to Pompey. In the meantime, in 58, Cloelius had tasked Clodius with detaining Prince Tigranes, the son of Tigranes II of Armenia (r. 95–55), by force if necessary, and he had been involved in a violent encounter with a group of Pompeians in which the *eques* Marcus Papirius was killed. In 56, again under orders from Clodius, Cloelius set fire to the Temple of the Nymphs in Rome, where the lists of those entitled to benefit as *frumentationes* were kept, to prevent Pompey from erasing the names recently added by Clodius.

An atmosphere of tension and collective unrest, chaotic and noisy, hovers over the Forum. Some commoners lay Clodius's body on the speaker's platform,[5] where, immediately afterwards, the tribunes Titus Munatius Plancus and Quintus Pompeius Rufus, close friends of the victim, give the funeral oration. After this, other commoners, led by Cloelius, remove the dead man from the Rostra and take it into the Curia Hostilia. The *exequies* conclude with the body being cremated on the spot, under pressure from the crowd, in an atmosphere of general commotion.

The corpse is placed on a huge pile of various materials (seats, desks, tables, documents, writing tablets), all stacked up. When the improvised pyre is set alight, the fire rapidly spreads to the roof of the building and from there to the adjacent buildings, one of which is the Basilica Porcia.

The Curia burns violently and disintegrates in tall flames of destruction. The huge bonfire burns for a day and a night. The glow of the flames adds to that of the sun and lights up the night like a sinister moon attracting moths. The crackle of burning wood will remain in the ears of those willing souls who try in vain to put the fire out. In the end, the entire structure is reduced to a heap of smoking ruins covered in ash.[6]

While the embers of the Curia were burning, a large crowd in the throes of excitement gathers outside Milo's residence and forcibly tries to enter it, with evidently awful intentions, but it is repulsed and dispersed by guards, who let fly with arrows.

The Curia blaze continues as a rowdy crowd swarms out of the city through the Esquiline Gate and reaches an area where flowers are grown for use in cult practices and the ornamentation of tombs, and where there is also a sacred wood, within which is the Temple of Libitina, the goddess of funerals and burial rites. Those who handle funerary rites are in the habit of meeting there, and it is also there where

---

5   On the display of Clodius's body: Asc. *Mil.*, pp. 32–33; A. C. Q. Clark, *Asconii Pediani Orationum Ciceronis quinque enarratio* (Oxford: Oxford University Press, 1907).

6   On the cremation of Clodius: Cic. *Mil.*, 90; Asc. *Mil.,* p. 33; A. C. Q. Clark, *Asconii Pediani Orationum Ciceronis quinque enarratio* (Oxford: Oxford University Press, 1907); Plin., XXXIV.21.

the *fasces* are kept, which, during funerals of magistrates *cum imperio*, are borne by the *lictors*, pointing downward.

The crowd force their way into the temple and seize the *fasces* during the chaos, accompanied by a loud mix of voices and noises. Then they return to the city and take the *fasces* first to the house of Publius Plautius Hypsaeus and then to that of Metellus Pius Scipio Nasica. Later, they move to the Pincian Hill, a low rise that overlooks the Campus Martius and is home to villas and gardens, and, in front of Pompey's townhouse, protected by armed guards, acclaim Pompey dictator. The collective unrest subsides in the early afternoon when feasts are held in honor of the deceased in the streets and squares. Then it resumes. In the end, the crowds return to the Forum where they will remain, their clamor unceasing, all night.

Milo returns to Rome on the evening of January 19 and learns that the friends of Clodius have spread malicious rumors about him to cast him in a sinister light. They say he stormed Clodius's country villa at Bovillae—that he had gone out in search of Clodius's son but, having not found him, tortured a slave to death to find out where he was; that he had the throats of the villa overseer and another two slaves cut; that he had killed another 11 men who had tried to defend the property, together with others; that two of his own men had suffered injuries.

Milo tries in vain to silence these rumors, freeing 12 of his slaves and distributing 400 sesterces to each citizen through the tribes. When he realizes the futility of his efforts and the growing hostility around him, he goes to Pompey to offer to withdraw his candidacy. Pompey feels embarrassed. He dissuades Milo from withdrawing from the contest, not to show him friendship but to avoid making it seem that he has power over him, that is, that Milo is one of his men.

Gangs of criminals are running riot and clashing violently with each other in every corner of the city. On the 19th, or more likely on the 20th or 21st, Clodius's men besiege, storm, and devastate the house of the *interrex* Marcus Aemilius Lepidus, consul in 46, because the five days of his mandate had expired to no avail (he should have called the elections for the civil magistracies for the following year but hadn't done so). Milo's gang shows up as well, also to demand that the elections are called. The two gangs confront each other. Lepidus barely manages to save himself.[7]

Protests are loudly voiced, other voices are raised in retorts, and insults are bandied about in an atmosphere filled with tension. On January 23, the tribune of the plebs Pompeius Rufus, who was closest to Clodius, holds a *contio* in which he accuses Milo of wanting to make an attempt on Pompey's life.[8] It isn't true, but nothing is off-limits in this game.

On the 27th, another tribune of the plebs, Marcus Caelius Rufus, holds a *contio* in the square in the Forum. He defends Milo saying that Clodius hadn't been attacked

---

7   Cic. *Mil.*, 13; Asc. *Mil.*, p. 43; *Schol. Bob.*, p. 281.
8   Asc. *Mil.*, p. 51 C.

by Milo, but rather it had been him who had attempted to ambush Milo and, instead, he had come off the worst. Milo and his men had done nothing other than defend themselves; if they had killed Clodius, it had been in self-defense. Caelius is probably acting in this way at the instigation of, or after being inspired by, Cicero, his former teacher and his friend. Caelius had reconciled with Cicero after the latter defended him in court against the accusations of having stolen Clodia's jewelry and having attempted to kill her, ensuring his acquittal.

When Caelius is finished, Milo speaks. He accuses Clodius of having been destitute, and a friend of the destitute who had set fire to the Curia. The *contio* ends in violence. Some of Clodius's supporters—the tribunes of the plebs belonging to the Populares faction, some citizens, and slaves—all armed with swords, pounce on the crowd, killing anyone within reach, no matter whether they were friends of Milo's or not, or whether citizens or foreigners. Mainly, they are targeting those who are well-dressed or are wearing a gold ring on their finger, signifying, in effect, that they are senators. Then the violence spreads to the Curia, and the Temple of Castor and Pollux, propagated by men bearing firebrands and scythes, while other armed men range over the entire Forum.[9] The turmoil degenerates into hellish chaos, with fires, robberies, looting, and every other crime or felony. On the pretext of searching for friends of Milo, armed men enter homes by force, turn them upside down in search of valuables, and remove anything of value that they find and can easily take away with them. Caelius and Milo flee, disguised as slaves.

Other *contiones* follow, in which Pompeius Rufus and his colleagues Caius Sallustius Crispus and Plancus Bursa, who convened them, insist that Milo is planning to kill Pompey and ask the "intended victim" whether he can prove it. Pompey responds that a certain Licinius, an innkeeper near the Circus Maximus, told him that some of Milo's servants, who Licinius named and described as utterly drunk, had confessed that they were ready to kill Pompey and that, later, one of them had stabbed him so that he would not report them. Milo is asked if he owns the slaves who have been named as conspirators. Milo answers that he has freed some of them and doesn't know the rest.

The flurry of rumors continues, increasing the levels of uncertainty and confusion. There is talk of Milo making hideouts, and weapons caches available in the city.[10] The situation remains unsteady, confused, tense, and dangerous for the next five weeks, during which Pompey maintains a passive attitude, while Cloelius works the plebeians up against Milo, pointing to him as Clodius's assassin and showing the people the texts of the proposed laws that Clodius would have wanted to put forward, had he been elected.

9   Cic. *Mil.*, 91.
10 Cic. *Mil.*, 64.

The *Senatus Consultum Ultimum* of February 52

Public order is dangerously unsettled, the elections for the magistracies for 52 cannot be held, the safety of citizens has been jeopardized, and the authorities are powerless to remedy the situation. It is worth dwelling on this final issue. Rome lacks a police force, and there can be no question of the army intervening. Firstly, it is prohibited for troops to enter the city (this is a measure designed to prevent *coups d'état*). Secondly, it is rare that the legions are camped on the Campus Martius. Usually, they are quartered in Capua, a city in Campania, about 170 km south of Rome. The only constitutional organ that can do anything in circumstances such as these is the Senate. It can charge a consul or a praetor with forming a militia.

The Senate gathers again between 3 and 10 February 52, outside the city, probably on the Pincian Hill, both because the Curia is unusable due to the fire and to allow Pompey to participate at the meeting (Pompey has been invested with a military command, and therefore he cannot pass over the *pomerium*). The meeting takes place under the protection of Pompey's soldiers. The agenda is full of items. After the ritual preliminaries, the Senate resolves to recover the half-burned body of Clodius, left abandoned in the rubble of the Curia and prey to stray dogs, and to grant him funeral honors and a burial. Then it agrees to rebuild the Curia and hands responsibility for so doing to Faustus Cornelius Sulla, son of the dictator Lucius, who died in 78. Sulla had been quaestor in 54 and is Pompey's son-in-law. He will call the new building the Curia Cornelia, in memory of his father, who had enlarged the Curia Hostilia in 82.

The subject of debate moves on to another topic. Marcus Calpurnius Bibulus takes the floor. Bibulus, remember, had been consul in 59, "the year of the consuls Julius and Caesar." He is Cato's son-in-law and, like him, is a hyper-conservative. Recently, he has frequently attacked Pompey in the Senate, blaming him for the gang warfare unleashed in the city by Clodius and Milo, so much so that Pompey had been convinced that Bibulus was one of those who wanted to kill him. Moreover, Bibulus voted against the proposal to task Pompey with command of the military undertaking that would have restored Ptolemy XII Auletes to the throne of Egypt. When, just recently, the Catonian faction ceased being hostile toward Pompey, Bibulus's outlook also changed, and he put forward the idea of a joint consulship for Caesar and Pompey.

Bibulus goes even further. To bring the emergency that has been sparked in the city after the death of Clodius back under control, to overcome the impasse caused by the impossibility of electing new magistrates, and to avoid having to appoint a dictator—the precedent represented by Sulla's dictatorship still weighs heavy— he suggests appointing an *ad hoc* magistrate, specifically a *consul sine collega*, "single consul," and suggests Pompey as a candidate. It is worth drawing attention to the fact that the political system doesn't recognize the position of *consul sine collega* and that this nomenclature avoids giving the name "dictator" to the magistrate to be appointed to the office, even though in practice it means the same thing. A long discussion follows, during which Cato announces himself to be in favor of Bibulus's proposal, explaining that any form of power is preferable to anarchy and that Pompey, if he becomes the single consul, will solve the present difficulties in the best way and will save the city.[11]

The nominee would have the powers of both consuls in his hands. But the Senate rejects this proviso. After a long discussion, which at times gets very lively, a compromise is reached. The Senate declares that it will allow Pompey to select a colleague in two months' time. That is, it gives Pompey the authority to choose his colleague and collaborate with another.

The tribunes of the plebs belonging to the Populares faction press Pompey to co-opt Caesar, his former father-in-law and current fellow triumvir, but Pompey chooses Quintus Caecilius Metellus Pius Scipio Nasica, praetor in 55, his current father-in-law, in whom he has absolute trust. The fact that Scipio Nasica was in court due to being tried for electoral fraud doesn't present an obstacle, as the case is withdrawn.

The Rapprochement of Pompey with the Optimates

The nomination of Scipio Nasica as Pompey's colleague in the consulship reflects a rapprochement between Pompey and the Metelli and, more generally, with the Optimates. In fact, Scipio Nasica, born in 98 from the marriage of Publius Cornelius Scipio Nasica (praetor in 93) with Licinia, had been adopted by Quintus Caecilius Metellus Pius, *pontifex maximus* from 81 to 63 and consul in 80. Therefore, he now is a full-fledged Metellus, and the Metelli are the spearheads of the Optimates in the Senate, tied to other families of illustrious and ancient nobility, such as the *Scaevolae*.

To seal the deal with Scipio Nasica, Pompey remarries again, this time to Quintus Caecilius Metellus Pius Scipio Nasica's daughter Cornelia Metella, the widow of Publius Licinius Crassus, son of the triumvir Crassus, who fell at Carrhae with his father.

Cornelia Metella is a beautiful woman with a pleasant character, well versed in geometry and philosophy, and an expert lyrist. She is Pompey's fifth wife. His previous wives, as a reminder, were Antistia (86–82, whom Pompey had divorced), Aemilia (married in 82, who left Pompey a widower); Julia, (Caesar's daughter, married in 61, who also predeceased her husband); and Mucia Tertia (who, after her divorce from Pompey, got married again to Marcus Aemilius Scaurus, praetor in 56).

---

11 Plut. *Cat. Min.*, 47.3–4.

To make himself free to marry Julia, Pompey had divorced Mucia Tertia after 18 years of marriage, reproaching her for committing too much adultery, including with Caesar himself. (Pompey, by marrying Julia, had wedded the daughter of someone who had had an affair with his wife!) In 54 Julia died in childbirth, and Pompey started to gradually grow further apart from Caesar. This drift started from the fact that Pompey was increasingly being placed in a mediatory position between Caesar and his political adversaries, something that had never previously happened. This was accentuated during the Gallic Wars, during which time Pompey gradually became increasingly cognizant of the fact that Caesar's successes could overshadow his own. The more Pompey distanced himself from Caesar, the more he drew closer to the Optimates, his old friends. He had gravitated toward them before making the Triumvirate pact; it must be said in this regard that Quintus Mucius Scaevola Pontifex, the father of Mucia Tertia and therefore Pompey's father-in-law, was one of the most prominent Optimates, as was his relative Quintus Mucius Scaevola Augur.

In short, the marriage of Pompey to Cornelia Metella restored the entente between Pompey and the Optimates, which had been broken by his repudiation of Mucia Tertia. The rapprochement of Pompey with the Optimates marks the definitive end of his political association with Caesar, therefore the death of the Triumvirate. This agreement had already begun to falter because of the death of Julia. The subsequent death of Crassus deprived it of the element that was keeping it in a state of equilibrium.

The Optimates are hostile to Caesar not only because he leads the opposing *pars* but also because they are shocked by the power and the glory that he has derived from his own sensational victories in the Gallic Wars, and they fear him no less than Pompey. They would like to get rid of Caesar, a fearsome rival. To remove him from the political scene, they are waiting for the right occasion to drag him to court with a reasonable hope of finding him guilty and sentencing him to death or exile. They are ready to accuse him of a series of wrongdoings that they allege he committed during his consulship in 59, as well as others that are also attributable to him. To do so, however, they must wait until Caesar's current appointments to the office of proconsul end because while he remains in post, he will be protected by immunity from prosecution. Unable to do anything else, the Optimates are trying to remove Caesar from his offices before their natural expiration. They know this is within their grasp because the Senate of Rome is the constitutional body in charge of the administration of the state, and they have a majority within it.

Among the Optimates, the group most hostile toward Caesar is its extreme right wing, that is, the Catonian faction. Cato is opposed to Caesar for personal as well as political reasons. On the one hand, he fears that Caesar wants to abolish the *res publica* and have himself appointed as dictator for life, in effect, that he wants to make himself king (in the past, Cato thought the same of Pompey; now he argues that the only Roman who is able to stand up to Caesar is Pompey); on the other hand, he hasn't forgiven Caesar for having damaged the integrity of his half-sister Servilia by making her—a married woman—his lover.

Ultimately, to sum up, a convergence of interests between Pompey and the Optimates has arisen, which is the result of the crisis of the Triumvirate, primed by the death of Crassus and explosively set off by the death of Julia.

After becoming consul together with Scipio Nasica, Pompey intervenes to put an end to the gang warfare and prosecute those responsible for the disorder and crimes committed after the Clodius's death. One of the measures he adopts is to order the arrest and incarceration pending trial of Milo and Saufeius, accused of being the instigator and perpetratorof Clodius's assassination.

The Trials of Milo and Saufeius

Pompey returns to Rome before the conscription drive is complete. Later, in the preliminary phase of the trial of Milo and Saufeius, he grants the request of Clodius's two nephews to interrogate the slaves of Milo as well as those of his wife. Clodius's nephews are both called Appius and are the sons of Caius Claudius Pulcher, the brother of Clodius. Caius Claudius Pulcher had been praetor in 56.

Milo turns up to the preliminary hearing with a retinue of people of significant reputation and prestige: Cicero, Hortensius, Cato, Faustus Cornelius Sulla, Marcus Claudius Marcellus (praetor in 54), and Marcus Calidius (praetor in 57). But this will not prevent him from being remanded for sentencing together with Saufeius.

After 23 or 24 February 52, Pompey presents two of his own legislative projects to the Senate of Rome that will create tougher punishments for the *crimen ambitus* and the *crimen vis* and drastically reduce the duration of trials by convening the cross-examination of witnesses and the orations of the prosecution and the defense, which could last up to two and three hours, respectively, on the same day.

The *crimen ambitus* relates to electoral corruption. The bill allows anyone who has been a magistrate since 70 to be challenged, while also guaranteeing immunity to anyone who, once convicted, can ensure the conviction of another for a more serious crime.[12] All evidence suggests that this reflects Pompey's intention to consider his regime as totalitarian and to clear the decks of his enemies. The retroactivity of the bill is opposed by Cato. In turn, Hortensius criticizes the bill, arguing that Clodius's murder, the burning of the Curia, and the assault on Lepitus's house are indeed crimes against the state, but they can be judged according to the legislation in force, which, at the very most, should only be modified to streamline the procedure. The tribunes Plancus Bursa and Sallustius prevent the Senate from deciding in favour of the procedure by using their veto.[13]

---

12 See L. Fezzi, *Il dado* è tratto. Cesare e la resa di Roma (Roma-Bari: Laterza, 2017), 119.
13 Cic. *Mil.*, 14.

The *crimen vis* regards acts of physical violence carried out against magistrates and senators, perpetrated with a view to impeding the normal and free course of public gatherings and, more generally, of the functions of the state. This crime has been provided for by the *lex Plautia de vi* (89?) and is punishable by death, without prejudice to commuting the capital punishment to a lifelong exile at the request of the condemned. In Pompey's draft law *de vi*, explicit reference is made to a concrete case to which the law, once it has been approved, can and must be applied. In fact, it explicitly says *de caede … in qua P. Clodius occisus esset*, that is, of the murder of Clodius (but also of the burning of the Curia Hostilia and of the assault on Lepidus's property). It is precisely for this reason that the tribune of the plebs Marcus Caelius Rufus judges the bill to be specifically aimed at Milo and threatens to use his veto (but he will not follow through on this). Pompey retorts that he is ready to defend the *res publica* by force of arms, if necessary. Around 26 March, Pompey's legislative proposals are approved by the people gathered in assembly. The *lex Cornelia de ambitu* and the *lex Cornelia de vi* thus enter into force.

Milo's trial is held from 4–8 April 52. Saufeius will be tried separately, albeit soon. Presiding over the court is the former consul Lucius Domitius Ahenobarbus. The charge is *crimen vis*. The trial acts on the accusation made against Milo by Pompeius Rufus and the lawsuit filed against him by Appius Claudius Pulcher, Marcus Antonius, and Publius Valerius Nepos.

Cicero—who until now has never missed an opportunity to accuse Clodius of any atrocity, calling him a corrupt, violent demagogue—takes up the defense of the accused, along with Cato and Hortensius. He has already skillfully defended a man accused of *crimen vis* in court in 56. On that occasion, the defendant was the tribune of the plebs Publius Sestius, who was accused of having sent an armed gang against that of Clodius to ensure Cicero's official recall from exile (*In Defense of Publius Sestius*). In his oration *In Defense of Titus Annius Milo*, Cicero imputes Clodius for having introduced violence into political discourse and describes the somber days in which Clodius and his entourage of slaves and clients had been rampant in Rome.[14]

As for the circumstances in which Clodius met his death, Cicero espouses the hypothesis of Caelius, according to which Clodius hadn't been attacked by Milo, but had instead ambushed him and had ended up coming off worst. Therefore, the defense's argument is that Clodius had premeditated the attack on Milo, who, having been assaulted, had defended himself, killing his attacker. As proof of Clodius's murderous intention, Cicero cites both the threats that he had made to Milo in public, prior to 18 January, and his hasty departure from Rome due, in his opinion, to his restlessness aimed at catching Milo in an ambush.[15]

---

14 Cic. *Mil.*, 87.
15 Cic. *Mil.*, 29.

Fulvia, Clodius's widow, is present at the trial, accompanied by her mother. She testifies in tears, eliciting deep feelings of emotion from those present.[16] Further testimonies on the assault on the inn where the injured Clodius had been taken prior to being dragged outside and killed are given by some residents of Bovillae. Moreover, during the hearing, the arguments of the prosecution are shared and made by Pompey. This shows that Milo has become an embarrassing issue for the Optimates, one that must be jettisoned, and the path to doing so is already clear.

When the trial reaches sentencing and the jury must establish whether the accused is guilty or not, 41 jurors—comprising senators, *equites*, and tribunes—out of the 54 present and voting, find him guilty. As such, Milo is sentenced to exile. He will seek refuge in Massilia in Gallia Narbonensis. However, he hasn't left the scene for good; this isn't the last we'll hear of him.

The trial of Saufeius takes place in the same month, April 52. At first, the accused is defended by Cicero and Caelius; later, he is defended by Cicero and Marcus Terentius Varro Gibba. In the end, he is acquitted.

---

16   On Fulvia's deposition: Asc. *Mil.*, pp. 32–33, 40; A. C. Q. Clark, *Asconii Pediani Orationum Ciceronis quinque enarratio* (Oxford: Oxford University Press, 1907).

CHAPTER XXII

Caesar's Friction with the Senate

A Question of Prorogations

Once the opportunity to become consul alongside Pompey vanishes, there is nothing left for Caesar to do other than to focus on the objective of being appointed for 48. This means that to run as a candidate in July 49, he will have to present himself in person and as a "common man" to the consul who presides over the polling station in Rome. And herein lies the problem.

It is worth reminding ourselves that Caesar currently holds the proconsulship of Gallia Narbonensis, and the proconsulship of Gallia Cisalpina and Illyricum. These roles were conferred to him by law (*lex Pompeia Licinia de provincia Caii Iulii Caesaris*) in 55. Both have a duration of five years and expire on 28 February 50.

We should also recall that Caesar is in the midst of a campaign in Gallia Transalpina, and everything suggests that hostilities will last for a long time yet. It isn't a given that this conflict will have ended by July 49. Even if it were, however, Caesar doesn't want to relinquish his offices, still less his *imperium* associated with the former, before becoming consul on 1 January 48 (he takes it as read that, if he runs, he will be elected). This is principally because being a magistrate in office guarantees him immunity from prosecution, protecting him from any future legal cases.

If he is taken to court, he risks not being able to run as a candidate, either because he is subject to legal proceedings or because he has been sentenced to a punishment that precludes him from holding public office. To avoid running this risk, he must ensure the date his proconsulships end is prorogued from 1 March 50 to 31 December 49. This would allow him to maintain his legal immunity until 1 January 48.

The problem could be resolved through the approval of one law that extends Caesar's mandates and another law that authorizes Caesar to participate in the elections *in absentia*, justifying his candidacy by the safeguarding of the public interest. There is no lack of precedents. Caius Marius, Caesar's uncle, had been a candidate *ex officio* for the consulship. This didn't happen just once but on several consecutive occasions because he appeared to be the only commander capable of leading the army to victory in the Cimbrian War (113–101). Caesar is thus obligated by circumstances to hold onto his public offices until 31 December 49.

In April 52, the tribune of the plebs Marcus Caelius Rufus takes advantage of the wave of excitement caused by the victory at Alesia to put forward a plebiscite that seeks to secure Caesar's candidacy for the consulship for 48 if, on the date the elections are called, the Gallic War is not yet over and there is thus a need to ensure continuity in the running of military operations in Gallia Transalpina. Before undertaking this initiative, to cover himself, Caelius had secured the support of Cicero, not so much because the latter is his teacher and mentor, but rather because he is on good terms with both Caesar and Cato and has a huge influence in the Senate, particularly on those who are indecisive, of whom there are always many.

All other nine tribunes of the plebs—Caelius is the 10th out of 10—support the plebiscite. Cato is strongly opposed to it. He says he considers it outrageous that Caesar cannot be arraigned to answer for his crimes in court because he is always protected by immunity. He refuses to compromise. He tries to isolate it politically, arguing the good name of the *res publica* is at stake. But it is all in vain. The proposal is sent on to the *comitia tributa*, which will vote on it and approve it. A law thus comes into force that authorizes Caesar's candidacy *in absentia* for the elections for the consulship for 48.

It is clear Caelius had been able to have his plebiscite approved because Pompey let it happen. Soon afterwards, however, Pompey's helpful demeanor toward Caesar is contradicted by the presentation of two draft laws, which, all the evidence suggests, were aimed at silencing the Catonian faction.

The first aims to create a general law abstracting from and binding a *senatus consultum* of 53 that established that senior ex-magistrates could not be appointed to the governorship of another province before five years since the expiration of their previous governmental mandate had elapsed. This was intended to avoid the risk that they abused their functions to recoup their electoral expenses and pocket some additional money into the bargain.

The second is a general law on magistrates. Among other things, it states that aspiring candidates must present themselves in person to the consul presiding over the elections in Rome.

Both bills are approved by the people gathered in assembly. The *lex Pompeia de provinciis consularibus* and the *lex Pompeia de iure magistratuum* thus enter into force. It escapes no one's notice that these laws conflict with the law that allowed Caesar to run as a candidate *in absentia* for the consulship for 48, rendering this privilege impracticable. In short, Pompey has given Caesar what he wants with one hand, and then taken it away with the other.

Caesar Enlists Troops

Until now, Caesar has shown flexibility, but he no longer wants to be subject to the machinations of his adversaries, whom he regards as a clique of envious, petty individuals. He fears that Cato and Pompey want to repay him for the world of good he has done for the state with the humiliation of a trial like Milo's, which had been held in a place surrounded by armed men, with an intimidated defense, and a hasty sentencing decided under pressure from the onlookers. He is anxious at the thought that they want to deprive him of his dignity— understood as his rank, political position and related privileges—and his reputation, and that they are willing to do anything to prevent him from accomplishing the success that is rightfully due to him for his great military achievements in Gaul, Germania, and Britannia and from realizing his grand plan for glory in his life, to which he has felt predestined since childhood.

As for Pompey in particular, Caesar sees him as an invidious and ungrateful man. Pompey—he considers—fears that he, Caesar, could overshadow his glory and pretends to forget about the help he has been given. Caesar also sees Pompey as a hypocrite because he bragged about having restored the prerogatives of the tribunes of the plebs, which had been annulled by Sulla, but then refused to allow the holders to exercise them.

However, Caesar does not waver from his goal. When he showers the electorate with money to bribe them and flatters and seduces his fellow citizens with his charisma, he sends a clear message to all those who have ears to listen; he is announcing a conscription drive in both of his provinces. He impertinently asserts that he is authorized to do so by the *senatus consultum* that authorized Pompey to enlist troops. But he knows perfectly well that this resolution by the Senate was only addressed to Pompey and that it referred only to *Italia propria*, not Gallia Cisalpina. *Italia propria*, remember, is that part of the Italian peninsula that lies south of the imaginary line that joins the mouth of the Magra in Tuscany to the mouth of the Rubicon in Emilia-Romagna. Gallia Cisalpina, on the other hand, corresponds to northern Italy, understood as the remaining part of the Italian peninsula between the Alpine arc, the Ligurian Sea, the Apennines, and the Adriatic Sea. It is evident that Caesar's actions are fracturing the constitution, which sets him against the law, the state, the Senate, Pompey, and all the interlacing powers and interests that wrap themselves around the highest offices of state.

By order of Caesar, as many recruits as are needed to form a legion are enlisted in Gallia Cisalpina. The new unit is called the *Legio V Alaudae*, from the tall crest that decorates the helmets of its soldiers, typical among Gallic warriors. It isn't a "regular" unit of the Roman army because it hadn't been enlisted based on a recruitment notice issued by the Senate of Rome. This means that it is maintained by Caesar himself, with his own money, unlike the two legions stationed in Gallia Cisalpina and the seven legions stationed across Gallia Transalpina,[1] who instead are paid by the state.

The signal is received loud and clear, and it is understood in its exact, intimidatory meaning. Pompey proposes and obtains approval for a bill that modifies the *lex Pompeia de iure magistratuum* by exempting Caesar from the obligation to present himself as a candidate in person.

Caesar's Building Interventions in the Area of the Forum

Since 54, Caesar has been promoting a program of building works with a view to improving his standing with the Senate, increasing the vast levels of approval he holds among the middle classes and the urban plebeians, widening the scale of the political, administrative, and religious center of the city, and celebrating himself. To meet the related costs, he has used his own share of the spoils of war accumulated in Gaul.

The projects include the construction of a new forum (Forum Iulium, or the Forum of Caesar), which will be added to the existing one (which from now on will be called the Forum Vetus, where *vetus* means old), the construction of the Basilica Iulia, the demolition of the Grecostasis and the *Comitium*, and the demolition and subsequent reconstruction of the Tribune of the Orators (*rostra*) and of the Curia Hostilia. All these interventions will be focused on the northern side of the Forum Vetus, which will therefore be reorganized.

Caesar has chosen a densely populated area of the city center for his building site. This means that although the lands to be expropriated to carry out the work are all suitable for construction, the amount of compensation to be paid to the owners is huge: 60–100 million sesterces.[2] The total cost of the works, therefore, is gigantic. The Roman people will judge this to be a crazy amount of money and will shake their heads in indignation.

But Caesar wants to show he is capable of overcoming any opposition and so he plows ahead undaunted, at the cost of casting hundreds of citizens out of their homes and exposing himself to the most uncharitable criticisms. The date of the start of construction work on the Forum Iulium is provided by the ceremonial laying of the foundation stone. This takes place at the end of April 51. Caesar will succeed in his project, but he won't live long enough to see his architectural "jewels" completed. Its first inauguration will take place—while work is still ongoing—on 26 September 46 (the anniversary of the Battle of Thapsus) and will pertain to the Basilica Iulia and the Forum Iulium. A second will occur at the start of the following October,

---

1   During the Gallic Wars, Caesar could count on 10 legions, but he had to hand two legions over to Pompey by order of the Senate. While waiting to be deployed in the war against the Parthians, which is currently being planned, these two legions are quartered in Capua.

2   Based on the exchange rate at the end of the I century, this equates to between 120/180 and 200/300 million euros.

coinciding with the celebration of the triumph for the victories won in Spain. The works will be suspended after the death of Caesar in 44, but will be resumed by his grandson Octavian, who will bring them to completion in 29.

Caesar proposes to Cicero, who accepts, that he takes on the task of supervising the acquisition of the worksites. On completion of this job, Cicero is appointed proconsul of Cilicia and is responsible for its government for 51 and 50. He has never suggested he would be open to taking on the office of a provincial governor; in fact, he has openly said that he prefers debates in the Senate and, more generally, political life in the capital, being with his family, and enjoying the pleasures of long stays in his villas. Ultimately, however, he could not shirk his duty. In the same round of appointments, Cato and Bibulus are appointed to the governorships of Sicily and Syria, respectively. Each appointment is for a two-year term. A military command is also linked to each office. Sicily, Syria, and Cilicia are each manned by two legions.

After Pompey's nomination as *consul sine collega* (52), Cato had retired to a private life, but he has remained a Pompeian. His appointment as governor of Sicily puts him back on the public scene. His office will have its seat in Syracuse, a city of grand traditions, situated on the coast at the very southeastern cusp of the island.

As for Bibulus, some say that the proconsulship is his reward for the support that he has been giving Pompey. In February 51, Bibulus leaves for Antioch on the Orontes, accompanied by his two sons, without imagining that he is leading them to an appointment with death. When the Parthian Pacorus invades Syria in 50, Bibulus sends his children to Alexandria in Egypt to negotiate the return of the Gabiniani to Syria so that he can use them for the defense of the province. The Gabiniani, we recall, are the Roman soldiers whom Gabinius, governor of Syria, left in Egypt after having brought Ptolemy XII Auletes (r. 80–58 and 55–51) back to power, to protect the royal family and ensure the political stability of the country. Since their arrival, however, the Gabiniani have integrated themselves into Egyptian society and married native women, and their ranks have been swelled by bandits and marauders of Syrian and Cilician origin. They have no intention of returning to active service in the employ of Rome. As soon as Bibulus's sons arrive in Alexandria, they are captured and tortured to death. Therefore, the slaughter of these two innocent youths must be placed within the context of the political situation in Egypt.

In this country, the current reigning monarchs are the legitimate heirs of Ptolemy XII Auletes: Cleopatra VII Philopator, little more than 20 years old, and Ptolemy XIII Theos Philopator, 13 or 14 years old.[3] They have two siblings: a sister, Arsinoe, and a brother who will, in the future, ascend to the throne with the regal name Ptolemy XIV. Arsinoe is younger than Cleopatra VII. Ptolemy XIV is younger than Ptolemy XIII. The law of the Pharaohs, taken up by the Ptolemies, allows royal princesses

---

3   Cleopatra VII's year of birth is unknown; it seems as though it should be placed around 70/69. Ptolemy XIII, meanwhile, was born in 62/61.

to be crowned as queens insofar as they are the wife of their brother-sovereign. Cleopatra VII has married Ptolemy XIII, becoming her father's true successor, since she is now old enough to know her own mind,, unlike Ptolemy XIII, who is little more than a child.

Not long after Cleopatra VII has ascended to the throne, a famine hits Egypt. As Alexandria has problems with its food supply, a joint edict from Cleopatra VII and Ptolemy XIII protects the transport of grain from Upper Egypt to the capital, threatening confiscations and punishments in the event of irregularities in the shipment of the harvest.[4]

On 27 October, the sovereigns send a letter to the *strategos* of the Heracleopolite Nome—the territory surrounding the city of Heracleopolis[5]—ordering him to deliver the entirety of the harvest, warning him that any deductions therefrom will be charged to him personally.[6]

---

4   *C. Ord. Ptol.* 73. *C. Ord. Ptol.* = M. Lenger, *Corpus des Ordonnances des Ptolémées* (Bruxelles, 1964). On the content of the edict: L. Capponi, *Cleopatra* (Roma-Bari: Laterza, 2021), 26.

5   Heracleopolis was the capital of the XX Nome of Upper Egypt (near the modern city of Beni Suef) and an important religious and cultural center.

6   *BGU* 8.760. *BGU* = *Berliner griechische Urkunden (Aegyptische Urkunden aus den Koniglichen [poi Staatliche] Meseen zu Berlin)* (Berlin, 1895). On the content of the letter: L. Capponi, *Cleopatra* (Roma-Bari: Laterza, 2021), 26.

CHAPTER XXIII

The Situation Turns on Itself

New and Old Friends

Caesar can count on many friends, including the holders of the highest offices of state, but he must also look around him at his many enemies, chief among whom are Pompey, the consuls of 50, and the unshakeable Catonian faction. Most of the Senate and the magistrates are neutral. They do not feel personally involved in the clandestine fighting between Caesar and Pompey, between Caesar and the consuls, and between Caesar and the Catonian faction caused by rivalries, jealousy, and boundless personal ambitions. One of the neutral senators is Cicero. As usual, he strives to keep himself equidistant from the warring parties and on good terms with both. Currently, he is the proconsul of Cilicia.

Among Caesar's friends, it is worth reminding ourselves of Aulus Hirtius, Caius Asinius Pollio, Mark Antony, Caius Cassius Longinus, and Caius Scribonius Curio.

Hirtius has been Caesar's legate since 54 and is currently his attendant. He doesn't have a fighter's temperament. He is a dour sort, devoid of a sense of humor, and is unloved by the soldiers. Caesar thinks highly of him for his ability to think analytically, to gather information, sift through it and quickly see the connections, to compile memoranda and documents, and for the efficiency with which he works.

Pollio comes from a rich family from Teate (Chieti in Abruzzo). He is an orator and a scholar, the future historian of the civil wars. When he was younger, he served in the army under Pompey's command. He then became friends with Caesar and has been at his side ever since.

We already know Mark Antony. After studying rhetoric in Greece, he served in the army in Syria, under the proconsul Aulus Gabinius as a cavalry commander, distinguishing himself for his courage and contempt for danger. Following this, he joined Caesar's high command in Gaul (54) and served as quaestor (52–51). He is a soldier with aristocratic ideas and with strong, perhaps excessive, self-esteem. Caesar respects him as a tough fighter and an expert in military matters. With help from Caesar, of whom he is an avid supporter, Antony took Hortensius's place in the college of augurs and was elected as tribune of the plebs (50).

In 49, Cassius Longinus is 26 or 27 years old. He belongs to the *gens Cassia*, which has provided the state with numerous magistrates over the years, including six consuls since 171. In the 60s, he married Tertulla, the daughter of Marcus Junius Brutus and Servilia Caepio, and seemed to be cozying up with the Optimates faction. He survived the disaster at Carrhae in 53 and fought against the Parthians at Antioch on the Orontes after Pacorus had led them on an invasion into Syria. After having been elected in 50 as a tribune of the plebs for 49, he sided with Caesar, abandoning Pompey.

Curio had been tribune of the plebs in 50. Cicero fundamentally holds him in contempt because he had been the lover and cohabitant of the young Mark Antony, with whom he has remained close (it isn't Curio's sexual inclination that shocks Cicero, even if he is somewhat old-fashioned when it comes to customs, but the fact that he and Antony cannot see each other for any other reason). It reaches the extent that when he speaks in public about the son of Curio senior, Cicero calls him "Curio's little daughter."

Curio has been the darling of the people of Rome ever since, in 53, returning from the province of Asia where he had carried out some assignments, he built a splendid theater-amphitheater in the city at his own expense and laid on some spectacular funeral games. He said he embarked on this undertaking to honor the memory of his deceased father, but his true intention was to capture the hearts of the electorate to have a chance at being elected to the tribunate.

Curio's theater-amphitheater is the realization of a highly daring architectural project. Two different stages were built, complete with seating, both precariously suspended on a rotating pivot so as to be able to put on two shows at the same time and then, at noon, when they finish, immensely complicated machinery is activated that rotates the theaters, bringing them together and forming a single amphitheater that hosts gladiatorial games. Spectators risk their necks because the structure is tremendously unstable, but they are also greatly entertained. The games are as exciting as ever owing to the panthers that are sent into the arena.

To build and run the theater, as well as to lead the comfortable, glittering, lavish lifestyle to which he has become accustomed, Curio burned through his substantial assets and got up to his neck in debt. By staying close to Pompey and leveraging on their common Sullan past, he managed to convince him to take on all his debts, only to get heavily into debt again. Pursued by creditors and at the height of despair, he turned to Caesar, hoping to obtain similar benefits from him as he had received from Pompey. It is worth saying that Curio had always been very critical of Caesar, and he had not kept his opinions about him a secret. The tension between them had intensified over time and had become public knowledge. But, Curio could give Caesar what he was craving: a tribune of the plebs with an easy word and quick intellect, with enough nerve and courage to oppose Cato, Pompey, and their friends among the magistrates and senators, using his veto if necessary to prevent their legislative proposals from being approved; these individuals are the same people with whom

Curio had been hand-in-hand only recently. Caesar jumped at the chance and said that he was ready to provide guarantees for Curio's mountain of debts.[1] Thus, Curio became a reformed anti-Caesarian.

Caelius had pointedly ended his relationship with Clodia, the sister of Clodius, after having been her lover, while he had also always been an enemy of Clodius, proof of which is in the fact that he had supported the latter's enemy Milo. Thus, after the death of Clodius, Caelius and Curio found themselves on opposing sides.

Curio remained faithful to the memory of his erstwhile friend and ally Clodius, and he proved to be such a comfort for his widow Fulvia that, when he proposed to marry her, she enthusiastically agreed (52).[2] He thus went to live in Fulvia's beautiful house, situated on the slopes of the Palatine on the corner between the Via Sacra and the Clivus Palatinus B. (originally, this was the house of Marcus Aemilius Scaurus before Clodius took ownership of it), becoming a neighbor of both Cicero and Caelius.

As well as their rhetorical skill, Curio, Cicero, and Caelius all share the quality of knowing how to navigate through dangerous waters. This, in a city that is buffeted every day by a violent whirlwind of ambition, rivalry, and intrigue, is a talent that garners respect. In addition, Curio and Caelius also have a common passion for panthers, which they do their best to import from Asia. On occasion, out of courtesy, Curio has given Caelius a hand in procuring some, a gesture that did not go unappreciated by Caelius.

Among Caesar's agents who protect his interests in Rome, there are also Lucius Cornelius Balbus and Caius Oppius. We have already met them, but it's worth reminding ourselves about them. They are among the most active but they work in the shadows and in silence asinconspicuous figures.

Waiting for the Prorogation

Caesar is waiting in Gallia Belgica for the decision of the Senate of Rome on whether or not they will grant his request to obtain an extension of 22 months to the expiration date of his proconsulship (from 1 March 50 to 31 December 48) which he has presented as the need to ensure the command of military operations remains continuous. But nothing happens and Caesar begins to lose patience, to the extent that, before summer 51, he renews his request through his friends Mark Antony, Caius Cassius Longinus, and Caius Scribonius Curio. Finally, the Senate discusses the case, but, before making its decision, wants to learn the consuls' opinion.

The consuls of 51 are Marcus Claudius Marcellus and Servius Sulpicius Rufus. The former is a Pompeian, while the latter is a distant relation of Caesar and a friend

---

1   This is said to have been in the tens of millions of sesterces: 10 million according to Vell. Pat. II.48.4, 60 million according to Val. Max., *Memorable Deeds and Sayings* IX.1.6.
2   On the marriage of Fulvia to Curio: Cic. *Phil.*, II.11, II.113, V.11.

of Cicero and of the lawyer and jurist Trebatius Testa, who was a military tribune of Caesar's in Gaul.

Marcellus and Sulpicius have been asked to debate a subject that, due to its extreme delicacy, requires utmost caution. They are likely to lose out personally, just as it's likely that you'll burn yourself by picking up a hot potato. In the end, they decide to remain silent; their successors in the consulship can do it, if they want to. Mainly, it is Marcellus whofavours this tactic of demurral. One of the reasons that explain his behavior is the fact that Marcellus, despite being a distant relative of Caesar, is nevertheless one of his most ardent political opponents, and has been ever since Caesar said he was anxious to get a divorce for his great-niece Octavia Minor, the wife of Sulpicius, to marry her to Pompey, who had been left a widower by Julia.

The new consuls are elected in early September 51, and they will take up their office on 1 January 50. These are Caius Claudius Marcellus Minor and Lucius Aemilius Lepidus Paullus. The former is the younger brother of Marcus Claudius Marcellus, who had been consul in 51. He too is a distant relation of Caesar, and he too is among the bitterest of his political opponents for the same reason as his brother. The latter is the son of Marcus Aemilius Lepidus, who had been consul in 78. When, in 63, he had been quaestor, he had supported Cicero in his actions against Catiline. He, too, is an ardent anti-Caesarian.

Both consuls, therefore, are political opponents of Caesar. To prevent them from joining forces against him, Caesar will see to it that they quarrel with each other, so that their political activity is paralyzed. To that end, he buys the support—at a high price—of Lepidus, who will use the money he has received from Caesar to cover part of the costs for the renovation of the Basilica Fulvia.

As winter 51/50 approaches, Caesar stations half of his eight legions in Gallia Belgica, and the other half in Gallia Narbonensis before setting off to Rabenna. Before leaving, Caesar delegates the functions of government and command of the troops to his second-in-command, the lieutenant with the rank of praetor, Titus Labienus (November 50).

Labienus is a skilled commander, strong fighter, and ingenious tactician and strategist. He was Caesar's closest collaborator during the Gallic Wars and is almost as famous throughout the Roman world as Caesar is. Labienus has fought against the Tigurini (58), the Treveri (54), the Belgae (53), the Parisi, and the Aulerci. In 52, he put down a popular uprising that had broken out in Lutetia (Paris). Caesar trusts him implicitly.

The Tension Rises

In 50, Caesar modifies his request to extend his proconsular offices, asking for a shorter prorogation (until 1 August 49), but the consul Marcellus Minor is opposed to this and induces his senatorial colleagues to postpone the decision.

In early September 50, the new consuls are elected and will enter office on 1 January 49. They are Caius Claudius Marcellus and Lucius Cornelius Lentulus Crus. The former is the homonymous consul of 50. The latter is the brother of Lucius Cornelius Lentulus Spinther, who had been consul in 57.[3] He is a man who loves luxury and so is always loaded with debts.

Both the consuls-elect are among Caesar's most tenacious opponents. Moreover, Lentulus Crus is a personal enemy.

On 29 September 50, the consuls-elect, in agreement with each other, secure the Senate's decision that the provinces to be assigned to the ex-consuls for 49 are Syria, Gallia Narbonensis, Gallia Cisalpina, and Illyricum. This means that Caesar will not be able to have the extension he requested, with the consequence that he will not be able to hold onto his legal immunity beyond the date he leaves office, with the subsequent risk that he will not be able to run as a candidate for the consulship for 48.

In the late autumn of 50, at the same time as the consular elections for 49, a rumor spreads that Caesar is preparing to enlist four new legions. The news aggravates Pompey and the Catonian faction more than the fact that their discreet invitation, made to Caesar the previous spring, to drop his military command has fallen on deaf ears.

Developments are not long in coming. The consul Marcellus Minor, at Pompey's suggestion, and in agreement with Lentulus Crus, presents two motions in the Senate. The first seeks the abrogation of the *lex Pompeia Licinia de provincia Caii Iulii Caesaris* and aims to get Caesar to leave his offices prematurely on the premise that the Gallic War has now been won and all that remains to be done is to disband the army. The second aims to ensure that Caesar cannot run as a candidate for the consulship for 48 *in absentia*.

Caesar still has a lot of friends in the Senate, and they come to his aid. In short, when the two motions are put to a vote after being discussed, they are rejected.

Since the Senate has clearly split, some of its members do their utmost to restore unity. One is Curio, the tribune of the plebs. On 1 December 50, at Caesar's suggestion, Curio proposes to the Senate that both Caesar and Pompey are ordered to disband all their legions and return to Rome, given that the swords of both men are threatening the Republic and the freedom of its political institutions. The proposal is discussed, put to a vote, and approved with an overwhelming majority: there are 370 votes in favor, with just 20 or 22 against.

However, the consul Marcellus Minor doesn't accept the outcome of the vote and declares that he will do his duty even without the Senate's vote. He immediately goes to Pompey, together with Lentulus Crus and other senators. Pompey receives these

---

3   Publius Cornelius Lentulus Spinther, remember, had been consul in 57. In that role, he spent heavily to ensure that Cicero was redeemed and brought back from exile. Later, he had recommended that Ptolemy XII Auletes be restored to the throne of Egypt. In 56–53, he had been governor of Cilicia. In 51, he celebrated a triumph.

visitors at his villa in Alba. During the meeting, Marcellus, in the midst of a tense and agitated crowd, "orders" Pompey, in both his and his colleague's name, to take up arms against Caesar in defense of their homeland (effectively, he is delegating control of an army to him, entirely arbitrarily). Pompey "obeys," accepting the sword, a symbol of military command, that Marcellus offers him. The incident marks the definitive break in the relations between Pompey and Caesar and between their supporters, who are found not only in the Senate and among the magistracies but also in every nook and cranny of Roman society.

The whole month of December 50 passes without a breakthrough in the impasse, partly because Pompey, after having started to enlist new troops, has fallen ill, and without him the political game remains at a standstill.

Caesar takes advantage of this to order the Legio XVIII Gemina (the Thirteenth Twin Legion), quartered in Gallia Belgica and commanded by Caius Trebonius, to join him in Rabenna. Caesar had recruited the Thirteenth in 57, ahead of the invasion of Gallia Belgica. It is composed of 5,000 infantry and 300 cavalry, almost all Gauls from Piedmont and Lombardy, whom Caesar had given citizenship against the will of the Senate. It is commanded by Trebonius.

On 26 December 50, Caesar writes to the Senate. He has the Thirteenth with him and has ordered Caius Fabius and Caius Trebonius each to send him another legion, namely the Legio VIII Gallica (?) and the Legio XII Fulminata (Twelfth Lightning Legion), one of which is found in Gallia Narbonensis and the other in Gallia Belgica. Both these legions are veterans of the Gallic Wars.

In the meantime, Cicero has returned to Italy after not wanting his proconsulship to be extended. Between 29 December 50 and 4 January 49, he is at *Formianum*, his beautiful villa in Formiae (Formia in Campania), of which he is very fond. This property is found on the coast at Vindicio, at the point where the Pontone plain widens on the border with Caieta (Gaeta). As it is exposed to pleasant winds, it is a fine place to spend hot summers.

Formianum is Cicero's *buen refugio*, his favorite place, where he dedicates himself to his studies, to philosophical reflections, and to his writing, and where he receives frequent visits from friends and acquaintances, of whom the most constant are Caius Arrius and Sebosus, a "friend of Catullus," who keep him updated on political affairs. "Caius Arrius"—Cicero says in a letter to Atticus—"is my next-door neighbor, or rather, he almost lives in my house, and even declares that the reason for his not going to Rome is that he may spend whole days with me here philosophizing!"[4]

There, Cicero puts together a schedule of his upcoming engagements. Before returning to Rome, he will go to Pomptinum (near the Pontine Marshes, a swampy area in Lazio) and Anxur (Terracina). Then, he will visit Pompey at Albanum on 2 January 49, before returning to Rome on his birthday, 3 January.[5]

---

4   Cic. *Att.*, II.14.
5   Cic. *Att.*, VII.4, 5.

CHAPTER XXIV

Crossing the Rubicon

The Intransigents Prevail

On 1 January 49, the tribune of the plebs from the Populares faction, Mark Antony, reads a letter in the Senate despite the disapproval expressed by the consuls Claudius Marcellus Major and Lentulus Crus, in which Caesar lists his great military victories, highlighting how they have benefited the state, and declares that he will relinquish command of his legions if Pompey does the same; otherwise, war is inevitable.

The tone and the substance of the missive are threatening, but do not match those of other letters Caesar has sent in recent days, in private, to Cato and other prominent senators, in which he says that he is ready and willing to renounce the proconsulship of Gallia Narbonensis and to dismiss the eight legions that fought in the Gallic Wars if he can retain his proconsulship of Gallia Cisalpina and Illyricum, and the command of two legions, until 31 December 49.

The Senate discusses the issue in a crescendo of strident tones, raised to an unusual level of harshness by Cato and his friends and political allies. The political atmosphere is heated. Quintus Metellus Pius Scipio Nasica presents a motion that aims to get the Senate to order Caesar to leave his offices at their natural end, under penalty of being declared a public enemy. Scipio Nasica is Pompey's father-in-law and had been his consular colleague in 52. Everyone knows that Pompey places absolute trust in him and that when he gets up in the Senate to speak, it is as if it were Pompey speaking. Scipio's motion is approved despite the Populares faction's tribunes of the plebs, Mark Antony and Caius Cassius Longinus, having used their veto, which is ignored.

On 4 January 49, Cicero returns to Rome from Cilicia; he is welcomed back by a cheering crowd.[1] On 6 January, he approaches Pompey and, under the illusion that he can still exercise a level of influence over him, tries to convince him to accept Caesar's proposal. Without success. Cato also remains steadfast in his position (he doesn't want to give Caesar the chance to become consul for a second time).

---

1   Cic. *Fam.*, XVI.11.2.

The Senate had continued its discussions on 2 January and does so again on 5 January. The voices remain heated, at times harsh and violent. Again, there is a prevalence of those holding an anti-Caesarian position, rigid, inflexible, alien to concessions or compromises, supported by the consuls, the Pompeians, and the Catonian faction. For the umpteenth time, Scipio Nasica reiterates his opposition to any extension to Caesar's term of office. In the end, the Senate, by a majority, shares then adopts the anti-Caesarian position, disregarding the vetoes of Antony and Cassius. As such, all attempts at mediation have been rejected, and all exhortations for prudence fall on deaf ears. The opinion that prevails is that of the intransigents, who do not compromise, nor entertain transgressions or deviations from the path of obstinate refusal.

Caesar is currently in Rabenna, where he is constantly updated on all important events happening in Rome thanks to a network of friends and private messengers. On learning of the Senate's position towards him, his face darkens. He furrows his brow, a line marking his forehead. The frown crossing his face is the only sign of his inner agitation. He remains silent, but this isn't to say that he will remain inactive.

On 7 January, the Senate, at the instigation of Cato and the consul Marcellus, issue a *senatus consultum ultimum*, with which it declares a state of emergency and instructs the consuls to intervene by taking extraordinary decisions, even at the expense of citizens' freedoms, in the greater interests of the state (*ne quid res publica detrimenti caperet*, "so that the state suffers no harm"). Antony and Cassius are expelled from the Senate and warned—or tangibly feel—that their physical safety is no longer guaranteed. Though the violence used against them isn't physical but psychological, it nevertheless constitutes a clear violation of their rights and guarantees. In the future, this argument will also be frequently made by Caesar to justify his actions.

On the night of 7/8 January 49, Antony and Cassius, together with Curio and Caelius, get away from Rome, disguising themselves as slaves aboard a wagon, to join Caesar in Rabenna. Recently, Caelius has definitively freed himself from the tutelage of Cicero and become closer to Caesar, espousing his cause. Before leaving Rome, he passes by Cicero's house to say his goodbyes and recommend to him that he remain neutral in the civil war that is brewing. The two, we recall, live on the Palatine, not far from each other.

The *Senatus Consultum Ultimum* of 8 January 49

The Senate meets again on 8 and 9 January 49. It decides to do so in the Temple of Bellona to allow Pompey to participate in the debate. Bellona, we recall, is the Italic goddess of war, assimilated into the pantheon of the Romans. Her temple rises on the Campus Martius, near the Temple of Apollo Sosianus and the Theater of Marcellus, and therefore outside the *pomerium*, albeit not far away from the city walls.

On 8 January, the college imposes some regulations in preparation for the outbreak of civil war that now appears inevitable. Among other things, it issues a second *senatus consultum ultimum*, which authorizes Pompey to levy up to 130,000 men in Italy, puts the public treasury at his disposal, allows him to exact tribute from cities, and even to make use of possessions of temples and private wealth.

The same day, the Senate assigns promagistrates to their provinces, appointing, among others, Scipio Nasica to the office of proconsul of Syria and designating Lucius Domitius Ahenobarbus as Caesar's replacement as governor of Roman Gaul and Illyricum. This latter office entails the command of a legion.

We have already looked at Lucius Domitius Ahenobarbus. He is an aristocrat and the brother-in-law of Cato. He is an ultra-conservative, and therefore a Catonian. He had been curule aedile in 61 and praetor in 59. As praetor, he had been opposed to Caesar's and Crassus's activities in favor of the plebeians and had been accused by Caesar of hatching a plot to kill Pompey. After his first attempt to be elected to the consulship (in 55 for 54), which failed due to the hostility he faced from the Triumvirate (born from the fact that he had threatened to remove Caesar from Gallia Cisalpina during his electoral campaign), he tried again and, this time, was successful. He was elected alongside the Pompeian Appius Claudius Pulcher. After his consulship, Ahenobarbus refused the governorship of a province. Later, after the death of Crassus, when Caesar and Pompey's relationship had already broken down, he opted to take Pompey's side. In 52, he had been the investigating magistrate during the trial following the death of Clodius. In the autumn of 50, he put himself forward as a candidate for the position of augur, which had become vacant after the death of Quintus Hortensius Hortalus in the summer. Caesar, however, had been able to ensure Mark Antony's appointment to the post. That same year, Ahenobarbus was elected to the praetorship for the following year (taking on the office for the second time, having already been praetor in 59).

In 50, as propraetor, Ahenobarbus comes to be designated as the governor of Roman Gaul and Illyricum in Caesar's place. He will never carry out his duties due to the outbreak of the civil war.

Caesar has already learned of the Senate of Rome's decisions before Antony, Cassius, Curio, and Caelius reach him in Rabenna. This latest news removes any remaining doubts. On the night of 10/11 January 49, Caesar has a dream: he thinks he is having incestuous intercourse with his mother.[2] On 11 January, he spends his day normally so as not to alert Pompey's spies: he goes to the theater, he examines the building plans for a large arena designed to host gladiatorial games, and he and others attend a meal offered by a civic magistrate. In the meantime, he has sent the tribune Hortensius to a bridge over the Rubicon with the instruction to guard it and wait for his arrival. Hortensius is in command of two cohorts of the Thirteenth,

---

2   Plut. *Caes.*, 32.9.

making 1,000 men in total.[3] To avoid excessive unrest and bloodshed among the local civilian population, he and his men have been ordered by Caesar to use only swords in the event of conflict.

The Rubicon is a small mountain stream that, since 59, has marked the border between Gallia Cisalpina and *Italia propria*. It runs across Romagna for 35 km between Ariminum (Rimini) and Caesena (Cesena) and flows into the Adriatic Sea. It springs in hilly terrain and descends to wind its way through a plain. At a certain point on its course, it is spanned by a stone bridge to allow the Via Aemilia across. This is the place where Caesar has ordered Hortensius to wait for him.[4]

"Alea iacta est"

On the night of 11/12 January, Caesar sets off in secret on a hired cart pulled by two horses, taking a back road known only to a few. He is accompanied by Aulus Hirtius, Caius Asinius Pollio, the commander of his Germanic bodyguards, and a few others.[5] The night is moonless; in fact, it is pitch black. The small group takes odd turns to make it seem that they aren't heading south to any spies who may be around. They get lost in a wood, but they find their way back to the road after getting directions from a shepherd whom Caesar and his companions, without identifying themselves, had dragged out of bed while he slept in front of the rest of his family. Eventually, the group abandons the cart and continue on foot. At dawn on 12 January 49, they reach the bridge over the Rubicon and join Hortalus and his men.

Caesar consecrates a herd of horses to the river then lets them run free, to go wherever they want. Then he turns his back on those nearby and pauses to look—thoughtfully—at the shallow water, which is flowing slowly. He is troubled. His dark eyes, usually piercing, seem lost in the distance. Caesar, by nature, is stern and inscrutable. He doesn't let his emotions seep out, instead always remaining alert, pensive, and cold. No one has ever seen him hesitate, let alone lose heart, in any of the many critical or even desperate situations in which he has found himself with his soldiers in nine years of war. No one has seen him tired, anxious, or simply sad. But this is different, and everyone is aware of it, because this time it isn't a case of waging war on the Gauls, on the Germans, or on other enemies of Rome, but on other Romans.

---

3   The legions are each formed of 10 cohorts (I–X); the First Cohort is composed of 1,000 men, while the others are each formed of 480 men.

4   More than 300 years of debate, often very lively, have not been enough to determine exactly which watercourse should be identified as the Rubicon: the Pisciatello near Cesena, the Fiumicino near Savignano, or the Uso near Rimini. It seems that the course of the ancient Rubicon changed during the early Middle Ages.

5   Plut. *Caes.*, 32.7.

Caesar had never deluded himself about the possibility of reaching a compromise agreement with Pompey, the consuls, and the Catonian faction, a view borne out by the facts. His political opponents managed to induce much of the Senate into the mistaken belief that he wanted to consolidate the victory he had won by force of arms with terror, in imitation of Sulla. Instead, Caesar had always maintained that he repudiated the Sullan precedent and sought to achieve the maximum possible consensus.

Caesar considers that the balance of power isn't in his favor. He has control of the provinces of Gaul, but south of the Alps, he only has 5,000 infantry and 300 cavalry available to him, all belonging to the Thirteenth Legion. The Senate, on the other hand, controls Africa and through Pompey, the Iberian provinces, as well as, crucially, the entirety of the East, where Pompey's clients are found and where Scipio Nasica is currently governor of Syria. Caesar's enemies, therefore, not only hold sway in *Italia propria* but also everything surrounding it. Caesar dismisses the idea of yielding to their impositions—giving up his proconsular mandate, handing his military command to Ahenobarbus, and returning to Rome as a private citizen, with the risk of not being able to run for the consulship for 48—*a priori*.

There are therefore two alternative possibilities: to challenge fate, throwing himself headfirst into the fray, where his enemies are considerably stronger than him, or to abandon Gallia Cisalpina, entrenching himself beyond the Alps, and try to resist attempts to flush him out until the coalition of his enemies falls apart. He knows he needs to decide quickly. Impulsively and predictably, he decides to wage war on his homeland (when Caesar finds himself in a tight spot he invariably throws himself forward, no matter the cost). For the purposes of propaganda, he will maintain that the conflict broke out because the Senate trampled over the right of veto of the tribunes of the plebs Antony and Cassius, interfering with the performance of their functions; it threatened them, violating their status as sacrosanct and inviolable magistrates; it adopted a *senatus consultum ultimum* in the absence of an emergency situation; it did not designate the command of the army to a magistrate elected by the people but to a private citizen (Pompey); and it harmed Caesar's personal *dignitas*, understood as his authority, prestige, respect, estimation, and credibility.

Just when Caesar is about to take the most important decision of his life, a tall man approaches him out of nowhere, sits on the ground next to him, takes a flute out of his shoulder bag, and begins to play. The melody brings numerous legionaries to him, including the trumpeters. Suddenly, the man stops playing, gets to his feet, snatches a nearby trumpeter's instrument and blows deeply into it, sounding the call to battle. Then he throws himself into the shallow water and runs toward the opposite bank. The action arouses a collective excitement. Caesar takes advantage of this and shouts: "Take we the course which the signs of the gods and the false dealing of our foes point out. *Alea iacta est!*" ("The die is cast!"). This being said, he mounts his horse, spurs it on and fords the river at a gallop. Everyone follows, either running on foot or at the gallop on their own horses.[6]

The move is one of open and irreconcilable rebellion against the Senate and the consuls. It is the key moment in the life of Caesar and in the history of the *res publica*, and it is one of the most important junctions in the entirety of Roman history. It will trigger incalculable consequences that will lead to civil war, to the dictatorship of Caesar, to his assassination, to the Second Triumvirate, to another civil war, to a new set of mass proscriptions, and finally to the obsolescence of the *res publica*, a form of government that had lasted for 460 years, and the dawn of the Principate, in effect to the transition from government by a few to government by one. The horrific I century, which had already witnessed the Social War, the Terror, the Civil War of Marius and Sulla, and the Sullan proscriptions, has not yet plumbed its deepest depths, despite the countless sorrows, destruction, and suffering already caused.

Pompey and Part of the Senate Leave Rome

Caesar and 1,000 men of the Thirteenth, in the days following 11 January, travel at speed down the Via Popilia and enter Ariminum (Rimini) without a blow being struck and occupy it. They are joined there by the remaining eight cohorts of the Thirteenth, arriving from Rabenna. Caesar carries out an inspection of his troops and gives an address to them. He stirs the soldiers up by showing them the tribunes of the plebs Antony and Cassius, saying that these men of great prestige and magistrates of the Republic have been vilified, persecuted, and forced to flee in servile clothes on hired carts. He affirms that the affronts caused to them by the Senate cannot be left unpunished. He tears at the clothes on his chest and is moved to tears. He asks the soldiers, who are all lined up, and his friends for their personal loyalty, promising that they will receive material benefits if they follow him.

Caesar is being melodramatic and is distorting the truth because it suits him to do so. Everything that has happened and is happening, reduced to the essential, derives from the fact that he wants to become consul for a second time and remain proconsul in the meantime, even beyond the natural expiration of his offices, in order to retain the immunity from prosecution that magistrates are entitled to and therefore to avoid being vulnerable to legal actions brought against him by his political adversaries. All this, notwithstanding electoral law (given the fact that he wants to run for office) and the rules that regulate the assignment of promagisterial

---

6   The episode is recounted by Gaius Asinius Pollio (76 BC–4 AD) in his *Histories* and is then recounted by Gaius Suetonius Tranquillus (70–126 AD) in *The Lives of the Twelve Caesars*. See Suet. *Iul.* 32. Plutarch (46/48–125/127 AD), in his account of Caesar's crossing of the Rubicon, doesn't mention it. *See* Plut. *Caes.*, 32.8.

offices. To get what he so ardently wants, Caesar is stopping at nothing, even going so far as attempting a *coup d'état*, knowing that it will result in a civil war. The key to understanding Caesar's way of thinking and acting is in two words: limitless ambition.

Between 8 and 12 January, the Senate, after many arguments, decrees that Cicero can celebrate a *supplicatio*, rather than the triumph he had asked for. On 12 January, it appoints him as supervisor of the seaboard and part of Campania (Capua and its territory) and to superintend the levy and general affairs.[7] In the meantime, in *Italia propria*, the call for a general mobilization has essentially fallen on deaf ears. Pompey draws his conclusion from this. The risk of catastrophe remains on the horizon as the tension rises. Surprisingly, between 12 and 16 January 49, he declares in the Senate that he isn't capable of defending the city, arousing anger and dismay. The praetor Marcus Favonius, a Catonian, accuses him of having deceived his friends when he said that all he had to do to make 10 legions spring from the earth was to stamp one foot on the ground.[8]

In reality, what Pompey claimed in the Senate about not being able to defend the city isn't correct. He could call the six highly loyal legions stationed in Spain to him, as well as the legions stationed in Campania in Nuvla (Nola) and have them converge on Rome. These are the two legions—the Fifth and the Seventh—that Lentulus Crus "loaned" to Caesar for the Gallic Wars and which Caesar then returned, obeying an order from the Senate, for them to be deployed in a war against the Parthians. The Spanish Legions could leave from Valentia Edetanorum (Valencia), Carthago Nova (Cartagena), and Tarraco (Tarragona) and disembark at Ostia and Neapolis in a few weeks. It would take the legions at Nuvla only a few days to reach Rome. Before the start of spring, Pompey could therefore have at least 60,000 men available to him for the defense of the city of Rome.[9]

On 17 January 51, Pompey convenes a meeting of his loyalists at his villa in Alba.[10] Consuls, ex-consuls, and many other senators are present. Among them, Marcus Tullius Cicero, Marcus Calpurnius Bibulus, Lucius Domitius Ahenobarbus, Publius Cornelius Lentulus Spinther, Cnaeus Cornelius Lentulus Marcellinus, Appius Claudius Pulcher, Quintus Caecilius Metellus Pius Scipio, and Marcus Claudius Marcellus are worthy of note. Pompey calls them friends and urges them to follow him to Capua in Campania (where the legions are camped) with their families and

---

7   Cic. *Att.*, VII.11.5, XIV.3, VIII.11b.1; *Fam.*, XVI.11.3, XVI.12.5.

8   Plut. *Caes.*, 33.

9   For more on this topic: *Précis des guerres de César par Napoléon*, écrit par M. Marchand *sour la decré de l'empereur (1819)* (Paris, 1836), 125; Th. Mommsen, *Römische Geschichte*, vol. V (Leipzig, 1885), chap. X; L. Canfora, *Giulio Cesare. Il dittatore democratico* (Bari-Roma: Laterza, 2006), 186–187.

10   Cic. *Att.*, IX.10.2.

servants. To overcome criticisms and resistance, he says that to stay in Rome at a time like this means preferring tyranny to liberty.

That same day, or at some point over the two following days (18–19 January 49), Pompey leaves Rome in complete chaos and many of his followers at the mercy of the enemy.[11] Many others follow him in the procession. Among them are numerous senators, including Cicero. Perhaps there are also some of Cicero's family members: his son Marcus, his brother Quintus, and his nephew. His wife Terentia, his daughter Tullia, and his sister-in-law—the wife of Quintus Tullius Cicero—remain in Rome.

The consul Lentulus Crus, in agreement with the Senate, delays his departure from Rome to collect and move the Treasury of the Roman People, which is kept beneath the Temple of Saturn at the foot of the Capitoline to the southwest of the Rostra, overlooking the paved road that leads to the Clivus Capitolinus. It is the oldest temple in Rome, after the Temple of Jupiter Capitolinus. Stored inside, amid the marble blackened by candles and by the centuries, are the eagles of the old legions that conquered the world and the unusual cult statue of the god, filled with oil, and wrapped with woolen bandages. Various state offices are in its basement, including the aerarium (the state treasury). But Lentulus's effort will not succeed, partly due to his haste, partly due to the opposition of the quaestors of the *aerarium*. Lentulus gives up and sets off in turn for Capua, where he will take command of his legions.

The Stop-off in Capua

Cicero isn't convinced by what he's doing and is tormented by the dilemma of whether to follow Pompey or not. Eventually, he returns to Rome and remains there. There is more than one defection from Pompey's camp. Another is the ex-consul Servius Sulpicius Rufus, a friend of Cicero. In turn, Lucius Calpurnius Piso Caesoninus initially follows Pompey to Capua, but then he goes back to Rome and declares himself neutral.

Piso Caesoninus is the father of Calpurnia, Caesar's third wife, whom he married in 59; therefore, he is Caesar's father-in-law. He had been consul in 59, proconsul of Macedonia from 57 to 55, and censor in 50. In February 49, even though his mandate has now expired, he hasn't yet handed back his insignia of office. In recent times, he offered to act as an intermediary between Caesar and Pompey, but he was forced to desist due to the opposition of the Optimates.

There is also bad blood, let us recall, between Cicero and Piso. The former cannot forget that the latter didn't object to Clodius's legislative initiative that sought his

---

11 Plutarch gives an effective description of the general uncertainty and altercations between citizens on opposing sides caused by Pompey's decision to leave Rome.

condemnation to exile, so as not to set himself against the tribune, and that he even attended the ritual vandalizing of Cicero's house after its confiscation. In a written oration, Cicero accused him of the heinous management of public affairs during his governorship of Macedonia; he ridiculed him, caricaturing his physical appearance and his habits; and he was scathing in his criticism of his fondness for Epicureanism and the hospitality and protection he gave to the Epicurean philosopher Philodemus of Gadara, the author of numerous works, including epigrams with erotic content that sing of carefree love, aimed at pure pleasure for the senses. In reality Cicero's invective had been unjust. Piso Caesoninus is a friend of Caesar's and his election to the consulship came after Caesar had married his daughter; Caesar was a consul at that time but Piso reached the highest office of state after having always won when he had run as a candidate for the lesser magistracies, so it cannot be said that he crossed this finishing line only and exclusively because he had been supported by Caesar. Furthermore, Piso is a capable person, with significant intellectual ability and a strong personality, eloquent and cultured, with literary and philosophical interests.

The consul Marcellus followed Pompey, his colleague Lentulus, the senators and their families and domestic servants to Capua. He doesn't believe that the legions in Capua are strong enough to repel Caesar's forces if they are attacked, so he liberates the gladiators from the local training school and gives them their freedom on the condition that they fight against Caesar. But he is criticized by other senators for this. He will soon abandon the idea and let the gladiators disperse over the countryside. Soon he will follow Pompey and the senators to Dyrrachium and will be one of the commanders of Pompey's Adriatic fleet.

During the short time that Pompey spends in Capua, he is joined by Titus Labienus, the former legate of the Thirteenth and second-in-command of Caesar's army, the most valiant and reliable of the latter's legates. Labienus has chosen not to follow Caesar in his war against the state, despite owing his career, his fame, and his honors to him. He told him of this openly, handing back his offices and decorations. Caesar let Labienus leave, albeit with regret. Hirtius, on the other hand, was pleased about Labienus's departure because he had always been resentful of him and jealous of his close relationship with Caesar.

It is difficult to understand why Labienus defected. It's possible that he considered that Caesar couldn't win a war against Pompey. If so, the reason would be found in his erroneous reading of the strategic balance of the moment. However, his political repositioning could also have been due to other considerations: Labienus and Pompey are countrymen—both of them are originally from Picenum; Labienus's family is from Cingulum (Cingoli), while Pompey's is from Oximum (Osimo)—and as such, Labienus may have given preference to his own, older personal ties with Pompey; Labienus may have seen his own central role being downsized due to the rise of other members of the *consilium*, such as

Aulus Hirtius, Mark Antony, and Marcus Aemilius Lepidus; or Labienus might have seen Caesar as a threat to the *res publica* and chosen to remain loyal to the latter.[12] By passing under Pompey's banner, Labienus swears his fealty to him and brings him priceless information.[13]

Labienus isn't the only official whom Caesar completely trusted who abandoned him after his crossing of the Rubicon. Another is Quintus Tullius Cicero. Yet another is Lucius Roscius Fabatus.

12 F. Santangelo, *Roma repubblicana. Una storia in quaranta vite* (Roma: Carocci, 2019), 293.
13 Cic. *Att.*, VII.13a.3.

CHAPTER XXV

Outbreak of Civil War

Attempts to Avoid Conflict

From Ariminum (Rimini), Caesar writes letters to Lentulus and Cicero. He forewarns the former about the disasters that are about to hit Rome. He asks the latter to report to Pompey that to avoid a war, he is willing to retire to private life, provided he receives sufficient guarantees. Cicero reaches Pompey in Teanum Sicidinum (Teano) in Campania and duly relays the terms. Pompey charges the praetor Lucius Roscius Fabatus, previously a legate under Caesar during the Gallic Wars, to notify the latter of the *senatus consultum ultimum* of 7 January. It is as if to say there is no turning back. Roscius will be accompanied on his mission by Lucius Julius Caesar, Caesar's cousin, being the son of the homonymous consul of 90 and the brother of Julia Antonia, the mother of Mark Antony. The two make for Ariminum, pass the message on to Caesar, and implore him not to harm the city and to set aside his anger. Caesar reiterates that he is willing to compromise and endure anything for the good of the state. He proposes that Pompey leave for the Spanish provinces, that the armies be disbanded, that everyone in Italy lay down their arms, that fear be dispelled from the city, that free elections be held, and that the administration of the state be left to the Senate and the Roman people. To facilitate all of this, he calls for Pompey to come to him, or to allow Caesar to go to him: a dialogue between them will smooth out any differences.

Roscius and Lucius Caesar return to Capua and relay the news to Pompey. Pompey sends them back to Ariminum with a counter-offer: Caesar will leave the city, return to Gallia Transalpina, and dismiss his legions; if Caesar does what he asks, Pompey will go to Spain. Pompey then leaves Capua and goes to Larinum (Larino in Molise), one of the main centers that line the coast between the mouth of the River Sangro and the mouth of the River Fortore (southeastern Abruzzo and Lower Molise). Larinum is an ancient center of the Frentani, an Oscan-speaking Italic people who have close ties to the Romanized Samnites. On 6 February, Pompey moves again, this time going to Luceria (Lucera), a city located in Tavoliere in Puglia at the confluence of the Molisano and Campanian valleys.

At the same time, Domitius Ahenobarbus and his numerous cohorts take up a position at Corfinum (Corfinio in the province of L'Aquila in Abruzzo), a city in the center of the Italian peninsula, near the River Aterno, at 345 m above sea level. Corfinium is the ancient capital of the Paeligni. It was the first capital of the Italic federation at the time of the Social War (91–87). It has been a *municipium* since 90. It is connected to Rome by the Via Valeria. Ahenobarbus establishes his headquarters there, then he sets up garrisons in the area, sending six cohorts to Alba Fucens and seven cohorts to Sulmo. He kept the remaining cohorts in Corfinium for himself.

Caesar fears that the Senate wants to deprive him of his offices and allow Pompey to retain his. This is demonstrated by the fact that the office of *consul sine collega* was not a substitute for Pompey's proconsulship of Spain but an addition thereto. As for Pompey, Caesar holds that he isn't paying much attention to the general interest but, instead, to his own personal interests, believing himself to be indispensable. Caesar no longer even trusts him. What happens if he accepts Pompey's proposal and Pompey then doesn't go to Spain?

Caesar believes that there is no longer any room for negotiation and resigns himself to the inevitability of the conflict. As a first step, he will seize Picenum (Marche) and then Umbria, the regions where Pompey's lands are found. Picenum is a region of great strategic importance, both as regards the recruitment of new troops and the provision of supplies, as well as being the area Pompey comes from and where he has a vast clientele, inherited from his father. As such, Caesar orders three cohorts to occupy Pesaurum (Pesaro) and Fanum Fortunae (Fano), and the Thirteenth to occupy other coastal centers that surveil the Via Flaminia. In addition, he orders Mark Antony to occupy Iguvium (Gubbio) and Arretium (Arezzo) in Etruria (Tuscany) with five legions. Caesar retains two cohorts for himself.

Caesar Advances into Central Italy

Caesar has chosen to demonstrate understanding and generosity in his attempt to restore a general consensus and bring about a lasting victory. He wants to distinguish himself from those who, in the past, have not been able to avoid being hated, nor to keep the fruits of victory for long, such as Sulla, whose precedent he wants to avoid following. This explains why Caesar's troops don't sack towns and round up dissidents, still less carry out purges. Caesar even frees Pompeian prisoners of war; he lets them go, safe and sound, to return to Pompey. This strategy gives excellent results. Cities open their gates to Caesar and welcome him as a god incarnate. But there is great fear too. Wherever the Thirteenth goes, many residents abandon their homes and flee in panic.

Caesar takes control of Picenum almost without a sword being drawn. He occupies Ankon (Ancona), Oximum (Osimo), Firmum Picenum (Fermo), and Beregra (Civitella del Tronto), as well as the rest of the region. When, later, he shows up at the gates of Asculum (Ascoli Piceno) with the Twelfth and Thirteenth, the city surrenders without a fight.

Some of the Pompeian forces pass under the banner of Caesar. The Legio VIII Gallica and the Legio XII Fulminata are joined with the Thirteenth at Fanum Fortunae. Six of the 13 cohorts that had been levied by the Pompeian Lucius Vibullius Rufus from among the Marsi in Umbria and the Peligni in Picenum also join up with Caesar.

The remaining seven cohorts beat a retreat led by Lentulus Spinther, and take refuge in Corfinium, where they reorganize themselves under the command of Vibullius Rufus and Domitius Ahenobarbus. Vibullius Rufus sends a message to Pompey to ask him to join them at Corfinium, but he receives no response.[1] In turn, the Pompeian Caius Hirrus, with his five cohorts, retreats from Cameria (or Camerta, Camerino) toward Umbria, whence he too will make for Corfinium.

On hearing of the loss of Picenum, Pompey panics and, even though he can count on a military force that is at least twice the size of Caesar's, without considering the legions in Spain and Africa, he nevertheless decides to fight the war well away from Italy. Perhaps this is because he wants to emulate Lucius Cornelius Cinna, Caius Marius's successor as leader of the Populares and consul from 87 to 84, who, when the war against Sulla broke out, planned to move the theater of war to Greece to spare Italy from a repeat of the horrors of the Social War (91–87) and the civil wars between the Marians, led by Marius's son, Caius Marius the Younger, and Sulla. However, the relocation didn't occur in the end because Cinna was killed in a military revolt in Ankon (Ancona), where he had concentrated his troops ahead of the crossing to the opposite coast of the Adriatic.

Consequently, Pompey relocates to Brundisium to board a ship for Dyrrachium, which has a considerable amount of food supplies. There are also other legions that are faithful to him in Epirus, and he will thus be able to put a larger army together.

The Fall of Corfinium

On 15 February 48, Caesar camps near Corfinium with two legions. On 16 February he is joined by the Eighth, who have reached him from Gallia Transalpina,[2] and by other troops: 300 cavalrymen, sent to him by the ruler of the Norici, and 22 cohorts, levied by him in Gallia Cisalpina.

On 18 February, he starts to build an 8-km-long *vallum* around Corfinium. As time passes, the atmosphere becomes stifling. Fear grips the minds of the defenders.

---

1   Caes., I.17.1.
2   The Eighth Legion was utilized by Caesar in Gallia Transalpina in 58. It fought at the Sabis and took part in the siege of Gergovia. It was given the name Gallica Victrix in honor of its service. Its emblem is the bull.

Some cannot bear the agony and commit suicide. Domitius Ahenobarbus attempts to flee in secret, but he is discovered, captured, and imprisoned.

Vibullius negotiates his release through Lentulus Spinther. Spinther meets Caesar in his camp and begs him to forgive him, reminds him of their friendship, and regales him of all the help he has given him, which is considerable (thanks to Spinther, Caesar became part of the College of Pontiffs, was appointed propraetor in Spain, and was supported in his campaign for the consulship). Caesar interrupts him mid-speech. He says that he has not crossed the Rubicon to harm anyone but because he had been intolerably offended by his political enemies and because he needed to defend the honor and prestige of the tribunes of the plebs who had been chased out of Rome. He did it to win freedom for himself and to free the Roman people from oppression from a small faction (Cato and his friends and political allies). He promises that he will refrain from carrying out reprisals if he can enter Corfinium without a fight. Spinther is encouraged and returns to Corfinium.

Abandoned by Pompey and by Ahenobarbus and besieged by the Eighth, which has now finished building a *vallum* around the city, Vibullius and his men end up surrendering without a fight (21 February). As is his custom, Caesar is generous to those who have surrendered; he holds back from sacking the city; incorporates the Pompeian soldiers who surrendered into his own legions; and allows many to go free, including four senators, among whom are Ahenobarbus and Spinther, Ahenobarbus's son, some *equites*, the military tribunes who directed the defense of the city during the siege, the local *duumviri*, and some *decurions* whom Ahenobarbus had gathered from the nearest *municipia*. He even hands the large sum that the *duumviri* had collected and that Ahenobarbus had deposited in the city's treasury to them, almost 6 million sesterces. Acting in this way, he wants to show that he is as benevolent to men as he is disinterested in riches, especially regarding public funds.[3] As for the cohorts of Spinther, as well as the cohorts from Alba Fucens and Sulmo, he absorbs them into his own army, putting them under Curio's command.

Vibullius remains loyal to the Optimates and is sent to Spain to join up with Pompeian soldiers there. Ahenobarbus makes for Cusi (Orbetello), from where he will embark for Massilia, where he will take part in the defense of the city, currently under siege by Caesarian forces.

Caesar's plan stems from his awareness of the strategic importance of Sardinia and Sicily, whose grain supplies keep the social peace both in Rome and throughout Italy. Therefore, Caesar orders Valerius to invade Sardinia with one legion and Curio to invade Sicily with four legions and then to aim to conquer Roman Africa. He will try to prevent Pompey from leaving Brundisium with the Eighth, Twelfth, and Thirteenth, veterans of the Gallic Wars, and with another three freshly recruited legions.

---

3   Caes., I.23.1–4.

Caesar heads down the Adriatic coastline by forced march and takes possession of Puglia. At this time, he captures and then liberates three of the praetor Publius Rutilius Rufus's cohorts, whom he intercepted while they were attempting to reach Pompey in Luceria, having come from Anxur (Terracina in Lazio).

On 5 March, Caesar writes a letter to Cicero to request a meeting with him. He wants to take advice from him and ask him to use his influence over those (few) remaining senators who haven't abandoned Rome to follow Pompey. The same day, he also writes a letter to his friends Oppius and Balbus, who are in Rome. He reports that he has captured two of Pompey's engineering officers—one of whom is the *praefectus fabrum* Numerius Magius—and that he released them on the condition that they take proposals of peace to Pompey and that they return with his answer. If they want to demonstrate their gratitude—writes Caesar—those officers will have to plead with Pompey to prefer to be friends with Caesar rather than with those who have been unceasingly hostile toward both him and Caesar, that is, with those who, with their nefarious plotting, have reduced the *res publica* to the state in which it presently finds itself.

Brundisium hoves into view for Caesar on 9 March. Pompey has barricaded himself in the city with two legions while he waits to be able to depart for Dyrrhachium. On 4 March, Pompey had already sent the two consuls, two legions, and 10 auxiliary cohorts (among whom, perhaps, are the formerly Caesarian Fifth and Seventh Legions, renamed the First and Third) ahead to Dyrrhachium. Not having enough ships available to him, he hasn't yet been able to embark himself, nor embark the remaining legions.

Caesar has his troops make camp below the walls of Brundisium, after which he receives Numerius Magius, his mission complete, in his personal tent. Magius reports that Pompey is not asking Caesar to compromise but to capitulate. Caesar finds the request unacceptable and sends Magius away with a final counter proposal. Magius returns to Pompey to pass it on, but Pompey ignores it. Caesar will wait for Magius's return in vain. Thus, the last, faint thread of hope of avoiding the worst from happening is broken. On 14 March, Caesar writes to Quintus Pedius, his nephew and collaborator, that there are no longer any alternatives to war.

Caesar Borrows the Roman Treasury

To have himself appointed dictator and obtain the means required to finance the war, Caesar quickly leads some of his legionaries from Brundisium to Rome and has them camp outside the *pomerium*. He distributes grain to the population and reassures them: their fears of reprisals are unfounded—he has come to Italy to defend his own personal dignity, the rights of the tribunes of the plebs, and the general interests of the Roman people. The people accept his grain but remain distrustful of him. They have not forgotten that Caesar had been declared a public enemy.

It is at this time that Caesar confiscates and auctions off the possessions of those Pompeians who have left the city. This will arouse much speculation. Servilia, for example, acquires vast amounts of real estate at derisory prices. Among other properties, she will be able to get her hands on the beautiful villa of Quintus Pontius Aquila, located near Herculaneum (Ercolano) in the center of a small nascent town (Portici). Pontius Aquila is a Roman aristocrat. His family's coat of arms is an eagle with the initials Q.P.A. beneath its talons.

Many commentators are amazed at how Servilia has been able to make so many beautiful properties her own at such low prices. Cicero, with his typically acerbic wit, will say: "It's a better bargain than you think, for there is a third off" (in other words, Servilia has acquired them with a discount of a third: *tertia deducta*). This sentence should be looked at more closely, as it contains a double meaning. The key to understanding lies in the word "third", which can be understood both as the third part of the sum (the market value of the individual property put up for auction, or the base price of the auction) and as Tertia, the third daughter of Servilia, a pretty young woman. The double meaning arises in relation to the gossip according to which Servilia, after having given herself to Caesar, made her own daughter submit to the latter's wishes as well. Cicero is very skilled at ironizing, casting invective, and using sarcasm. He plays on the meanings of words as few others can, often catching his interlocutor by surprise. It is typical of the orator to use "jokes" that are also quite cutting against enemies and adversaries, but Cicero overindulges: he ridicules anyone who ends up in his sights, and this causes much rancor toward him.

In February and March, Cicero spent most of his time at Formianum, where he was joined by his wife Terentia and his daughter Tullia. He isn't happy with the task he has been assigned, which makes him an enemy of Caesar. He doesn't want to offend Caesar, but he doesn't want to set himself against Pompey either. He makes no preparations for war and informs Caesar of his inertia and of his own peaceful intentions.[4] He thinks about sending his son Marcus and his nephew Quintus to Athens but then changes his mind. He keeps them under his supervision in his villas until 7 June.[5] From 15 April to 20 May, he hosts them in his villa in Cuma. He is worried and anxious about the progress of the civil war and is especially uncertain about whether to side with Pompey or with Caesar (the problem is theoretical and is used as an alibi in discussions with others; whenever there are risks to be run, making a tactical choice, Cicero places himself in the middle—to mediate, he says—trying to keep one foot in two camps).

Caesar convenes a meeting of the Senate of Rome for 1 April on the Campus Martius to explain his rationale. There are fewer senators present than have remained in the city, following the departure of the majority of the Senate in Pompey's wake.

---

4   Cic. *Att.,* VII.11, V.17, VIII.3.4–5, XId.5, XII.2; *Fam.,* XVI.11.3; Plut. *Cic.,* 37.3.
5   Cic. *Att.,* VII.13a.3, VII.13b.2, XVII.1.4, XVIII.1.20, XVIII.2, XXVI.3.

Caesar denounces the injustices he has suffered and reminds them of his own, numerous attempts to avoid conflict, all thwarted by Pompey's equivocating; he invites the Senate to join with him to govern the state and to send messengers offering peace to Pompey, though he adds that he is also ready to go it alone. He asks to be appointed dictator and to be authorized to withdraw the financial means he needs to win the war from the *aerarium*. What the Senate of Rome has always feared, and what it has not been able to avoid, is being realized; they see in this the end of the *res publica* and the clandestine restoration of the monarchy.

The senators present refuse, albeit while full of fear. Caesar takes note of this. Shortly afterward, to general consternation, he has the Forum occupied by troops and, after threatening to kill Caecilius Metellus, the quaestor of the Treasury who had implied resisting, forces the doors of the Temple of Saturn open. Caesar plunders its coffers and appropriates 15,000 gold bars, 30,000 silver bars, and 30 million sesterces in cash. However, he commits to returning them and pledges the entirety of the booty accumulated during the Gallic Wars as collateral.

In the meantime, before heading back toward Pompey in Greece, to protect his back, he has ordered six legions under the command of Caius Fabius to go ahead of him to Spain and to engage the seven Pompeian legions found there in combat.

Military Operations

The Pompeian legions in Spain are reinforced by contingents of Cantabrian and Aquitanian auxiliaries and can count on significant economic resources and on the magnetism of Pompey (Pompey is renowned in the Iberian provinces for having fought and won the Sertorian War there in 80–72). Three of these are found in Hispania Citerior and are commanded by Lucius Afranius. Afranius, remember, had been praetor in 72 and consul in 60, together with Quintus Caecilius Metellus Celer. More recently, he has been proconsul and governed one of the provinces of Roman Gaul. He has been in Spain since 53.

Two legions of Roman citizens and 30 cohorts of auxiliaries can be found in Hispania Ulterior under the command of Marcus Petreius, who has been at work in Spain since 55. The two remaining legions, in addition to 30 cohorts of auxiliaries and 5,000 cavalry, are in Lusitania (central and southern Portugal, plus the Spanish region of Extremadura), led by Marcus Terentius Varro. Varro, we recall, is politically active among the ranks of the Optimates. He has been tribune, quaestor in Illyricum, and legate and proquaestor in Spain. He fought in the Piratic War, patrolling the waters between the Ionian and the Aegean Seas with his fleet. In 49, he is a propraetor.

After a two-week stay in Rome, Caesar leaves for Spain, leaving the running of the city to the urban praetor Marcus Lepidus and the government of Italy to Mark Antony. One of those who goes with him is Marcus Caelius Rufus. It is worth highlighting how, on Caesar's departure, Antony becomes the arbiter of the situation in Italy. All this happens in the month of April.

In the meantime, Curio has disembarked in Sicily. Cato abandons his position, not even making an effort at resisting. He flees with his troops to the province of Africa to join Publius Attius Varus, Pompey's legate and formerly the provincial governor. After having been abandoned by his troops at Oximum in Picenum, he had been sent by Pompey to North Africa to oversee the Pompeian resistance there. Varus commands two legions, one of which is formed of fresh recruits, while the other is the one that is stationed in the province and has Juba I, king of Numidia, as an ally.

Curio leaves two legions in Sicily (perhaps he doesn't trust them, seeing as they were previously loyal to Pompey; he may fear they will abandon him at the first opportunity) and disembarks at Cape Bon, near Aquilaria, not far from Clupea (Kelibia, Tunisia). Firstly, he sets up a naval blockade of Utica with 12 warships, before occupying Castra Cornelia, around 1.5 km away. This is where the legion that is stationed in the province is normally based, but they have just abandoned it as they have been moved to Hadrumentum. Curio then defeats Varus's troops who had been camped outside Utica and forces them to take refuge in the city.

At the same time, the praetor Caius Valerius Triarius disembarks in Sardinia. He will keep this island loyal to the Pompeian faction, sending the latter a considerable amount of steel to supply its army with weapons in 47. Later, the city of Caralis (Cagliari) will side with Caesar, followed soon after by the entire island. It expels Pompey's lieutenant Marcus Aurelius Cotta and welcomes Caesar's own lieutenant, Quintus Valerius Orca. The Pompeians attempt to reconquer the coastal cities, and while Sulci surrenders, Caralis resists. For this reason, Caesar will later punish the former with a heavy repression and reward the latter.

Caesar's Clemency

In May, Caesar is in Gallia Narbonensis and, with three legions, besieges Massilia, then leaves Caius Trebonius and Decimus Brutus in charge of directing the siege while he sets off with 30 squadrons of light cavalry (900 cavalrymen). He joins his legions from Gaul in June near Ilerda in Hispania Citerior (Lerida in Catalonia), where his men have already begun fighting against Pompey's legions. Right from the very start of the campaign, it is all a series of clashes, pursuits, small sieges of opposing camps, tricks, and errors by commanding officers. At one point, the Pompeians move toward Tarraco (Tarragona in Catalonia) but they are intercepted and forced back to Ilerda, where they are surrounded. The Battle of Ilerda lasts for many days and ends on 2 August 49 with a Caesarian victory. Afranius, Petreius, and Varro surrender and give themselves up to the enemy. Petreius asks to be killed, such is the shame he feels at the defeat he has suffered, but Caesar forgives him, just as he forgives all the others, and lets them go free. Afranius and Petreius will join Pompey in Greece, while Varro lingers. Caesar thinks highly of him as a scholar with very wide intellectual horizons and entrusts him with the task of building a large public library, divided into two sections, one with Latin texts and the other with Greek texts, following the model of similar Hellenistic collections, exemplified by those in Alexandria and Pergamum. The project will be carried out in Rome within the wider context of the building interventions that Caesar proposes to carry out around the Forum.

The legionaries that surrendered, because they are Roman citizens, are given a free choice as to whether to enroll in Caesar's army, settle down in Spain as civilians, or be discharged once they have returned to the River Var, which marks the border between Gallia Narbonensis and Italy.

Caesar then returns to Brundisium, arriving there after Pompey has embarked for Dyrrhachium and reached his destination. Caesar sets off from there for Epirus, with a small army, made up of those war veterans of Pompey's Spanish Legions who have passed under his own banner. He leaves the bulk of his troops in Italy (four legions and 800 cavalry), placing them under the command of Mark Antony, and he orders the latter to join him in Epirus as soon as possible.

Operations in the Strait of Otranto and the Ionian Sea

Bibulus has sided with Pompey, who has put him in charge of the fleet of the Adriatic, with the primary task of preventing Caesar and his troops from reaching Epirus via Brundisium and the Strait of Otranto. But Bibulus loosens his surveillance as winter is coming and the sea is rough. He believes Caesar would not dare to attempt the crossing, so the ships that should be involved in the blockade remain safely at their moorings in port. Caesar—as often happens—does exactly the opposite of what his enemy expects him to do, and, therefore, on the evening of 6 November 49, he lands unopposed with three legions in the Ionian Islands, about 90 km from Bibulus's position. On hearing the news, Bibulus is flabbergasted. Only then does he decide to resume the blockade and increase the number of ships required to prevent further crossings and isolate Caesar where he is.

Caesar takes Corcyra (Corfu) after a week-long siege and integrates the 30 cohorts of Domitius Ahenobarbus that had surrendered into his own forces. By doing so, he puts together six legions. Later, making a mockery of Bibulus's blockade, he deploys his ships outside the port of Brundisium. This happens when Pompey is about to embark for Dyrrachium with 15 cohorts. Another 15 cohorts, led by Lentulus Crus and Claudius Marcellus Minor, have already left Brundisium and are currently sailing for Dyrrachium.

Pompey successfully breaks Caesar's blockade and lands near Dyrrachium, where he joins the consuls. He storms the city and sets up his base of operations there.

Caesar returns to Epirus and takes Oricum and Apollonia, two ancient cities, one situated at the southeastern end of the Bay of Vlorë and the other on the right bank of the River Vjosë (near the modern village of Pojan), important agricultural centers and slave markets. Oricum was born as a Greek colony. It is strategically important for communication with Corcyra and for navigation between the opposite shores of the Adriatic through the Strait of Otranto, and therefore it is an excellent port of call for traveling between Italy and Epirus. It has already functioned as an important military base for the Romans during the wars against the Illyrians and the Macedonians.[6]

Apollonia is also a Greek colony. It was founded by a group of Corcyraeans and Corinthians in 558 and has grown and developed over time. In 148, it became part of the Roman province of Macedonia. Up to 100 ships can be moored in its port. It is the corresponding port to that of Brundisium on the opposite coast of the Adriatic and is the starting point for the Via Egnatia, the extra-urban road that connects the eastern Adriatic coast to Thessalonica, passing through the Balkans, Macedonia, and Thrace.

Caesar waits for Antony to bring him the reinforcements he has asked for, but he is late. Antony doesn't have sufficient transport ships; moreover, Bibulus's fleet has crossed the open sea and has already sunk some of his ships, which were intercepted and attacked while attempting to break the blockade. Antony will join Caesar in three months' time. Neither Bibulus's ships, during the crossing of the Strait of Otranto, nor those of Pompey, during the disembarkation in Epirus, will be able to stop him, despite maneuvering appropriately. In the meantime, Bibulus falls ill. He will die before the winter of 49/48 in a port in Epirus, near Corcyra, leaving his wife, Portia, and a son, Lucius.[7]

Caesar's Second Consulship

Caesar returns to Rome. The Romans hail him, and the Senate spontaneously (so to speak) offers him the dictatorship. Caesar, who requested this before, now makes the *beau geste* of refusing it, but he accepts the consulship for the following year (48). It is noteworthy that this office will not be conferred on Caesar through a vote of the people gathered in assembly but by law by the *comitia centuriata*. Caesar's colleague as consul for 48 is Publius Servilius Vatia Isauricus, consul in 79, proconsul in Cilicia from 78 to 74, vanquisher of the pirates of Cilicia and the bandits of Isauria, censor in 55, and a friend of Cicero. When Caesar was young, he served under him in the

---

6   Caesar provides us with a vivid description of Oricum in Book 3, Section 12 in his commentary on the civil war.

7   Having been widowed by Bibulus, Portia gets married again to Marcus Junius Brutus (Quintus Caepio Brutus), the son of Servilia, and pushes her husband and her son Lucius to conspire against Caesar (44).

early days of the military operations in the Mediterranean seaboards of Anatolia that began in 78.

Remaining in Rome, Caesar governs the state, trying to make himself loved by the people and maintaining a position of restraint. As usual, he doesn't mandate proscriptions or confiscations of property but instead sets free those who fought against him, even conferring offices and honors on some of his enemies, to the extent that after his death (15 April 44), the Romans will dedicate a temple to the goddess Clementia, the personification of the virtues of mercy and clemency, believing that clemency was a characteristic of the deceased dictator.

He sorts out internal affairs, including introducing a regulation for debts that works in favor of the debtors; extending Roman citizenship to the inhabitants of Gallia Cisalpina; recalling exiles back to their homeland; creating many new senators, selecting them from among his supporters, regardless of their origins, which in some cases are very humble (the number of senators thus rises from 600 to 900; from now on, the balance of power within the Senate, previously hegemonized by the Optimates, will be in Caesar's hands); rewarding war veterans by assigning plots of arable land to them; dissolving all trade unions, other than the most ancient (the gangs that had been headed by Clodius and Milo cease to exist); and freely distributing grain to 150 families in need.

As he does so, two pieces of important news reach him. One is good news: the announcement that Massilia has fallen. The other is bad, tragic in fact: the two legions that had been led to Africa by Curio in pursuit of Cato have been massacred by the army of Saburra, the general of Juba I, king of Numidia and an ally of Pompey. Curio is dead.[8]

Both are reported to him in full detail. Caesar thus learns that, during the siege of Massilia, a naval battle had been fought just opposite the city during which ships were boarded and men fought hand-to-hand. As the bodies of the dead and dying plunged into the waters below, falling into the gaps between one ship and another, the water took on the color of blood. Many soldiers, while they were fighting on the decks of ships or trying to remain afloat, were shot by stray arrows. Many others were overwhelmed as masts and shrouds collapsed, broken clean off by chained shot. The horrible sight of mangled bodies could be seen everywhere. One ship, because all those fighting on board had crowded onto one side, tilted further and further until it capsized and sank within a few minutes, dragging men and cargo with it. Soldiers fought with all possible weapons, whether proper or improper, some even using an oar or a plank. Some even tore the spear or arrow that had pierced them from their wound and, holding back the viscera that threatened to spill out, found the force to hurl it back at the enemy in a gesture that was as heroic as it was desperate. In the meantime, the fires of the torches had spread over the ships

---

8   On the death of Curio: Caes., 42; App. *B. Civ.*, 2.45–46; Luc., 4.793–793; Flor., II.13, 34.

and an inferno was now raging. Half-sunken wrecks burned, and the salt water was unable to put out the flames that devoured them. The sea was littered with debris and corpses. The victors, mindful of Caesar's instructions, refrained from carrying out reprisals against the residents of Massilia due to the fame and antiquity of the city and to its previously fine relations with Rome. Domitius Ahenobarbus managed to avoid capture, boarding the only ship that escaped the siege, and joined up with Pompey in Thessaly.

As for Curio, he had been preparing to besiege Utica when he had been informed of the arrival of Juba's army. He launched an attack on the Numidians even though he was leading an army weakened by disease, the season was hot with the sun high in the sky from the early hours of the morning, he didn't know the terrain, he had no knowledge of how the enemy fought, and he probably underestimated their strength. Exhausted by fatigue, heat, and thirst, he stopped with his troops on a rise near the Bagradas River to rest. On 11 August 49, seeing the enemy approach, he rashly accepted the fight and suffered a crushing defeat. As the disaster became clear, he preferred to die rather than to be captured by the enemy and threw himself into the fray; he and almost all of his men were killed. Curio's severed head was delivered into the hands of Juba I. The Roman prisoners were executed. One of the commanders who escaped, Caius Asinius Pollio, managed to get back to Sicily with a few men.

CHAPTER XXVI

Pharsalus

The Mustering of Troops

In January 48, Caesar witnesses the mustering of 12 legions at Brundisium, then embarks for Epirus with 15,000 infantry and 500 cavalry (seven legions) on 12 ships. He disembarks at Paleste, about 100 km south of Dyrrachium, and returns to Brundisium straight away to bring the remaining five legions across. But a violent storm catches him by surprise in the Strait of Otranto. His ship, as well as the rest of the fleet he is commanding, are taking on more water than they can bail out. They can no longer maneuver themselves, colliding with one another with great crashes of broken planking. In the end, almost all of them sink, dragging men, animals, and cargo with them into the depths. Caesar has a brush with death but is saved by a miracle.

In the meantime, Pompey has arrived in Candavia, a mountainous region on the border between Illyricum and Macedonia. To prepare himself for the encounter with Caesar, he has gathered 10 legions (22,000 infantry and 1,000 cavalry), two sizeable fleets, and a large amount of financial aid and supplies, thanks to the assistance he has received from across the Aegean world from Anatolia, from the Roman East, and from Egypt.

Caesar sends the ex-consul Cnaeus Domitius Calvinus to Macedonia with two legions and 500 cavalry with orders to engage Quintus Caecilius Metellus Pius Scipio Nasica. Domitius Calvinus was consul in 53, and he will be again in 40. Scipio Nasica, after having been propraetor of Cyprus (58–56) with the task of making the island into a Roman province (Cyprus had been seized from the Ptolemies), was praetor (54) and proconsul of Syria (49). He is Pompey's father-in-law, having married his daughter Cornelia Metella (born from his marriage to Aemilia Lepida) to him in 52.

Caesar besieges Dyrrachium and entrenches himself outside the city. Awful news then reaches him: he left two fleets at Oricum (at the southeastern end of the Bay of Vlorë in southern Albania) and Nymphaeum, a headland in Illyricum near Lissus, but one of them has been destroyed by Cnaeus Pompey the Younger, the son of Pompey Magnus, while the other has been set alight.

Pompey, with 36,000 men, reaches Dyrrachium from Candavia along the Via Egnatia and makes camp a short distance from Caesar's encampment, in a better position than his. Caesar besieges him. But Caesar doesn't attack, nor does Pompey attempt to break the siege. The standoff continues for a few weeks. When Pompey learns that Caesar has found himself in a tight spot due to problems with his water supplies, he makes a sortie. The fighting goes on for a whole day. At first, Pompey has the worst of it; he loses a couple of thousand men compared to a few dozen fallen soldiers on the opposite side. The battle goes on over the following days, and fortunes ebb and flow. In the end, the odds are proven wrong: Pompey wins hands down. Many of Caesar's soldiers turn tail and run, and many are crushed, trampled on, and killed by the mass of their fellow legionaries. Caesar himself is nearly killed: a terrified legionary is about to attack him, brandishing his sword, when a *lictor* cuts his arm clean off with a blow from a double-headed axe.

Caesar has lost 960 legionaries, 5 tribunes, 43 centurions, and 32 standards when, prudently, he decides to fall back to Apollonia (Pojan in Albania). Pompey's victory, inflated by the sole consul's propaganda, elates Greece, which leaps wholeheartedly onto the winning side. In the heat of battle, however, Pompey made an error: pressured by Labienus, in turn ill-advised by an oracle, he chases the fleeing Caesarians instead of focusing on their encampment. Had he done the opposite, the war would have taken a different turn, one more favorable to him.[1]

Caesar leaves four cohorts in Apollonia, one in Issa (Lissa), and three in Doricum, abandons the wounded, and moves inland. As Caesar is crossing the River Genusus (Shkumbin) at Asparagium (a town near Dyrrachium), Pompey's cavalry intercepts his rear. Pompey arrives; Caesar and Pompey find themselves face to face, separated by the river. Caesar disengages his army, crosses the Pindus mountain range, and enters Thessaly at Eginion (near modern Kalabaka in Thessaly). His intention is to force Pompey to come to the aid of Metellus Scipio Nasica, who is currently in Larissa in Thessaly, a city loyal to Pompey. If he succeeds, the conditions for a decisive pitched battle will present themselves.

Pompey takes the bait. He returns to Asparagium and convenes his *consilium*. It is suggested to him that he return to Brundisium, destroy Caesar's ships that are stationed in Messana (Messina in Sicily) and Valentia (Vibo Valentia in Calabria), free Rome, strip Caesar of Gaul and Spain, and only after all this face the enemy in a final showdown. But he doesn't agree because he wants to prevent Scipio Nasica from succumbing to Caesar. Therefore, he marches eastward along the Via Egnatia, with the intention of surprising Domitius Calvinus who is camped at Bitola. In the meantime, Caesar is enlisting every man he meets and Fufius Calenus threatens Athens.

---

1   F. Santangelo, *Roma repubblicana. Una storia in quaranta vite* (Roma: Carocci, 2019), 294.

Domitius flees toward the upper course of the Haliacmon. Pompey doesn't follow him but instead heads south. Meanwhile, Caesar has arrived at Gomfi, a city in the foothills of the Pindus, in a position that dominates the deep gorges that cut through from Thessaly to Athamania and Ambracia. The local population refuse to supply him with food and barricade themselves behind the city walls. Caesar storms Gomfi in half a day, plunders it, and razes it to the ground. It is a clear message to other Thessalian strongholds, a terrible warning not to take Pompey's side but to pass under Caesar's banners instead. His men can finally fill their bellies, which have been empty for days, and even gorge on food and get drunk. This is what the Germans do most of all, making fools of themselves. Before long, all the cities of Thessaly have submitted to Caesar, except for Larissa.

Metropolis (near Paleokastro in Karditsa) is one of the corners of a fortified quadrangle that monitors access to the Thessalian plain. Its inhabitants used to take refuge there in the event of danger. Caesar parades the prisoners from Gomfi before the walls of Metropolis and ensures that the inhabitants open its gates to him. Then he continues his march and camps on the road that leads to Larissa, via Palaeofarsalos and Pharsalos/Pharsalus (Farsala), at the point where it crosses the River Enipeas (near the modern village of Vasilis).

On 29 July, Caesar makes camp on the plain of Pharsalus, an agricultural area in southeastern Thessaly (south of Larissa and west of Volos, probably on the northern banks of the Enipeas, immediately north of the city of Palaeofarsalos and close to Cynoscephalae). Pharsalus is the successor to the Homeric city of Phthia, the capital of Peleus's kingdom, the father of Achilles, and famous for its Myrmidons (the soldiers commanded by Achilles). It was one of Thessaly's major settlements and the seat of one of its *tetrarchs*. It became a Roman city after the fall of the Kingdom of Macedon, of which it formed a part. Armies often pass through on their way to war, with all the good and bad that can derive from that (more bad than good, to tell the truth). This helps to explain why it is protected by fortification walls in Cyclopean masonry.

Caesar is joined at Pharsalus by Domitius and his two legions and 500 cavalry. His army is thus increased to eight legions, i.e., 80 cohorts for a total of 22,000 infantry, and 1,000 cavalry, in addition to non-combatants.

On 31 July, Pompey also arrives at Pharsalus at the head of 12 legions and a number of cavalry contingents supplied by his allies. The legions are subdivided into 120 cohorts for a total of 40,000 infantry. Of the cavalry, 2,700 are European Gauls and/or Germans, 500 are Italics from Egypt (Gabiniani), 600 are Galatians (Gauls from Galatia in Anatolia), and 3,200 are other mounted troops from Asia. Pompey is accompanied by numerous senators and *equites*. He waits on the slopes of Mount Dogandzis, 5 km northeast of Caesar's camp. There, he is joined by Scipio Nasica and his legions. His infantry thus totals 47,000 men, of whom 2,000 are war veterans.

The Pompeians outnumber the Caesarians by more than two to one and have a seven-to-one advantage in their cavalry numbers. As such, they are certain of victory. They are so confident that they have prepared the victory banquet and decorated the tents with laurel wreaths. They are already thinking of what they will do after the victory to take revenge on their enemies and profit from their defeat. They are drafting the bills that they want to propose and have approved after their victory. They are listing the enemies they want to capture and execute. They are even reserving which properties and goods of the Caesarians they want for themselves. They are arguing about whether Lucilius Hirrus can stand for office *in absentia*, given that the man in question is absent, finding himself in the Parthian Empire on a mandate from Pompey.[2] Civic and religious offices are divided up. Scipio, Lentulus Spinther, and Domitius Ahenobarbus are all fiercely competing for the position of *pontifex maximus,* currently held by Caesar.[3]

Pompey believes Caesar is in trouble, and therefore he judges that it isn't necessary to meet him in a pitched battle; all he needs to do is to wear him out and, in the end, he will give in. His high command is of the opposite opinion. They believe that Caesar has no way out and that they should press him, give him no respite, and provoke him to offer battle. They pressure Pompey, quivering for action and champing at the bit, and are not satisfied until they manage to force Pompey's hand. They don't realize that they are playing into Caesar's hands, who, in the meantime, is thinking about how to prepare his men for battle, how to raise their spirits, and how best to deploy them on the field ...

The Battle

On the night of 8/9 August, Pompey has a premonitory dream. He sees himself entering his theater on the Campus Martius and consecrating the spoils of his victory to Venus, the goddess to whom the temple at the top of the *cavea* is dedicated. But this is no dream but a nightmare, and he wakes up with a start. Venus, in fact, is the tutelary deity of the *gens Iulia*, the family line to which Caesar belongs. The next day—9 August 48—Caesar leads his troops to the foot of Mount Dogandzis and deploys his legions. He arranges them where the ground is flat, among the wheat fields, where the ears move like waves on the sea in a light breeze. The Tenth, on the right flank, under the command of Faustus Cornelius Sulla; the Seventh, Eighth, and Ninth, with the auxiliaries and Balearic slingers, on the left flank, under the command of Mark Antony; the Eleventh, Twelfth, and the most recently levied legions—the Twenty-Fifth, Twenty-Sixth, and Twenty-Ninth—are positioned in the center, under the orders of Domitius Calvinus. Caesar leaves between two and seven

2   Caes., III.82.3–4, III.83.1–3.
3   Caes., III.83.1.

cohorts to guard the camp and the baggage. A unit of 120 volunteers is placed on the front line, at the very end of his right flank. This is led by a veteran reservist, the 37-year-old Caius Crastinus, a man of considerable valor and who is held in high esteem by Caesar.

Crastinus has served as a legionary for 17 years (he took up arms in 65), 12 of which have been under Caesar, to whom he is utterly loyal and devoted. He served first in the Eighth, then in the Ninth, and, since 61, in the Tenth. He has served as the *primus pilus* centurion of the First Century of the First Cohort of the Tenth Legion.[4] He fought at the Battle of Alesia and, later, against the Helvetii. For him and for many of his fellow soldiers—those from the Hispanic regions, that is, the Eighth and Ninth—their term of service is already over. The campaign that Caesar is leading against Pompey is the last campaign of Crastinus's draft; the battle Crastinus is preparing to fight at Pharsalus will be his last before being discharged.

Pompey has deployed his men on the slopes of the hill in a widened formation to unnerve the enemy. On the left wing are the First and Third, with the archers and slingers, all under the command of Lucius Domitius Ahenobarbus (the First and Third are the legions that, after fighting in the Gallic Wars under Caesar's command, were handed over to Pompey by decree of the Senate to fight in a war against the Parthians; the Third was formerly Caesar's Fifteenth), and the entirety of the cavalry, led by Titus Labienus. He has placed his "Syrian" Legions in the center under the command of Scipio Nasica. On the right is the Gemina Legion, brought from Cilicia, and the Iberian cohorts of Lucius Lentulus. Positioned between the center and the right flank are the Twenty-Fourth and the Twenty-Eighth, two Italic Legions previously led by Caesar. Seven cohorts and a few units of Thracian and Thessalian auxiliaries have been left to guard the camp under the command of Lucius Afranius, whose lieutenant is one of Pompey's sons, the 25-year-old Cnaeus.

Caesar is very close to the enemy position and slowly advances closer and closer. On the far side of the enemy lines, he sees a potentially advantageous situation for him. He is aware that Labienus is in the habit of attacking the enemy on their weaker side and then sweeping toward the center to meet the stronger side. To counter his ex-lieutenant's tactic, he detaches six cohorts, the most experienced, from the right side of his formation, separating them from the Tenth, and keeps them in reserve. By doing so, he guarantees the availability of a mobile unit on the one hand, which can be used for any eventuality, and, on the other, he tempts Labienus with a falsely weakened right flank.

Caesar harasses Pompey to prompt him to descend from his position, but his troops remain motionless for a long time. Then, finally, Pompey cedes his advantage of holding the high ground and starts to descend toward the plain in battle formation. This is a clear signal; it means that the encounter is about to begin.

---

4   Caes., III.91.1.

The legionaries and auxiliary forces of both sides—70,000 men in all—are ready to fight, impatient to start the carnage. The tension is so high that the air itself seems to be vibrating. Caesar's men, set out in *maniples*, lined up behind their shields, struggle to overcome their anxiousness and nerves as the enemy approaches. The signal to attack is given by Caesar's standard being lowered twice and by the blasts of trumpets from Pompey's camp.

The battle unfolds as Caesar had expected. At the start, 7,000 of Labienus's cavalry attack the Tenth. The latter cannot withstand the onslaught, but Caesar uses his reserve and catches the enemy cavalry in a vice. Labienus and his men have to fall back. As they flee, they leave their missile troops unprotected. The Caesarian reserves annihilate them, then they rush behind the exposed flank of the Pompeian formation. This move determines the course of the battle. The bulk of Pompey's army—seeing their cavalry in flight—lose heart, retreat, break ranks, then flee in disorder for the nearby hills. Domitius Ahenobarbus is swamped by cavalry. Cicero, in his *Second Philippic*, will state that Domitius was killed by Mark Antony.[5]

The First retreats from the battlefield, making for the coast and Pompey's fleet, which is waiting at anchor. Titus Labienus has fled, as have Marcus Junius Brutus and a group of senators. Brutus, we recall, is the stepson of Decimus Junius Silanus and the son of Servilia, and the nephew of Cato. He is also, perhaps, Caesar's illegitimate son.

Another 18,000 men save themselves. Many of these will succeed in reaching Buthrotum.

Some 20,000 soldiers, breaking away from their respective units (the Fifteenth, the Gemina, and the Syrian Legions), reorganize themselves in Pompey's camp. On the arrival of the Tenth, around midday, they are forced to retreat. They make for Mount Dogandzis, where 4,000 other Pompeians are deployed. One of these is Domitius Ahenobarbus. While he tries to reach the troops caught on the mountainside, he faints from fatigue and weakness, exhausted by the recent, intense physical and mental exertions and by a continual lack of sleep. Caesar's soldiers will find him unconscious on the ground and kill him. In the meantime, thousands of other scattered Pompeians and Pompeian auxiliaries plunder the camp. As for Pompey, as soon as he realizes that the battle is lost, he retires to his tent.

Pompey's Escape

When the Tenth attacks the camp, while looting rages and chaos reigns, the generals Favonius, Lentulus, and Spinther gather at the entrance to Pompey's tent, horses held at the bridle, ready to take flight. Favonius enters the tent and finds Pompey lying on his bed. He warns him about the attack, but Pompey only responds with

---

5   Cic. *Phil.*, II.71.

a dazed expression. Favonius shakes him to jolt him out of his stupor, and, with the help of Pompey's secretary Philip, a Greek freedman, gets him to his feet, puts an ordinary cloak around him to disguise him, and gets him into a saddle. Afterward, he, Pompey, and the other generals, and perhaps Philip too, spur the horses to a gallop, charging through the rear gate to the encampment and escaping from view.

In the immediate hours that follow, Caesar—at the head of the Seventh, Eighth, Ninth, and Tenth—chases, intercepts, and attacks the Pompeians who, having retreated to Mount Dogandzis, have abandoned their position and are marching for Larissa. These 24,000 men are cornered on a hill near a river. Exhausted, hungry, and thirsty, they surrender unconditionally and are taken prisoner. Caesar gives the order to release 20,000 of these prisoners and incorporate them into his army and to execute the rest. Then he orders his troops to march on Larissa.

The Hispanic Legions—the Eighth and Ninth—and the Tenth mutiny. Pharsalus was supposed to have been the Hispanic Legions' last battle, as their term of service is now up, and they are demanding they be discharged and receive their severance pay (20,000 sesterces each). In turn, the Tenth demand they also be paid. Furious, Caesar calls his other four legions to him, hands the mutineers the task of escorting the prisoners of war and sends them to his encampment on the banks of the Enipeas. He decides to postpone punishing the leaders of the revolt until later. In the meantime, he marches on Larissa.

On the way, he receives a message from Marcus Junius Brutus. He is in Larissa with a group of senators. After their flight from Pompey's camp, he and the senators hid in the hills before managing to reach the city. Brutus gives advance notice to Caesar that the city has surrendered. In the meantime, Pompey and his companions, spurring their horses at a gallop, have arrived in Larissa. Along the way, a large unit of Labienus's cavalry, scattered but intact, has joined up with them (from now on, this unit will be Pompey's escort).

Caesar arrives in Larissa after Pompey has moved away with his generals and his escort. As he enters the city, he embraces Brutus, who begs him to forgive him. Not only does Caesar spare his life but he even appoints him as praetor (Caesar, remember, has the power to appoint magistrates).

Caesar returns to Pompey's camp at Pharsalus. Faced with the sad sight of what he finds there, he doesn't rejoice in the victory. Caius Asinius Pollio (76 BC–5 AD)—*eques* and *homo novus*, judicial orator, author of a history in 17 books, a Caesarian loyalist, and combatant at Pharsalus—will write that, at the sight of so many fallen Romans, killed by other Romans, scattered across the battlefield, Caesar exclaimed that if he wanted this, it was because he had been forced to do it, and that it was not he who wanted a civil war but the Optimates, who had fooled Pompey, forcing him to do what he would never have done had it been up to him.

Later, Caesar moves to the battlefield where the fallen are lying in their thousands and looks disconsolately at the panorama. The losses amount to 15,000 Pompeian soldiers, including 10 legionary commanders and 40 legates, and 200 for the Caesarians, including 30 centurions.[6] One of these centurions is Crastinus. He was one of the first to launch himself at the enemy and fought with extraordinary courage until a sword blow caught him in the face. Caesar will pay him solemn honors and will remember him in his commentary on the Civil Wars.[7] The Caesarians take 24,000 prisoners, accumulate vast spoils of war, and collect 180 standards, including nine legionary eagles.[8] Caesar celebrates the victory with his men, distributing prizes and honors, before ordering that the Tenth be decimated as punishment.

Decimation is a sanction that was most recently applied by Crassus during Spartacus's Revolt (73–71). It consists of killing one soldier in 10. Each cohort is divided into groups of 10 legionaries, and each group chooses one of its members to be stoned or beaten to death. Those who must die eat a last meal based on barley instead of wheat, and, on the eve of their execution, are sent to sleep in the open air, outside the encampment. The Hispanic Legions protest, the Seventh, Eleventh, and Twelfth join their voices to the chorus, and Caesar's senior officers advise him not to follow up on the sentence to avoid an uncontrollable riot. In the end, Caesar changes his mind. The next day, he sends all his legions back to Italy, led by Mark Antony, except for a legion of ex-Pompeian volunteers and the cavalry, with whom he will go after Pompey. The ex-Pompeian volunteers are the two cohorts of the Sixth that surrendered on 9 August at Pharsalus. In all, Caesar takes around 900 men with him.

In the meantime, Pompey's group—some 40 men—have cantered toward the sea without stopping to take a rest, not even at night. Once they have arrived on the coast, they board a cargo ship leaving for Mytilene/Lesbos, an island off the rugged Aegean coast of Anatolia. He will be joined there by his wife Cornelia and his son Sextus, to whom he will show his optimism about the outcome of the war. Afterwards, following some initial hesitation and having discarded a series of alternative hypotheses, he definitively settles on asking the Ptolemies in Egypt for asylum and protection. Thus, he embarks for the Nile country with his wife and son. He doesn't know that he is going to his death.

---

6   The losses declared by the victors are not reliable because they are always lower than the actual figure; other sources, putting Caesar's commentary on the Civil Wars to one side, speak of at least 1,200 Caesarians being killed at Pharsalus. The estimate of the number of fallen Pompeians supplied by Caesar is not reliable either; in the future, Pollio will speak of 6,000 legionaries killed in addition to an unspecified number of non-combatants (slaves).

7   Caes., III.91, III.99.2.

8   Caes., III.99.

CHAPTER XXVII

The Alexandrian War and Conquest of the Cimmerian Bosphorus

The Death of Pompey

In the spring or summer of 49, Pompey sends one of his sons to Alexandria to ask for troops, ships, and money in preparation for the inevitable civil war. Cleopatra VII seizes the opportunity to get rid of the Gabiniani, sending 500 of them to Pompey together with 60 ships loaded with grain. The Roman Achillas, commander-in-chief of the Gabiniani and of the Ptolemaic army, reacts to this, in agreement with the highest-ranking state officials, Pothinus and Theodotus of Chios.

Achillas, Pothinus, and Theodotus are a group of schemers intent on securing mutual favors. Pothinus is the finance minister and acts on behalf of Ptolemy XIII, whom he tutors; he is a eunuch (as all court officials are) and a shrewd man, adept at plotting. Theodotus is a rhetorician and teacher and is an adviser to Ptolemy XIII.[1]

The three conspire against Cleopatra VII, bending Ptolemy XIII to their ends. In the autumn of 49, Ptolemy XIII sends his sisters into exile and remains on the throne as the sole ruler of Egypt, while Theodotus becomes regent (he will govern Egypt in his name and on his behalf).[2]

Cleopatra VII initially finds refuge and protection in a temple in the Nile Valley as the guest of Callimachus, the *strategos* of the Thebaid (the territory around the city of Thebes in Upper Egypt); then in Ascalon (Ashkelon in Israel), a *civitas libera et immunis* in the western Negev, with Antipater the Idumaean, the ruler of Judea, who is grateful to the Egyptian royal household since Ptolemy IX Soter Lathyros wrested Ascalon from the Hasmoneans of Judea in 104.[3]

In Judea, Cleopatra VII hires an army of mercenaries and tries to use them to recover her throne, going to war against her brother Ptolemy XIII and clashing with his army near Pelusium, a city situated on the very eastern end of the Nile Delta (Tell

---

1   Plut. *Brut.*, XXXIII.3; *Pomp.*, LXXVII.2. According to Appian, Theodotus was born on Samos. App. *B. Civ.*, II.84.
2   Caes., III.108.
3   Str., XVII.11.

el-Farama, 30 km southeast of modern Port Said and on the border with Palestine). The Ptolemaic army is under the overall command of Ptolemy XIII, who follows his troops, who are commanded by Achillas and other generals. While Cleopatra VII is fighting her brother on the battlefield at Pelusium, Pompey enters the arena, fresh from his defeat at Pharsalus and fleeing from Caesar who is pursuing him.

Pompey has arrived in Egypt with about 50 triremes and quadriremes, aboard which are his wife Cornelia, his son Sextus, and a militia of 2,000 slaves, made available to him by clients and traders. After leaving Thessaly, the ships followed the coast of Anatolia, heading past Cyprus, passed by the ports of Syria and Palestine (whose inhabitants prevented them from stopping so as not to compromise themselves with Caesar), before finally entering Egyptian waters and dropping anchor in the canal port of Pelusium.

Pompey sends a messenger to Ptolemy XIII, requesting asylum. He trusts he will be able to find refuge and protection in the Nile country as an act of gratitude to him after he helped to restore Ptolemy XII Auletes to the throne. In fact, Pompey worked hard for this, convincing the Senate to intervene militarily in Egypt to put Ptolemy XII back on the throne and even hosting the latter in his own villa in Alba. And there is no doubt that Aulus Gabinius re-established Ptolemy XII on the throne in agreement with Pompey, to whom he was very loyal.[4]

On 28 September 48, Ptolemy XIII sends a message to Pompey to say that he is ready to welcome him, that he is waiting for him on the beach together with his court dignitaries, and that he will send a ship to pick him up. In fact, it isn't wise for Pompey to bring his ship close to shore due to the risk of running it aground on the shoals. Before long, a small launch is approaching Pompey's ship. It is being handled by a number of Egyptians, but Achillas and the leader of the Gabiniani, the military tribune Lucius Septimius, are also on board. Achillas and Septimius are in military uniform and are armed with swords.

Pompey says his goodbyes to his wife and son, who will remain on the ship, and, preceded by two centurions and by his freedman Philip and servant Scythes, goes to take his place on the small vessel. When Pompey steps onto the boat, Septimius, who served under him against the pirates in 67, welcomes him deferentially, hailing him as *imperator*. The rowers sink their oars into the water, and the boat moves away from the ship and heads toward the beach. Septimius remains on his feet, standing beside Pompey, while everyone else is seated. The journey is short and conducted in silence. When the hull scrapes against the shore, Pompey gets to his feet and prepares to get off. Just then, Septimius, with a sudden movement, draws his sword and thrusts it into Pompey's side, without giving him time to defend himself. Immediately afterward, Achillas also strikes Pompey. Pompey collapses without a

4   After this, Gabinius managed to restore order in Syria. In 54, he was replaced by Marcus Licinius Crassus and returned to Rome, where he was subjected to three trials for malfeasance. He was found guilty and sentenced to exile, also having his assets confiscated.

sound and soon breathes his last. Thus dies the Roman Alexander, the hero of the *res publica*, the sole consul, the ex-triumvir, the former son-in-law of Caesar and both his enemy and his friend. Caught unawares, Scythes and the two centurions have no time to react and are also killed.

The tragedy unfolds within a few moments. Cornelia, Sextus, and the crew on the ship anchored in the harbor have seen everything, albeit from a distance; they are horrified but unable to intervene. Their ship raises its anchor and quickly leaves the harbor. Ptolemy XIII and his entourage withdraw. Pompey's body is decapitated with a dagger (the head, once separated from the torso, is taken away), stripped of its clothes, and left naked on the shore. The freedman Philip is spared: it is left to him to build a pyre and burn what remains of Pompey's body.

The order to assassinate Pompey was nominally given by Ptolemy XIII; *de facto*, it came from the regent Theodotus.[5] Acting in agreement with Achillas and Pothinus, he decided to have Pompey killed, thinking that, by doing so, he would ingratiate himself with Caesar and obtain his support against Cleopatra VII. Primarily, he wanted to make Caesar forget that Egypt, under Ptolemy XII Auletes, had supported Pompey during the Civil War, promising him a subsidy of 17.5 million drachmas (about 80 million sesterces, based on an exchange rate of 1 drachma = 4.5 sesterces) and subsequently paying him half. But the conspirators have made a serious miscalculation.

The Battle of Alexandria

On 2 October 48—just four days after Pompey's assassination—Caesar arrives in Alexandria with 3,200 legionaries, 800 mounted auxiliaries, and 10 warships from Rhodes. He enters the Royal Palace, surrounded by armed men, and preceded by *lictors* each of whom carries *fasces*, a bundle of rods with an axe-head tied into them. He is welcomed by the senior courtiers; the sovereigns are absent. Once the introductions are over, Theodotus shows the embalmed head of Pompey to Caesar, together with the signet ring of the deceased. He is expecting a sign of gratitude and instead is speechless when Caesar reacts to the sight of the macabre remains entirely differently. Caesar turns his gaze away and becomes misty-eyed, then orders that Pompey's remains be buried in a small plot of land outside the city, dedicated to Nemesis.[6]

Summoned by Caesar to the palace. Ptolemy XIII and Arsinoe return to Alexandria. Fortuitously, Cleopatra VII's voyage from the Palestinian frontier has taken place by sea. She arrives at her destination at night and reaches the palace

---

5   Plut. *Pomp.*, 77; Dio Cass., XLI.3; App. *B. Civ.*, II.84.

6   App. *B. Civ.*, II.90. *See* also Lucan's reconstruction of the episode in *Pharsalia*. Pompey's head was buried outside Alexandria, but exactly where is unknown. The burial site was devastated during the war that the emperor Trajan (r. 98–117) waged against the Jews in Egypt. The Jews hated Pompey for having conquered Jerusalem in 63.

on board a small boat, which approaches the complex in silence. She will present herself to Caesar in an unusual, unexpected, and rather amusing way.

A certain Apollodorus—possibly the brother of Callimachus, the *strategos* of the Thebaid who had hosted Cleopatra as his guest after her flight from Alexandria—bribes the palace guards and is able to reach Caesar's apartments undisturbed. Being carried on his shoulder is Cleopatra VII, wrapped in blankets, which are tied together with a cord and enclosed in a flaxen sack, the kind used to carry linen. He requests and is granted permission to be admitted to Caesar's presence, and, when he is standing in front of him, he opens the bundle, from which the woman emerges.[7] Caesar is struck by Cleopatra VII's brazenness, but he is fascinated by her conversation and her grace. Cleopatra VII, with the musical intonations of her voice, her polished eloquence, and her highly refined intelligence, captivates and seduces him.[8]

Caesar writes off the unpaid half of Pompey's war expenses (about 40 million sesterces) that is owed by the Egyptian state, but he asks for, and receives, 10 million sesterces to continue the fight against the Pompeians. He insists that Cleopatra VII and Ptolemy XIII stop fighting one another. He agrees that Egypt shall remain a client state of Rome, passing up on the opportunity to turn it into a Roman province (he fears the political problems that would be created were it to fall into the hands of an unscrupulous governor).[9] He declares that he wants to respect the will of Ptolemy XII Auletes, which Pompey went against. Consequently, he restores Cleopatra VII to the throne, where she will sit alongside Ptolemy XIII. Furthermore, he proclaims the restitution of Cyprus to the Ptolemies, restores the Kingdom of Cyprus, and puts Arsinoe and Ptolemy XIV on the throne. In 58, we recall, Rome tore Cyprus away from the Ptolemies, confiscating the property of Ptolemy on Cyprus, and annexing the island, adding it to the province of Cilicia. Because of this, Ptolemy committed suicide. With this act, Caesar thus nullifies the Clodian laws in relation to Cyprus and the island once more becomes an independent state, governed by a pair of Ptolemies (though it will not remain so for long).

Caesar doesn't expect problems to arise among the Gabiniani, nor at court. But he is mistaken. He underestimates the fact that the Gabiniani no longer respond to the authority of Rome. It also escapes him that the clique in power in the country don't want Cleopatra VII and Ptolemy XIII to make peace with each other, nor do they intend to submit to Cleopatra VII, because they believe she lacks support among the people of Alexandria. Moreover, to free Egypt from its status as a client state of Rome, the clique considers Caesar's claim to 10 million sesterces as interference in the internal affairs of Egypt.

---

7   Plut. *Caes.*, 49.1–2.
8   Dio Cass., 42.34.3–6; Plut. *Caes.*, 49.
9   Suet. *Iul.*, 35.2.

Pothinus and Theodotus plot to kill Caesar during a banquet held at the Royal Palace to celebrate the reconciliation of Cleopatra VII with Ptolemy XIII. Their plan is thwarted by an anonymous barber, who hears of it by chance and runs to tell Caesar. Caesar has Pothinus executed,[10] while Theodotus flees for Asia.[11]

Achillas sends for the army of Ptolemy XIII, which is stationed in Pelusium. In turn, Caesar summons a legion of ex-Pompeians to him who surrendered after the Battle of Pharsalus and who are currently in Syria under the command of Cnaeus Domitius Calvinus.[12] Caesar also asks for help from client kings in the East— Mithridates of Pergamum, the Nabateans—the Pompeians in Asia, and Hyrcanus II, the High Priest of the Temple of Jerusalem. All those who are asked respond positively. Hyrcanus II orders the Jews of Alexandria to rally to Caesar's side while he awaits reinforcements, which he will lead himself.

Caesar takes Ptolemy XIII and Arsinoe IV hostage and, on hearing that the Egyptian army is marching on the city, forces the former to send two old friends from Rome, Dioscorides and Serapion, to Achillas with orders to stop. However, the situation deteriorates when Achillas has the message-bearers killed, puts himself at the head of the army, and marches on Alexandria.

The army of Achillas is sizeable—20,000 infantry and 2,000 cavalry—but also heterogeneous: it comprises regular soldiers from the Ptolemaic army, Gabiniani, and Macedonian, Greek, Persian, Thracian, Rhodian, Arab, Nubian and Libyan mercenaries, not to mention ex-slaves and ex-pirates from Syria and Cilicia. It attacks the walls, is able to breach them, and occupies most of the city.

Caesar retreats to the innermost and most inaccessible part of the Royal Quarter. From there, however, Caesar can control the Great Harbor, where 22 Egyptian ships and 50 Roman ships are at anchor. In theory, Caesar could disengage, boarding his men onto the ships and setting sail. In practice, though, he cannot, as the Etesian winds are whipping up the sea.

Achillas tries to take possession of the Great Harbor. If he succeeds, he would be able to prevent Caesar from receiving reinforcements and supplies from the sea.

Caesar sees the danger and orders the Ptolemaic fleet to be set ablaze.[13] A shower of incendiary arrows falls on those ships, which catch alight (they will burn like torches). Very quickly, the fire, blown by the wind, spreads to the dock and brushes at the warehouses where heaps of sacks of grain and 40,000 rolls from the Library,

---

10 Plut. *Caes.,* 49.
11 Theodotus was killed in Asia between 43 and 42. It is uncertain whether this was at the hands of Caesar's assassin, Marcus Junius Brutus, or on the orders of Gaius Cassius Longinus, who is said to have had him crucified. App. *B. Civ.,* II.90; cf. Plut. *Brut.* XXXIII.6; *Pomp.* LXXX.6.
12 Caes. *BAl.,* 9.
13 Caes., III.111.6.

copies of the originals, are stored ahead of being exported.[14] Caesar captures the island of Pharos, which controls access to the Great Harbor, and hunts down and kills its inhabitants.

It is just then that Arsinoe IV escapes from the Royal Palace and rallies the people of Alexandria, who are ready to race into the streets to riot. They revolt against the Romans for two reasons: because they do not accept being ruled by a woman (Cleopatra VII) and because they are indignant at Caesar's demands for 10 million sesterces. Arsinoe IV promotes her own servant, named Ganymedes, to the rank of general. Ganymedes kills Achillas[15] and taints the aqueduct that feeds the Royal Quarter with sea water, making the water undrinkable.

Caesar curbs the panic that is spreading among his men by having deep wells dug, and he will find abundant fresh water and aquifers.[16] The legion from Syria also arrives at this point on board a fleet, but the wind prevents them from being able to enter the harbor. Caesar goes to meet them with his ships to supply them with fresh drinking water.

Ganymedes attacks Caesar on his return to the harbor with the few Egyptian ships that were saved from the fire, but he is repelled. Ganymedes quickly fills the gaps in his ranks (he rapidly prepares 22 quadriremes, five quinqueremes, and many other smaller ships which he equips with expert crews) and engages Caesar's fleet again. The battle is very hard-fought; Caesar loses 400 men and risks his own life (he dives into the water from a sinking ship and swims for a long way under a hail of Egyptian arrows until he reaches and clambers aboard another ship that is further out).[17] Retaking the command, he withdraws from the battle due to the many losses suffered.

---

14 Dio Cass. XLII.38.2. It is commonly believed that Caesar set fire to the Library of Alexandria. This isn't correct. Nor is it correct that the scrolls lost in the incident were books imported from abroad, waiting to be stored away in the Library. The stored books that were burned were ones that were ready to be exported. L. Canfora, *La biblioteca scompasa* (Palermo: Sellerio, 1988), 7–79, 130–132, 139–143. The real end of the Library of Alexandria came during the war between Emperor Aurelian (r. 270–275 AD) and Zenobia, Queen of Palmyra. At that time, the entirety of the Bruchion district, including the Royal Palaces, was destroyed, except for the Museum. Ammianus Marcellinus, speaking of Alexandria, mentions the disaster in *Rerum gestarum* XXII.16.15. The activity of the Library continued through the Serapeum, albeit in a reduced form, given that this contained only 42,800 works, whereas the Library that had been destroyed had contained 700,000. The Serapeum was in turn destroyed in 391 AD when a mob of fanatics led by Theophilus, patriarch of Alexandria, stormed it and destroyed it. On this incident: E. Gibbon, *Storia della decadenza e caduta dell'Impero romano*, vol. II (Torino: Einaudi, 1987), 1031–1034; see also A. Baldini, "Problemi della tradizione sulla 'distruzione' del Serapeo di Alessandria," *RSA* 15 (1985): 97–152.
15 Caes. *BAl.*, 4.
16 Caes. *BAl.*, 7.
17 App. *B. Civ.*, II.90; Dio Cass., 42.40.4.

The Alexandrians send an envoy to ask Caesar to release Ptolemy XIII, handing over Arsinoe IV and Ganymedes in exchange, whom they consider failures. Caesar agrees.[18] The Egyptian army then returns to the attack, led by Ptolemy XIII. He defeats Euphranor, commander of Caesar's fleet, in a bitter naval battle off Canopus.

In the meantime, Antipater of Ashkelon has crossed the eastern border of Egypt at the head of 3,000 Jews. He captures Pelusium, wins a battle at Leontopolis (Kafr Al Meqdam), and accepts the spontaneous surrender of the population of Memphis (Mit Rahina) (November 48).

For his part, Mithridates, King of Pergamum, arrives in Egypt with an army and defeats the Ptolemaic forces at Iudaion Stratopedon. Ptolemy XIII is unsuccessful in his attempts to prevent Mithridates from joining his forces with those of Caesar on the shores of Lake Mareotis. Lake Mareotis is a body of brackish water located in the western part of the Nile Delta and separated from the Mediterranean Sea by the narrow strip of coastal land on which Alexandria stands. The decisive battle is fought on 27 March 47 on the banks of the Nile. Ptolemy XIII is defeated[19] and dies when his ship sinks[20] (when his body is found, he is still wearing his golden breastplate[21]). Caesar makes a triumphal entry into Alexandria.

The inhabitants of Alexandria file past Caesar as supplicants, and he forgives them. Arsinoe IV will be taken to Rome. In 46, she will be exhibited during Caesar's quadruple triumph.

Having become the new master of Egypt (thus sealing an old aspiration of his), Caesar allows himself a holiday in the company of Cleopatra VII. The two take a cruise down the Nile with a retinue of 400 boats.[22] They travel onboard the royal barge, where luxury and decadence reign supreme. They would have gone as far as Ethiopia, had Caesar's troops not refused to follow them.[23] Cleopatra VII then marries Ptolemy XIV, thus making a commitment that follows the Egyptian-Ptolemaic tradition but which is principally aimed at quelling arguments among the Alexandrians, who do not want to be governed by a woman (their support for the monarchy is the foundation on which the country's political stability is built).[24] But she is 22 years old while he is only 10, so she is still the one holding all the power in her hands. In the meantime, major political developments have unfolded in Anatolia. Before turning to these, a brief contextualization is necessary.

---

18 Caes. *BAl.*, 23.
19 App. *B. Civ.*, II.90 [(…) He fought the last battle against the king on the banks of the Nile, in which he won a decisive victory (…)].
20 Plutarch narrates that "many fell and the king himself disappeared." Plut. *Caes.* 49. For more details: Caes. *BAl.*, 31.6; Liv. *Per.*, 112.7; Dio Cass., 42.43.4.
21 Flor., 2.13.60; Eutr., 6.221; Oros. 6.16.2.
22 App. *B. Civ.*, II.90. *See also* Luc. 10.268.
23 Suet. *Iul.*, 52.1.
24 Recounting the incident, Dio Cass. says that the marriage happened as "a mere pretence." Dio Cass., 42.44.4.

"Veni, Vidi, Vici"

In 63/62, during the political reorganization of Anatolia after the Third Mithridatic War (73–63), Pompey rewarded Deiotarus, a faithful ally of Rome, with Lesser Armenia in addition to Galatia, which he already ruled. In addition, he assigned the Kingdom of the Cimmerian Bosporus[25] to Pharnaces II (r. 63–47) to reward him for the help the latter gave him in the war against his father, the deceased Mithridates VI, King of Pontus.

Deiotarus, during the civil war that tore the *res publica* apart, united his forces (Legio XXII Deiotariana) with those of Pompey; after the defeat at Pharsalus, when the surviving Pompeian forces scattered, he returned to Galatia, where, later, he was defeated by Pharnaces II.

In December 48, Pharnaces II attempts to profit from the chaos that has broken out in Anatolia since the Battle of Pharsalus and the death of Pompey by invading Lesser Armenia (a region situated between Pontus and Greater Armenia) and defeats Deiotarus at Nicopolis, the urban center of a Roman colony founded in 63 by Pompey in Lesser Armenia after the conquest of the Kingdom of Pontus in the Third Mithridatic War.

Subsequently, Pharnaces II invades Cappadocia as well, which borders Lesser Armenia to the north, and deposes its king, Ariobarzanes III (r. 51–42), himself a devoted friend to the Romans. Caesar orders Domitius Calvinus to restore order to Cappadocia and reinstate Ariobarzanes III to the throne. Pressed by the Thirteenth, Pharnaces retreats from Cappadocia but takes revenge on the Roman citizens residing in Pontus, robbing and killing them. He then turns his armies toward Syria and succeeds in making life difficult for Domitius Calvinus.

In April 47, Caesar leaves Alexandria for Cappadocia, leaving three legions in Egypt led by one of his most trusted men, Rufio, to enact his instructions and keep Cleopatra VII and Ptolemy XIII in check. In the meantime, he has rewarded Alexandria's Jewish community for the help they provided him during the war by conferring Roman citizenship on them. Caesar reinstates Deiotarus on the throne of Galatia, and, on 2 August 47, both of them face Pharnaces II at the Battle of Zela (Zile in Turkey).

Caesar has set up two encampments: one near Zela and another on a hill that controls the road from Zela to Tokat. When the army of Pharnaces, 20,000 strong, is sighted on that road, Caesar deploys the Sixth on his right flank, the city of Pontica's and Deiotarus's legions in the center, and the Thirty-Sixth on the left. The battle, bitter and bloody, lasts for five hours and ends with a Roman victory. Caesar

---

25 The Kingdom of the Cimmerian Bosporus embraces the Crimean and Taman peninsulas, almost completely encircling the Sea of Azov, which is navigable to the Black Sea through the Strait of Kerch. It is a Hellenistic-type state with a mixed population that speaks Greek and participates in Greek civilization.

had a sentence of just three words engraved on a memorial stone to commemorate his victory, but these were destined to go down in history: *Veni, vidi, vici* ("I came, I saw, I conquered").

In September 47, he returns to Alexandria, where Cleopatra VII has given birth to Ptolemy XV (Ptolemy XV Caesar, Caesarion), the result of her lovemaking with Caesar. Cleopatra VII's propaganda asserts that the child is the fruit of a sacred union: Zeus-Ammon, the highest divinity in the state religion of Ptolemaic Egypt, is said to have assumed the form of Caesar to couple with the queen-pharaoh. Caesar sees his beloved again, cradles his little boy in his arms, then leaves, heading for Rome via Antioch on the Orontes, recalled by a problem that has dragged on for some time—since the end of the Alexandrian War—and has brought about a crisis at the center of which is the tribune of the plebs, Publius Cornelius Dolabella.

Dolabella is Cicero's son-in-law, and since 49 he has been a friend and ally of Caesar, for whom he has commanded a fleet in the Adriatic. Following in the footsteps of Catiline and Caelius, he demands that a draft law assenting to the cancellation of all debts be approved in order that his incredible debts may also be canceled. Because two of his colleagues—the tribunes of the plebs Lucius Trebellius and Caius Asinius Pollio—had blocked the initiative using their right of veto, Dolabella, to have his plebiscite approved, used large mobs for terrorizing and intimidatory purposes, in imitation of Clodius and Milo.

In order not to be hindered, he asked the *magister equitum* Mark Antony to leave Rome for a while. Antony—very happy with Dolabella's initiative since he too has significant debts—went along with it, visiting his war veterans in Capua. Dolabella and his followers then occupied the Capitoline. The Senate, incredibly worried, issues a *senatus consultum ultimum*, with which it declares a state of national emergency, and asks Antony—currently the highest legal authority in Italy—to intervene to reestablish public order. Antony rapidly returns to Rome at the head of the Tenth. His soldiers move from the Capitoline into the Forum, where they carry out a massacre (1,000 victims) but are unable to regain control of the situation. Having arrived back in Rome, Caesar is furious with Dolabella and Antony, but especially with the latter whom he relives of the position of *magister equitum*. He is replaced with Marcus Aemilius Lepidus, the former governor of Hispania Citerior (48–47), consul (46), and his close confidant.

In the future, Caesar, Dolabella, and Antony will reconcile with each other. This will allow Dolabella to be reelected as tribune of the plebs and Antony to be elected in 45 to the consulship for 44 alongside Caesar.

CHAPTER XXVIII

The African Campaign

Pompeian Refugees in North Africa and Their Allies

Roman Africa is a rich province due to its highly fertile soil, which provides plentiful crops of cereals, fruit, and vegetables; what is left over from its internal needs is exported, primarily to Rome. It is one of Rome's granary provinces; Rome heavily depends on it for its food supply—hence its great strategic importance. Its capital is Utica, a city situated at the mouth of the Bagradas (Medjerda River in Tunisia) near the ruined plain of Carthage.[1] In the civil war between Caesar and the followers of the deceased Pompey, it has taken the side of the latter.

Cato has reached Utica after having abandoned Sicily, of which he was the governor, after the island had been invaded by the Caesarian Curio. On hearing the news of Pompey's death, he put himself at the head of 10,000 legionaries and marched for the city from Taucheira/Arsinoe in Cyrenaica (Libya), a journey of more than 2,000 km, completed in less than four months in conditions of extreme hardship. In Utica, he is reunited with numerous other Pompeian refugees, among whom is Pompey's father-in-law Quintus Caecilius Metellus Pius Scipio Nasica, and he has formed a Senate with 300 members, bringing together the senators who survived the Battle of Pharsalus and local businessmen residing in the city.

The Senate of Utica has the task of assisting (and supporting) Cato in his decisions. It is politically opposed to the government in Rome, whose legitimacy it does not recognize. In 47, it confirms Scipio Nasica as Pompey's successor in the office of consul, following the decision already taken in Thessalonica in 48, after the Battle of Pharsalus by the senators who had followed Pompey into war, and it gives him the urgent task of continuing the fight against Caesar without contemplating the possibility of surrender or a potential, probable pardon.

Among the other Pompeian refugees in Utica, other than those already mentioned, the following are worthy of note: Marcus Petreius, Titus Labienus, Lucius Afranius,

---

1   The present-day site is found 8 km from the coast, 32 km northeast of Tunis.

Cnaeus Pompey, Caius Considius Longus, Publius Attius Varus, and Publius Cornelius Sulla. It is worth saying a few words about each of them.

Petreius had been taken prisoner at Pharsalus, but he received a pardon from Caesar and was set free. He took refuge in the Peloponnese and traveled from there to Utica.

Labienus, after the defeat of Pharsalus, retreated to Buthrotum with 1,600 cavalry, made up of Gauls and Germans; later, he moved with them and Lucius Afranius to Corcyra (Corfu in Greece) and, subsequently, to Cyrenaica. When he was in Cyrene he wanted to meet Cato but Cato didn't want to see him, given his past with Caesar. After this, Cato's aversion to Labienus subsided, and Labienus and his soldiers were allowed to join the Pompeian army.

Cnaeus Pompey is the eldest son of the deceased Pompey Magnus and his third wife, Mucia Tertia. After the Battle of Pharsalus, he joined his father on Mytilene, the capital and port of the Greek island of Lesbos, together with his mother and his younger brother, Sextus. He then left for Egypt with the rest of his family, where he watched on, helplessly, as his father was assassinated. In 47, he joined the resistance against Caesar in Roman Africa.

Considius Longus was praetor in 58 and propraetor of Africa in 50. Currently, he is the commander of the garrison at Hadrumentum (Sousse in Tunisia), a *civitas libera et immunis* found at the center of a vast swath of territory, planted with olive trees, and which has a very busy seaport.

Attius Varus was praetor in 53 and 52 and, subsequently, propraetor of Africa. Recently, he handed his powers over to Metellus Scipio, becoming one of his legates.

Publius Cornelius Sulla is the nephew of the deceased dictator Lucius Cornelius Sulla and a cousin of Faustus Cornelius Sulla, himself the son of Sulla and Metella Dalmatica. He married Pompeia, the daughter of Pompey and Mucia Tertia. As such, while Pompey was alive, he was Pompey's son-in-law.

He is a controversial character. He had been elected to the consulship for 65, but he was stripped of his office and expelled from the Senate because he was found guilty of electoral fraud. In 62, he was put on trial again because he was accused by Lucius Manlius Torquatus, among others, of a series of crimes that infringed and were punishable by the *lex Plautia de vi*: in particular, of having tried to establish a base of support for the conspiracy of Catiline in Pompeii, using his network of clients and friends for this purpose; of having tried to assassinate the consuls of 63 (this was included as part of the conspirators' plan); and of having fomented unrest in Spain. As for the latter charge, he was accused of having sent Publius Sittius Nucerinus—an Italic *eques* with interests in Italy, in the provinces, and abroad—to Spain to instigate riots and garner support, though whether this was to come from resident Italics or from the native Spanish is uncertain.[2] Cicero defended him, giving the oration *Pro*

2 Sall., 21.3.

Sulla to prove the groundlessness of the accusations[3] (another judicial orator who participated in the trial was Quintus Hortensius Hortalus). It was true that Sittius had been to Spain, but he did so to see to his own affairs, as he had in the past, and in any case he left again in 64, months before the conspiracy was unmasked. Sittius went from Spain to North Africa to attend to other business that he had with the king of Mauretania. In the meantime, he had delegated the task of managing his possessions in Italy to Sulla, and the latter carried out the task so well that, by selling some properties, he had managed to pay off most of his debts. The arguments put forth by Cicero were held to be convincing, and the accused was thus acquitted.

Cato, the other Pompeian refugees in Utica, and the Senate that had been set up in the city, are aiming to transform Roman Africa, where Pompey's clientele still carry significant weight, into an alternative Roman state to the *res publica* of Caesar.[4] The model that they use as a reference is the state that was created by Quintus Sertorius in Spain in the 70s. That state had also had its own Senate, an alternative to the one in Rome and which was opposed to it. The Spanish Senate had been formed by Sertorius with members of the Senate of Rome who had taken refuge with him and with his friends, chosen from among the Romans residing in Spain. This senate had its seat in Osca (Huesca in Aragon) and discussed important political problems, such as the question of the military alliance that had been formed between Sertorius and Mithridates VI, King of Pontus. It also denied the legality of the regime set up by the dictator Sulla in Rome.[5]

The Pompeians' allies in North Africa are Massinissa II (r. 81–46) and Juba I (85–46). Massinissa II is the king of western Numidia who has his base at Cirta, the historic capital of Numidia. He is a descendant of Massinissa I, founder of the unified Kingdom of Numidia, and is the grandson of Gauda (d. 88), who divided his kingdom between Massinissa II's father Masteabar and the latter's brother Hiempsal II.

Juba I is an arrogant and cruel man. He is a cousin of Massinissa II and is the king of eastern Numidia, that is, of most of Numidia. He had been Pompey's ally because he had helped his father, Hiempsal II, recover his throne, which had been taken from him by Hiarbas in 81, and because he had added a strip of territory along the coast to his lands. But he would have allied himself with Pompey in any case, as he was still angry at Caesar over an old incident. While Hiempsal II was alive, a certain Mesintha—a young man from a noble family and a client of the young Caesar—offended Juba by tugging at his beard during a court hearing. After Hiempsal's death, Juba had wanted to arrest Mesintha, but Caesar, attentive and loyal toward his clients, hid him in his own home and then took him with him to

3   Cic. *Sull.*, 56–59.
4   App. *B. Civ.*, II.397; Caes. *BAfr.*, 88; Plut. *Cat. Min.*, LIX.3.
5   On the Senate in Spain: Plut. *Sert.*, XXII.5; App., *B. Civ.*, I.507.

Spain.[6] Numidia, during the reign of Hiarbas, provided Domitius Ahenobarbus with support. In 81, Pompey subjugated it in just 40 days and restored both Hiempsal II and Massinissa II to their thrones.

Caesar Lands in Africa

Caesar, having placed the Dolabella issue into the capable hands of Marcus Aemilius Lepidus, decides to face the Pompeians on African soil. He could have waited for them to bring the theater of war back to Italy to take Rome, but he preferred to take the initiative. Accordingly, he concentrates his forces in Sicily ahead of the naval crossing to North Africa. Specifically, he sends the legions of Roman Gaul, the Fifth from Hispania Ulterior, the Eighth and Ninth from Hispania Citerior, and his Spanish cavalry to the island. At a later point, Caesar is joined by the Twenty-Fifth, Twenty-Sixth, and Twenty-Seventh, all of whose provenance is the southern end of the Italian peninsula, and by the Twenty-Eighth, who come from Egypt. Caesar also commands two final legions, the Nineteenth and the Twentieth, survivors of the ill-fated African campaign of Curio. These legions will not take part in the African campaign but will remain in Sicily.

On 17 December 47, Caesar reaches Lilybaeum (Marsala), a port city at the very western end of Sicily. He is at the head of a huge army, formed of the Twenty-Fifth, Twenty-Sixth, Twenty-Eighth, and Twenty-Ninth, almost all the Fifth, and a few cohorts of the Tenth. The Seventh, Eighth, and Ninth, and the majority of the Tenth, have been delayed and are behind schedule. The former are traveling from Rome; the rest, from Brundisium. They will arrive in Africa later.

Among the legionary commanders who will follow Caesar to Africa are Oppius, Pollio, and Sallust. Mark Antony has remained in Rome. The relations between him and Caesar are no longer as good as they once were. It isn't just the Dolabella issue that has left its mark. Caesar can no longer bear Antony's arrogance. A recent incident caused a rift between the two: on taking possession of Pompey's house, which had been confiscated, Antony had complained that he had to pay for it (he would have liked Caesar to have given it to him for free).

On 25 December, Caesar sets sail with 3,000 legionaries and 150 cavalry (the rest of the army will follow). A headwind hinders navigation, so much so that part of the fleet is scattered. On 28 December, Caesar lands on the shores of Africa near Leptis Minor (Lamta in Tunisia).[7]

On 1 January 46, Caesar sets up camp near Ruspina (near Monastir in Tunisia) and awaits the rest of the army that embarked with him (and who will join him on

---

6   Suet. *Iul.*, 71.
7   So-called to distinguish it from Leptis Magna, found in modern Khoms in Libya. Leptis Minor is found 15 km southeast of the modern city of Monastir in Tunisia.

4 January) as well as the delayed legions.[8] Since there is not enough food to feed the troops, nor enough forage for the animals, he decides to obtain supplies from the surrounding area, where the season's harvest remains abandoned in the fields. Therefore, he leaves the camp and goes inland. With him are 30 mixed infantry cohorts (including the cohorts from the Tenth), 400 cavalry, and 150 archers. When he is 5 km away from his base, he is suddenly attacked by the cavalry of Labienus, reinforced by units of infantry and local archers. The bitter fight goes on for hours. During the battle, Labienus's horse is hit by a javelin; it rears up in pain, throwing its rider from his saddle.

In the end, Caesar manages to break the encirclement with yet another sortie and leads his troops on a forced march toward Thapsus (Rass Dimasse in Tunisia),[9] pursued by Labienus. Before long, Caesar is attacked by Petreius, who is at the head of 1,600 Numidian cavalry and units of infantry. He draws to a stop on a hill, where he repels the enemy (or is only saved because Petreius was seriously injured and called the retreat), and, as evening approaches, heads back to his camp at Ruspina.

In the first weeks that follow, Caesar remains in Ruspina, waiting for the bulk of his army to arrive from Sicily. While he waits, he builds three independent *valla*, two of which start from his camp and from Ruspina, which slope down toward the sea from a plateau that rises a few kilometers from the coast and protect a port with moles and towers. The third *vallum* connects the Roman encampment to the city, circumventing the entire plateau and forming a single fortified structure, which is elevated and difficult to capture. Since construction timber is scarce, Caesar has it brought to him from Sicily. But the Pompeian fleet enters the Strait of Sicily and intercepts some Caesarian transport ships.

Caesar, since he lacks the numbers to do so, avoids meeting the enemy in a pitched battle. However, there are several skirmishes. There are rumors that the Pompeians are preparing an assault with an enormous army, reinforced with contingents of war elephants. This disheartens Caesar's soldiers. Toward the end of January 46, the arrival of the first reinforcements from Sicily gives them fresh courage. They are joined by two legions—the Thirteenth and Fourteenth—some squadrons of cavalry, and a few units of auxiliary light infantry, all under the command of Caius Sallustius Crispus. This group, before reaching Ruspina, landed on Cercina, the largest of the Kerkennah Islands, where they seized a shipment of grain. The Kerkennah Islands

---

8   Caes. *BAfr.*, 11–18; App. *B. Civ.*, II.95. Ruspina is the name the Romans gave to the ancient Phoenician port of Rous Penna in 146, when they took control of the town. They erected walls around it and built bath houses there.

9   Thapsus (Ras ed-Dimas in Tunisia) was a city located on the coast, south of Hadrumentum. It was a thriving maritime emporium during the era of the Carthaginian Empire. At the beginning of the Third Punic War, like Utica and other cities, it sided with Rome. After the Romans' victory, it became a *civitas libera et immunis* within the Roman province of Africa. Many Roman and Italic merchants are found there. During the Civil War, it has sided with the Pompeians.

are situated in the north of the Gulf of Gabès, lying off the harbor town of Taparura (Sfax). They are low, flat, and windy. Cercina is the seat of the homonymous Roman colony and plays an important role in the trade relations between Rome and the northern regions of the Kingdom of Numidia.

Caesar's Allies

Caesar now has a good number of legions available to him, but he doesn't have control over the local territory. Moreover, he has few specialist units and only a single legate, Lucius Nonius Asprenas. His allies are the Gaetuli; the ruler of Mauretania, Bocchus II; Bogud, Bocchus II's brother; and a soldier of fortune, Publius Sittius Nucerinus.

The Gaetuli, like the Mauri and the Numidians, are a Berber population, but, unlike the Numidians, who are mostly farmers, they are overall a nomadic people. Organized in groups, they constantly move between the southern slopes of the Aurès and Atlas Mountains to the coast and the desert oases. Their landscape is that of the pre-desert and desert zones of the Sahara's interior, bordering Numidia and Mauretania to the north and the lands of the Garamantes to the east. They are, therefore, the lands of the "seas of sand," immense boulders, oases, rock formations shaped by the wind, mountains split by the scorching heat and the endless dry seasons, and the dried riverbeds of the occasional water course, which suddenly begin to overflow when the occasional heavy rain falls and causes them to flood. The Gaetuli are very primitive: they dress in animal skins, raise horses, and live in isolated groups.

Bocchus II rules the eastern part of Mauretania. His kingdom has its capital at Caesarea (Cherchell in Algeria) and, since Caius Marius ceded it to Bocchus I for his help in capturing Jugurtha, includes the formerly western part of Numidia.

Bogud exercises sovereignty over the western part of Mauretania, which is bathed by the Atlantic Ocean. His wife is the beautiful Eunoë, a tall, lithe 16-year-old, whose nose and plump lips are barely distinguishable through the veil that covers her face. It seems that Eunoë had an affair with Caesar.

The rulers of the Mauri want to free themselves from Juba I to have a direct relationship with Rome. Caesar has recognized them as friends and allies and has promised he will involve them in the political reorganization of North Africa once he has defeated Juba I and seized his kingdom.

We have already spoken of Publius Sittius, *en passant*, when looking at the occasion on which Publius Cornelius Sulla was on trial on various charges connected to his alleged participation in the Catilinarian Conspiracy.[10] He is nicknamed Nucerinus because he is the son of a rich landowner from Nuceria Alfaterna, one of the main cities of Campania, where he was born and later distinguished himself as a

---

10 On Sittius's role during Caesar's African campaign: Caes. *BAfr.*, 25, 36, 48, 93–96; App. *B. Civ.*, IV.54; Dio Cass., XLIII.3.1–2.

businessman. Serving in the army of Sulla, he fought in the Social War. He was suspected of having also participated in Catiline's conspiracy. In the meantime, he amassed large sums of money thanks to successful financial and commercial transactions, but then he got himself into financial difficulty after speculating too optimistically on large imports of wild beasts and gladiators. Swimming in debt and being chased by creditors, although still rich, he left Italy in 65 to go on a business trip to Spain and Mauretania, where he possessed a vast amount of property.[11] In Italy, there is a widespread opinion that Sittius is a cowboy of the worst sort, a corruptor, and an unscrupulous businessman. If he sets foot in the Peninsula again, he will be arrested and put on trial for his debts. Therefore, Sittius keeps well away from Italy and focuses on his economic interests in North Africa. In 57, Cicero, who is friends with Sittius, wrote him a letter in which he dealt with his difficult situation, owing both to family problems (separation from his son) and to the fact he had been indicted on charges related to his involvement in the system regulating the provision of food in Rome.[12] Caesar came to know Sittius in 62 (though Dio Cass. will say that Caesar didn't know of Sittius before his arrival in Africa). Recently, Sittius—who maintains his own militia and his own ships—has offered assistance to Caesar in his fight against the Pompeians. Caesar, accepting the offer (having considered the possibility he was willing to open a second front against Juba I), promised him that he will settle with his creditors, or at least alleviate his debts, and have him administrate Cirta and the surrounding territory after he has captured them from Juba I and organized it into a colony.

Caesar Moves North

Scipio Nasica's troops are encamped near Uzita, 9 km away from Ruspina. Initially, neither side offers battle but instead clash in a series of skirmishes, useful to establish their respective strengths and ability to adapt. In the meantime, the legates Quintus Pedius and Quintus Fabius Maximus, who are operating in Spain on Caesar's behalf, have informed him that two Pompeian legions have deserted and switched sides. These are legions that, in 47, had rebelled against the praetor Quintus Cassius Longinus, who governed the Iberian provinces with vicious greed, and forced him to flee. Cassius died when his ship sank as he attempted to escape.

At the start of March 46, Caesar receives a second wave of reinforcements. In turn, Scipio Nasica receives the help of Juba I: three legions, 800 cavalry, 300 light infantry, and 30 war elephants. The Pompeian army in Africa now numbers 40,000 men (about 10 legions), plus auxiliary and allied forces, among whom are 10,000 cavalry and around 100 war elephants. On 15 March 46, Caesar receives a third wave

---

11   Cic. *Sull.*, 56–59.
12   Cic. *Fam.*, 5.17.

of reinforcements from Sicily. At this point, he leaves his camp at Uzita and marches on Aggar (Henchir Sidi Amara, a town situated on the plain of Kairouan, about 60 km east of Maktar in Tunisia). Lucius Afranius and Juba I follow him at a distance. On 28 March 46, Caesar is joined by a fourth and final wave of reinforcements (4,000 legionaries, 400 cavalry, and 1,000 slingers and archers).

A few days later, on 4 April 46, he sets off down the coast with five legions of war veterans and one or two legions of fresh recruits. After marching for 24 km, he comes in sight of a promontory, where two isthmuses separated by the salt lagoon of Moknine connect a rocky outcrop to the mainland. At the far end of this promontory is the harbor town of Thapsus (Rass Dimasse in Tunisia). Thapsus was a thriving maritime emporium during the era of Carthage's hegemony. At the start of the Third Punic War, like Utica and other cities, it sided with Rome. After the Roman victory, it became a *civitas libera et immunis* within the Roman province of Africa. Numerous Roman and Italic merchants can be found inside the city. During the Civil War, it sided with the Pompeians. The city is held by a large garrison. Within it are the Pompeians Petreius, Sulla, Varus, and Marcus Porcius Cato, son of Cato the Younger. Caesar advances along the eastern isthmus, positions himself between the city and the lagoon, and orders access to the isthmus to be blocked by three lines of fortifications. Nonius Asprenas, commander of the Seventh and the Eighth, is charged with carrying out the work.

The Battle of Thapsus

Scipio, Afranius, and Juba I advance toward Thapsus. They stop about 12 km from the city and set up separate entrenched camps. The camp of Afranius and Juba is on the eastern isthmus, while Scipio's is on the western isthmus. Scipio then leads some of the troops, reinforced by 16 war elephants, along the western isthmus. There he meets Caesar, in a confined space where the cavalry and elephants have little room to maneuver and the entire army, if forced to retreat, will end up slipping into a bottleneck. Scipio entrenches himself about 1.5–2 km away from Caesar's position and prepares for battle. The units are deployed in close order, with the legionaries in the center and the elephants, native cavalry, and light infantry on the flanks. The elephants are placed in front of each wing, with eight elephants on each side.

On 6 April 46, Caesar decides to attack. He deploys his troops on the battlefield: the four veteran legions in the center, the cavalry, archers, and slingers on the flanks, half of the Legio V Alaudae behind each wing, and one legion behind everyone, left in reserve to counter any sorties by the Thapsus garrison. The Fifth, we recall, was the first Roman legion to be composed of provincial soldiers, enrolling Gallic natives. At first, Caesar paid the unit with his own money, then it became fully part of the Roman army and received its pay from the state. It fought in the Gallic Wars, distinguishing itself for its valor and ardor. Some of its cohorts are specialists in combating war elephants.

The Tenth is placed toward one side of the center, on the right. The Eighth and Ninth are positioned at the opposite end. In the middle are the Thirteenth and Fourteenth. Caesar commands the right wing of the army. While he is deploying his troops on the ground, he feels faint and is taken to shelter in a mobile tower. He has a severe headache. This is the first manifestation of the illness that Caesar will suffer from for the rest of his life. It isn't certain whether this is epilepsy or another illness. Most likely, it is another disease he has contracted that causes headaches, sudden fainting, and sleeping disorders. Octavian, after Caesar's death, will publicly claim that his adoptive parent suffered from this illness to justify his own attempt to deify the deceased (the Romans consider epilepsy as the "sacred disease," a sort of divine mark on man).[13] However, it could be something else: migraines, malaria, neurocysticercosis, a parasitic infection of the brain contracted during the Alexandrian War (a condition that can remain asymptomatic for years, except for the onset of epileptic attacks), or a chronic infection, such as neurosyphilis, cerebral tuberculosis, or typhoid.[14] Nor can it be excluded that he may have been suffering from a benign tumor, such as a meningioma or a glioma, or from repeated ischemic attacks (temporary disruptions in the blood supply to parts of the brain tissue) due to a genetic predisposition.[15] Caesar's father, we recall, died suddenly and unexpectedly while tying a sandal, seemingly for no reason. Another of Caesar's ancestors died in a similar way in the past. In addition, Ptolemy Caesar, or Caesarion, the son of Caesar and Cleopatra, suffers from similar ailments from early childhood.

While Caesar is temporarily prevented from exercising command by his poor health, an unauthorized charge by the Caesarian Fifth Legion against the left side of the Pompeian line begins the battle. The Pompeian left wing is surrounded. The Fifth moves behind it, while the Tenth attacks it from the front. The Pompeians respond by sending in their war elephants, which start to charge, but are pummeled by projectiles from the slingers. The pachyderms go wild, stop in their tracks, then turn around, charging back toward the Pompeian front line, sowing chaos in its midst. They crash into the auxiliary troops lined up behind, who flee in disarray, and wreak devastation through the encampment. The Numidian cavalry make the most of the confusion to desert and take flight.

The Eighth and Ninth are also advancing. When the left flank of the Pompeian army collapses under the irresistible pressure being put upon it, the rest of the army disintegrates too. The soldiers flee in disorder and *en masse*, some toward Scipio's

---

13 The Greek historian Plutarch identified the episode at Thapsus with an epileptic attack, and this hypothesized diagnosis has, over time, enjoyed reasonable support.

14 On the hypothesis that it might be neurocysticercosis: R. S. McLauchlan, "Julius Caesar's late onset epilepsy: a case of historic proportions," *Can. J. Neurol. Sci.* (*The Canadian Journal of Neurological Sciences*) 37, no. 5 (2010): 557–561.

15 F. Galassi & H. Ashrafian, "Has the diagnosis of a stroke been overlooked in the symptoms of Julius Caesar?," *J. Neur. Sci.* (*Journal of the Neurological Sciences*) 36, no. 8 (2015): 1521–1522.

camp, some toward the camp of Afranius and Juba I. The Eighth and Ninth force their way into those camps and kill everyone they find there, including those who—in their thousands—lay down their weapons and raise their arms in a sign of surrender, in an orgy of blood that their commanders are unable to stop.

It has been claimed that Caesar played no part in the battle. This may not be true, Caesar could have participated after overcoming the worst of his symptoms, but it is not documented—Caesar will never speak of his health troubles, nor will any of his officers. The fact remains, though, that the battle started in his absence and without orders from him.

The losses are counted. The Caesarians report a few hundred fallen. The Pompeians, somewhere between 5,000 and 10,000, including some senators and *equites* (according to some, the number of Pompeian dead amounts to 50,000, but this figure seems exaggerated). Of the ex-consuls and ex-praetors, some committed suicide to avoid being captured and subjected to an undignified death, while others were killed on Caesar's orders after being taken prisoner. Caesar authorizes the Fifth to adorn their insignia with the image of an elephant. Sixty elephants have been captured. Caesar tries to incorporate them into his army, but when the animals don't obey their orders, he sets them free.

Thapsus resists and is besieged. On 7 April 46, Caesar sends two legions to occupy the city of Thysdrus, defended by the Pompeian Caius Considius Longus, leaves three legions at Thapsus to continue the siege, and leaves for Utica with five legions. Considius Longus will be besieged and attempt to escape, but he will be caught and killed by Gaetuli horsemen.

After the battle, Caesar resumes his siege of Thapsus, which eventually falls. Some of the Pompeians manage to escape, some by sea, others by land. Pompey's sons, the First Legion, and other stragglers land in Gades (Cádiz in Spain). Labienus and Varus initially take shelter in the Balearic Islands, then move from there to Hispania Ulterior and join up with Pompey's sons again.

Scipio Nasica runs into a storm and takes refuge in a sheltered bay (Hippo Regius—Annaba in Algeria) but is ambushed by Sittius. Seeing no way out, he falls on his sword, the typical way for Roman soldiers to commit suicide.

Afranius takes 1,000 men and makes a break for Mauretania with the idea of going from there to Spain and reuniting with the other Pompeians, but he is captured in an ambush by Sittius. Caesar sentences him to death for having broken his promise not to take any further part in the Civil War (it is also possible Afranius is killed by out-of-control Caesarian troops, together with the proquaestor Lucius Julius Caesar).

A similar fate befalls Faustus Sulla. He is trying to escape to join up with the Pompeians in Spain when he is captured by Sittius. Caesar will put him to death, but he will pardon Sulla's wife, Pompeia, the daughter of Pompey Magnus, and their children.

Juba I and Petreius take flight to Zama, but the residents refuse them entry so as not to jeopardize their own position with the victors. Since Juba and Petrius have no chance of salvation, they head off in search of death. To that end, they challenge each other to a duel. Petreius kills Juba with relative ease, then he orders a slave to kill him. The fate of Massinissa is unknown. Perhaps he fell in battle, or perhaps he was cut down while attempting to flee.

Arabio, Massinissa's son, manages to leave North Africa with a contingent of armed men and joins the Pompeians in Spain. He will fight against Caesar until the Pompeians' final defeat at Munda, after which he will return to North Africa and attack Sittius, who will be killed, possibly in an ambush. He will recover part of his kingdom (Cirta and the surrounding lands) and allow the former soldiers of Sittius to remain on their lands. In 44, after the death of Caesar, he will ally himself with Octavian.

Marcus Porcius Cato is one of the prisoners of war, but Caesar decides that he is to be set free. It will be his job to deliver news of the disaster to his father in Utica.

The Death of Cato

On 9 April 46, Cato the Younger convenes the Senate of Utica[16] to urge them to resist. The Senate decides not to adopt a hostile stance toward Caesar, believing that, if it opposed the victor, the battle would be lost from the start. Cato doesn't want to give up, because he loves liberty, but he doesn't want to admit defeat either, still less give Caesar the satisfaction of forgiving him. On 12 April, he quietly dines, reading and discussing some passages from *Phaedo*, one of Plato's dialogues, with some friends. He seems calm, but in fact he is preparing himself for death. During the night (12/13 April), he pulls a dagger out from beneath his pillow and tears open his stomach. He falls out of bed with a thud. The servants who are sleeping on the other side of the door wake up and run to him. His son Marcus and others help the dying man, pushing his insides back into his belly and stitching the wound. Then they take his dagger away from him and withdraw so that he can sleep. Once he has been left alone, Cato thrusts his hands into the wound and pulls out the stitches. He will bleed to death. On hearing the news of Cato's suicide, Caesar is struck deeply, and, addressing the dead man in spirit, exclaims: "Cato, I grudge you your death, as you would have grudged me the preservation of your life."[17]

On 15 April 46, Caesar enters Utica in triumph. This leads to the capitulation of the Pompeians in Africa and to the political reorganization of North Africa. Caesar abolishes the Kingdom of Numidia and divides its territory into two parts:

---

16 App. *B. Civ.*, II.397.
17 Plut. *Caes.*, 54; Plutarch, "Regum et imperatorum apophthegmata (XV)," in *Opuscoli di Plutarco*, vol. 1, trans. M. Adriani (Napoli: G. Nobile, 1841), 676.

he annexes eastern Numidia for Rome, adding it to the Roman province of Africa, and confers the western part to Bocchus II. He renames the province of Africa from Africa *vetus*, calling it Africa *nova* and rules that it will be garrisoned by four (or five) legions: the Twenty-Sixth, Twenty-Seventh, Twenty-Ninth, and Thirtieth, and perhaps also the Twenty-Fifth. Sittius is given what he was promised, which is Cirta and its surrounding territory, that is, part of the abolished kingdom of Massinissa II; he will subdivide these lands among his soldiers.[18]

The victory at Thapsus is the preface to the restoration of peace in North Africa. At this point, there is only one more score to be settled, the one with the sons of Pompey—Cnaeus and Sextus—who are in Hispania Citerior with some of the Pompeian commanders who survived the debacle of North Africa. Spain thus becomes Caesar's next strategic objective, the last one to be achieved to put an end to the civil war.

Caesar sends the Fifth, Seventh, Eighth, Ninth, and Thirteenth back to the south of the Italian peninsula, the Twenty-Eighth (perhaps only half) to Syria, and the Sixth and the Tenth to Spain, except for two cohorts of the Sixth, which he keeps with him. He starts to warm to the idea of conducting a campaign against the Parthians (who, since the Battle of Carrhae, have remained in an intermittent state of war with Rome) after defeating the Pompeians in Spain once and for all.

At the same time, the military tribune Aulus Fonteius; Caius Avienus, a military tribune in the Tenth; and the centurions Titus Salienus, Marcus Tiro, and Caius Clusinas were dismissed from the army for acts of indiscipline and robbery. After this, Caesar leaves for Italy, taking the two cohorts of the Sixth with him, leaving four legions in North Africa.

On 15 June 46, he lands at Caralis (Cagliari) on Sardinia. On 25 July, he is in Rome. In the meantime, the Senate of Rome has heard the news of his victory at Thapsus and has decreed a *supplicatio,* and that an honorific statue of Caesar be placed in the Area Capitolina in front of the Temple of Jupiter Optimus Maximus.[19]

This is the first in a series of similar statues of Caesar that the Senate will decide to erect in every city and all the temples of Rome within the broader scope of the conferral of a wider, incredibly vast series of honors, such as have never been seen for an individual in the *res publica* before. It depicts Caesar in heroic nudity with one foot placed on a globe, which represents the world and is a symbol of power and hegemony.[20]

---

18 This isn't certain.
19 Dio Cass., 43.14; Cic. *Deiot.,* 34.
20 This reimagining is hypothetical. See P. Zanker, "Le irritanti statue di Cesare e i suoi ritratti contraddittori," in *Giulio Cesare. L'uomo, le imprese, il mito (Catalogo della mostra, Roma, Chiostro del Bramante, 23 ottobre 2008–3 maggio 2009)*, ed. G. Gentili (Milano: Silvana Editoriale, 2008), 73.

However, it isn't so much this that irks Caesar's political opponents as much as the inscription that appears on the statue's base as a dedication. This, in fact, defines Caesar as a *hemitheos*, "demigod." This causes a political outcry, which Caesar resolves by having the dedication changed.

In addition, in the first months of 44, the mint of Rome puts a series of coins into circulation that feature Caesar, the globe, and Venus Genetrix. On the reverse side of the coins, Venus Genetrix—the goddess from whom the *gens Iulii* claim to descend—is depicted as holding the Victory of Caesar (as if she were about to give it to him), with a shield resting on the globe.

CHAPTER XXIX

The Spanish Campaign

Caesar Defeats the Pompeians in Spain

In 55, Pompey had levied four legions in Italy. In 52, one of these, the Second, fought against the Lusitanians, an indigenous people from the western part of Spain, garnering considerable experience. Following this, it was kept in Spain.

In 49, the first year of the civil war between Caesar and Pompey, Lucius Afranius and Marcus Petreius, who had been tasked by Pompey with governing the Spanish provinces in his stead, conscripted a new legion—the Vernacula—through the enlistment of Roman citizens and war veterans who had fought under Caesar's command in 61. During the civil war, Caesar besieged them in Ilerda (Lleida in Catalonia) and forced them to surrender.[1] After the capitulation of Ilerda, the Second and the Vernacula moved, in whole or in part, under the banners of Caesar and were placed under the command of Quintus Cassius Longinus, governor of Hispania Ulterior in 48–47, and fought in North Africa against the Pompeians. In 47, they mutinied and were sent back to Hispania Ulterior, specifically to Corduba, the capital.

In 46, when the Spanish provinces were governed by Marcus Aemilius Lepidus (Hispania Citerior), and Caius Trebonius (Hispania Ulterior), the Pompeians Cnaeus Pompey the Younger, his brother Sextus, the First Legion, Labienus, Varus, and others who had survived the Battle of Thapsus mustered their forces in Spain and went on the attack against Trebonius. Cnaeus Pompey managed to subjugate the entirety of Hispania Ulterior, except for Corduba and the city of Ulia (in the modern province of Córdoba), partly thanks to the fact that Trebonius was hated as much by the local population as he was by his own soldiers (three legions, including the Second and the Vernacula) due to his abuse of his office to draw personal benefits. Then he enlisted new troops and increased the size of his forces to 13 legions, plus a few

---

1   Ilerda is a city situated on a high hill on the right bank of the River Sicoris (Segre), which is spanned by a stone bridge that bears the road that runs from Tarraco (Tarragona in Catalonia) to Osca (Huesca in Aragon).

thousand cavalry and light infantry. Cnaeus besieged Ulia. To shock its inhabitants and induce them to surrender, he arrayed corpses as if to form a terreplein, with shields and spears set up like a palisade, and then, above all this, set the heads of the dead on pikes, all facing toward the city.

In the meantime, on Sextus's arrival, the Second and the Vernacula mutinied and forced Trebonius to flee. This resulted in Corduba falling into the hands of the Pompeians. Sextus took possession of Corduba, and the Second and the Vernacula joined him. Therefore, these legions became Pompeian troops once more, as they had originally been. Consequently, in 45, all of Hispania Ulterior, including its capital Corduba, is in the hands of the Pompeians. They have 15 legions available to them, plus a few thousand cavalry and light infantry, as well as a sizeable fleet. Labienus commands the cavalry, Varus the navy.

Caesar recalls Trebonius to Rome and replaces him with Quintus Pedius and Quintus Fabius Maximus. Pedius is one of Caesar's nephews and served under him during the Gallic Wars (58–51/50). Fabius Maximus is the son of a consul of 121 (Quintus Fabius Maximus Allobrogicus) and the great-grandson of a consul of 145 (Quintus Fabius Maximus Aemilianus). In 59, he and Marcus Caelius Rufus had filed a lawsuit against Caius Antonius Hybrida and won, despite the fact the accused had been defended by Cicero. He was curule aedile in 57 and, in 48, praetor. Pedius and Fabius Maximus are already in command of one legion in Hispania Ulterior when Caesar sends them the Sixth and Tenth as reinforcements, in addition to a third legion redeployed from Sardinia. Caesar also sends a naval contingent and a unit of marines to Spain under the command of Caius Didius.

In November 46, or toward the end of December 46, Caesar sets out for Spain again with his senior officers, his attendants, and his Germanic bodyguard. Having reached Massilia by land, he continues the journey by sea. This forces him to give up his Germanic bodyguard, as the ship is not equipped to carry horses. He disembarks in Tarraco, after having obtained another bodyguard, and reaches Pedius and Fabius Maximus in Obulco (Porcuna in Andalusia), a city located on the administrative border between the two Spanish provinces.

Caesar starts to head for Corduba but falls ill again, as he did at Thapsus. On this occasion too, once the worst has passed, he recovers and regains full possession of his faculties.

The Pompeians lift the siege of Ulia to be able to focus on the defense of Corduba. Despite what it seems, however, Caesar doesn't intend to take Corduba at all. Instead, one night, he carries out his sleight of hand. With one single march of 28 km, he reaches Ategua, where the enemy has left the baggage train. Ategua is a town on a hilly plateau near the River Guadajoz and is about 32 km from Corduba, in an area well supplied by water and where plains, orchards, and meadows alternate over the rolling hills. The town is enclosed by stone walls, interspersed with stone towers.

In the meantime, Varus and his ships have been intercepted by Didius and have sought refuge in the port of Carteia (El Rocadillo, at the head of the Bay of Gibraltar, between Algeciras and Gibraltar), while the Eighth and Ninth, Caesarian legions, have defected to the Pompeians, not wanting to fight against the Second and the Vernacula as they are also formed of Hispanics. The example of the Eighth and Ninth is followed by the Thirteenth, the legion with which Caesar crossed the Rubicon. Command of the Eighth is given to Cnaeus Pompey the Younger. Command of the Ninth and the Thirteenth is given to Sextus Pompey.

On 15 January 45, Cnaeus Pompey sets up camp near Ategua and manages to get one of his officers, Munatius Flaccus, into the city to organize the defenders and assume command. Flaccus shows how far the brutality of a cruel and thuggish man can go. First, he has all those inhabitants who sympathize with Caesar massacred and their bodies thrown from the walls, then he calls out to the husbands in the enemy camp by name so that they can witness the slaughter of their wives, who are killed with their children. He dashes some children down against the ground in the presence of their parents, while others are impaled on stakes.

Caesar persists and ends up victorious. On 19 February, Ategua falls, and Caesar is acclaimed *imperator*. This is the third time this has happened. Caesar was acclaimed *imperator* for the first time at the end of his term as praetor in Spain (60). The second time came in Gaul after his decisive victory over Vercingetorix.

A Visit as Welcome as it Is Unexpected

Cnaeus Pompey has a smaller force but is perched on the high ground of Munda (Montilla in Andalusia), a position that is further secured by the marshy grounds below. Caesar prepares to drive him out. Just then, however, he receives an unexpected but very welcome visitor. His great-nephew Caius Octavius Thurinus has come to find him, accompanied by one of his friends, the noble and cultured Caius Cilnius Maecenas.

Caesar has a total of four nephews and nieces, plus three great-nephews and great-nieces. His two nephews are Lucius Pinarius and Quintus Pedius, the children of Julia Major, Caesar's sister; his nieces are Atia Major and Atia Minor,[2] the daughters of Marcus Atius Balbus and Julia Minor, another of Caesar's sisters. His great-nephew and great-nieces are Caius Octavius Thurinus the Younger, Octavia Major, and Octavia Minor. Caius Octavius and Octavia Minor are the children of Caius Octavius Thurinus the Elder and Atia Minor. We have already met Thurinus the Elder, but it is worth pausing to examine some of his relatives.

---

2   Atia Minor married Lucius Marcius Philippus, consul in 56, who gave her a daughter, Marcia, who will marry Paullus Fabius Maximus, consul in 11.

Atia Minor is a very well-known matron in the high society of the capital. A widow, she remarried her brother-in-law, Lucius Marcius Philippus, consul in 56 and the widower of Atia Major, and together they had a daughter, Marcia. After the Battle of Pharsalus (48), the two brought their children back to Rome.

Caius Octavius Thurinus the Younger was born on 23 September 63 in his father's house in Rome on the northeastern side of the Palatine, in a place called *ad capita Bibula*, which looks toward the valley between the Palatine, Caelian, and Esquiline hills (where the Colosseum will be built in the future).

In 45, when he goes to find Caesar at Munda, he no longer lives in this house but in another situated on the northwestern side of the Palatine, above the Scalae Anulariae and immediately below the house of Cicero, which has a fine view over the Forum and the Capitoline. In the past, this house was owned by Caius Licinius Calvus, an individual of short stature, well-off, if not rich, a neoteric poet and an orator of Attic eloquence, a friend of Catullus, and an opponent not only of both Caesar and Pompey but Cicero too. Licinius Calvus went up against Cicero in several significant trials, such as that of Vatinius. He was the husband of Quintilia, but he was soon left a widower, and he dedicated some sweet and poignant verses to her. He died at little more than 30 years old, which was said to be due to studying and working to excess, which had weakened his body.

In 45, Octavius is 18 years old. He is a skinny individual of frail health, but his face is sensitive and his movements graceful, and he is well-educated and cultured. He is serious and practical by nature and very reserved to the point that, some say, he is a little sad. Among people, he appears somewhat cold and detached, except with his family members and close relatives. His way of thinking is based on the traditional criteria of Republican morality. Caesar thinks highly of him. He finds him to be an intelligent and serious young man and has set about ensuring that he progresses.

In 48, he saw to it that Octavius became engaged to the daughter of one of the most prominent senators, his consular colleague Publius Servilius Vatia Isauricus. In 47, he took Octavius under his own tutelage, somehow prising him away from his mother. He has also discretely stepped in to have Octavius coopted into the College of Pontiffs, then elected to the praetorship, and then designated as *praetor urbanus*. The then 17-year-old Octavius gave a good account of himself, fulfilling the duties of his office with great seriousness, calm, and poise, uncommon qualities in a youth of his age. Caesar thus had good reason to be pleased with his protégé.

As mentioned, Octavius was accompanied by Maecenas. The latter is a young man, 22 years old (he was born in 68) and therefore five years older than Octavius. He descends from an ancient and aristocratic family of equestrian rank from Arretium (Arezzo), which boasts of descending from the princely Etruscan lineage of the *Cilnii*. He was educated to the highest levels, so he is a highly cultured man. He is the author of modest literary works, both in prose and in verse, and is a refined connoisseur of art. He has inherited an enormous fortune (he owns the immense gardens known as the *Horti Maecenatis* in Rome). Maecenas is a known homosexual, his favorite being the freedman Bathyllus,[3] a young actor who specializes as a *pantomimus*.[4]

Munda: The Last Battle

On 17 March 45, Caesar deploys his troops on the field, putting the Third on his left flank and the old guard on the right, including the Tenth. Not long after, the battle starts; it will be both extremely uncertain and bloody, as well as the most bitter of all those that Caesar has fought up to this point. At one time during the fighting, Caesar fears his legions are about to give in, and he races to the front line to incite them to go on. Leaving his head unprotected, he throws himself headlong into the enemy. The gesture raises the spirits of his legionaries again.

Cnaeus Pompey takes a legion from his right flank to reinforce his left flank, which is about to give way, but a Caesarian charge causes the maneuver to fail. As the sun is setting, the Mauritanian, Bogud, with his horsemen, clambers up the hill and prepares to attack the enemy encampment, situated near the walls of Munda and left unguarded. Labienus, with five cohorts, tries to stop him. He leaves the battlefield, rushing for the Pompeian camp to try to reach it before Bogud to defend it. But the move is misunderstood. The Pompeians think he is falling back, break their lines, throw down their arms, and flee. Caesar's cavalry pursues them and massacres them. One of the victims is Labienus; another is Varus.[5] Cnaeus Pompey manages to escape and boards a ship to Carteia (Gibraltar). But his fate is sealed: within a few weeks, he will be captured and executed for treason by being beheaded. Sextus Pompey collects his brother's remains and flees by sea. From now on, he will move from place to place, operating as a pirate and causing no end of trouble for the future triumvirs Antony, Lepidus, and Octavian.[6]

The losses declared by Caesar after the Battle of Munda are 1,000 dead and 500 injured, while the number of Pompeian fallen amounts to 33,000. The Second, the Vernacula, and other legions have been wiped out. All the eagles of the Pompeian

---

3   On this relationship: Cornutus, V.123; Tacitus *Ann.,* I.54; Dio Cass., LV.17; Sen. *Q. Nat.,* VII.31.1–3; Anonymous, *Elegiae in Maecenatem.* Hor., XIV.10–15 traces a parallel between his own heterosexual love for Phryne and that of Anacreon for another Bathyllus, in homage to Maecenas' love.
4   Pantomime was a silent stage performance in which the actors were limited to gestures, facial expressions, the movement of their body, and to dancing, occasionally with a musical accompaniment. It emerged in Greece as an offshoot of mime and became more widespread in Rome from the end of the I century.
5   Marcus Porcius Cato, son of Cato of Utica, survives, but will fall at the Battle of Philippi in 42 while fighting in Brutus's army.
6   App. *B. Civ.,* II.440.

legions have been captured. The severed heads of Labienus and Varus are brought to Caesar, who orders that their remains be buried with full honors. Once again, the troops acclaim him as *imperator*.

Among the prisoners of war, those who were pardoned by Caesar on previous occasions but returned to fight against him once again are executed, while those for whom someone has interceded are pardoned and set free—Caesar allowed each of his friends to be able to save a man. Among the latter, worthy of note are Caius Cassius Longinus, brother-in-law of Marcus Junius Brutus and Crassus's quaestor in the war against the Parthians in 53 and subsequently the protector of Syria; Cnaeus Domitius Ahenobarbus, son of the deceased Lucius Domitius Ahenobarbus; and Marcus Vipsanius Agrippa, a friend of Octavius's.

It is worth dwelling on the latter. Agrippa was born in 63—some say in Arpinum (Arpino) in Lower Lazio, others say in Pisae in Etruria—into a family that was probably well-to-do but not noble. He is thus the same age as Octavius. He and Octavius have been close friends since childhood. Both fought at the Battle of Munda (45) as cavalry officers on opposing sides. Captured and taken prisoner, Agrippa is set free by Caesar following Octavius's intercession. He will remain Octavius's friend throughout his life and will marry his sister Octavia. When Octavius becomes Octavian and then Augustus, Agrippa will be his most faithful partner. A renowned military commander and a skilled public administrator, he will hold the consulship three times, will be the architect of many of Octavian's military victories (for example, at Actium in 31), and will reform the state administration and the treasury. He will also attend to matters of engineering and architecture, building roads, aqueducts, and the Pantheon in Rome.

The Senate Bestows Further Honors on Caesar

The Battle of Munda puts an end to the civil war between the Caesarians and Pompeians, which began in 49 with the crossing of the Rubicon. It consolidates Caesar's position at the center of the institutional apparatus of the Roman state. After the Battle of Thapsus, in fact, the Senate of Rome conferred the office of dictator to Caesar for 10 years. Following the Battle of Munda, it appoints him *dictator perpetuus*, "dictator for life."

After Munda, the Senate also decides that further honors should be given to Caesar, including putting up more statues. As a result, on 21 April 45 during the games held as part of the celebrations of the Parilia, an ivory statue of Caesar is carried in procession through the Campus Martius.[7] The Parilia is the festival of Pales. During the festival, following the lighting of fires, men and their flocks are

---

7   Dio Cass., 43.45

cleansed with sacred soot. This takes place every year on 21 April, the anniversary of the founding of Rome.

Another statue, dedicated to Caesar at the behest of the Senate of Rome, is placed in the Temple of Quirinus. This also causes political uproar, seeing as Quirinus is the deified form of Romulus, the founder of the city, and the inscription describes the subject represented in the statue as *theos aniketos*, "invincible god."[8]

A third statue of Caesar is placed in the Area Capitolina, next to a group of sculptures representing the seven Roman kings and an eighth of the Brutus who defeated the last of the Tarquinii. This might be seen as conferring the status of king on Caesar, were it not for the fact that the statue of Caesar is placed closest to that of Brutus, who freed the city from monarchy and is portrayed with his sword drawn. This suggests Caesar's political adversaries have had a say in the location of the statue. And that they intended it to mean that Caesar would be killed—and that the one to kill him should be Caepio Brutus, the descendant of the Brutus portrayed.[9]

8   Dio Cass., 43.45; Cic. *Att.*, 12.53.2, 13.4.2.
9   See P. Zanker, "Le irritanti statue di Cesare e i suoi ritratti contraddittori," in *Giulio Cesare. L'uomo, le imprese, il mito (Catalogo della mostra, Roma, Chiostro del Bramante, 23 ottobre 2008–3 maggio 2009)*, ed. G. Gentili (Milano: Silvana Editoriale, 2008), 75.

CHAPTER XXX

An *Ephebe* on the Victor's Chariot

A Fourfold Triumph

To say that Caesar, in 46, celebrates a triumph for his victories in Gaul, Egypt, Asia, and North Africa would be to severely understate the reality because he doesn't just celebrate one single triumph but four, two in August and two in September. Pompey had had three triumphs, and so Caesar must have one more than him.

The spoils of war exhibited during the triumphal procession consist of arms and armor, but also of silver, gold, and other precious metals. It is an enormous and immensely valuable collection. The gold alone weighs more than 10 tons. The spectators watching a single procession, crowded along both sides of the triumphal path, see 2,892 golden crowns paraded in front of them, donated by rulers and cities, as well as innumerable treasures, amounting to a total value of 65,000 talents.

All these riches—Caesar has announced, arousing a wave of enthusiasm—will be distributed among his legionaries in payment of their promised rewards. The tribunes and cavalry prefects will receive 20,000 denarii each, centurions will each receive 10,000 denarii, and each soldier will be given 5,000 denarii (more money than a legionary earns in the entirety of his 16 years of service).

The painted panels that are displayed in the parade depict the most memorable incidents of the campaigns—one, the suicide of Metellus Scipio, another, that of Cato. During the Parthian triumph, a huge sign is exhibited: *"veni, vidi, vici,"* the phrase with which Caesar announced his victory at the Battle of Zela in Pontus on 2 August 47.

At the end of August, during the Gallic triumph, Vercingetorix is displayed to the jubilant crowd, laden with chains, on top of a chariot. He has been held in prison in Rome for five years. He will be taken back there after the procession and executed. He will die of strangulation at the same moment that Caesar climbs the Capitoline to offer his victories at the foot of the statue of Jupiter Optimus Maximus.

The principal ornaments of the Egyptian triumph are Arsinoe IV and other high-ranking prisoners, who are put on display in chains. Arsinoe will be allowed to live and will be sent to the sanctuary of Artemis at Ephesus, the capital of Roman

Asia, where she will live in peace until 41, when she is killed on the orders of Mark Antony, instigated by Cleopatra VII.[1]

Another of the prisoners of war who are shown to the delirious public—this time looking on at the African triumph—is Juba, the five-year-old son of the deceased Juba I, King of Numidia. Caesar spared him and took him with him to Rome. Juba will be taught and educated like a Roman aristocrat and will occupy a prominent social position. In 19, he will marry Cleopatra Selene II, daughter of Mark Antony and Cleopatra VII. In 25, he (and, in due course, also his wife) will become the ruler of Numidia and Mauretania. They will also have a son, Ptolemy of Mauretania, destined to become their successor. Juba II (52 BC–23 AD) will be a scholar, the author of numerous works in the fields of literature, grammar, art, theater, history, geography, and medicine. Among other things, he will send a scholarly expedition to the legendary Fortunate Islands, an archipelago in the Atlantic Ocean somewhere off North Africa, vaunted as a place where the climate is pleasant, the vegetation is lush, men don't have to strive to produce food because there is enough to forage, and an eternal and happy life is reserved by the gods for heroes.[2]

In the days of his four triumphs, a square in Rome is named after Caesar. "The Games of Caesar's Victory" are established, to be celebrated on 20 July every year from now on, in memory of Caesar's daughter Julia. And 100 denarii, wheat, olive oil and meat are freely distributed to the poorest inhabitants of Rome.[3]

The games, which are magnificent, consist of theatrical performances, sports and athletics competitions, gladiatorial bouts (during which there is considerable bloodshed), chariot races, wild beast hunts (400 lions and numerous giraffes, animals never before seen in Rome, are killed in the arena), a battle between two armies each made up of 500 infantry, 30 cavalry, and 20 war elephants,[4] and even a naval battle, which takes place in a lake specially dug for the purpose in the Campus Martius, near one of the banks of the Tiber.

All these celebrations are the biggest and most spectacular that have ever been seen in Rome. Many of them take place under large silk awnings, unfurled to shade the spectators from the sun. Immense crowds attend, even coming from outside the city and making camp wherever possible. In the densest gatherings, where people are packed tightly together, many are crushed, including two senators. A famous playwright, Decimus Laberius, acts in one of the theatrical performances at Caesar's request. Before going onto the stage, he has to renounce his status as

---

1   App. *B. Civ.*, V.9; Joseph, XV.89.
2   The Fortunate Islands, or the Isles of the Blessed, are spoken of in Hes. *Theog.* 166–173; Pind. *Ol.*, II.61–76; Diod. Sic., V.19–20; *Mir. ausc.*, 84; Plin., VI.203–205; Ptol., *Geog.*
3   Caesar's legionaries do not appreciate the gesture, and some rebel in protest. Caesar suppresses the disorder with an iron fist, having one of the rebels executed, and then has another two beheaded in the Campus Martius. Their severed heads are put on display next to the Regia.
4   Some sources state that the battle with the elephants took place separately.

an *eques*—which he did reluctantly—because it is commonly believed among the Romans that the performing arts is not a pastime that befits a wealthy citizen. He is rewarded, however, with 500,000 sesterces and a golden ring. The ring symbolizes the restoration of his equestrian rank.

On the last day of the celebrations, Caesar lays on a sumptuous public banquet for 200,000 guests (22,000 tables, all set with the best food and wines), after which, crowned with flowers, he enters the Forum *Iulium*,[5] which is still under construction.

The Inauguration of the Forum *Iulium*

The Forum *Iulium* is the forum Caesar wanted to gift to the city. It is close to the existing Forum *Vetus* (due to the necessity for an urbanistic integration of two areas with similar functions) and is intended solely for civic functions, thereby removing its potential to be a place to carry out commercial activities. Specifically, it has been built in the area overlooking the Clivus Argentarius, extending in part to the eastern slopes of the Capitoline.

The architectural complex is 175 m long and 74 m wide, and it is composed of three elements: a rectangular open space, long and narrow, paved in travertine; a colonnaded portico with a white marble floor; and a temple. The designer probably used the Greco-Hellenistic sanctuaries dedicated to deified rulers as a template. The portico encloses the square on three sides, and the temple encloses the fourth side of the forum (on one of the shorter sides) opposite the entrance. It is dedicated to Venus Genetrix, that is, not so much—or not only—to Venus as the goddess of military fortune, and more generally as the goddess of success, but as the fabled progenitor of the *gens Iulia*. Venus was the mother of Aeneas, who in turn was the father of Ascanius, who was the founder of the *gens Iulia*. Caesar vowed to dedicate the building to Venus Genetrix in 48, before the Battle of Pharsalus. The temple is located at the end of the square, in an axial position, and is built on a raised platform made of concrete. It can be accessed from the square by two side staircases built into the platform. It has eight Corinthian columns on the façade and nine of the same order on each of its sides. The back is blind (that is, without columns) and was built against the earth. The platform's cladding, the columns, the architrave, and the entablature on the façade are all in marble. The entablature is decorated with a frieze with acanthus spirals. The *cella* is vaulted and ends in an apse, where one can find a cult statue of Venus, the work of a Greek sculptor from southern Italy, Agesilaus, perhaps a native of Tarentum, who is active in Rome. In the interior, ancient yellow marble columns line the walls on either side, surmounted

---

5   Dio Cass., reporting on the construction, calls the inaugurated complex the Great Forum, and it is understood that this name was given to it to distinguish it from the old one (Forum *Vetus*, or the Republican Forum). *See* Dio Cass., XLIII.22.2.

by an architrave, decorated with winged *putti*, and a gilded statue of Cleopatra VII has also been placed inside.[6]

The complex's very rich decoration also includes two statues of Caesar, fountains outside the temple, works by the painter Timomachus of Byzantium, collections of sculpted gems, and a chest decorated with pearls from Britannia.[7] One of the statues depicts the dictator as *imperator*, standing and in military dress, wearing a loricated cuirass (the first statue with a cuirass set up in Rome);[8] the other, placed in the center of the square, portrays Caesar on horseback.[9] This one is a work by Lysippus, the great Greek artist, who had sculpted it to depict Alexander the Great in the act of riding Bucephalus, his favorite horse, and which Caesar has taken for himself; the head of the rider is no longer that of Alexander, and has instead been replaced with that of Caesar. The paintings depict Medea and Ajax and they cost an enormous sum, as much as 80 talents.[10]

The statues mentioned above spark political controversy. Caesar's political adversaries see a violation of a customary norm in the statue with a cuirass, commissioned by the Senate with the endorsement of Caesar, and Caesar's intention to compare himself to Alexander the Great in the equestrian statue. The norm invoked by the dissenters is the one that prohibits soldiers from entering Rome bearing arms. They believe that, by extension, no statue portraying a warrior should be allowed in the city either.[11] However, they are forgetting about the statue of Junius Brutus placed on the Capitoline, which depicts Rome's liberator from monarchic oppression with his sword drawn.

After the inauguration of the Forum *Iulium*, Caesar returns to his own house, accompanied by an immense crowd and by 20 elephants bearing torches. The house in which he currently lives, with his wife Calpurnia, is no longer the Regia, or the Domus Publica, the seat of the *pontifex maximus*, but the first *domus* found on the Via Sacra after the Regia and which constitutes an extension or guesthouse of the Regia itself.

Octavius Appears in Public at Caesar's side

Caesar's fourfold triumph and the inauguration of the Forum *Iulium* are staged to make the Senate and the Roman people forget that some of the victories that Caesar

---

6   On the statue of Cleopatra VII: App. *B. Civ.*, II.102.
7   In 29, on Augustus's initiative, a gilded bronze statue of Cleopatra VII, a spoil of war, will be added to the works already mentioned.
8   Plin., 34.18.
9   An allusion to this statue can be found in Stat. *Silv.*, I.85.
10 A talent is equivalent to 26.2 kg of silver.
11 See P. Zanker, "Le irritanti statue di Cesare e i suoi ritratti contraddittori," in *Giulio Cesare. L'uomo, le imprese, il mito (Catalogo della mostra, Roma, Chiostro del Bramante, 23 ottobre 2008–3 maggio 2009)*, ed. G. Gentili (Milano: Silvana Editoriale, 2008), 74.

is taking credit for came against Roman citizens, waging war against, among others, the sons and the lineage of a man (Pompey) who had been one of Rome's greatest.[12] This is most evident in the Spanish campaign. Caesar's propaganda, seeking to justify it, presents it as a war fought against Juba I and local rebels, supported by treacherous Romans. The Pompeians, however, recognize that this conflict has been a civil war. Therefore, they consider the fact that Caesar is celebrating a triumph as an unprecedented act, as it celebrates a military victory achieved by Romans against other Romans. In the future, Caesar's version will be corroborated by the fact that Sextus Pompey joined up with Spanish bandits, and it was the governors of Hispania Ulterior, Caius Carrinas (in office in 45 and 44) and Caius Asinius Pollio (in 44, after Caesar's death), who paid the consequences, especially the latter, who suffered a catastrophic defeat.[13]

It is important to note that, during the processions, not only were Caesar's two legates in Spain, Quintus Pedius and Quintus Fabius Maximus, paraded as triumphators,[14] but so was a young man with a slender build and delicate features, dressed in splendid clothes with a gold chain around his neck: Caius Octavius Thurinus, Caesar's great-nephew.

Caesar, as we know, has a special relationship with Octavius, and he wants him to be at his side at every moment of the celebrations. Therefore, Octavius is first paraded on the triumphal chariot, drawn by four white horses, and preceded by 72 *lictors*. Then he attends the public games and participates in the final banquet.

At the same time, Caesar also has him decorated for his services in Spain. Octavius, during his sojourn in Spain, collaborated in the handling of Caesar's affairs, often acting as an intermediary in the administration of justice and in the reorganization of the provinces.

---

12 Plut. Caes., 56.8–9.
13 L. Canfora, *Cesare. Il dittatore democratico* (Roma-Bari: Laterza, 2006), 298.
14 Dio Cass., XLIII.42.2.

CHAPTER XXXI

More Than a Dictator for Life, Almost a King

An Extraordinary Accumulation of Powers

The powers of a dictator pervade every area of the state's activity, and those of a dictator for life are exercisable indefinitely. But Caesar is more than a perpetual dictator. He is also *imperator* for life (this title has become an element of his name and, as such, can be passed down to his heirs), as well as tribune of the plebs for an undefined period and even consul for five years (starting from 44). He also holds the office of prefect of the morals (*praefectura morum*). This means that he has essentially unlimited control over Roman citizens, including senators, over whom he can wield the same authority that, in the past, was held by the censor.

Therefore, Caesar has brought together a wide-ranging series of offices and traditional magisterial powers, always previously conferred on separate individuals, for himself, and has combined the office of consul with proconsular *imperium*. With this, the division between civil power and military power, which had recently occurred under the dictatorship of Sulla, is overlapped, allowing Caesar to hold control over the armed forces as well.

It goes without saying that, by claiming all the above-mentioned offices for himself, Caesar also enjoys innumerable privileges.[1] As dictator, he can be preceded at public appearances by 72 *lictors*: 24 for each of the preceding two dictatorships and 24 for the third. He can sit in the *sella curulis* in the Curia indefinitely, between the two consuls in office. He can speak first in discussions in the Senate (not because one of his offices is that of *princeps senatus* but because he presides over its sessions). He can wear the purple and the laurel wreath of a triumphator (something that he cares about deeply because it allows him to hide his baldness) at any time. In the theater, he has a raised seat relative to the orchestra. He has been able to substitute the name of Quintus Lutatius Catulus in the dedicatory inscription on the Temple of Jupiter Capitolinus in Rome with his own. Numerous honorific statues have been dedicated to Caesar, both in Rome and in all the other cities of the *imperium*. One

---

1   For a summary of his honors: Suet. *Iul.*, 76.1.

of these has been placed alongside the sculptures of the kings on the Capitoline. Caesar has also officially obtained the use of a state litter and the use of a *tensa*, the sort used to transport statues of the gods during processions, to carry sacred vestments and objects.

Needless to say, Caesar's status is one of unprecedented privilege. Looking through the entire history of Rome, it is possible to trace only one similar precedent in this regard: Lucius Cornelius Sulla became dictator for life by law in 83, he too after he had won a civil war—just as it is unnecessary to point out that such a large concentration of honors on one person cannot fail to arouse envy and jealousy.

Grandiose Building Projects

Having triumphed over both internal and external enemies, Caesar wants to usher in a new era of peace and prosperity. To this end, he launches some major projects, among which are: the codification of a new Civil Law, resulting from the thinning of the current regulations so as to retain only the best and most necessary ones; the reclamation of the Pontine Marshes to obtain farmland to be distributed both to war veterans who want to remain in Italy and to farmers who have suffered as a result of armies marching through their lands; the construction of a new road that will link the Adriatic coast to the Tiber, passing through the Apennines; channeling the waters of the Fucino into a newly built canal to irrigate the vast and dry surrounding plain; and the construction of a large public library, with distinct sections for Latin and Greek works.

Caesar promises to put experts in charge of the above-mentioned projects (Marcus Terentius Varro is to oversee the library) and ensures that the Senate approves the building works, foregoing the option of approving them himself with his own edicts (this would be the quickest method but, were he to use it, it would expose him to accusations of abuse of power).

Furthermore, as dictator, Caesar wants to restore politics and society and, in this direction, makes his clemency a weapon. He pardons many of his political opponents, who can thus return to Rome. One of those who is pardoned is Marcus Claudius Marcellus, consul of 51 and a friend of Cato. Marcellus had been opposed to Caesar's candidacy for the consulship, had tried to have him recalled from Gaul, and had been opposed to the conferral of citizenship rights to the inhabitants of the colonies founded by Caesar in Gallia Cisalpina. Following the defeat of the Pompeians, Marcellus had gone into voluntary exile on Mytilene/Lesbos. In early September 45, Lucius Calpurnius Piso Caesoninus, consul in 58 and Caesar's father-in-law, raises the issue in the Senate of the pardoning of the exile Marcellus, which had been requested by the cousin of the individual involved, Caius Claudius Marcellus, consul of 50, and by his wife, Octavia Minor, the sister of Octavius. Octavia throws herself at Caesar's feet and begs his forgiveness for her husband.

Caesar gives it to her. Cicero will laud Caesar's magnanimity in the Senate, giving the oration *Pro Marcello*, the first of three that are aimed at thanking Caesar for his clemency (the others will be *Pro Ligario* and *Pro rege Deiotaro*).

However, despite having been pardoned, Marcellus will not return to Italy. He will be killed in Athens, and Caesar will be wrongfully suspected of having been behind the assassination.

The Laws to Reform the Provinces and *Municipia:* Octavius, Deputy *Magister Equitum*

Between the second half of 45 and the first months of 44, Caesar uses his powers to bring forward and obtain approval for a series of draft laws that initiate a process that will radically reform the state and its government (*leges Iuliae*). Standing out among these is a law that increases the number of provinces from 14 to 18, which confirms the 10 provinces established by Sulla and the four later established by the Senate, which had subsequently been reduced to three by joining Cyrenaica to Crete (*Lex Iulia de provinciis*), and a law that reorganizes the administration of the *municipia* and sets down some rules of a social nature (*Lex Iulia municipalis*).

The new provinces are Gallia Comata, Illyricum, Achaea, and Africa Nova. The new system, furthermore, establishes that the provincial promagistracies will last no longer than two years for ex-consuls (in the consular provinces) and no longer than a year for ex-praetors (in the praetorian provinces) and that prorogations are not permitted.

With the *Lex Iulia municipalis*, all cities and colonies become *municipia*. The same law also bans wagons from circulating through cities during daylight hours to ease vehicular traffic congestion, except for the transport of materials to be used in the construction of religious buildings; charges aediles with maintaining the cleanliness of public places such as the forum and squares; and excludes passive homosexuals from holding high public offices, such as that of a senator.

One of Caesar's powers allows him to appoint civic magistrates, priests, provincial governors, and military commanders at his discretion and for the length of time he desires. He appoints the 18-year-old Octavius, his great-nephew, as the second-in-command of the cavalry, directly reporting to the *magister equitum* Marcus Aemilius Lepidus, and sends him to Apollonia in Epirus (near Fier in Albania) to participate in the preparations for a war against the Parthians.

Lepidus is a patrician, the son of Marcus Aemilius Lepidus and brother of the consul of 50, Lucius Aemilius Lepidus Paullus, who is the one who was bribed with a large sum of money by Caesar not to fulfill his duties. Paullus used the money to build the Basilica Aemilia in Rome, and then took care, on Caesar's behalf, of the construction of the Basilica *Iulia*, built on top of the demolished Basilica Sempronia. Since then, Paullus has been friends with Caesar and, in his absence from the capital, his spokesman and the coordinator of the tribunes of the plebs from the Populares faction. In 52, after the death of Clodius, Lepidus was appointed *interrex*, but he failed to do what was required of him (convene the *comitia centuriata* to allow the renewal of the magistracies). Besieged in his own home by Clodius's supporters, he barely managed to escape. Afterward, thanks to the support of Caesar, he became praetor (49), governor of Hispania Citerior (48–47), and consul (46). In addition, in 46, he became *magister equitum*, the second-highest office of state after that of dictator.

The Conspiracy

All the absolute and extraordinary power that is concentrated in Caesar's hands outrages and worries the Optimates. They consider the dictatorship of Caesar as the negation of the entire Republican constitution, even if one cannot speak yet of a monarch but, at most, of a *dominatus*, a regime theorized by Cicero in his *De re publica*, a political science treatise in six books, begun in 54 and probably published in 51. The *dominatus*, Cicero writes, repudiates consent—the element that characterizes the people as belonging to the center of power—and thus the law and the citizenry itself. Facing the *dominus*, adds Cicero, are not citizens but *res*, 'things,' objects over which others hold dominion.[2]

Caesar's political opponents are also indignant over some of the measures adopted by him, such as the appointment of all eight *praefecti urbi* (in the past, this public office was embodied in one single individual) and the debasement of the office of consul, which the dictator declares he holds in name only and delegates the duties thereof to others. Moreover, when the office becomes vacant due to the sudden and unexpected death of Quintus Fabius Maximus, Caesar assigns it for a single day to a senator, Caius Caninius Rebilus, who had asked him for it and is therefore allowed to hold it for one day only.

Their irritation reaches its peak when, in front of the Temple of Venus Genetrix, Caesar, while remaining seated, receives the entire Senate, which brings him a series of decrees conferring lavish honors on the dictator ("Some think that when he attempted to get up, he was held back by Cornelius Balbus"[3]). To their eyes, the fact that Caesar had been infuriated by the failure of the tribune of the plebs Pontius Aquila to rise to his feet as he passed by him and his colleagues, the only one not to do so, "in one of his triumphal processions" does not bode well,[4] nor the incident when an unknown person adorned a statue of Caesar with a fillet and laurel and

2 Cic. *Rep.*, 3.31.43.
3 Suet. *Iul.*, 78; see also Liv. *Per.*, 116.
4 Suet. *Iul.*, 78.

was thus arrested by the tribunes of the plebs (around 26 January 44);[5] still less the response of the dictator ("I am Caesar") to the crowd when they hailed him as king.

At the beginning of 44, anti-Caesarian opposition intensifies and prompts a political conspiracy that has as its objective the assassination of the dictator for life, which is to take place during the meeting of the Senate scheduled for the Ides of March (15 April 44) in the Curia of Pompey. The planned assassination attempt originates from a profound and secret pact, both cerebral and sentimental, sealed by an oath, among a limited number of senators, whose purpose is to restore the long-standing prerogatives of the oligarchy—those that Caesar has overridden—subject to the ousting of the dictator, and to avoid a new civil war.

The conspiracy is the tangible manifestation of two groups working together, and its leader is Caius Cassius Longinus. We have already met Cassius. In 53, he fought with Crassus at *Carrhae* and, subsequently, defended the Roman province of Syria from Parthian attacks. In 49, he was tribune of the plebs. He commanded part of Pompey's fleet during the Civil War. In 45, he had been pardoned by Caesar after the Pompeians' defeat at the Battle of Munda and fought under his banners against Pharnaces. Recently, he abandoned Caesar and hatched a political conspiracy against him.

One of the two groups associated with these conspiratorial ends is the *eteria* of Cassius, a politically active and well-structured clique that operates clandestinely as a secret association.[6] The other is made up of ex-Caesarians, that is, of people who had been extremely faithful to Caesar, only then to abandon him and move over to side with his political opponents while pretending that nothing has changed and continuing to act as if they are loyal to Caesar.

Among those who form part of this secret association is Caius Trebonius, suffect consul in 45. Another is the legionary commander Decimus Junius Brutus Albinus, born around 81 into a noble family of conservative leanings and which boasts of descending from the consul of 509, Lucius Junius Brutus, founder of the *res publica*. His grandfather had been a great general and statesman. His father hadn't been a military man. On his death, he had been adopted into the family of Postumius Albinus, himself an Optimas. Brutus Albinus had been a friend of Clodius and worked intensively with Caesar for at least a decade, going back to 56. That year, at just 25 years old, he had led the fleet to victory at the Battle of the Morbihan Gulf, which laid the basis for the conquest of Brittany and, subsequently, for Caesar's first landing

---

5   Dio Cass., 44.9; Suet. *Iul.,* 79.1.

6   The existence of a secret association led by Cassius can be deduced from the Greek word *eteria* used by Plut. *Brutus* 7.7, which has this meaning in the Attic dialect, and from the narrative of the conspiracy against Caesar provided by App. *B. Civ.* II.121, 122, 123, 142, etc., with particular reference to the use of phrases like "Cassius and his friends" or "the party of Cassius." On this point, see L. Canfora, *Cesare: il dittatore democratico* (Roma-Bari: Laterza, 1999), 336–342, esp. 339.

in Britannia. In 52, he commanded some ground forces in the campaign to suppress the Revolt of Vercingetorix. At the Battle of Alesia, he had been the one to launch the counterattack, followed by Caesar. He is a quick-thinking, tough, resourceful man who likes to fight; he seems made for a military life. Proud and competitive, he ardently aspires to fame.[7] In 50 and 49, he had been a quaestor in charge of the Treasury and minted coins to celebrate Caesar's victories in Gaul. During the Civil War (49–45), he led Caesar's fleet to victory in the Battle of Massilia, snatching away Pompey's exclusive claims to naval success. He was praetor in 48 and, from 47 to 45, propraetor for Gallia Narbonensis, repressing the rebellion of the Bellovaci. For the remainder of 45, he was again praetor in Rome. But political office has never interested him as much as military command. He fought in the Civil War between Caesar and Pompey on Caesar's side, causing a rift with the rest of his family and his brothers-in-law, who sympathized with Pompey and Cato. Gaul is his passion, so much so that he speaks, behaves, and dresses as a Gaul. He possesses a team of gladiators. He married Paula Valeria, who had divorced her husband, previously a provincial governor. Decimus Junius Brutus Albinus is one of the few people whom Caesar trusts implicitly. Caesar would never think that he could be betrayed by him, so much so that he has named him in his will and is thinking of appointing him as governor of Gallia Cisalpina for 44 and 43 and putting him forward as a candidate for the consulship for 42.

The two groups are linked by the urban praetor Marcus Quintus Servilius Caepio Brutus. We have met him many times already. He is a promising judicial orator and is inclined to the study of philosophy. Cicero dedicated his *Brutus* to him, a Platonic dialogue on Roman oratory written in 46, which has Cicero, his friend Atticus, and Brutus himself as its protagonists. Brutus provided assistance to Cato during the mission the latter undertook in Cyprus, where Brutus took advantage of the circumstances to make a great deal of money through the practice of usury. Rumors abound that he is the illegitimate son of Caesar because his mother Servilia had been Caesar's mistress. After the Battle of Pharsalus, in which he fought among the Pompeian ranks, he had been pardoned by Caesar and continued to enjoy his favor to the extent that he was propraetor legate in Gallia Cisalpina and urban prefect in Rome.

Cassius attempted to bring Brutus into the folds of his *eteria* when the latter was already plotting Caesar's assassination. He did so in various ways, sending some of his friends (members of the *eteria*) to him in order that he paint Caesar as a tyrant who wants to make himself king and cover the city's walls and monuments with graffiti to that effect, scrawled by an anonymous hand. Brutus was still ill-disposed toward Cassius, who had tried to prevent him from becoming urban prefect for 44 (assuming that the contest between the two for this magistracy hadn't been a *mise-en-scène*,

---

7   B. Strauss, *La morte di Cesare* (Roma-Bari: Laterza, 2015), 11.

"so that they might not seem to have a common understanding with each other"[8]), but he was a dyed-in-the-wool Optimas, educated in the school of Cato, and thus was not indifferent to the solicitations of Cassius and his friends, who saw in him, in the context of the conspiracy, the common ground between the Pompeian soul and the ex-Caesarian soul. So, little by little, he overcame his hesitations regarding the necessity to save the *res publica*, thereby thwarting, with the killing of Caesar, the attempts by the dictator to subvert it. In the end, he agreed to take part in the plot because, ultimately, when he decided what he wanted, he desired it greatly.[9]

The wheels of the political conspiracy against Caesar are already in motion in the summer of 45, when an attempt is made to involve Mark Antony in it as well. With this in mind, Trebonius approaches Antony in Narbona. Antony refuses, but he keeps his mouth shut; he doesn't warn Caesar, nor does he report anyone's name to him.

Antony and Fulvia

Antony married Fulvia after she had already been widowed twice: first by Clodius, with whom she had had a daughter called Clodia (not to be confused with the Clodius's sister, also called Clodia), and then by Curio.[10]

Fulvia was born from the marriage between Marcus Fulvius Bambalio ("The Stutterer") and Sempronia Tuditana. On her father's side she descends from a family originating from Tusculum, but which moved to Rome and supplied numerous Roman consuls between 322 and 125. Cicero has no respect for Fulvia's father, considering him a nonentity.[11] Her mother comes from a family that used to be rich and noble but has since fallen from grace, and it seems that Fulvia received a substantial fortune from her.

Fulvia married Clodius in 62 and had two children with him: Publius Clodius Pulcher and Clodia Pulchra. She became a widow in 52, showing the wounds of her spouse to those who came to pay their respects to his body on the Palatine. Later, she had been a witness for the prosecution in the trial against Milo, which caused her a considerable amount of pain. She subsequently remarried, this time to Caius Scribonius Curio, tribune of the plebs in 50, who would fall in North Africa in 49 while fighting against the Pompeians. Later, she remarried once again, to Antony, who gave her two children: Marcus Antonius Antyllus and Iullus Antonius. Antyllus means 'little Anton', referring to the mythological figure of Anton, a son of Hercules, held to be the progenitor of the *gens Antonia*. The name Iullus, conversely, is an

---

8   On the hypothesis that this disagreement was staged: App. *B. Civ.*, II.112.
9   Plut. *Brut.*, 6.7: "And it is said that Caesar, when he first heard Brutus speak in public, said to his friends: 'I know not what this young man wants, but all that he wants he wants very much'."
10 Plut. *Ant.*, 10.3.
11 Cic. *Phil.*, III.16.

archaic variant of the name of another mythological figure, Iulus, or Ascanius, the son of Aeneas and the progenitor of the *gens Iulia*.

Mark Antony gave these names to his sons to demonstrate the noble origins of the *gens Antonia*, pay homage to the family of Caesar, and underline the privileged relationship that he had with the latter. Since 53, he has lived with his family in a *domus* on the slopes of the Palatine, on the corner of the Via Sacra and the so-called Clivus Palatinus. It was originally owned by Marcus Aemilius Scaurus and, later, by Clodius. After the death of Clodius, the house remained the property of Fulvia, who continued to live there.

Cicero the Philosopher

Cicero had retired from public life in 50, but he remains a senator. In January 49, he does his utmost to broker peace between Caesar and Pompey. In 48, after Pharsalus, he ditches the Pompeians.

In 47, he divorces Terentia, a petulant and whiny woman who had been a burden on his life but who had given him two children: Tullia and Marcus. He does so after accusing his wife of conducting unlawful business and profiting in his absence from the possibilities that opened from managing the family wealth, thanks in part to Philotemus. Terentia counters that the real reason for the divorce is her husband's desire to marry the beautiful and rich Publilia, who is also much younger than her. In fact, in December 46, Cicero does marry Publilia, who is probably about 15 years old at the time, and who brings him a dowry as rich as that of Terentia.[12] But it isn't a happy marriage.

In 45, Tullia dies in childbirth with the baby she was carrying. Cicero had never paid all that much attention to his daughter, but he mourned her death greatly, saying that he had felt a lot of affection and tenderness for her. Tullia dies in her father's house on the Palatine. From that moment on, Cicero detests that house. This is also because the death of Tullia delivers the *coup de grâce* to the already unstable marital relationship between him and Publilia. Cicero leaves that house and at first goes to live with his friend Atticus on the Quirinal Hill, then in his own villa in Astura (Torre Astura, on the coast of Lazio, south of Anzio and Nettuno), where Tullia's ashes had been buried.

In 45, Cicero enjoys the fruits of an industrious life, the most recent of which is a new out-of-town villa in Puteolis (Pozzuoli in Campania). Cicero has just inherited it from a businessman, Marcus Cluvius, in co-ownership with Caesar. Before very

---

12 Terentia remarries as well, marrying the historian Sallust. After being widowed by him, it seems she marries twice more: first to Messalla Corvinus, then to Vibius Rufus. She dies at the age of 103. Her marriage to Messalla Corvinus is attested by Plutarch. The one to Vibius Rufus is attested by Dio Cass., but he is perhaps confusing Terentia with Publilia.

long, the villa will be "invaded" by Caesar's soldiers, and Cicero will have difficulty in housing them.

Also in 45, Cicero writes the *Academica*, a philosophical work in the form of a Platonic dialogue, in another of his villas, the one in Cumae. This villa in Cumae will also be the setting of another of Cicero's Platonic dialogues—*De finibus bonorum et malorum* (On the ends of good and evil)—in which he, Lucius Manlius Torquatus, and Caius Valerius Triarius discuss whether the Epicurean doctrine, according to which what gives pleasure is identified with what is good, is correct.

As a political man, Cicero is someone who defends the *res publica*, which he still sees as a city-state as it was at its inception, and not a universal empire as it has become at this point. As a philosopher and a scholar, he believes that politics must be instilled with moral values. It is for this reason that he was close to Cato until shortly before his death. He sees in Caesar a powerful man who is gifted with no shortage of talents but "who does not know the shadow of morality" (in the sense that he cares more for his own personal benefit than for the well-being of all) and who has more than a million deaths on his conscience, whilst in Mark Antony, he sees a man who yearns to be dictator but whose unrestrained ambition has gone unnoticed by everyone.

CHAPTER XXXII

Cleopatra in Rome

Pretextual Accusations

In 44, Caesar is 56 or 57 years old. As he has grown older, he has put on a little weight and is growing bald, which upsets him badly. He has got used to combing the few remaining hairs down from the crown of his head. He makes considerable use of his privilege of being able to wear a laurel wreath to hide his brow, his favorite of the privileges that have been granted to him or seized by him.[1] Nor is his health what it once was. Recently, he has often been victim to bouts of fainting and nightmares; moreover, on two occasions, he has been struck by a mini-stroke in public, which caused dizziness, numbness in the limbs, and resulted in him falling to the ground. In 46, at Thapsus, as the battle approached, he passed out and was carried to shelter.[2] He suffered from a similar attack the following year in Corduba,[3] and more recently twice more in Rome, in the Forum. These transient ischemic attacks could have damaged Caesar's physique and undermined his character. This hypothesis is supported by the fact that Caesar has been dejected for some time and suffers from rapid mood swings. One day, during one of Cicero's orations, he began to tremble, turned pale, and let a bundle of documents that he held in his hand drop to the floor. Suetonius will recount that Caesar enjoyed excellent health except toward the end of his life, when he suffered from bouts of fainting and from sleeping disorders. Despite the fact he is no longer a young man, and despite his issues with his appearance and health, Caesar nonetheless remains a handsome and captivating man. As always, women love and desire him, and he reciprocates their feelings with gallantry and love.

---

1   Suet. *Iul.*, 45.
2   Plut. *Caes.*, 53.
3   Or at some point up to three years before Thapsus. Plutarch, who recounts the episode in Corduba, could have mixed up the years of the two visits that Caesar made to Spain toward the end of his life.

Ever since he was very young Caesar has had many lovers, usually married aristocratic women: Servilia Caepio, the half-sister of Cato and the wife of Marcus Junius Brutus and then of Decimus Junius Silanus; Postumia, the wife of Servius Sulpicius Rufus; Lollia, the wife of Aulus Gabinius; Tertulla, the wife of Marcus Licinius Crassus;[4] and Mucia Tertia, Pompey's third wife. This isn't a complete list. To these women, we must also add two queens: Eunoë, the wife of Bogudes, King of Mauretania, and Cleopatra VII, consort of Ptolemy XIV, king-pharaoh of Egypt.[5] The victorious Caesar allowed himself two months of rest with Cleopatra VII, sailing up the Nile in her ship and having a child, Caesarion, with her. It shouldn't be forgotten that, while he was flirting with the queen-pharaoh in Egypt, Caesar was married to Calpurnia who was waiting for him to return to Rome.

That Caesar is a philanderer is common knowledge among his fellow citizens and his soldiers. Proof of this comes in 45, when his war veterans, while they are parading down the Via Sacra at the end of a triumphal procession and making jokes and laughing at their victorious commander's expense, strike up a chorus, while snickering, of a light-hearted refrain: "Citizens, lock up your wives: we're bringing the bald adulterer home."[6] The same soldiers, however, also sing: "Caesar conquered Gaul, Nicomedes conquered Caesar: look, Caesar who conquered Gaul is celebrating a triumph, not Nicomedes, who conquered Caesar!" This latter refrain needs an explanation. The Nicomedes in question is Nicomedes IV Philopator (r. 94–74), King of Bithynia. To explain why Caesar is mentioned in relation to this sovereign, we need to take a step back.

In 80, Caesar was a conscript officer in the service of Marcus Minucius Thermus, propraetor of Asia. Thermus's army was stretched as it sought to capture Mytilene/ Lesbos, an island off the Aegean coast of Anatolia. Tasked with obtaining the supply of warships that had been promised by Nicomedes IV but always delayed, Caesar stayed as the king's guest for several months in the palace in Nicomedia, the capital of Bithynia. He visited the king assiduously and they became friends. On his return to Rome, he resumed his activity as a judicial speaker, again setting himself against the Optimates. Before long, he became the subject of gossip. It was said that he had had passive sexual relations with Nicomedes IV. The smears were corroborated by the fact, after having been to the court of the king once, Caesar rapidly returned there, saying that he wanted to recover credit he had granted to a freed slave who had become one of his clients. He was once again received as a guest of the king,

4   It seems that Crassus didn't feel too interested in the affair. In fact, he may have encouraged his
    wife, as her relationship with Caesar might then help their own. Tertulla may also have had other
    lovers in addition to Caesar, seeing as she had a reputation for infidelity. It was rumored that one
    of her sons bore more of a similarity to a senator named Axius than to Crassus and was therefore
    a son of the former rather than the latter.
5   Suet. *Iul.*, 52.
6   Suet. *Iul.*, 51.

who, on his departure, gave him a bag of money as a gift, enough to enable him to lead a comfortable life for a long time.

It is likely that there is a secret part of Caesar's soul that contrasts with his virile, cool-headed, courageous, and determined side and consists of a feminine sensibility, albeit one kept in check. If true, he was doubly intimate: just as he cannot resist the charms of beautiful women, so he does not disdain intimacy with men.

Confirmation of what is being said about the double nature of Caesar is given by other rumors, according to which Caesar, as a young man, had loved a boy called Sarmentus[7] and that, during the Gallic Wars, one of his secretaries had the task of procuring young slaves for him with a slender physique and who were very attractive, if not beautiful. They had the license to spend any amount just to get them but would omit the related disbursements from the records out of modesty, though not because Caesar was ashamed of the reason for the expense, but rather of the exorbitant prices that he had had to pay.

The accusation of *impudicitia*[8] has followed Caesar his whole life. Since Caesar became dictator, gossip about this has been used instrumentally against him by his political opponents. As such, Caesar is criticized, mocked, and even insulted for his alleged *impudicitia*.

The mud-slinging machine is in full operation. His detractors act in plain sight, persistently and ferociously. Dolabella, previously a cast-iron Caesarian, defines Caesar as "the queen's rival, the inner partner of the royal couch"; Curio, the father, calls him "the brothel of Nicomedes" and "the Bithynian stew"; and Bibulus, in the edicts in which he insults his colleague, uses the term "the queen of Bithynia" who "had formerly been in love with a king, but now coveted a kingdom." Marcus Brutus relates that, during a banquet, a certain Octavius (Marcus Octavius, aedile in 50?), a madman who says anything that comes to mind, greeted Pompey and Caesar, calling them respectively "king" and "queen." Caius Memmius reproaches Caesar for having served Nicomedes IV as his cupbearer together with other homosexuals, offering as proof the fact that some Roman businessmen claimed to have been eyewitnesses of a compromising incident as proof. Cicero writes that Caesar, dressed in a light, flowing robe, had been carried in the arms of Nicomedes IV's servants and laid down in a bed with the finest sheets and soft pillows, waiting for the arrival of the sovereign. Not satisfied with this, Cicero, when Caesar is in the Senate defending the cause of Nysa, Nicomedes's daughter, refers to the benefits that he had received from her father, saying "Let's get over it, as it is well known what you have given to him and

---

7   The story, whether true or false, will be passed on by Plut. *Ant.*, 59.

8   Among the Romans, *pudicitia* meant virginity or sexual virtue/modesty, both for a woman and for a man. A man lost it, thus exhibiting *impudicitia*, if he gave himself to be a passive partner in a homosexual liaison. Sexual relations—real, not imaginary—between people of the same gender were common among the Romans and were entirely lawful, other than for a couple of practices considered reprehensible by common morality and punishable by law.

he to you." In other words, Cicero affirms in the Senate that Caesar is defending the daughter of the King of Bithynia "for obvious reasons."[9] Caius Licinius Calvo—poet, orator, and Catullus's friend—writes on Caesar's homosexuality as follows: "All that Bithynia and Caesar's bugger ever possessed." Cicero also calls Caesar "The husband to all wives and wife to all husbands" (evidently, he is alluding to the fact that Caesar did not limit himself to the King of Bithynia alone).

The reason why his political opponents persist in presenting Caesar as an *impudicus* is not moral at all, but lies in their desire to put him into political difficulty. Caesar has concentrated such a collection of civic and military powers and honors on himself that it makes his government appear like a monarchy, which makes him the primary target of criticism from those who, for various reasons, remain tied to the traditions of Republican *libertas*.

The fact that Cleopatra VII has arrived in Rome, holding Caesarion in her arms and her brother-husband Ptolemy XIV by the hand, and is now holding court in the city, offers the dictator's political opponents another tool with which to damage his image. Cleopatra VII's sojourn in Rome will last for two years (46–44), during which she will live in a splendid building in the *Horti Caesaris*, away from prying eyes.

Caesar's political opponents heap accusations on him, often unfair, often artfully formulated, for the sole purpose of making life difficult for him. He is accused of coupling with Cleopatra VII while he remains married to Calpurnia, of having tried—unsuccessfully—to have a law passed that would have allowed him to have two wives (the Senate, meanwhile, was pressing Caesar to disavow Calpurnia and marry Cleopatra, enticed by the prospect of acquiring Egypt through inheritance), of ignoring his public duties to keep track of his lover and of the renovation of the *Horti,* and of having granted royal honors to a foreigner and recognizing her divine status as the reincarnation of Isis. More seriously, they spread the rumor that Caesar aspires to tyranny and, under the influence of Cleopatra VII, wants to establish a Greco-Hellenistic-type monarchy, or perhaps a monarchy inspired by the paternalism of the early kings of Rome. Their objective is to arouse popular indignation, leveraging on the fact that many Romans—such as Cicero—are envious of Caesar and have an aversion to him, but also and especially because, in Rome, the word *rex* is full of negative connotations, unless this refers to the *rex sacrorum* which, however, is something else entirely.

Some Incidents Suggest a Conspiracy Is Underway

In November 45, while pronouncing an oration in defense of Deiotarus, king of Galatia, Cicero warns Caesar that having his statue placed among those of the ancient

9   Suet. *Iul.*, XLIX.

kings has aroused a swarm of malevolent rumors about him.[10] On 26 January 44, while returning to Rome from the Feriae Latinae on Monte Albano, Caesar, dictator for the fourth time, is unexpectedly greeted by a passer-by as king. Caesar replies quickly and curtly that his name is not *rex* but Caesar. These incidents suggest that a conspiracy is underway. Caesar knows this, but he refuses to believe that anything bad will befall him because he also knows he is a guarantee of system stability. With his death the *res publica* would fall into civil war, and this is something that his political opponents, who say they love the Republic and want to defend it from him, would not want.

A third incident confirms that someone around Caesar, insisting on falsely attributing the desire to become king to him, is aiming to create the conditions for a situation that would justify killing him as a measure to safeguard the Republican system and the political independence of the state. This happens on 15 February 44, the final day of Lupercalia, a pastoral festival observed annually to purify the city of Rome by promoting health and fertility. During a frenzied race along the ancient *pomerium* by a crowd of half-naked young people who hold in their hands the leather straps made of sacrificed animals' hides with which they whip passers-by, Mark Antony, one of the runners, approaches Caesar's box. He publicly offers the dictator a crown in the form of a Hellenistic diadem. Caesar refuses the offer. Cassius Longinus intervenes and, with Publius Casca alongside him, places the crown on Caesar's lap. The audience watching the scene loudly urges them to place the crown on the dictator's head, and Antony twice tries to gird the head of Caesar with it, Caesar disdainfully refuses on each occasion, while the audience acclaims Caesar as king. Caesar, at the height of irritation, snatches the crown from Antony's hands and throws it into the crowd. To understand Caesar's reaction, one must consider that the diadem has been a symbol of regal power since the times of the Hellenistic monarchies, and Caesar's refusal to wear it constitutes a symbolic rejection of the role of king.[11]

However, another tradition reports that Caesar didn't throw the crown into the crowd but ordered it to be placed in the Temple of Jupiter Optimus Maximus on the Capitoline. Shortly afterward, someone decorates some of the statues of Caesar around the city with the royal diadem. The tribunes of the plebs Lucius Cesetius Flavus and Caius Epidius Marullus tear the diadems from the statues and imprison the first people in the crowd who had acclaimed Caesar as king.[12]

It is not clear whether Antony's gesture was staged following a prior agreement with Caesar. In any case, it doesn't stop the organization of the conspiracy unfolding

---

10   Cicero *Deiot.* 12.33.
11   Cicero *Phil.* 2.33.84–2.34.87; 3.5.12; 13.8.17; Nicolaus of Damascus *Aug.* 21.
12   Dio Cass. 44.9.1–3; Plut. *Ant.* 12.24; *Caes.* 61.8; App. *B. Civ.* 2.108; Nicolaus of Damascus *Aug.* 20. The end of the episode, as it is presented, is perplexing: Caesar dismissed the tribunes, having seriously offended them in public, but the public then insulted the tribunes.

against Caesar, which aims at the physical elimination of the dictator as a measure to safeguard the Republican political system and the political independence of the state. The date that the conspirators decide that action should be taken is the Ides of March (15 March). As this date approaches, the tension builds.

In a meeting of the conspirators that takes place shortly before the Ides of March, Cassius expresses his opinion that Antony should also be killed out of fear that he will speak, and, even if he does not, he will still be a dangerous man (remember that Trebonius approached Antony to persuade him to join the conspirators, but while the latter refused to take part in the plot, he also didn't denounce it). But Brutus opposes this, perhaps under pressure from Trebonius, and Cassius's motion is not passed. Antony is safe, but Trebonius will have to take care of keeping him well away when the plan to assassinate Caesar is set in motion.

CHAPTER XXXIII

Twenty-Three Stab Wounds

Baleful Omens and Other Warnings

On 14 March 44,[1] a few events occur in Rome that transcend the natural order of things and seem to be ominous omens. In the *Horti Caesaris,* the freed herds of horses dedicated by Caesar to the Rubicon stop grazing, refuse to feed, and weep constantly. A little bird that flew into the Curia of Pompey with a sprig of laurel in its beak is attacked and killed by a flock of other birds, of various species, that had taken off from a nearby grove. A lioness gives birth on the street. Some graves open, casting the dead out. It rains blood on the Capitoline.[2]

Recently, the number of omens has increased, suggesting there is a widespread awareness of the gravity of the moment. A member of Caesar's bodyguard has told Calpurnia things that have frightened her. The soothsayer Spurinna, while Caesar was offering a sacrifice, had warned him to beware the Ides of March (Caesar, who had no love for Spurinna, dismissed him with contempt, despite knowing that sometimes soothsayers could interpret divine signals from earthly circumstances). His friend Caius Aemilius Balbus had whispered in Caesar's ear: "The Ides of March are near; whatever comes, when you go to the Senate, have yourself protected by your Spanish bodyguards."

Balbus also recently reported to Caesar that the settlers brought to the colony at Capua, under the *lex Iulia agraria* of 59, were demolishing some ancient tombs to build country houses in their place when, in one of them, they found a vast quantity of vases of ancient workmanship and a bronze tablet bearing an inscription in Greek words and characters. The inscription said that Capys, the founder of Capua, was buried in that tomb, and it warned: "Whenever the bones of Capys shall be moved, it will come to pass that a son of Ilium shall be slain at the hands of his kindred, and presently avenged at heavy cost to Italy."

---

1   The ancient sources providing the circumstances surrounding the death of Caesar are primarily Suet. *Iul.* and Plut. *Caes.*

2   On the events connected to Caesar before his assassination: Suet. *Iul.,* 81; Plut. *Caes.* 63–65; Plut. *Brut.,* 14–16.

It seems as if Caesar isn't paying attention to anything or anyone, but it is just a façade. On the evening of the 14th, he is entertained at the house of the urban prefect Marcus Aemilius Lepidus for dinner, at which Decimus Junius Brutus Albinus, the *praetor pellegrinus,* is also present. (Caesar doesn't know that Decimus Brutus is one of the conspirators; he is not the least bit suspicious of him and has even named him as a secondary heir in his will.) The evening is characterized by a sinister, troubling atmosphere. Caesar returns home, wondering whether he has eaten his last supper.

On the night of the 14th to 15th, there are more premonitory signs. The doors and windows of Caesar and Calpurnia's bedroom swing open by themselves, for no apparent reason; the spear of Mars trembled in the Regia, a sign that something terrible is about to happen; and Caesar and Calpurnia have strange dreams. He dreams of flying silently above the clouds and shaking the hand of Jupiter. She dreams that the pediment above Caesar's house is collapsing and that she is crying for her murdered husband, whom she holds in her arms. But it doesn't end there. On the morning of the 15th, Caesar, during a sacrifice, cannot find the offering's heart. A meeting of the Senate has been convened to be held in the Curia of Pompey, and he is preparing to leave the house to take part, with the intention of giving a speech. Calpurnia tries to dissuade him from doing so, while flocks of birds seem to want to stop him leaving the house too, but he resists these overtures.

The Death of Caesar

Caesar knows that all the signs that have been observed can be interpreted as divine portents with fatal consequences. It seems that he is continuing to pay them no heed. In reality, due to both the omens and his poor health, he is hesitant. He is tempted to stay at home and postpone his participation in the Senate. But then Decimus Brutus arrives. He has come to accompany him to the Senate. Decimus Brutus urges Caesar not to disappoint the senators, who have already been waiting for him for a little while, and, toward the end of the fifth hour (nine o'clock in the morning), he sets off. He has dismissed his Spanish bodyguard so he leaves the house without an escort, in the company of Decimus Brutus. Just then, a statue of Caesar, placed near the entrance, falls to the ground and shatters. Caesar pays it no heed, not even turning his head, and he leaves in a litter, preceded by *lictors.*

As can be seen, Caesar hasn't listened to the warnings, neither the supernatural ones, nor those of his wife and his friends. Furthermore, he disbanded his bodyguard. It could be that he is consciously setting out to meet his death because he is exhausted, or in physical decline, or perhaps he feels reassured by the fact that the senators have sworn to safeguard his life.

It could also be that he is aware that forces greater than him are trying to use the pretext of his death to cause the civil war to break out again, and he prefers to face his enemies openly, once and for all, rather than wait for them to spring their traps, to defeat them and thus prevent the *res publica* from falling back into violence and chaos.[3]

On their way through the streets, Caesar and Decimus Brutus encounter the consul Mark Antony, who joins them, while a mass of people crowd around their litters and hail Caesar *imperator, dictator, rex!* (This shows that the people are not against the idea of Caesar becoming king and do not fear that he, once he has put on the crown, will behave like a tyrant). Finally, the trio reaches the Curia of Pompey.

The conspirators' plot begins to unfold as soon as Caesar, Decimus Brutus, and Antony are about to enter the room where the Senate is due to meet, making their way through the quadriportico crowded with senators and the public. The first of the conspirators to spring into action is Trebonius: he engages Antony in deep conversation, keeping him occupied under the vaults of the portico. Meanwhile, Caesar—himself under the quadriportico—sees Spurinna and points out to him, in reference to the latter's previous warning, that "the Ides of March have come ..." (meaning, "as you can see, nothing has happened!"), but receives the response that "but they have not yet passed."

Caesar and Decimus Brutus enter the room while Antony is still being distracted by Trebonius. A stranger is quick to come to Caesar's side and hand him a parchment, which the dictator will never read. The scroll contains information essential to Caesar's safety; in it, the plan and some names of the conspirators are revealed—Brutus, Cassius, Casca, Trebonius, Cimber, Decimus Brutus, Quintus Ligarius. He is advised to be careful, and vows are made to beseech the gods to protect him.

Caesar makes a sacrificial offering to the man he defeated at Pharsalus on an altar at the foot of the statue, then he takes his seat on a golden chair a few steps beyond. He looks around at a confused scene. The conspirators, about 60 in number, gather around him, as if they are about to honor him. Lucius Tillius Cimber asks him something. Caesar, who has a stylus in one hand and is preparing to write something on a wax tablet, replies with a gesture, as if wanting to postpone the matter to another, more appropriate moment. But Cimber grabs the folds of his toga at the shoulder and yanks it down. Caesar immediately springs to his feet and decries the violence. It is the prearranged signal.

Caius Servilius Casca attacks the dictator from the front, stabbing him in the throat. A gasp leaves Caesar's lips, but he doesn't say a word—instead he grabs Casca's arm and thrusts his stylus into it, which he is holding like a dagger. Then he steps back toward the statue, his back to it so that he can at least protect himself from behind and looks around. While the other conspirators converge on him with daggers in hand, throwing themselves at him and overwhelming Caesar with a hail of blows, the other senators cry out and flee in terror. No one dares to step

---

3   Suet. *Iul.*, 86.1–2.

forward and defend the victim. Stabbed repeatedly, Caesar's body is weeping blood from the wounds (none of which are fatal except for the second one, inflicted by Cassius Longinus, who thrust his dagger into Caesar's face), drenching the base of the statue, then he loses his strength and staggers. He is about to slump to the ground when he recognizes Caepio Brutus among his assailants and gives him an astonished and pained expression, saying, "You too, my son?" But the phrase dies in his throat because Brutus, without saying a word, stabs him in turn, sinking his blade between his ribs (the victim's body will bear the marks of 23 dagger blows). Caesar collapses to the floor, in his death throes at the foot of the statue of Pompey, covers his head with the hem of his toga, then breathes his last.

A Situation of Extreme Tension

The news of Caesar's death spreads like wildfire through Rome, arousing immense shock, bewilderment, and confusion, while the conspirators—abandoning their aim of throwing the victim's body in the Tiber, as is traditionally done with those who have been accused of having wanted to make themselves king—leave the Curia of Pompey in disorder, scale the Capitoline and barricade themselves there for fear of violent responses by the lower-class plebeians and the deceased dictator's war veterans (who are flowing into Rome in increasing numbers).

Then they go down to the Forum, and Brutus speaks from the Rostra to a silent crowd on the theme of liberty. One of those who takes to the floor is Lucius Cornelius Cinna, the homonymous son of the consul of 87, 86, 85, and 84 and the brother of Caesar's first (or second) wife, Cornelia. He delivers a fierce oration against Caesar, accusing him of having tried to take away the freedom of Roman citizens. This sparks a wave of anger in the audience and the conspirators must flee once more, again returning to the Capitoline to take shelter.[4] In the meantime, the bloody corpse of Caesar, after having remained on the floor for a long time, has been placed on a gurney by three slaves and is taken home.

Before long, the situation descends into chaos. The streets and squares are full of people gathered at intersections, exchanging news, and animatedly discussing the latest developments. Scuffles break out, barely kept in check by the Legio X Equestris. The Tenth currently preside over Rome, under the command of the *magister equitum* Marcus Aemilius Lepidus.

The legion was used in 67–65 by Caius Calpurnius Piso[5] to put down a revolt by the Allobroges and from 58 to 50 by Caesar for the conquest of Gaul and the expeditions to Britannia. It fought at Genava, at the Arar, at Bibracte, in

---

4   Plut. *Brut.*, 18.
5   Piso was one of the Optimates and had previously induced Cicero to accuse Caesar of conspiring with Catiline.

Alsace, at the Atlona at the Sabis, in Britannia, perhaps at Avaricum, certainly at Gergovia, and most notably at Alesia. Highly loyal to Caesar, who trusted it over all the others, it was transformed in part into his mounted personal bodyguard. This occurred when the peace treaty was agreed with Ariovistus (thus explaining its name, *Equestris*, 'mounted'). At the beginning of the war between Caesar and Pompey, it was stationed near Narbo Martius/Narbona (Narbonne in France). It took part in the siege of Massilia and then in the war in Spain. Later, it was transferred to Macedonia and fought at Dyrrachium and at Pharsalus, where it formed the right wing of Caesar's army, the one that defeated Pompey. It subsequently took part at the Battle of Thapsus. It was disbanded in 46, and its veterans were settled around Narbona. At the end of 46, at the request of these veterans and on the orders of Caesar, the Tenth was reconstituted by Mark Antony, *magister equitum*. In 45, it fought at Munda. The Tenth was Caesar's favorite legion. Thus, Lepidus finds it a straightforward task to ensure that it remains loyal to his memory and loyal to both himself, and the consul Mark Antony, formerly two of Caesar's lieutenants.

The Opening of Caesar's Will

Presently, Antony is the strongman of the situation. Between 15 and 16 March, he obtains a compromise agreement from the leaders of the conspiracy (who from now on will be called the Liberators, who "liberated" Rome from Caesar), which he obtains with the following terms: Dolabella will replace Caesar as consul, the Liberators will be granted amnesty, the laws laid down by Caesar will be respected, and the victim will receive a state funeral. Therefore, he calls a meeting of the Senate for 17 March in the Temple of Tellus in Carinae. Cicero will speak for him to the senators.

The Senate of Rome ratifies the agreement reached between Antony and the Liberators, undertakes to recognize the validity of Caesar's last acts and of the dictator's will, and assigns the government of Macedonia to Antony, that of Syria to Dolabella, and the joint government of Crete and Cyrenaica, which were organized into a Roman province in 74, to Brutus and Cassius. Lepidus is rewarded for the support he has pledged to Antony with his appointments to the governorship of Gallia Narbonensis and to the post of *pontifex maximus*, the highest religious office that is currently available.

This is followed by the reading of Caesar's will, which is carried out in public in the Forum before the funeral rites of the assassinated dictator begin. The testament was drawn up on 15 September 45. Its content is already known to a few members of Caesar's inner circle. In fact, it was previously opened in Antony's own house, in the presence of senators, magistrates, many of Caesar's friends, including some of his soldiers, and relatives, after the father-in-law of the deceased dictator, Lucius

Calpurnius Piso, had obtained it from the Vestal Virgins, who had been holding it for safekeeping.[6]

It emerges that the testator has adopted his great-nephew Caius Octavius Thurinus as his son, who, if he accepts, will become the deceased's only legitimate male child (Caesarion, the progeny of Caesar and Cleopatra VII, is illegitimate, because he was born out of an extra-marital affair). As the document is read out, it is revealed that Caesar has left three-quarters of his immense fortune to his great-nephew Octavius, the son of Atia, herself the daughter of Caesar's sister, Julia Minor, and the remaining quarter to two of his nephews, Lucius Pinarius and Quintus Pedius, the sons of Julia Minor. He also named many people whom he had believed to be utterly loyal to him and who then betrayed him by conspiring against him. One of these people is Decimus Brutus, who had been named among his heirs in the second degree, that is, among those who would have the rights due to the first-named if they don't accept their inheritance (Antony is another heir in the second degree). Others are suggested as possible tutors for Octavius if it becomes necessary to designate one. Caesar's final wish concerns his fellow citizens. The testator leaves 300 sesterces to the head of each household among the urban proletariat and his own magnificent and highly envied gardens (*Horti Caesaris*) to the Roman people.[7]

The will mentions neither Cleopatra VII nor Caesarion, as is only logical. Caesar, whose status in Rome is unsurpassed, could hardly name the sovereign of a foreign state as the heir to his wealth and political legacy. Cleopatra had taken this as read. What she had not expected, however, was that Caesar would leave his gardens, where she is currently living, to the Roman people. In practice, that part of the will is essentially her eviction notice. Moreover, the little consideration that Caesar gave to her by not mentioning her among his last wishes makes her seem weak, and this puts her in danger. Rome is no longer a safe place for the queen-pharaoh of Egypt and her son, the prince and her heir.

Bad weather is ravaging Rome at this time. The Tiber is swollen. The current is carrying trees and carcasses with it. The floods have made mooring impracticable. The private dock where the royal ship is lying at anchor is unusable. To return to Egypt, Cleopatra VII has to make alternative arrangements.

At dawn on 20 March 44, a long line of wagons and carriages, loaded with people, crates, and luggage, escorted by the Royal Guard, moves off from the *Horti Caesaris*, heading for Ostia, Rome's maritime port at the mouth of the Tiber. Aboard these vehicles are the Ptolemaic royals and their large retinue of servants and assistants. The cortège joins the Via Ostiense and follows it to its end. Upon entering Ostia, it rumbles noisily below the windows of houses, like a royal parade, waking up

---

6   Suet. *Iul.*, 83.1.
7   Suet. *Iul.*, 83.2. In fact, the *Horti Caesaris* will be passed on to Sallust, and only after his death will they return to being public property and, in part, to the people.

their inhabitants and startling them. At the port, the royals and their retinue board small ships, suitable for sailing along the coastline, ready to depart for Puteolis, Rome's main Italian port city and the point of departure for voyages to the East. After arriving in Puteolis, they will transfer everything to a large ship suitable for navigating the open seas and head back to Alexandria.[8]

A Tumultuous Funeral

On 20 March 44, the body of Caesar, placed in an ivory casket with coverlets of purple and gold, and with the bloodied toga of Caesar also on display, is carried into the Forum, borne aloft by the arms of current and ex-magistrates, and placed in a shrine in front of the Rostra.[9] Antony delivers the eulogy before the open casket, while the emotions of those present are gradually rising. A herald reads the *senatus consultum* in which "all human and divine honors" had been decreed on Caesar, as well as the "oath with which they had all pledged themselves to watch over his personal safety."[10] A wax effigy depicting a bloodied and disfigured Caesar is lifted up and swung back and forth, while Antony, grasping the dead man's toga, brandishes it so that the bloodstains and tears caused by the dagger blows can be clearly seen.[11] Antony's act amounts to an instigation for a lynch mob and marks the betrayal of the compromise agreement Antony had himself reached with the Liberators. Indeed, the people explode with anger. There are cries for revenge, ripples of movement run through the crowd, and the event quickly becomes noisy, disorderly, and violent.[12]

The plan for the funerary rites is that the corpse will be cremated on the Campus Martius, next to the tomb of Julia, Caesar's daughter, and a golden shrine that resembles the shape of the Temple of Venus Genetrix. Instead, the crowd, on a mystical yet furious impulse, seize possession of the casket and carry it in their arms, raucously, to the top of the Capitolium (one of the two summits of the Capitoline, the other being the Arx) and into the Area Capitolina. They consider the deceased as a god and make clear their desire to cremate his body in the *cella* of Jupiter Optimus Maximus in the Temple of the Capitoline Triad. The armed guards and priests stop them from doing so, both to avoid the sacred place from being corrupted and out of fear that the burning pyre could stoke a major fire, as happened at the cremation of Clodius in the Curia Hostilia in 52.

The crowd thus leaves the Area Capitolina and swarms downhill onto the Via Sacra, taking the casket back into the Forum. And it is there, amidst the most

---

8   See A. Angela, *Cleopatra. La regina che sfidò Roma e conquistò l'esternità* (Milano: Harper & Collins, 2018), 143–146.
9   Suet. *Iul.*, 84.1.
10 Suet. *Iul.*, 84.2.
11 Plut. *Brut.*, 20.4.
12 App. *B. Civ.*, II.146.

sacred and inviolable places in Rome, that the body of Caesar is cremated upon an improvised pyre, despite the prohibition that has been in force in that part of the city since time immemorial. As the flames rage, some of the mob approach them, grab some of the burning embers, and disperse toward the houses of the Liberators with the intention of setting them ablaze. They will not succeed in their aim due to the defensive barricades set up by the conspirators, but, in the confusion, there will be one death, the victim of mistaken identity. The enraged mob lynch, decapitate, and carry around the head, thrust onto the end of a pole, of the poet Caius Helvius Cinna[13]—the author of *Zmyrna*, friend of the deceased Catullus, and protected by Caesar, of whom he was a relative—erroneously believing him to be the praetor Lucius Cornelius Cinna, who, the day before, had spoken out angrily against Caesar.[14]

The disorder is led by an eye doctor called Amatius, probably a slave or a freedman, who is claiming to be the natural son of Marius the Younger, and therefore the grandson of Caius Marius and the first cousin once removed of Caesar (Marius had married Caesar's aunt, Julia Major). Amatius is at the head of an armed gang, which intends to terrorize the Liberators,[15] and is quite a well-known character, both within and outside of Rome, among many veterans' colonies and *municipia*. In Rome, he is known to many colleges, as well as by the Octavii and Cicero. Caesar, on his return from the war in Spain, had forced him to leave Italy. Later, Amatius returned to Rome. He says that he wants to give voice to the total disillusionment of the urban proletariat with the compromise agreement reached between Antony and the Liberators.[16]

In the meantime, both Brutus and Cassius have left Rome in a hurry.

---

13 Suet. *Iul.*, 85.
14 Here, we are following Plutarch's version (*Caes.*, 68.2–3; *Brut.*, 20.7; *Ant.*, 14.8), according to which the victim is said to be the poet Gaius Helvius Cinna. Other authors, such as Suetonius, Valerius Maximus, Appian, and Dio Cassius, in the telling of the same incident, speak of a tribune of the plebs also called Gaius Helvius Cinna.
15 App. *B. Civ.*, III.2.3.
16 Plut. *Brut.*, 20.5–7; *Ant.*, 14.7–8.

CHAPTER XXXIV

One Day in March in Apollonia

Octavius Accepts Caesar's Name and Inheritance

Apollonia (near present-day Fier in Albania) is a city in Epirus (in the Roman province of Macedonia) on a hilly plateau from which the fertile plain of Musacchia extends, on the right bank of the Aoös (Vjosë), a navigable river that connects the Adriatic coast to the interior. It is the starting point, we recall, of the Via Egnatia, the road that represents the overseas extension of the Via Appia that leads to Thessalonica, the capital of Macedonia, and, beyond, to the River Evros in Thrace, hundreds of kilometers distant.

In March 44, Octavius, Caesar's great-nephew, is in Apollonia. He is a senior cavalry officer, reporting directly to the *magister equitum*, Marcus Aemilius Lepidus, and acting as his deputy. Thus, if Lepidus were to die or be otherwise prevented from carrying out his obligations, Octavius would be the one to replace him, temporarily taking on all his responsibilities. After being appointed by Caesar, the latter sent him to Apollonia both because troops are converging there ahead of the campaign against the Parthians that Caesar had decided to undertake, and to further his intellectual training. Octavius reached his destination in the company of his inseparable close friends: Caius Cilnius Maecenas, Marcus Vipsanius Agrippa, and Quintus Salvius Salvidienus Rufus.

We have already met Maecenas. He is an aristocrat of Etruscan origin. Agrippa is Octavius's childhood friend, who asked for and obtained his liberation from Caesar when he was a prisoner of war, after the Battle of Munda. Salvidienus Rufus, like Agrippa, is an individual of humble origins. As a young man, he was a shepherd.[1]

Octavius is in the company of Agrippa and their tutor—the 60-year-old Greek rhetorician Apollodorus of Pergamum, an advocate of the Attic oratorical style—when a messenger arrives on horseback. The courier is one of Octavius's mother Atia's freedmen. Exhausted by his long journey, he staggers as he hands Octavius a sealed case. Octavius breaks the seal, opens the case, pulls out a sheet of parchment, and reads the text, which is set out in cursive, the Romans' quicker method of writing.

---

1   Dio Cass., 48.33.1.

It is a letter from Atia. She informs her son that Caesar has been killed in the Senate, that Caesar has adopted him in his will, that Caesar has designated him as the almost universal heir to his immense fortune, and that Rome is shocked and terrified. She warns him of the dangers that he may be about to face and advises him to look after himself. Octavius remains silent for a few moments, motionless, then, in a voice curbed by emotion, he says, "Caesar is dead." Those present don't understand and look at him questioningly. He repeats himself, his voice clearer this time, stunning those around him: "Caesar is dead."

When the news of Caesar's death becomes public knowledge, Octavius's escort is strengthened, and his fellow officers show that they are close to him and loyal to him. The young man is deeply shaken, sincerely saddened, and worried about what is to come. He already knew that Caesar would adopt him, and so this news doesn't surprise him. But the circumstances have changed in the meantime and now require careful consideration. Octavius takes Agrippa and Apollodorus aside and discusses what to do with them. But they have little knowledge or evaluations on which to reflect. The three do not know who Caesar's assassins are and therefore they do not know how many or which friends they can rely on. Octavius needs to make a decision, but he is struggling with the uncertainty. He could put himself at the head of the legions in Apollonia and depart for the East. Instead, he chooses to return to Rome and claim the rights owed to him as Caesar's adopted son and heir. Agrippa, Maecenas, Salvidienus, and Apollodorus will accompany him on his journey. Octavius has no authorization to do so, nor the responsibility, but before he leaves, he takes some of the money set aside for the Parthian War and collects the annual tax of the province of Asia, which he will use to recruit a militia in Campania.[2] The little group leave the camp, escorted by a unit of cavalry, and head for Dyrrachium, the major seaport of Epirus and one of the most important in the Adriatic Sea, where they will embark for Italy. They take the Via Egnatia and follow it as far as the waypoint at Claudiana, where they turn off for Dyrrachium.

After they arrive in Dyrrachium and their escort has departed to return to Apollonia, Octavian and his traveling companions board a ship for Italy and set sail. The wind is blowing in the right direction, that is, there is a tailwind, however slight, and the ship drifts leeward.

However, the ship isn't heading toward Brundisium, the closest Italian port to Dyrrachium, but toward Hydruntum (Otranto) in Salento, about 85 km south of Brundisium. Octavius prefers to land there because he doesn't know if the legion stationed in Brundisium is on the side of the Caesarians or the Liberators. The travelers disembark at night, not revealing their real identities to anyone, and rest for a few hours, taking care not to attract attention. As the sun rises, they set off for Brundisium. At Lupiae (Lecce), about 50 km north of Hydruntum, two soldiers on

2   W. Eck, *Augusto e il suo tempo* (Bologna: Il Mulino, 2010), 13.

patrol stop them. One recognizes Octavius; he saw him with Caesar in Spain and remembers him well. The soldier gives him reassurances: the legion in Brundisium is loyal to the memory of Caesar, so he and his friends are in no danger.

In Brundisium, Octavius and his companions are welcomed with full honors. They receive confirmation that Rome is in turmoil, and they learn that there are about 60 conspirators (and also discover their names); that the Senate has condemned the assassination, but that it has allowed those responsible to flee far from Rome and scatter; that Dolabella had approved of the crime and co-opted the consulship to become Mark Antony's colleague in office; that the latter, after having spoken out against Caesar's assassins in public, had invited them to dinner, only then to inveigh against them; and that the people are aggrieved and infuriated.

Octavius writes to his mother and his stepfather Philippus to inform them he has returned to Italy and receives a quick response: his parents urge him to abnegate Caesar's name and inheritance so as not to expose himself to the dangers deriving therefrom. Octavius is of the opposite opinion. Recent events have brought about a profound change in him. He feels as though the mission to restore stability to the *res publica* has been entrusted to him. He has great self-esteem and confidence in the future, firstly because, in Apollonia, a famous astrologer and astronomer—Theogenes—had foretold that he would become the most powerful man in the world and even deified *post mortem* and, secondly, because it seems to him that only a part of the nobility have given their support to the Liberators, while the rest of the aristocracy, together with the urban plebeians, are on the Caesarians' side, as are Octavius's own friends, those of Caesar, the magistrates appointed by Caesar (among whom are many provincial governors), and Caesar's war veterans, who mainly live in Campania. Octavius publicly declares that he is accepting Caesar's inheritance out of a sense of duty, and his name as a sign of respect. Agrippa, the entire legion in Brundisium, and those of Caesar's war veterans who have come to him from afar, acclaim him as leader, *dux*, and general, pledge their eternal loyalty to him and loudly call on him to lead them into battle because they hold an ardent desire to avenge the death of Caesar.

Octavius is a coldly rational, calculating, lucid, reasoned sort, who is in full control of himself and his impulses. He does not get carried away by a wave of enthusiasm. He thanks and dismisses everyone, then, with his friends, leaves Brundisium, heading overland for Puteolis, where his stepfather has a villa. From there, he will continue to Rome when the time is right.

His acceptance of his adoption implies a change to his certified identity, according to the rules of Roman onomastics.[3] From now on, Octavius will no longer be called

---

3   Let us remind ourselves that the rules of Roman onomastics stipulate that the adoptee takes on the *cognomen* of the adopter, added to which is the *cognomen* of the adoptee's natural father with the suffix *-anus*.

Caius Octavius Thurinus, but Caius Julius Caesar Octavianus (though he will sign his name as Caius Julius Caesar, omitting the rest), or, more simply, Octavian (as he will be referred to henceforth).

Cicero's *Volte-Faces*

Cicero's position regarding the assassination of Caesar and his assassins isn't clear. It seems he was not present in the room when the dictator was stabbed to death and therefore did not witness the scene. But he would have been in the area, possibly even outside the hall, by the entrance, under the portico. This idea is supported by the fact that Cicero, in his *Second Philippic*, which was never delivered, mentions that he saw Trebonius preventing Antony from entering the Curia alongside Caesar.

Whether Cicero was aware of what was about to happen is uncertain. Conversely, what is certain is that Cicero was convinced that, despite the power and the glory of Caesar, it was not inevitable that his dictatorship would mark the end of the *res publica*, that the latter could recover, and that its history was not yet over.[4]

As for the question of whether Cicero is on the side of the Caesarians or of the Liberators, a series of serious, precise, and concordant indications lead one to answer that he is on the side of the Liberators. There is, firstly, a note that Cicero sent to a certain Basilus on 15 March 44 (the day of the assassination) in which he rejoices at the killing of Caesar;[5] secondly, the letter written to Atticus on 27 April 44 in which Cicero speaks of "the joy with which I feasted my eyes on the just execution of a tyrant";[6] and thirdly, the passage in the aforementioned *Second Philippic*, in which Cicero makes it clear that, had he been a part of the knifing of Caesar, he would not have left the job half-done but completed it by also killing Antony.[7] The words he wrote to Atticus, reproduced just above, might mean that Cicero wasn't inside the meeting hall in the Curia of Pompey when Caesar was killed but entered it after the senators had abandoned it and left it deserted; that he saw Caesar's bloody corpse, lying on the marble floor, and walked around it to make sure that it was lifeless.

Was the conspiracy prompted by Cicero? There is a doubt in this regard, arising from an allusion that can be gleaned from another letter to Atticus, regarding the campaign by unknown hands of scrawling on walls and monuments carried out in the days leading up to the Ides of March, which prompted Brutus to put himself at the head of the conspiracy against Caesar. The allusion could mean that this campaign

4   Cic. *Fam.*, VI.15.
5   *Ibid.* Basilus will be assassinated by his own slaves in the autumn of 43 for reasons of personal vengeance.
6   Cic. *Att.*, XIV.14; L. Canfora, *Cesare. Il dittatore democratic* (Roma-Bari: Laterza, 2006), 355.
7   Cic. *Phil.*, II.14 [(...) if I had been the author of the piece, as it is said, believe me, I should not have been contented with one act, but should have finished the whole play (...)].

had been orchestrated by Cicero.[8] It should also be said that Mark Antony, speaking in the Senate on 19 September 44, when Cicero was absent, accused the latter of being behind the principle of the killing of Caesar, basing this on a few words that were said to have been uttered by Quintus Servilius Caepio Brutus immediately after he had stabbed Caesar himself (Brutus is said to have then called out Cicero's name and "congratulated him on liberty being recovered").[9]

Cicero is in his villa in Asturia, on the Lazio coast, when Octavian arrives in Puteolis. Cicero wants to get to know and evaluate the young man and his friends, so he goes to visit him in Puteolis. He meets the three youths (Maecenas has since joined Octavian and Agrippa), speaks with them, observes them, and listens to them. He forms an opinion that they are unreliable, naïve, and slightly confused individuals, incapable of representing a danger to the Liberators. He will suggest in a letter to Caepio Brutus that he try to lure Octavian to his side, taking advantage of him to weaken Antony and then tossing him aside to wipe out Caesar's lineage. Caepio Brutus, remember, is one of the most prominent of the Liberators alongside Cassius and Decimus Brutus. The detail just mentioned here unequivocally confirms that Cicero is on the side of Caesar's killers.

Some time after his return to Rome, Octavian delivers a speech to a crowd that has gathered in the Forum Vetus. He praises Caesar and says—unthinkingly—that he wants to stay out of public life and that therefore he will not replace his adoptive father on the political stage. Cicero celebrates, convinced that he was correct in his judgment, thinking that Octavian is a simpleton and a conceited one at that, and certain that he has him in the palm of his hand. He decides to go and visit him again as soon as possible.

Presently, Antony is the highest legal authority in Rome, and thus the arbiter of its domestic and foreign policies and of the administration of the state. After Caesar's funeral, he has remained in Rome, taking possession of Caesar's files and claiming to be carrying out the deceased dictator's last wishes, even when—Cicero argues—they are his own inventions, manipulating Caesar's orders at his own discretion, with the complicity of his wife. Recently, he has taken possession of the house of the deceased Pompey Magnus and has moved into it with his family. He lives in luxuriously furnished rooms, feasts off precious crockery, and receives clients and postulants. Cicero says that it is in this house that the fate of the state is being decided.[10]

Fulvia is present when Antony is dealing with governmental matters in their house. In 44, she witnesses the negotiations between her husband and Deiotarus's

8   Cic. *Att.*, XIII.40.1.
9   Cic. *Phil.*, II.12. It must be underlined, though, that it isn't certain whether this detail of the incident actually occurred.
10   Cic. *Phil.*, II.39.

302 • BEFORE AUGUSTUS

ambassadors for the restitution of the lands that the King of Galatia obtained from Caesar in 47 in exchange for 10 million sesterces; she doesn't remain silent, out of the way, as she should, but voices her own opinion, rightly causing Cicero to accuse her subsequently of greed.[11] In October 44, Antony, proconsul of Macedonia, summons the four legions stationed in that province to him in Italy, and he goes to welcome their arrival at Brundisium, accompanied by Fulvia. On disembarking in Italy, some of the legionaries defect to pass under the banners of Octavian. Antony orders a merciless decimation as punishment for the mutiny. Fulvia witnesses the execution of the rebels. According to Cicero, it was she who riled Antony up against the rebels (hence her reputation as a cruel woman).

Subsequently, having strengthened himself with these legions, Antony obtains a five-year term, handed to him by law by the Senate of Rome, as the governor of Gallia Cisalpina, shedding his role as governor of Macedonia and taking Decimus Brutus's province from him, which had previously been given to him by Caesar. Because Decimus Brutus resists, Antony besieges Mutina (Modena). The siege is ongoing.

Considering that it is up to Antony to put the ratification of the act of Octavian's adoption on the Senate's agenda, without which he cannot obtain his inheritance, Octavian goes to see Antony, accompanied by Agrippa, Maecenas, and Rufus. The four must wait outside in the house's atrium, under the gaze of the death masks of Antony's ancestors; herethey pass the time by watching the fish darting about in the shallow pool set in the floor beneath the opening in the roof before they are admitted to the study where the master of the house conducts his business. This room in a Roman atrium house is called the *tablinum*, which is decorated with a mosaic floor and painted murals and opens out onto lush gardens, furnished with stone benches and fountains, enclosed by a colonnaded portico, and embellished by herms, mosaics, and murals.

Antony and Octavian already know each other, having seen each other in passing on a couple of public occasions. The tone of the meeting is formal. Antony says he vaguely remembers that Caesar spoke to him about his great-nephew on the day that the triumph for the victory at Thapsus was celebrated. (It would have been difficult not to have spoken about him, given that Octavian was at Caesar's side at all times during the celebration of that triumph). Then he watches Octavian carefully while he speaks to him and looks at him condescendingly. He ends the discussion rather abruptly.

In the meantime, Amatius and his partisans pay divine honors to the deceased dictator at an altar that they have set up on the very spot where Caesar's body was cremated, at the foot of a column bearing a dedication to "Caesar, *pater patriae*." This form of worship gave rise to the cult of Divus Julius, which immediately became very popular among the urban plebs. Antony intervenes and has Amatius

---

11   Cic. *Phil.*, II.37, 44, V.11, VI.4.

arrested and illegally put to death, to great scandal in the Senate, though this was done entirely for show (Amatius had made accusations against Brutus and Cassius; ultimately, the Senate, which is in the control of the Liberators, is happy to be rid of him). Amatius's supporters rise, finding support among the urban plebs. There are loud calls in the Forum for Caesar to be publicly venerated as a god. This time, the army intervenes and forces them to disperse. Meanwhile, some statues of Caesar have been torn from their pedestals by persons unknown, taken to specific workshops, and are being destroyed. Amatius's followers attack these workshops and try to set them ablaze, but they are stopped and executed, either by being killed on the spot, thrown from the Tarpeian Rock, or, if they are slaves, crucified.[12]

Brutus in Greece

Marcus Tullius Cicero is the only male child born from the marriage of the homonymous orator and Terentia. His father took care of his education from the very start and took him with him to Cilicia when he was proconsul and governor of this province in 51 and 50. In the autumn of 50, while he was fighting against the tribes of the Amanus, he kept him at a safe distance, sending him to Deiotarus, King of Galatia, together with his cousin Quintus, his fellow student.

In 48, Cicero fought at the Battle of Pharsalus as a unit commander in Pompey's army. After the defeat, he was pardoned by Caesar. After Caesar's murder, his father sent him to Athens to study rhetoric and philosophy. In Athens, Marcus (the son) attended lessons by the rhetorician Gorgias and the Peripatetic philosopher Chrysippus. He is one of the young generation of families of good standing who welcome Caepio Brutus congenially when he arrives in the city.

Brutus is still in Athens, listening to its philosophers, when he is joined by other Republicans: Cnaeus Domitius Ahenobarbus, Marcus Valerius Messalla Corvinus, and Marcus Licinius Lucullus. Ahenobarbus is the son of Lucius Domitius Ahenobarbus, whom he followed to Corfinium in 49 and to Pharsalus in 48. He was pardoned by Caesar and had been able to return to Rome in 46. Following the Ides of March, he fled to Brutus in Athens.

Messalla is the son of Marcus Valerius Messalla Niger, who had been consul in 61 and censor in 55. He studied in Athens with Horace and the younger Cicero. He has always been a Republican and always will be. As well as being a former magistrate, he is also a writer and a patron of the sciences and the arts. In the future, he will encourage and have considerable influence on Latin literature, founding the so-called "Messalla Circle."

Lucullus is the son of Lucius Licinius Lucullus (consul in 74, commander-in-chief in the Third Mithridatic War until 66) and his second wife, Servilia Minor, Cato's

---

12 App. *B. Civ.*, III.3.

half-sister. Thus, he is the nephew of Marcus Terentius Varro Lucullus. Following the death of his father, in 57 or 56, Servilia Minor wanted Cato to become her son's tutor.

In November 44, Caepio Brutus, under pressure from his friends, embezzled money from the taxes collected in the Anatolian provinces and in Syria, while this was on its way to Rome, with the complicity of the quaestors who held it in their custody, Marcus Appuleius and Caius Antistius Vetus. Then he whips up the Republican cause, which is taken up by a growing number of supporters. He subsequently relocates to Thessalonica, where he receives the support of Quintus Hortensius Hortalus, the son of the famous orator of the same name and governor of Macedonia, who commands two legions and a unit of cavalry (he used to command six legions before sending four of these to Mark Antony in Italy). Hortalus's term has expired, but he refuses to be replaced by the urban prefect for 44, Caius Antonius, the brother of the consul Mark Antony and of the tribune of the plebs, Lucius.

Caius Antonius was Caesar's legate in 49 and had been ordered by him, together with Publius Cornelius Dolabella, to defend Illyricum from the Pompeians. In the event, Dolabella's fleet was destroyed, Antonius was trapped on the island of Curicta (Krk) in the Kvarner Gulf, and he had to surrender, being set free again after Caesar's victories. He has formed a legion by recruiting war veterans who fought under Pompey and sent it to Asia Minor under the command of the proconsul Dolabella.

In the early days of January 49, Caius Antonius disembarks at Dyrrachium, where he will share the command of an army of three legions with Publius Vatinius, governor of Illyricum, and where he will also accept the defection of a fourth legion. Brutus rushes to Dyrrachium with two legions and a unit of cavalry. At the end of January 43, he manages to put Caius Antonius in a tight spot. In the meantime, Vatinius's army falls apart: two legions defect and pass over to the Republicans. Brutus has thus come to have four legions at his disposal, plus his cavalry. Caius Antonius is forced to take refuge in Apollonia, where he will be besieged by Brutus.

Cassius, meanwhile, has arrived in Roman Asia before Dolabella. The province's outgoing governor Caius Trebonius and his quaestor Publius Lentulus give him help. Cassius enlists troops and opens his arms to a unit of cavalry that has defected, then marches toward Syria, where Quintus Caecilius Bassus and his legion are besieged in Apamea by six Caesarian legions, led by Lucius Staius Murcus, governor of the province, and Quintus Marcius Crispus, governor of Bithynia and Pontus. All the legions of Staius Murcus and Marcius Crispus very quickly defect to take their orders from Cassius. The siege on Caecilius Bessus and his legion is lifted, and they in turn join Cassius' army. Cassius's ranks are then further reinforced with the arrival of four legions from Egypt, commanded by Aulus Allienus. Cassius now has a very powerful army at his disposal, capable of dominating the eastern provinces.

The Philippics

In the final months of 44, there are some significant occurrences that no one expected. Antony delays putting the matter of Octavian's adoption before the Senate for ratification. Octavian, from his villa in Capua, recruits a private army of Caesarians (two legions) fully aware that by doing so he is exposing himself to an accusation of high treason because only the consuls can enlist a militia, and then only after the Senate has declared a conscription drive. At the same time, Octavian negotiates in secret with Cicero to draw him over to his side. Cicero sniffs to see which way the wind is blowing, accepts Octavian's courtship, and is convinced that, with the death of Caesar, normality has been restored to the *res publica*. Thinking so, he throws himself wholeheartedly into the political struggle against Antony, without realizing that the clock is ticking down on the *res publica* and that Caesar's murder has only accelerated its end. In one of his famous *volte-faces*, Cicero delivers a series of vehement orations against Antony in the Senate, in which he argues that Antony is seeking the dictatorship and that Octavian must be used to thwart this threat and revive the Republican order (that is, the supremacy of the senatorial aristocracy). To destroy Antony's image, Cicero paints a portrait of him that is anything but flattering. Among other things, he calls to mind that Antony had been the lover of Caius Scribonius Curio and he maliciously calls him "Curio's little daughter." These orations, because they recall those that Demosthenes of Athens (384–322) delivered against Philip II of Macedon (r. 360–336), will go down in history with the collective name of *The Philippics*.

The Battle of Mutina[13]

The Senate shares Cicero's theorem. Therefore, on 1 January 43, it appoints Octavian to the office of propraetor (Octavian is only 19 years old and has never been elected to any magistracy, let alone the praetorship); it confers *imperium* on him and authorizes him to use consular insignia; and it recognizes his right to sit among the rest of the Senate, as well as to take the floor and to vote with them, and his ability to run as a candidate for the consulship 10 years earlier than he is legally allowed to do. Seven days later, Octavian receives the *fasces lictoriae* and takes the auspices. The Senate then sends the consuls Aulus Hirtius and Caius Vibius Pansa, together with the propraetor Octavian, to the aid of Decimus Brutus, who is besieged in Mutina (Modena).

At present, Mark Antony risks being declared a public enemy. To avoid this, his wife Fulvia goes to visit the most influential individuals in Rome to entreat them, one by one, for their help and throws herself at their feet. She takes her

---

13 On the Battle of Mutina: App. *B. Civ.,* III.71; see also Dio Cass., XLVI.29–38*.

little boy—Marcus Antonius Antyllus, her son with Antony—with her and is also accompanied by her mother-in-law Antonia.

The civil war thus resumes, with new contenders: on one side, Mark Antony; on the other, the Senate of Rome, the consuls Hirtius and Pansa, and the propraetor Octavian, all intervening in defense of Decimus Brutus.

On 14 April 43, Pansa and his men are caught in an ambush by Antony at Forum Gallorum (Castelfranco Emilia, a town situated between Modena and Bologna). Pansa is seriously injured. Hirtius arrives with his men. A battle is inevitable. In the end, Antony is defeated (Cicero will praise Hirtius's victory in his *Philippics*), and the battlefield is littered with weapons, corpses, and wounded and dying men. Both sides lament the loss of around half their men. Octavian's entire cohort was wiped out.

What follows is another battle—on 21 April 43—under the walls of Mutina. The consul Hirtius is cut down while fighting near Antony's own tent after he had broken through into his camp. Octavian recovers his body and holds his position until he is driven out by Antony. In the end, Antony is defeated again, but he escapes (he will take refuge with Lepidus in Gallia Narbonensis). Decimus Brutus follows Antony, who takes flight from Italy dressed as a Gallic cavalryman. At the end of September 43, Decimus is discovered, executed, and decapitated by a Gallic tribe allied to Antony. His severed head will be delivered to Antony.

Mutina is liberated. One of the fallen on the side of the Liberators is Hirtius's legate Lucius Pontius Aquila, tribune of the plebs in 44. On 22 or 23 April, the consul Pansa also dies of his injuries. Before long, rumors circulate that Octavian was not uninvolved in the deaths of Hirtius and Pansa. No one saw Hirtius fall in combat. A certain Aquilius Niger claims that the consul was killed by Octavian in the thick of the fray. Moreover, the quaestor Torquatus has Pansa's doctor Glyco arrested, accusing him of having poisoned the consul's wounds.[14] But no one will investigate this thoroughly; Glyco is released, and Octavian is not prosecuted.

With the deaths of the consuls, Octavian has been left in sole command of the consular armies. On 9 May 43, a tribune of the plebs, in a public assembly, open to the participation of all the Roman people, presents him as the son and heir of Caesar. Taking the floor in turn, Octavian publicly says that he wants to exact justice on the Liberators and that he will make peace with Antony, Lepidus, and their followers, because there are many Caesarians among their ranks.

Shortly after, in agreement with Antony, Octavian follows up on his words with actions by marrying Clodia, Antony's very young stepdaughter.[15] In this way, an unexpected and major change to the alliances and a drastic change in circumstances occurs at the expense of the Senate. Octavian has used the Senate to become propraetor and has now sided against it, allying himself with his former enemy.

---

14 Letter of Marcus Junius Brutus to Cicero (19 May 43), in Cic. *Brut.* I.6; Suet. *Aug.* 11.
15 Suet. *Aug.*, 62.1; Plut. *Ant.,* 20.1; Dio Cass., 48.5.3.

In the meantime, the civil war has also exploded into life in the East. Dolabella has attacked Trebonius with two legions and defeated him in battle. Trebonius escaped, but he was captured in Smyrna (Izmir in Turkey) by Dolabella's men, and, after they killed him, they used his head for ball games (February 43). Trebonius was the first of the Liberators to die. He would soon be followed by many others (by 30, none will be left alive). Dolabella then barricaded himself in Laodicea *ad mare* (Apamea's port), a coastal city in northwest Syria, as he was enticed by the friendliness of its inhabitants and the convenient location of the city. There, he was besieged by Cassius, who had superior forces, and, after having defeated him at sea, he had a wall erected across the promontory on which the city rose to isolate it from the mainland and thereby force him to surrender.

In June 43, Laodicea *ad mare* is captured by treachery and left to be plundered, and it is largely destroyed. Dolabella commits suicide. What remains of Dolabella's legions is subsumed into the ranks of Cassius's forces. Cassius's army thus increases in size to 12 legions.

CHAPTER XXXV

The Second Triumvirate

Another *Coup d'état*

Cicero made a mistake in his judgment of Octavian, and now he fears him more than his senatorial colleagues. This prompts him to perform another extraordinary pirouette. He abandons the anti-Antony line he has followed up until now and delivers impassioned speeches against Octavian and manages to land a knock-out blow. The Senate attributes Octavian's success to Decimus Brutus so, at Cicero's suggestion, puts him at the head of the consular armies, declares Antony and Lepidus as public enemies, and puts Sextus Pompey in command of the fleet; he is a staunch defender of Republican values and is a bitter enemy of both Antony and Octavian.

Octavian doesn't allow himself to be intimidated. He promises the legions under his command that he will fulfill Caesar's promises, provide the veterans with land on which to settle, bring the Liberators to justice, and put an end to all this war; he says that the only path to salvation for himself and for his soldiers is for him to be elected consul through them. No sooner said than done. In July 43, around 400 centurions and soldiers present themselves to the Senate to call for Octavian to be proclaimed consul.[1] The Senate objects, stating that Octavian is too young to aspire to such a great honor (he is only 19 years old) and rejects the examples of historical precedents that are given, following his observation that, when they became consuls, Scipio Africanus, Scipio Aemilianus, and Pompey had all been much younger than the 40 years of age prescribed by the *lex Villia Annalis*.

The Senate doesn't fully understand the situation, but very soon it will do when—between July and August 43—Octavian marches on Rome at the head of his private army, divided into two groups, one of which goes ahead, led by Octavian himself, while the other follows at a distance. Octavian's march on Rome is the umpteenth in this city's history, but it is the one that will have the greatest impact on public life. He was preceded in so doing by Sulla, after the Battle of the Colline Gate, in 88, and by Caesar in 49, which caused Pompey and part of the Senate

---

1   App. *B. Civ.*, III.87.

to abandon the capital. Given that it is an act of violence led by an organ of the state's institutional apparatus that is using the state's own armed forces to overthrow the established power and undertake a political regime change, it is technically an attempted *coup d'état*.

The Senate convenes an urgent meeting and applauds the (false) news, brought by Cicero, that soldiers are currently being levied in Picenum. Then it mobilizes its conscripts, sets up the two legions that have arrived from Africa and the legion previously under Pansa's command to defend the capital, and—unsuccessfully—has them seek out, using subterfuge where necessary, Octavian's mother and sister to take them hostage.

Having reached the gates of Rome, Octavian occupies the far end of the Quirinal Hill, without meeting resistance, then has his troops camp outside the walls. Then, something extraordinary happens. Prominent citizens and the people of the capital run out of the city to greet him. The next day, protected by an escort, Octavian enters the city unmolested; receives a warm welcome and homage from individuals and groups out in the streets; meets his mother and sister in the Temple of Vesta, where they had taken refuge to escape from the Senate; and receives messengers from the legionaries deployed in the city's defense, who convey to him that they want to join his ranks and that one of their commanders, Cornutus, has committed suicide. Toward the evening, however, word spreads that two legions—the Fourth and the Martia—which passed under Octavian's banners in the summer of 44, have rebelled and defected to join the Republicans. This gives the Senate hope that it can still turn the situation around in its favor, so it sends an officer to Picenum to organize the enlistment of new soldiers. But the rumor is unfounded.

Cicero manages to meet Octavian and, while speaking with him, tries to justify his actions since the death of Caesar and lets him know that he is in absolute agreement with the proposal to make him consul. Octavian ironically replies that Cicero seems to be the last of his friends to have greeted him.[2]

Octavian announces "free elections" to be held the next day, and he thus convenes the *comitia centuriata* as a matter of urgency. On 19 August 43, the people gathered in assembly elect him to the consulship together with Quintus Pedius. Pedius, we recall, is the deceased Caesar's nephew. He had been a legionary commander during the Gallic Wars and remained at Caesar's side even during the war against Pompey. He was praetor in 48. Recently, he was named as a co-beneficiary in Caesar's will together with Lucius Pinarius (his cousin) and Octavian.

Octavian's attempted coup was a success. At the age of just 20, Octavian has become the master of the *res publica*. The victor makes sacrifices to the gods while 12 vultures circle in the sky overhead: the same presage that appeared to Romulus in 753 when he was competing with his brother to found Rome. Soon after, Octavian

---

2 App. *B. Civ.*, III.91–92.

promotes and obtains approval for a *lex Curiata* that ratifies his adoption and revokes both the amnesty granted to the Liberators and the decrees that declared Antony and Lepidus to be public enemies. For his part, Pedius promotes and obtains approval for the *lex Pedia*, which sentences the Liberators to death or exile and orders the confiscation of their goods and property.

In addition, Servius Sulpicius Galba is executed. After having been praetor (in 54), Caesar's legate in Gaul (from 58 to 50) with command of the future Legio XII Fulminata, and a defeated candidate for the consulship for 49, in which he put himself forward as a candidate for the Populares, he had betrayed Caesar by playing a part in the conspiracy.

A New Division of Power

The funeral of Lucius Marcius Philippus, Octavian's stepfather, had only recently been held in Rome when—on a gray, rainy day in autumn 43—Octavian, Antony, and Lepidus meet in a dry stone hut on a small, depressed islet on the Reno at a point where this river, which flows in flat countryside near Bononia (Bologna), widens as it approaches the sea. Each of the three has been accompanied by other people. Ten legions, in two blocks of five, are camped nearby, one close to the other, and are keeping an eye on each other. After crossing a bridge that connects the islet to the riverbank, on which each of them has posted 100 men, the three of them greet each other with false cordiality, which, in any case, is lukewarm. The hut is near the bridge; it contains just a single room, which has an earthen floor and a large, unrefined table in the middle of it. Octavian, Antony, and Lepidus, with their companions, sit down on benches and stools at this table. Octavian's companions are Maecenas, Agrippa, and Rufus. The purpose of the meeting is to agree on the partition of Caesar's political legacy, to determine their spheres of competence, and to establish an alliance against the Senate and the Liberators. The negotiations go on for two full days, day and night. Eventually, an agreement is reached. Octavian, Lepidus and Antony will jointly wield the power to govern Rome; each will be able to appoint urban magistrates and command provincial military forces.

The criterion that determines their respective spheres of competence is territory. Antony receives Gallia Cisalpina, Gallia Transalpina, the East, and Egypt. It is worthy of note that the eastern provinces are the richest and most populous parts of Rome's dominion; Antony intends to strengthen Rome's borders and expand them, putting Caesar's plan to launch a war against the Parthians into practice. Lepidus receives Gallia Narbonensis, Hispania Citerior, and Hispania Ulterior. Octavian receives Italy, Sicily (despite the fact that the Senate has already guaranteed control of the island to Sextus Pompey), the province of Sardinia and Corsica, and all of Rome's territories in Africa on the shores of the Mediterranean, except for Egypt.

Moreover, the parties agree a three-point program:

1) Octavian and Antony will face the army of Cassius and Caepio Brutus in Southeast Europe to punish Caesar's assassins and restore order in Italy, and Octavian will have 14 legions available to him for this purpose;

2) Octavian will renounce the consulship in order to fulfill his military obligations without the impediments and restrictions linked to this magistracy;

3) the consulship for 42 will be held by Lepidus and Lucius Munatius Plancus, who will remain in Rome to govern Italy and clean house, removing any enemies of the Triumvirs who are hiding among the senators and their supporters.

Prompted by the need to find the mountain of money required to pay the soldiers and prepare for the final showdown with the Liberators, the Triumvirs revive the proscription lists invented by Sulla during the First Civil War (83–82). Those who have been proscribed, remember, are those who, insofar as they have been declared public enemies, can be killed by anyone with impunity. Their goods are confiscated and sold at auction, and their slaves are set free. Anyone who kills a *proscriptus* receives a reward.

In the hut on the river, the Triumvirs compile a list of those to be proscribed, which includes the names of the Liberators, those of other influential individuals whom they do not trust, and those of their personal enemies. Among the names on the list are 17 of the richest and most powerful senators. Top of the list is Cicero. Antony hasn't forgiven him for what he said in his *Philippics*. The Triumvirs also agree that 130 senators shall be exiled.

On 27 November 43, the agreement reached in the hut is enacted into law by the *comitia centuriata*. The *lex Titia de triumviris rei publicae constituendae consulari potestate creandis* thus enters into force, which hands sweeping powers to the ruling parties, including proconsular *imperium*, creates the office of triumvir, and establishes that this is to be conferred for a period of five years. Octavian, Antony, and Lepidus are immediately appointed to this office. It is in this way that the Second Triumvirate legally comes into being. This pact was inspired by the analogous accord reached between Caesar, Crassus, and Pompey in 60, but it is legal and public, whereas the earlier one was just an agreement between private citizens that never held any official worth and was kept secret for a long time as part of the political plans of the individuals involved.

The Proscriptions

The publication of the *lex Titia* ushers in a new, bloody season of revenge. The Triumvirs have put up the list of wanted people in public places. This isn't the list that was penned in the cabin on the river but another, far more substantial one, as Antony and Lepidus have both added to it in the meantime. These insertions consist of the addition of names of individuals whom Antony and Lepidus want to be free of, whether this is because they have always hated them, because they have recently had disagreements with them, because they are friends of their enemies, or, *vice versa*, because they are enemies of their friends, or for the simple reason that they are very rich. When the names of those on the list of *proscripti* become well-known through the lists being put up in public, a manhunt is unleashed. The proscribed, if captured, are killed on the spot and beheaded; their heads are delivered to the authorities to collect the reward and they are then displayed on the Rostra. Some people, mistaken for *proscripti*, are killed by mistake. Some soldiers make the most of the confusion to eliminate their personal enemies and make themselves rich.

Those who know they are wanted men react to their misfortune in a wide variety of ways. Some of them allow themselves to starve to death, others hang themselves, drown themselves in the Tiber, throw themselves into a fire or off a roof, hand themselves in to the authorities, or offer money in exchange for their life. Some, in an attempt to disappear, hide down a well, in the sewers, or in a cellar or an attic, and remain there in silence, secretly watching everyone's movements and flinching at every sound.

Many are helped to safety by wives, children, relatives, or slaves. Many others are denounced by wives or children, slaves or freedmen, creditors or neighbors of their house or farm, eager to take revenge for a wrong they have suffered at the hands of the *proscriptus*. The most unfortunate are those who manage to escape, only to be shipwrecked and drowned at sea.

The Death of Cicero

On hearing the news that Pedius was seeing to the execution of the proscribed, Cicero made his way to his villa in Tusculum. In early December 43, he is still there. He is in the company of his brother Quintus and the latter's son, who shares his father's name.[3] The three decide to go to Astura, and board a ship to join Brutus in Macedonia. (Brutus holds the most authoritative position among the Liberators). They make the journey from Tusculum to Astura by litter. They are all in the grip of darkest desperation: every so often, they stop along the road with their litters side by side and lament with one other. The one in deepest despond is Quintus (the father): he does nothing but think about the countless difficulties they will encounter and repeats that he has taken nothing from his house. Cicero, in his haste to leave, has brought only a few provisions with him. The three decide that Cicero will continue the journey alone, while his brother and his nephew return to Rome to collect their money and everything else the trio needs. Thus, with hugs and tears, they part ways. Cicero cannot know it, but he will never see his brother or his nephew again. Once in Astura, he waits for them in vain, then he finds a suitable vessel and sails away.

---

3 The final hours of Cicero and his brother Quintus are narrated in Plut. *Cic.*, 47.1–7.

Cicero follows the coast southward as far as Circaeum. It is winter, and the sea is rough. Cicero's seasickness induces him to return to shore, partly because of his fear of the choppy seas, partly because he hasn't entirely lost faith in Octavian. He remains ashore while the ship sets sail again, against the advice of the helmsman, who had counselled him to leave again immediately.

He decides to travel by litter from Circaeum to Formiae. He is doubtful, uncertain. Having started the journey, he quickly changes his mind and has himself carried back to Astura. He has a restless night. He is haunted by nightmares and terrible thoughts. He assembles and disassembles numerous plans, each one more unclear than the last. He plans to sneak into Octavian's house and commit suicide upon his hearth to arouse the vengeful Furies against him. Then he considers that, if he fails, he would be tortured, and he shelves the idea. The next morning, he orders the captain of the ship, which in the meantime has returned to Astura, to take him by sea to his villa in Formiae and orders his servants to follow.

In the meantime, the vengeance of the Triumvirs has been exacted on Cicero's brother and nephew. Shortly after they separated from Cicero, they were sold out by their slaves to the assassins who were on their tail. They tried to hide themselves, but the young Quintus was found and captured. The prisoner was tortured by his captors to give up the location of his father's hiding place, but he resisted. Eventually, the older Quintus revealed himself to save his son, only for them to be killed at the same time.

Antony's soldiers are guided in their search for Cicero by the centurion Herennius and the tribune Caius Popillius Laenas (the latter, in 48, at the request of Caelius, had been defended in court by Cicero and acquitted). When Cicero arrives at Formianum, they are put on his trail by a cobbler, who had previously been one of Clodius's clients and still remembers the whole affair between the latter and Cicero perfectly clearly. They make all haste to Formianum, where they surprise Cicero in the gardens of his villa.

It is 7 December 43. The senator is on a litter, being carried by his servants in the gardens above the villa, 1,000 paces from the sea. When the soldiers appear, the litter-bearers look to defend their master, but Herennius and Laenas persuade them against it. Herennius approaches the litter, holding his unsheathed *gladius* in a trembling hand. Cicero has the presence of mind to exclaim, "What is this? I am certainly not your first victim!" Then he leans out of the litter and offers his neck to his executioner. Herennius cuts his head off with three badly struck blows, then he also cuts off his hands. The death of Cicero is cruel, bitter, yet glorious, as he always wanted it to be.

Antony pays Herennius 250,000 drachmas, 10 times more than the usual reward for killing a *proscriptus*. Later, during a banquet in his house on the Palatine, which is near Cicero's old townhouse, he places the head of the deceased before him on his table and leaves it there until he gets bored of looking at it. His wife Fulvia takes it in her hands and, after insulting it with vulgarities and spitting on it, she holds it between her knees, opens its mouth, pulls out its tongue—which has spoken so much ill of her and those dear to her—and stabs at it with a hairpin, all the time continuing to mock it.[4] Antony orders that the head and hands of Cicero be hung at the highest point of the Rostra, the platform in the Forum from which the Orator pronounced his diatribes against him. He then calls for a public assembly to convene precisely there. Fulvia, during the *contio*, hurls insults at the head on display.[5]

In total, rather than 147 senators, as had been agreed on the river, 300 senators and 2,000 *equites* were targeted by the proscriptions or were forced into exile and had their property confiscated, including brothers and uncles of the Triumvirs or their military commanders. Among others, these include consuls, praetors, tribunes in office, former magistrates, and candidates for the magistracies. The consul Pedius had insisted, to no avail, that the proscriptions only be applied to the people most heavily involved in the conspiracy against Caesar, who numbered 17 in all. Pedius suddenly and unexpectedly dies toward the end of his mandate. The cause of his death is unknown. It is possible that he committed suicide or died due to the stress of being unable to stop the spiral of political vengeance triggered by the Triumvirs and refusing to get involved in their bloodthirsty excesses.[6]

Some of the proscribed managed to escape to safety and, in the future, will return with great success. Consider, for example, Marcus Terentius Varro Lucullus. He will be rehabilitated by Octavian and will return to his studies and to his literary work.[7] His private library, however, has been destroyed. In the meantime, the project that he had been entrusted by Caesar to carry out in 47 (the creation of a large public library) was suspended after the dictator's assassination and the violence that ensued. It will be taken up again in 39, by Caius Asinius Pollio, in the form of a public library supported by private patrons. Varro will be the only living author to be depicted in the form of a bust in that library. He will conduct further studies and publish his works until his death, which occurs in 27 at the age of 90. By then, he will have produced at least 55 publications, and perhaps as many as 75, on a vast range

---

4   Dio Cass., 48.8.4. It is uncertain whether the incident reported is entirely true, only in part, or not at all. Some contemporary scholars have expressed their doubts. If one were to consider Fulvia's character, however, it seems likely that Dio Cass. is telling the truth.

5   Fate was benevolent to the son of Marcus Tullius Cicero, his namesake. In 44, together with others, he warmly received the fugitive Brutus in Athens, following the assassination of Caesar. In 30, he was suffect consul. Later, he governed Syria. He was an irascible sort and had a habit of drinking to excess. His death marked the end of the Cicero family line.

6   App. *B. Civ.*, III.6.

7   Unfortunately, the works of Marcus Terentius Varro Lucullus, all considerable undertakings that had a significant impact, have only survived in fragmentary form. What little is known about what has been lost is due to citations from later sources, which often pose problems of interpretation. Varro Lucullus is today considered one of the best historians of Republican Rome and one of the greatest scholars, intellectuals, and writers of classical antiquity.

of subjects. His works attest to his encyclopedic knowledge, his very wide-ranging intellectual horizons, his analytical method of developing his theme or solving a problem, and his ability not only to combine Greek with Latin culture but also to ensure that one influences the other and *vice versa*.

In early January 42, while the violence of the proscriptions is raging, the Triumvirs obligate 1,400 rich matrons to pay a special tax to finance the war against Brutus and Cassius; they are to deliver an estimate of their total assets, against which their contributions will be measured. The plan includes sanctions in the event of omissions or false declarations, as well as rewards for tip-offs or confidential information, including by slaves or freedmen.

A delegation of the matrons involved visits the women of the Triumvirs' families, receiving understanding from Octavia, Octavian's sister, and Antony's mother. They also go to the house of Fulvia, but she abuses them. The matrons had not been expecting to be treated with arrogance. Deeply offended, they gather in the Forum to ask for justice, and they manage to get Hortensia, the daughter of Quintus Hortensius Hortalus and Lutatia, to take up their cause.[8] It should be noted that Hortensia was chosen as their spokeswoman because no man had dared to support their case[9] and that she was also the first woman in the history of Rome to give an oration in the Forum. This had been banned ever since the reign of Numa Pompilius, not by a specific law but by the *mos maiorum*, because it would lead to an inversion of the correct functioning of public institutions.

At first, Hortensia justifies her intervention by the fact that the civil wars have deprived women of fathers, sons, husbands, and brothers, such that they no longer have any male family member who can represent them before the law. She then discusses their cause courageously and enthusiastically, asking how it can be that women have to pay taxes if they are excluded from public offices, military commands, and political institutions. In the end, the Triumvirs partially repeal the demand, imposing the tax on only 400 women and covering the remainder with a new tax on large estates. Immediately afterwards, however, they issue an edict that states that women cannot be represented in a lawsuit by other women.

8   App. *B. Civ.,* IV.32–34.
9   Val. Max., 8.3.3.

CHAPTER XXXVI

Philippi

"I Shall See Thee at Philippi"[1]

Antony, Octavian, and Lepidus have managed to reach an agreement with the Senate of Rome, overcoming its hostility toward them. This allows them to confront the Liberators, not just to avenge the death of the dictator but also to reclaim possession of the eastern provinces. The reckoning is a process that begins in the mid-summer of 42, when Octavian and Antony initially lead eight legions and then another 20 to Macedonia (Lepidus has remained in Italy to maintain the peace there), successfully defying—thanks in part to favorable winds—the naval blockade imposed by the powerful Republican fleet, led by Cnaeus Domitius Ahenobarbus, formed of 240 warships. The first eight legions disembark at Dyrrachium under the command of Caius Norbanus Flaccus and Lucius Decidius Saxa and march along the Via Egnatia to intercept the army of Brutus and Cassius. Antony follows them at a distance with most of their forces, which includes the Tenth Legion. Octavian, because he is feeling unwell, has remained at Dyrrachium. He is a young man of delicate health, and he became quite seriously ill during the crossing. He is feverish and unable to travel.

Amphipolis is a city located in central Macedonia, at the mouth of the River Strymōn (Struma), close to the gold mines of the Pangaion Hills. Antony leaves a legion there and then continues toward Philippi, a walled city at the foot of the Pangaion Hills (near Kavala), about 13 kilometers from the port of Neapolis. Norbanus and Decidius capture Philippi and take control of a narrow mountain pass of great strategic importance, guaranteeing a communication line with their eastern allies. But the numerically superior forces of Brutus and Cassius drive them out of there, and Norbanus and Decidius retreat west of Philippi.

---

1   Plut. *Brut.*, 36. The phrase was taken up by William Shakespeare in Act IV of his *Julius Caesar*, where the ghost of the dictator, which has appeared to Brutus, addresses him with these words, presaging his coming defeat, to which Brutus responds: "I shall see thee again."

The Battle of Philippi

Brutus and Cassius are holding an excellent position, about 3.5 kilometers west of Philippi, each one on a hill that lines the Via Egnatia, a few hundred meters away from each other, with Brutus to the north and Cassius to the south. The encampments are protected, to the south, by a vast marsh that is difficult to cross, and, to the north, by impassable hills. Each of them fortifies their encampment with ramparts, towers, and ditches. The fortifications of both camps are laid out to present a single line of defense.

Antony and Octavian arrive on the spot in the second half of September 42. Octavian has since got better and has rejoined Antony, but he is still recovering and is unsteady on his feet, so he is traveling by litter. He sets up camp in the north, close to Brutus's encampment, in a seemingly unsuitable place on the arid plain. Antony places his camp further south, close to that of Cassius.

Octavian and Antony have 19 legions available to them, almost all of which are at full strength (the other nine legions have been left behind), and a substantial cavalry force (Octavian has about 13,000 cavalry, while Antony has about 20,000). Their army includes several legions of war veterans left by Caesar in the East and who have remained loyal to his memory, save for the Thirty-Sixth. This Pompeian legion was cut to pieces at the Battle of Pharsalus. The survivors were then subsumed into Caesar's army.

The forces of Brutus and Cassius are formed of 17 legions of Roman citizens (Brutus commands 8, Cassius leads 9, while another 2 are in service with the fleet) and their respective auxiliary troops, supplied by their eastern allies (17,000 cavalry, of whom 5,000 are mounted archers). However, only two legions are at their full complement; all the others are at less than full strength.

The armies that are facing each other at Philippi are essentially numerically balanced: about 100,000 men on each side. The scales are tipping in the Triumvir's favor by a few thousand men. It is also worth mentioning that many of the legions who are preparing to fight each other at Philippi were fighting on the same side until only recently. This can be said for the Fourth, Fifth, Seventh, and Tenth on Antony and Octavian's side, and for the Twenty-Seventh, Twenty-Eighth, Thirty-Sixth, and Thirty-Seventh on Brutus and Cassius's side. Cassius tries to strengthen the loyalty of his men by paying 1,500 denarii to each legionary and 7,000 to each centurion.

The First Battle

Every day, the Triumvirs' 19 legions and 20,000 cavalry take to the field, ready for combat, and offer battle. Every day, they are refused. Brutus and Cassius remain on their hills, waiting for the enemy's supplies to run out, as they will not be able to be replenished by sea due to the blockade set up by Ahenobarbus's fleet. This situation continues for about 10 days. In the meantime, Antony has secretly cut a path through the marsh and suddenly assaults the enemy lines where they had not been expecting to be attacked, capturing their position. Brutus and Cassius have tried to block off his progress by digging out a defensive line. The works are in progress.

On 3 October 42, Antony first deploys the Triumvirs' troops, placing their Hispanic Legions (the best) on the flanks: the Tenth on the right and the Fourth on the left; then he sends his nine legions to attack Cassius's camp. Brutus has placed some of his men outside his camp. He is still completing his deployment and circulating the watchword when his right wing, led by Messalla Corvinus, charges forward against Octavian's troops. Brutus steams after them and hurls himself against the Fourth, hitting it hard and managing to outflank it. Antony sends reinforcements to the left wing, but the enemy does the same, thus increasing the pressure on Antony's left flank. In the end, Brutus manages to break the heroic resistance of the Fourth. Messalla's troops rush after Octavian's and into the enemy camp. Octavian's fleeing soldiers aren't pursued any further because Messalla's troops stop to plunder and wreak havoc in the encampment. This will give Octavian time to regroup. During the attack, three of Octavian's legionary standards fall into the enemy's hands. But Octavian isn't found in his tent. Before the battle, he hid away in the marsh because his physician and friend Marcus Artorius Asclepiades[2] had told him that he had been warned in a dream that he shouldn't remain in the camp, and Octavian took him at his word.

While Messalla is ransacking Octavian's encampment, the Tenth bulldozes through three of Cassius's legions and forces its way into his camp, slaughtering anyone in its path and sweeping through with iron and fire. Cassius, after unsuccessfully trying to stop his men from fleeing in terror, retreats to the highest part of the hill, from where he will be able to watch the ongoing slaughter in his camp. Distraught by the defeat and having heard no news of Brutus and believing him to be either fleeing or dead, he becomes alarmed. He mistakes a group of Brutus's cavalrymen for enemies who are coming for him to take him prisoner, panics, and orders his freedman Pindarus to kill him. Pindarus obliges (it may be that Cassius was assassinated by Pindarus). Cassius dies on the day of his 45th or 44th birthday (he was born in 87/86) after apparently turning the same dagger with which he had stabbed Caesar on himself. He will be called *ultimus Romanorum*, in the sense that he was the last

---

2   Asclepiedes of Bithynia (129–40) studied in Athens and Alexandria, and was an alumnus of the Garden of Epicurus, the philosophical school of the Epicureans. In 91, he moved to Rome, where he was first known as an expert in rhetoric and then as an eminent physician. Only a few fragments of his main works survive. Marcus Artorius Asclepiedes was a pupil of Asclepiedes of Bithynia, and he was a physician and friend of Octavian. He was with him at the Battle of Philippi. Among his patients are Mark Antony, Marcus Licinius Crassus, and Cicero. He will die in a shipwreck at the Battle of Actium in 31.

of the Romans who embodied the values and spirit of their ancestors.[3] In the end, the battle ends with neither side able to claim victory, with the destruction of two of the four camps, and with at least 9,000 dead among Brutus' and Cassius's men and 16,000 dead and wounded on Antony and Octavian's side (the Fourth has been almost completely destroyed). But this is only the first battle. A second, decisive one will follow.

Antony and Octavian have suffered twice as many losses as their enemies. Moreover, they are short of food. Brutus and Cassius's calculations that they would soon run out of supplies, which could not be replenished due to the naval blockade, were correct. As if that wasn't enough, Antony and Octavian receive news that the reinforcements they have been waiting for from Italy—two legions, one of which is the Martia, and some cohorts from the Praetorian Guard—will never arrive. The convoy of ships carrying them ran into the enemy fleet (130 ships), which attacked. The transport ships were rammed and nearly all of them sank, resulting in the loss of thousands through drowning or being shipwrecked.

The Second Battle

On 23 October 42, Antony and Octavian, to raise the morale of their troops who are exhausted by hunger, distribute (or promise to distribute) 10,000 denarii to each legionary and 25,000 denarii to each centurion. Then they order them to line up in battle formation and offer battle to the enemy. Prior to this, they also sent one legion south in search of food.

Brutus's senior officers want to accept the challenge (one of them is Marcus Favonius, a Pompeian from the beginning), but Brutus prefers to wait, wanting to defeat the enemy through hunger and exhaustion. He distributes another 1,000 denarii to each legionary to keep his soldiers from responding to the provocations of those who are insulting them.

Brutus, therefore, doesn't move. The hours go by, and the soldiers remain lined up under the sun, with their helmets low over their eyes, their cuirasses heavy, their rectangular shields resting vertically on the ground, with their left hands resting on them, and a bow, sling, spear, javelin, or sword clutched in their right hands.

His officers are tired of waiting: they fear that the men will desert. When the defections begin, Brutus decides to do battle. It is the afternoon of 23 October. Both sides forego the preliminary phase of exchanging arrow fire and javelin throws from a distance. War cries fill the air, and both sides charge forward on the attack, one against the other, with great fervor. When they meet, the warriors clash swords in bloody hand-to-hand combat or throw their javelins at each other at point-blank range amid splashes of sweat and blood. A deafening noise rises from the battlefield,

---

3   Tac. *Ann.*, IV.34.1.

from the clashes of iron, from the mass of people pushing and fighting in fierce hand-to-hand combat, and from the killing, while the ground shakes under the hooves of thousands of horses galloping into the fray on the charge. Thousands of men are running every which way, calling out and shouting orders. Everyone fights with great courage. The fallen are dragged away and fresh units of legionaries are sent onto the field and reinforce the ranks, extending the battle, as vast numbers fall. Commanders and centurions roam among the combatants, spurring their men on and throwing fresh reserve forces into the focal points of the fighting.

Brutus leads the left wing's charge with some success, while the right wing collapses, outflanked and overwhelmed by the enemy. He sees the deaths of his legate, Labeo, and his chief of engineers, Flavius. Among the others who fall are his cousin Marcus Porcius Cato, the son of Cato; the son of the orator Hortensius; and the Liberators Lucius Tillius Cimber and Publius Servilius Casca. The former is the one who, in the Curia of Pompey on 15 March 44, tugged at Caesar's clothes, thus giving the signal for the assassins to act. The latter is the one who stabbed Caesar first. By the time of the surrender, Brutus's army has been reduced to four legions. Many officers and numerous conspirators commit suicide, including the Liberator Pacuvius Antistius Labeo, father of Marcus Antistius Labeo, who will become a famous jurist. Brutus flees with a handful of men, but before long he stops and, despairing, commits suicide. When his body is found, Antony will cover it with a purple cloak as a sign of respect. They had been friends, and Brutus had even saved Antony's life when, on the eve of Caesar's assassination, Cassius had expressed his desire to kill him.

After the battle, some prisoners of noble rank negotiate the surrender, but no one wants to do so with Octavian. The four surviving legions from Brutus's army are incorporated into the victors' forces. Antony stays near Philippi with a few men to found a colony there. Of the surviving Liberators, some will continue to resist in the East, where they will eventually be defeated for good by Antony. Brutus's head, decapitated from his body, will be displayed on the Gemonian Stairs in Rome, where the bodies of traitors are commonly thrown.

Cleopatra VII Seduces Mark Antony

On the understanding that his interests in Rome will be looked after by his brother Lucius and his wife Fulvia, Mark Antony leaves for the East with the intention of obtaining economic and political support and fighting the Parthians. He is also passionate about Greek culture, therefore, during his travels, he stops in Athens, where he is given a warm welcome and called a "friend of the Greeks" and "friend of the Athenians." From there, he goes to Asia Minor and enters Ephesus in an ostentatious procession, preceded by women dressed as Bacchantes and men as satyrs or as Pan, while the people acclaim him as Dionysus, Giver of Joy and Beneficence.

In Ephesus, he has the Liberator Petronius, who had taken refuge in the Temple of Artemis, arrested then executed. Then he continues to Syria.

Having arrived in Tarsus in Cilicia, he invites Cleopatra VII to join him. He wants to meet the queen-pharaoh of Egypt firstly because he needs money and a political and military alliance, but also because he wants to exploit Egypt's strategic position for the purposes of foreign policy. It is in the interests of Cleopatra VII (as well as her son, and her kingdom) to consolidate power in Egypt and for her to maintain good relations with Rome, and with Antony in particular, who at the moment is the most powerful person in the world. She knows Antony is captivated by Hellenistic culture, so she presents herself to him with dramatic and memorable scenography and propagandistically announces her meeting with him as the occasion on which Aphrodite/Isis meets the New Dionysus/Osiris to ensure prosperity for all Asia. The title of New Dionysus is the one given to Antony by the people during his triumphant journey through Greece. It should be noted that, from the very beginning, Cleopatra has created a connection between her and Antony. Initially this is purely ideological—Aphrodite/Isis is the sister and wife of Dionysus/Osiris—but it will soon become physical.

The queen-pharaoh of Egypt sails up the Cydnus as far as Tarsus aboard a ship with a golden stern, sails that are red-purple in color, and oars shining with silver. Plutarch will describe the scene.[4]

Antony finds himself alone in the agora of Tarsus, because the throng that had been clustered around him have flocked to the pier to witness the queen-pharaoh's approach, convinced they are about to witness a historic event when, just before the arrival of Cleopatra VII, the air is filled with perfume and sweet music. As the ship approaches the pier, all eyes are trained on Cleopatra, who can be seen without a veil, as in the paintings of Venus rising from the waters, under a golden pavilion, surrounded by beautiful maids and by boys who are keeping her cool with large fans made of ostrich feathers.

When the ship arrives at the dock, Cleopatra doesn't move. Antony impatiently boards the ship to ask the queen to disembark. When the two meet, she asks him and the officers among his staff to join her for a banquet aboard her ship in a large interior room. The Egyptian writer Athenaeus of Naucratis (II–III century AD), citing the Greek historian Socrates of Rhodes (I century BC), perhaps a member of Cleopatra's court, will describe the banquet as an event that takes place among furnishings made of gold and adorned with precious stones, within a screen of curtains of purple and gold.[5]

4   Plut. *Ant.*, 26.
5   Ath., IV.147; Socrates of Rhodes, *Civil War* III.68 (FHG [=Fragmenta Historicorum Graecorum] 68).

Cleopatra's intention, Plutarch adds, is to seduce Antony. She trusts that she will be able to do so more easily than was the case with Caesar in 48, since she was young and inexperienced at that time, whereas now, aged 28, she has matured both physically and intellectually. She exhibits both her wealth and her personal charm to Antony. She is not just beautiful but also an intelligent, cultured woman. She uses her conversational ability to seduce him and has no need for interpreters since she speaks Latin, as well as many other languages. Unlike the other Ptolemies, who have always persisted in speaking only in Greek, she wanted to learn Egyptian too, and this allowed her to present herself to her subjects as the reincarnation of Isis.

Cleopatra doesn't have to work hard to win over Antony because he has admired her for no short amount of time. He had already been struck by her allure when he arrived in Alexandria in Caesar's entourage when she was just 14 years old.

The two relocate to Alexandria, where they will spend the early weeks of the winter of 41/40, taking turns to put on lavish banquets and becoming inseparable. They play dice, they drink, they go hunting, and they go on nocturnal jaunts disguised as slaves, which often result in Antony getting into fights.

The Battle of Perugia

In the absence of Antony, who is currently engaged with a campaign against the Parthians, Fulvia steers internal affairs, going over the head of the weak Lepidus, who is kept busy with his authorization to celebrate a triumph for his insignificant victories over some Alpine tribes, initiated by Fulvia herself. The celebration is held on 1 January 41, but Lepidus passes by almost unobserved in the triumphal procession, while Fulvia watches the parade go by and receives all the glory from the Senate and the people.

Later, Fulvia, when she notices that Octavian is acquiring more prestige than Antony thanks to his distribution of land to war veterans, postpones any further apportionments of land until her husband has returned. In so doing, she sets herself against both Octavian and the army at the same time.

Octavian, annoyed, breaks away from Antony by divorcing Clodia Pulchra, the daughter of Fulvia and daughter-in-law of Antony, with whom he has been living for two years. He sends her back to her mother, with a letter in which he confirms that Clodia is still a virgin. The marriage never having been consummated will give rise to a lot of talk. Some maintain that Octavian had always intended to break off his ties with Antony from the very beginning.

Octavian frees himself from Clodia to marry Scribonia, the sister of Lucius Scribonius Libo, Sextus Pompey's father-in-law. It is worth noting that Scribonia is much older than Octavian. He then hastens to occupy Gaul. In the meantime, because Lepidus has refused to give Sicily, Sardinia and Corsica to Sextus Pompey, he has taken them by force, making use of his 100 warships. In the future, he will return to undermine maritime communications to and from Rome.

At this point, Fulvia convinces Lucius Antonius (who is the brother of the Triumvir and therefore Fulvia's brother-in-law, and who owes his election to the consulship for 42 to her) to put himself forward as the defender of the Romans, Latins, and Italics who have been harmed by Octavian, whether directly through the proscriptions or indirectly through the expropriations. It isn't fully understood why she does this. Perhaps it is because Octavian has rejected her sexual advances,[6] or perhaps because Antony is cheating on her with Cleopatra VII and, as his betrayed wife, she wants a war to break out to ensure her husband returns to Italy.[7]

Fulvia and Antonius's faction, because there is a lot of discontent on show toward Octavian, rapidly gains hold. A militia is established. Fulvia wears military garb and involves herself personally in the process of recruitment. Lucius levies recruits in Praeneste (Palestrina), an ancient city in Lower Lazio, famous for its sanctuary and temple oracle of Fortuna Primigenia. Then he returns to Rome, where he promises the Senate that his brother will restore the *res publica*, and he obtains both command of the army and a mandate to move against Octavian. After this, he heads to Perusia (Perugia) together with Fulvia. The latter publicly urges the Perusians to support Lucius against Octavian.

When Octavian besieges Perusia, Fulvia, who is inside the walls alongside Lucius, dresses as a soldier and actively participates in the city's defense. Perusia capitulates due to hunger at the end of winter 41/40. Octavian sets the city ablaze, exterminates the entire local ruling élite (300 citizens of senatorial rank), saying that this is how he wants to commemorate the Ides of March, the anniversary of Caesar's death, then leaves the city to be sacked.[8] However, he avoids aggravating his already tense relations with Mark Antony by allowing Lucius Antonius to live and making him governor of an Iberian province.

Fulvia manages to avoid being captured; she goes to Brundisium, embarks for Greece, and joins her husband in Athens, where he has stopped on his way back from the East. His campaign against the Parthians has met with less success than expected, having only yielded the subjugation of the Kingdom of Armenia, reduced to a vassal of Rome with the task of acting as a buffer state between Rome and the Parthian Empire. Antony is temporarily in the city of the Acropolis ahead of continuing to Italy. He reprimands Fulvia in harsh terms, accusing her of having seriously damaged his relations with Octavian. Fulvia then falls ill. Antony leaves her in Sicyon, on the shores of the Gulf of Corinth, and boards a ship at Patrai (Patras)

---

6   Mart., 11.20.
7   App. *B. Civ.*, V.19; Plut. *Ant.*, 30.
8   App. *B. Civ.*, V.33.

for Brundisium. The two will never see each other again. Fulvia wastes away with grief and, in the middle of 40, she dies.[9]

The Pact of Misenum

Meanwhile, the 25-year-old Sextus Pompey, the only living son of the deceased Cnaeus Pompey and Mucia Tertia, after having been appointed by the Senate to the position of prefect of the fleet stationed near Massilia, has been proscribed. He recruits many other fugitives, and launches a naval war against the Triumvirs, blocking maritime trade with his agile fleet and threatening Italic ports.

The blockade on the grain supplies of Rome is a cause of great unrest among the population. The Senate cannot ignore it. It makes an attempt at mediation with Octavian and Lepidus on one side, and Sextus Pompey on the other. In the end, an agreement is found, which will go down in history as the Pact of Misenum. The Senate makes an offer to Sextus Pompey of the peaceable possession of two provinces—Sardinia and Corsica and Sicilia—authority over the province of Achaea (Greece), as well as a significant indemnity by way of compensation for the damage suffered following the confiscation of his paternal assets, which he accepts. All this is on the condition that Sextus supplies the inhabitants of Rome with grain from Sicily and Africa.

Antony Marries Octavia Minor

Antony, Octavian, and Lepidus meet in Brundisium and renew their ties of personal friendship and their political alliance, with the priority commitment to fight against Sextus Pompey. The accord is sealed by the marriage between Antony (who is now Fulvia's widower) and the 29-year-old Octavia Minor, the sister of Octavian, who has recently been widowed and is the mother of three children: Claudia Marcella Major, Claudia Marcella Minor, and Marcus Claudius Marcellus.

Octavia Minor is "a wonder of a woman … who, besides her great beauty, ha[s] intelligence and dignity."[10] Before 54, when she was 15 years old, she had married Caius Claudius Marcellus Minor, scion of the illustrious *Claudii* family and descendant of the Marcus Claudius Marcellus who fought against the Carthaginians during the Hannibalic War (Second Punic War, 218–201). In 51, Marcellus Minor became consul and adopted an antagonistic stance toward his brother-in-law Octavian. Octavian had demanded that Marcellus divorce Octavia Minor to allow the latter to marry Pompey Magnus, who had recently been widowed by Julia. This was not pursued, however, as Pompey had refused the marriage. Later, Caesar had

---

9   App. *B. Civ.*, V.62.
10 Plut. *Ant.*, 31.1–2.

been generous with him: after the victory at Pharsalus (48), he had spared his life and allowed him to continue living peacefully in Rome with Octavia Minor and their three children. Marcellus Minor died in 41, leaving Octavia pregnant with her fourth child.

To get married, Antony and Octavia must obtain a special dispensation from the College of Pontiffs since the prescribed 10 months of widowhood have not yet elapsed. It is forbidden by law for a Roman woman to remarry before the widow's mourning period has elapsed. This measure is designed to remove the risk of erroneous attributions of paternity.

Antony and Octavia honeymoon in Greece, where Octavia will give birth to the child she has been carrying, Antonia Major. The Athenians pay homage to the parents of the newborn as divine benefactors, the New Dionysus and the New Athena. Some eastern mints put coins into circulation bearing the portraits of Octavia and Antony, positioned side by side in profile.

Meanwhile, the restoration of the peace has allowed Tiberius Claudius Nero the Younger, his wife Livia Drusilla, and their three-year-old son Tiberius to return to Rome. This little family, after the events in Perusia, had needed to leave the capital to escape the purges. With the little Tiberius in her arms, Livia had followed her husband first to Praeneste, then to Campania, thence to Neapolis, and later to Achaea before finally reaching Sparta.

Octavian Marries Livia

Livia has hair that parts on her forehead, large eyes, a slightly pronounced aquiline nose, and a perfectly oval-shaped head. She is a girl with a refined simplicity and an understated, reserved, intelligent, courteous nature. She is well-loved by her relatives and friends. Beyond being fair or beautiful, she is charming and can arouse considerable passion. She was born from the marriage of Marcus Livius Drusus Claudianus and Afidia, at Fundi (Fondi), a town in Lower Lazio where the Drusi own vast amounts of property. Livia's father was born with the name Appius Claudius Pulcher, but after the death of his father (a praetor in 50 and a loyalist of the Liberators who committed suicide at Philippi), he was adopted by Marcus Livius Drusus. He thus became part of the *gens Livia* while he was still a boy. At 18 years old, Livia married her cousin Tiberius, who was 30 years older than her.

In 39, during an event at the circus in Rome, the eyes of the 24-year-old Octavian and the 20-year-old Livia meet for a moment. It is as if an electrical charge passes between them. Octavian falls in love with Livia at first sight, and this love is passionately returned. The tryst will not remain secret for long, partly because the two adulterers make no attempt to keep it hidden. During one banquet, Livia accompanies Octavian to a bedchamber, leaving the other diners and her poor husband astounded, only to come back a short time later with her ears glowing and her hair disheveled.[11] A scandal breaks out. Livia's husband, Tiberius Claudius Nero the Younger, disowns his wife, who is six months pregnant.

In turn, Octavian divorces Scribonia, who is also pregnant. This happens on the same day that she gives birth to their daughter Julia. On 14 October 39, Octavian and Livia marry, without waiting for the prohibition period following the divorce to expire (they have, in the meantime, obtained special dispensation from the *pontifices*).

It is true that Octavian and Livia love each other, but it is also true that their marriage is politically convenient both for her family, as it ensures its survival, and for Octavian himself, who, until this point, has not been pursuing political alliances with the most important families in Rome, including through matrimonial ties, in accordance with the strategy widely used among the patriciate. This explains why, on Octavian and Livia's wedding day, the latter's divorced husband, that is, Tiberius, leads his ex-wife up to the altar, just as a father would, to take the auspices.

Octavian and Livia's wedding is a simple ceremony. The wedding banquet is altogether different. This is held in Octavian's house, in a peristyle on the ground floor. During the festivities, Octavian and 11 other guests enter the scene disguised as gods and goddesses: Octavian has taken the guise of Apollo.

In the days following the banquet, Octavian is harshly criticized for how the wedding party unfolded, both by his political opponents and by some of his friends, including Mark Antony. He is reprimanded for having feasted in luxury at a time when the people of Rome were suffering from hunger (Sextus Pompey's naval blockade of the Italian coastline is still making it difficult for grain supplies reach Rome).

At the same time, the *pontifices* issue a second dispensation that allows Scribonia, Octavian's divorcée, to immediately remarry, this time to an old friend of Octavian: Caius Cilnius Maecenas.

Maecenas has always been part of Octavian's inner circle; he remained alongside him in the campaigns of Mutina, Philippi, and Perusia. A trusted adviser, one whom Octavian listens to, he is an astute diplomat and a capable administrator "of sleepless vigilance in critical emergencies, far-seeing and knowing how to act, but in his relaxation from business more luxurious and effeminate than a woman."[12] Due to Maecenas's influence, Octavian adopts more moderate political policies after his first alliance with Antony and Lepidus. Since the end of the civil war and Octavian's victory, Maecenas has retired to a private life and uses his immense wealth to surround himself with first-rate poets and writers whom he protects and finances, so much so that, in the future, he will become famous and respected for championing talented youths' literary and artistic exploits.[13] Among his *protegés* are the renowned

---

11   Suet. *Aug.*, 69.1.
12   Vell. Pat., II.88.
13   The modern Italian words *mecenate* and *mecenatismo* derive from Maecenas's inclination to protect and offer patronage to artists and scholars, motivated by reasons of prestige as well as taste.

Vergil, Horace, and Propertius, as well as other minor poets: Lucius Varius Rufus, Plotius Tucca, Caius Valgius Rufus, and Domitius Marsus. The purpose of this cenacle is twofold: to support the arts and to orchestrate political propaganda in favor of Augustus. The poet Publius Vergilius Maro (70–19) will write the *Georgics* for Maecenas and will introduce him to Quintus Horatius Flaccus (65–8), who, shortly after, will compose his *Odes*. Until now, Maecenas has kept himself out of the public eye, remaining in the shadows. His marriage to Scribonia suddenly puts him in the limelight.

The renovations to Octavian's house are still underway. The project involves the demolition of the six houses on the Palatine and their reconstruction according to a different plan, which also includes a temple. Three houses have already been gutted, and so Octavian and Livia take up residence on the first floors of the others.

On 14 January 38, in those rooms, Livia gives birth to Nero Claudius Drusus, the son of her previous husband. Drusus, like Tiberius the Younger, will not stay in his mother's house but will join his father, who lives close by. As an adult, he will be adopted by Augustus and will become known by the name Germanicus, in reference to the military victories that he will achieve in Germania. He will also be known to future generations as Drusus the Elder to distinguish him from the only natural son of Tiberius the Younger, Drusus the Younger, or Drusus Caesar.

CHAPTER XXXVII

New Theaters of War

The War Against Sextus Pompey

The promises made regarding Achaea and the payment of reparations for damages caused have not been kept, and so the war between Octavian and Lepidus on one side and Sextus Pompey on the other has resumed. Sextus uses the Aeolian Islands as a base of operations for his fleet, to regulate the movements of Octavian's ships in the Lower Tyrrhenian Sea, and to prevent Rome from receiving supplies from the East, via the Strait of Messina. Before long, Rome is suffering from starvation.

The situation improves when Octavian recovers control of Sardinia and Corsica, thanks to the betrayal of Menas (also known as Mena, or Menodorus), a freedman of Sextus Pompey and admiral of the Sardinian fleet. Menas defected from Sextus to join Octavian's ranks, to which he added 60 ships.

Octavian has already been defeated twice by Sextus when he places the fate of the war at sea into the capable hands of his loyal general Marcus Vipsanius Agrippa, freshly returned from Gaul, and is able to guarantee him military aid from Mark Antony thanks to the intervention of Maecenas. Then he renews the pact forming the Triumvirate with Antony and Lepidus (Treaty of Tarentum, 37). The trio reinforce their agreement to oppose Sextus Pompey, starting by denouncing the Pact of Misenum that made a provision, among other things, for Sextus to become consul and a high priest.

In 36—the last year of the war between Octavian and Lepidus on one side and Sextus Pompey on the other—Agrippa, sailing from Valentia in Brutium (Vibo Valentia in Calabria), occupies Stromboli—the most northerly of the Aeolian Islands—with an audacious *coup de main*. Later, he attacks the people of Lipara (Lipari), supporters of Pompey, and deports some of them to Puteolis. His ships are heading for Vulcano, another of the Aeolian Islands, when the Pompeians occupy Lipara again. Shortly after, Agrippa's ships clash with those of the Pompeian Demochares in the waters of Mylae (Capo di Milazzo, on the northeastern coast of Sicily). Demochares has 75 ships, 45 of which were sent to him as reinforcements by Pompey, who has set off to join him with another 60 ships. He loses 30 ships in the battle, while Agrippa only loses 5. Agrippa returns victoriously to Lipara but, very quickly, leaves again, heading for Sicily, because he has learned that Demochares has left the waters off Capo di Milazzo.

Later that year, Agrippa occupies Mylae and Tyndaris (Tindari, a city located on the northeastern coast of Sicily, slightly to the west of Mylae) and clashes with the 70 ships of Sextus Pompey near Naulochus, east of Mylae, recording another, stunning victory. The conflict is ended by the victory Agrippa wins near Miletus (Mileto), a city on the Tyrrhenian coast of Calabria. Soon after, Sicily falls into Octavian's hands.

Sextus flees to the East, but he is captured in Miletus (in Asia Minor) and is executed without a trial by Marcus Titius, the governor of the Roman province of Asia. This happens on the orders of Mark Antony, (or by Plancus, the governor of Syria, who was authorized to use Antony's name and his seal if absolutely necessary or in an emergency).[1] It is in contravention of Sextus's rights as a Roman citizen. He had only recently turned 30 years old (he was born in 67). A few days later, during the public games, the people of Antioch on the Orontes in Syria rise up against Titius for having put Sextus Pompey to death (within a few years, Octavian will accuse Antony of having had Sextus arbitrarily executed). All this happens in 35.

But this isn't the end of it. Lepidus, who is in Africa, reclaims Sicily for himself. Octavian refuses to accept this. Another war thus breaks out, this time between Lepidus on one side and Octavian and Antony on the other. But it doesn't last long. Lepidus is defeated, apprehended, and sentenced to exile in Circeii, a promontory on the Lazio coastline, south of Rome. His lands will be passed to Octavian, though he will remain *pontifex maximus* until his death in 13.

Meanwhile, Mark Antony is fighting victoriously in the East. Among other places, he captures Antiochia in Commagene, previously Samosata (Samsat in Turkey), the capital of the Kingdom of Commagene, which extends from the Taurus Mountains to the Euphrates. Antiochia in Commagene is located at a ford over the Euphrates on a route that leads from Damascus through Palmyra and Sura toward Armenia, going as far as the Black Sea.

The Disintegration of the Triumvirate

In 33, the second quinquennium for the Second Triumvirate ends. The pact is not renewed, and the kinship, friendship, and alliance between Octavian and Antony fall away. The reason for this is found in a private affair that becomes politically significant, and it can be summarized as follows.

Antony has fallen madly in love with Cleopatra VII, queen-pharaoh of Egypt, as she has with him. The two became lovers in 37 in Antioch on the Orontes, and they

---

1 App. *B. Civ.,* V.144.

have had three children: two boys—Alexander Helios and Ptolemy Philadelphus—and one daughter, Cleopatra Selene.

Antony, we recall, has already married Octavia Minor, Octavian's sister, with whom he has had two children (Octavia Major, born in 39, and Octavia Minor, born in 36). He divorces Octavia Minor so he can marry Cleopatra VII. Octavian interprets this move as an intolerable affront. This irrevocably undermines the relationship between the two. From this moment on, Antony will slander Octavian, insinuating that he had a love affair with Caesar and that this was why he had been adopted. It may well be that Octavian is bisexual; if so, this should not be surprising—many Romans are, to a greater or lesser extent. It is well-known, however, that Octavian has been with a lot of women and will sleep with many more; Antony himself has to acknowledge this. And talk about the pot calling the kettle black! Everyone knows that Antony, as a young man, prostituted himself for money and had been the lover of Caius Scribonius Curio. When Antony had been little more than an adolescent, Curio, the son of the rich patrician of the same name, fell for him, and Antony, already greedy for luxury and pleasure and already in a vast amount of debt, accepted his advances and even agreed to live with him, attracted above all by the possibility of silencing his own creditors.

The consuls for 32 are Cnaeus Domitius Ahenobarbus and Caius Sosius, both of whom are on Antony's side. Octavian, after getting his hands on the lands previously assigned to Lepidus and after Antony had given Cleopatra VII a lavish welcome in Tarsus in Cilicia, forces them to flee from Rome. Shortly after, Antony attacks Palmyra, a city-state in Syria.

The Attack on Palmyra

A dense oasis of palm and olive trees punctuates the monotony of the Syrian Desert, about 240 km east of Damascus. It is located in a basin not far from the Jabel Muntar, where the source of the Efqa, a spring of sulfurous water, is found. A settlement has existed around that source since time immemorial, known as Tadmur both to Assyrian traders from Kanesh (Kültepe in central Anatolia), who mention it in their archives, dated to the start of the II millennium, and to the writers of the Bible. In the past, the oasis of Tadmur has been occupied, successively, by Amorites, Canaanites, Arameans, and Nabateans. In the Hellenistic Age, the residential buildings contained within it, comprising clusters of dwelling houses corresponding to individual familial or tribal groups, were transformed into a city called Palmyra.

When, in 64, Rome created the province of Syria, Palmyra remained an independent enclave, albeit one linked to Rome; it was a free trade zone for the exchange of goods that traveled along the caravan routes that connect the Mediterranean to the Euphrates. Currently, Palmyra is a city-state, the capital of an Arab principality, similarly to Petra, Emesa, and Iturea. It controls a strip of land that is sparsely populated and infertile, if not entirely desolate. "It is a city famous for the beauty of its site, the riches of its soil, and the delicious quality and abundance of its water."[2] However, it is a city in the middle of the desert. "Its fields are surrounded by sands on every side, and are thus separated, as it were, by nature from the rest of the world."[3] The oasis is primarily inhabited by Arabs, but in the cultured environment of Palmyra, the dominant languages are Greek and Aramaic.

Antony attacks Palmyra under the pretext that its inhabitants are oscillating between the Romans and the Parthians (in a sense, this is true, because the Palmyrene merchants buy goods in the Parthian Empire that they then sell in the Roman province of Syria); in reality, he wants its riches. However, he doesn't manage to get his hands on them (they were transported to safety beyond the Euphrates before his arrival).[4]

The news that Antony has attacked Palmyra, a friend and ally of Rome, concerns the Senate of Rome, which takes the opportunity to denounce the fact that Antony is giving orders in the eastern provinces as though they were his own. It criticizes Antony for two reasons: because, by having himself accompanied by Cleopatra VII and Ptolemy Caesar[5] with all the pomp and trappings of the East, he is viewed as a Hellenistic ruler in pursuit of a political dynasty, in sharp contrast with Roman political tradition; and because it wants to avoid the political heart of the empire being moved to the East.

Indeed, this is the result that Antony is seeking. Evidence of this comes to light when Octavian illegally obtains the former triumvir's will (by having it taken from the House of the Vestals, where it had been deposited) and reads it out in the Senate. In the will it is written that, on the testator's death, the buffer states that are spread out along the borders of the Roman East will be inherited by Cleopatra's children.

The Senate declares Antony to be a public enemy, accuses Cleopatra VII of having appropriated the eastern provinces of the Roman state in league with Antony, and asks the people gathered in assembly for a declaration of war against Egypt, which is approved. It hands command of military operations, both on land and at sea, to Octavian, who, unlike Antony, who has shown 'orientalizing' tendencies, has always put himself forward as the defender of the ancient primacy of Rome and Italy.

---

2   Plin., V.21.
3   *Ibidem.*
4   App. *B. Civ.,* V.9.
5   Caesarion, the illegitimate son of Caesar, born from his love affair with Cleopatra VII.

CHAPTER XXXVIII

Octavian, the Final Winner

The Battle of Actium

In 31, Antony and Cleopatra concentrate their land and sea forces near Actium, with the intention of using it as a launchpad for an invasion of Italy. Actium is a small town on the western coast of Epirus, and thus in the Roman province of Macedonia. Specifically, it is situated at the tip of one of the two peninsulas facing one another, with a passage between them that allows ships to travel from the Ambracian Gulf to the Gulf of Arta.

Antony commands the fleet, while Publius Canidius Crassus leads the army. The fleet is made up of 500 ships and is stationed in the waters facing the entrance to the Gulf of Arta. There are 440 Roman ships, aboard which are 22,000 legionaries and 2,000 archers. The remaining 60 ships are Egyptian and have Cleopatra and the royal treasury on board. Of these ships, 230 are very large, with sails and three rows of oars, and are equipped with a bronze rostrum and weapon platforms, on which catapults and ballistae (a sort of large crossbow, capable of shooting bolts and stones and hitting a target with great precision) are positioned, but due to this, the ships suffer from poor maneuverability. Each has 286 rowers and can move at a maximum speed of 7.7 knots.

Canidius's army is formed of 12,000 horsemen and is camped on the side of the promontory of Actium that looks toward the open sea. It is an unhealthy area, and malaria is already starting to claim victims among his ranks.

Octavian's fleet, led by Agrippa, is preventing Antony's ships from breaking out into open waters. It is formed of 400 ships, aboard which are eight legions and five praetorian cohorts, a total of 40,000 soldiers, all war veterans. Like the enemy fleet, they also have archers and artillery. For the most part, these are *liburnae*—a type of light craft that lies low in the water and is very maneuverable—with skilled and well-trained crews. The larger ships each have 236 rowers and can reach a maximum speed of 9.5 knots. In sum, Agrippa's ships are smaller and fewer than those of Antony, but they are more maneuverable and quicker.

Three days of bad weather have prevented Antony's ships from trying to break the blockade. Now that the weather has improved, he girds himself for a confrontation. Consequently, he divides his fleet into three groups of 60 ships, burning the remaining 260, which comprise the smaller ships and the slower transports. He takes command of the right-hand group and hands command of the left-hand group to Caius Sosius. The center of his formation, it must be noted, is weaker than his flanks.

By 2 September 31, the defections have already started. Philadelphus of Paphlagonia, Rhoemetalces of Thrace, and even Domitius Ahenobarbus desert to join Octavian's ranks. Shortly afterward, they are followed by Amyntas, King of Galatia, with his 2,000 horsemen, the governor of Greece, and a diplomat, Quintus Dellius. The latter will reveal Antony's plan of attack to Agrippa.

The plan is this. Antony will attack the flanks of the enemy formation, drawing the forces deployed in the center toward the flanks and allowing Cleopatra to send her ship into the gap in the center, pass through it, and reach the open sea. If the tactic works, the enemy would have failed to achieve their goal, which is to seize the royal treasury, and will lose interest in continuing the fight. After the battle, the ships and the army will make their separate ways to a predetermined location, where they will reunite.

Therefore, even before Antony's fleet begins to move against the blockade and Canidius relocates further down the coast, Agrippa already knows everything about what the enemy will do. This will allow him to jeopardize his opponent's tactics.

The attempt to break the blockade is preceded by a series of events that come to be interpreted as ominous omens. On Cleopatra's command ship (called the *Antonius*), some swallows drive other swallows out of their nest under the stern and kill their nestlings. A statue of Antony near Alba (Albano Laziale, near Rome) oozes sweat and blood. The chariot of Jupiter in the Circus Maximus in Rome is destroyed. For many days torchlight rises in the sky over Greece before it shoots up, disappearing. Mount Etna erupts on Sicily, burying towns and villages beneath the lava.

At Antony's signal, the three groups advance toward the mouth of the gulf, while Octavian's fleet expands in front of them to bar the exit, forming two semicircular rows. The left wing of Octavian's fleet is commanded by Marcus Lurius, prefect of Sardinia, and the right wing, by Agrippa. In the center is Lucius Arruntius. Octavian is on board a *liburna* on the right wing.

The fleets move toward one another with great hesitation, and nothing happens before noon. Then Antony orders the attack. Sosius's group is first to push forward and closes in on the enemy as arrows, rocks, and ballista bolts hail down on them. Agrippa doesn't let their grappling hooks get attached to his ships and tries to lure the enemy ships toward the open sea, where he will have more room to maneuver and surround them with enveloping tactics. When the two fronts finally come into contact at each end of the combat zone, a furious melee begins. Some ships ram against others with a loud hollow sound. Whole rows of oars are sliced off with a crash. The hulls of the rammed ships explode into a thousand pieces under the impact of the rostra. Arrows (including incendiary arrows), ballista bolts, javelins, and stones rain down on the decks. Mortally wounded ships keel over onto one side and quickly capsize and sink, dragging men and materials down with them. Roaring flames flash amid the heavy black smoke that rises in columns above the burning ships. The fighting rages on the decks after ships are boarded amid shouts, cries, and spilled blood. Many sailors and soldiers die from smoke inhalation, some are burned alive, others are stabbed or trampled, while many more fall or throw themselves into the sea and either drown or are shot by enemies aiming down at them. The castaways desperately try to cling to all sorts of wreckage, swimming amid lifeless bodies, floating facedown in the water.

In the meantime, the wind has picked up. As it gets stronger, Cleopatra's 60 ships, which were positioned at the rear, begin to come forward and slip through the center of the enemy lines. It is an incredibly risky maneuver, but it succeeds. The group makes it safely through and, with the wind in their sails, quickly distance themselves from the carnage.

As envisaged in the battle plan, Antony follows in Cleopatra's wake. But then something unexpected occurs. The rest of the fleet should go after Antony, but only a few ships do so. The others either misunderstand what is happening (believing that Antony and Cleopatra are fleeing), perhaps because they don't know the detail of the plan (if so, why had they not been informed?) or cannot disengage themselves from the battle. As such, they remain where they are and continue to fight, in a state of general confusion and discouragement, without a commander-in-chief and without precise orders. They keep resisting until nightfall, when those that remain scatter. Many ships flee, while the others surrender.

Meanwhile, there has been another twist. Cleopatra's ships have not gone to the meeting point where they were supposed to meet the army but instead set their course for Egypt. As for Canidius's army, they observe the battle from the promontory. Seeing Antony and Cleopatra move into the distance, they realized they have been abandoned. The troops rebel against Canidius, who tried to escape by fleeing the camp at night, and pass over to Octavian's side *en masse*.

Antony and Cleopatra return to Alexandria safe and sound, together with their friends and supporters. Cleopatra had wanted to get back as quickly as possible because she feared that the news of their defeat would precede them and that the Alexandrians would rebel, overthrowing her and her son.

She has kept her ships and the royal treasury, but she has lost all her political support in the East. The client rulers of the Ptolemies have jumped onto the bandwagon of the victor, Octavian. She will retaliate by having Artavasdes of Armenia killed, together with all the courtiers whom she no longer trusts. At a military level, the real loser is Antony. He has lost not only most of his ships and his entire army, but also his reputation as a military commander. From now on, he will no longer be considered as the next great general of Rome after Caesar, but as a rebel on the run with a cowardly and irresponsible attitude in battle, having abandoned his soldiers in the thick of the fighting.

Octavian was unable to get his hands on Cleopatra's treasure, which he needed to pay his troops, so it must be expected that he will arrive in Egypt with his army at any moment. Egypt can't defend itself effectively against his legions, and so Cleopatra is preparing her escape, with the idea of founding a new kingdom with Antony somewhere else, possibly in Africa or in the East. But after being reassembled at their destination and launched back into the water, the ships are attacked and destroyed by Malichus, the king of the Nabataeans. Amid a tense and gloomy atmosphere, Cleopatra and Antony distract themselves however they can from the expectation of Octavian's arrival. Cleopatra begins the construction of a mausoleum for her and Antony and designates Caesarion as her successor, simultaneously organizing a means for him to escape to India in the event of danger.

In the spring of 30, Antony and Cleopatra approach Octavian through diplomatic channels. Cleopatra asks that her children Caesarion and Antyllus be allowed to inherit her throne. Antony gives Octavian the location of one of the last surviving Liberators: Publius Decimus Turullius, the commander of Brutus and Cassius's fleet. His hiding place is on Kos, an island in the Dodecanese. Octavian doesn't give a clear answer either to Cleopatra or to Antony. But Turullius is killed by Octavian's assassins, who were sent to hunt him down.

In the summer of 30, Octavian invades Egypt, simultaneously from east and west. He obtains the surrender of Pelusium, which is given to him without a fight by the governor Seleucus, and then besieges Alexandria. Lucius Pinarius, who commanded the four legions sent by Antony to Cyrenaica and Libya, switches sides and joins him, handing his entire army over to Cornelius Gallus. Shortly after, Gallus takes Paraetonium (Marsa Matruh), uselessly contested by Antony, who rushes to the place to try and regain control of the town.

Toward the end of the year, Octavian has the poet and writer Caius Cassius Parmensis, another of the Liberators, executed in Athens. His death marks the end of the Liberators, as none now remain alive. All met violent deaths. The following men all died prior to this: the *equites* Marcus Spurius, Quintus Ligarius, and Publius Sextius Naso; Caius Servilius Casca, the brother of Publius and the first man who stabbed Caesar; the former Pompeian Rubrius Ruga; and the senators Bucilianus and Caecilius.

Octavian's immense army advances on Alexandria. It is formed by the original nucleus of Octavian's forces, plus Canidius's army that defected after Actium, and by contingents of Octavian's friends and allies in the East, previously vassals of Antony and Cleopatra, one of whom is Herod of Judaea.

Octavian sets up his camp at Canopus (near Abu Qir in Egypt), 25 km from Alexandria. Canopus is a coastal town situated on the far western tributary of the

Nile Delta, the Canopic branch of the river. Before the foundation of Alexandria (331), it was the principal Greek port in Egypt.

It is already known that Alexandria will not be able to hold out for long. The defense of the city is entrusted to Canidius. On 31 July 30, Antony makes a sortie, launching himself with his cavalry at Octavian's entrenched encampment, but he is repelled and retreats into the city.

The Death of Antony and Cleopatra

Antony's attempt to find a way out of this impossible situation nearly succeeded, but Octavian has instead only tightened his stranglehold. On 1 August 30 Antony and Cleopatra's fleet, as well as their cavalry, surrender to the enemy *en masse* without a fight. At this point, everything falls apart. Word gets out that Cleopatra is dead. On hearing this, Antony loses heart and stabs himself with a dagger after a servant, whom he had ordered to kill him, had turned the weapon on himself instead, collapsing at his feet. But the news of Cleopatra's death is untrue. Perhaps it was she who started the rumor, predicting Antony would do what he then did, so as to have a free hand to negotiate with the victor, not so much with herself in mind as Caesarion and Egypt. When Antony, close to death, finds out, he has servants carry him to the mausoleum where Cleopatra VII has barricaded herself with her handmaids and breathes his last in her arms.

Cleopatra soon consoles herself and takes recourse to the same secret weapon that allowed her to win over Caesar and Antony. She tries to seduce Octavian, but she fails. Octavian treats her coldly and tells her that he will take her to Rome to adorn his triumph. Cleopatra realizes that it's all over, and she commits suicide.

> No one knows clearly in what way she perished, for the only marks on her body were slight pricks on the arm. Some say she applied to herself an asp which had been brought in to her in a water-jar, or perhaps hidden in some flowers.[1]

Octavian allows Antony and Cleopatra to be buried together, alongside each other. It is here and now that the legend begins of Cleopatra VII, the last queen-pharaoh of that name and the most famous; she will go down in history as "the most beautiful woman in antiquity" and as a symbol of feminine seduction.

A few days later, Caesarion is executed while he is returning to Alexandria, confident that no harm will come to him. Most likely this is on the orders of Octavian, as Caesarion is a potential rival because, despite being illegitimate, he is Caesar's only son.

The children of Antony and Cleopatra are invited to Rome to stay with Octavia, who will raise them as her own. Subsequently, both Alexander Helios and Ptolemy

---

1   Dio Cass., LI.14.1.

Philadelphus disappear in mysterious circumstances, as does the eldest of the children that Antony had with Fulvia.

As for Antony's other sons, born from his marriage to Fulvia: Antyllus, after his father's defeat, is executed on Octavian's orders, while Iullus will be looked after by his stepmother Octavia Minor, Octavian's sister and his father's widow.

Of his four children with Cleopatra, only Cleopatra Selene will survive: she will marry Juba II, King of Numidia and Getulia, who was raised in Rome, and will become the queen of the Roman provinces in Africa (Numidia and Mauretania). Her son Ptolemy—the last of the Ptolemies—will be killed on the orders of Caligula (r. 37–41 AD).

Having entered Alexandria as a conqueror, Octavian finally seizes the treasure of Cleopatra VII, loots the Royal Palace, confiscates the possessions of rich Alexandrians whom he suspects are still loyal to the Ptolemies, and imposes very heavy taxes on the city. Finally, he incorporates Egypt into the Roman state, but it will retain a special status insofar as it becomes his personal property.

Octavian remains in Egypt for a year, during which time he conducts himself before the people as the heir of the ancient pharaohs and as the guarantor of public order and collective prosperity; he thus becomes King of Egypt and starts to be venerated as a god in various temples dedicated to him, one of which is found as far away as Philae in Lower Nubia. When he leaves to go back to Rome, he entrusts the Country of the Nile to the care of a prefect of equestrian rank, who must report to him alone. He decides to hand this position of trust to the soldier-poet Cornelius Gallus, a friend of the poet Publius Vergilius Maro, the author of the epic *Aeneid*.

Octavian Celebrates a Triumph

In 29, Octavian, as the undisputed victor and as the absolute master of Caesar's entire legacy, presents himself to the Senate as the savior of the *res publica*. The Roman aristocracy is tired of wars, public disorder, arbitrary acts, and vendettas. He promises them a strong and authoritative government capable of restoring peace in the exhausted country. Then, in lavish style, he celebrates a triumph for each of the decisive victories he won in Illyricum, Asia, and Egypt.

The gold, silver, precious gems, and pearls that flow into Rome on the days of this triple triumph are added to the treasure of the Temple of Jupiter Capitolinus. The quantities arriving are so abundant that it results in reducing the value of silver in circulation by 5 percent, and the interest rates charged by money lenders by two-thirds. Meanwhile, numerous statues, the result of the looting carried out in Egypt, have arrived Rome, where they adorn its temples, forums, and villas.

As part of his triumphs, Octavian inaugurates the Temple of the Deified Julius, dedicated to Caesar, in the Republican Forum. A gilded bronze statue of Cleopatra

VII, part of the spoils of war, is added to the existing works of art in the Forum *Iulium* for the occasion.

It is worth noting that the Temple of the Deified Julius is the first temple in Rome to be dedicated to a deified mortal. On his cremation, Caesar—it is said—ascended to the heavens, taking his place among the gods.

The fact that Octavian is the adopted son of the deceased dictator permits him to proclaim himself *divi filius*, "son of the deified one"; therefore, this allows him not only to legitimize his ascent to power but also to place himself in a liminal space between the divine and earthly spheres, with the result that he can make a distinction between himself and common men.

Octavian Becomes the *Princeps*, the *Augustus*

On 16 January 27, Octavian—who was bestowed with *tribunicia potestas* and proconsular *imperium* for life at the age of 23—repeals the exceptional provisions assumed by the Triumvirs in the context of the fight against Caesar's assassins (that is, he voluntarily renounces the extraordinary powers he had been invested with to repair the Republic) and publicly announces that the Republic has finally been restored and that therefore the state can start functioning regularly again. With this announcement, the Senate, in recognition of what Octavian has done for the state, confers on him the *cognomen augustus*. Octavian's official name thus becomes *Imperator Caesar Divi Filius Augustus*. From now on and until the day he dies (19 August 14 AD), Octavian will be called Augustus, "he who is revered." No one, after 27, will be able to find a better word than Augustus to summarize what happened on the Roman political scene that year.

The *cognomen augustus*, however, would have been a vague and indistinct form of authority, designed to be connected to the religious sphere too (the word in fact has the same etymology as *augurium* and *inauguratio*), had it not been followed by the commendation of the *ius agendi cum patribus et cum populo* and a whole host of extraordinary honors and new powers.

The most extraordinary honor of all is the one that is linked to a newly coined role: that of *princeps universorum*, "leader of all", the man to whom complete custody of the *res publica* and its traditional functions, to which he ideally remains subordinate, have been entrusted. The *princeps* is the leader of the state and holds the position of guarantor of political stability, acting as a point of balance between the conservative leanings of the aristocracy and the reformist ones of the plebeians, the army, and certain provinces. He is able to govern because he has been granted *auctoritas omnibus praestiti, cum imperio* by the Senate, which is somewhat greater than *tribunicia potestas*, which is given to magistrates, insomuch as it gives the *princeps* the right to convene popular assemblies and the Senate; to make decisions on foreign affairs, including whether or not to wage war; and to appoint the most senior magistrates. His *imperium*, in particular, hands the *princeps* supreme command of all the armed forces (that is, control of military power) for 10 years, which can be extended.

Caius Julius Caesar Octavianus has thus become the *princeps*, the *augustus*, and from now on, he will be called Augustus. The story of the Roman Republic, which lasted for 500 years, has reached its epilogue. The *ancien régime* has been replaced by a new form of state called the Principate that will usher in the Imperial Era. After Octavian, all the highest holders of power in Rome—first the *principes* and then the emperors—will be defined as such with the title of Augustus.

At the same session in which the Senate confers the title *princeps* on him, Octavian accepts his reelection to the consulship, serving alongside his most faithful ally Marcus Vipsanius Agrippa, who is holding his second successive consulship himself. Furthermore, following the precedent set by Cnaeus Pompey Magnus in 52, Octavian accepts the attribution of an extraordinary command for a period of 10 years over provinces *non pacificatae*, among which are Gallia Transpadana, the Iberian provinces, and Syria.

It is important to underline that the conferral of this extraordinary command grants Octavian Augustus, as consul, control of almost the entirety of the army because almost all the Roman provinces outside of the Italian peninsula are *non pacificatae*, and practically the entire Roman army is stationed in these provinces. At the same session, the Senate decrees that the door jambs of the entrance to the house of Augustus be decorated with laurel wreaths—symbols of glory and triumph.

Further Reading

Provided here is a selection of publications, limited to the major actors, supporting cast, and extras whose events are discussed in the book, and to other characters mentioned in the text.

Aulus Gabinius
Santangelo, F. *Roma repubblicana. Una storia in quaranta vite.* Roma: Carocci, 2019, pp. 239–246.

Caecilii Metelli
Simmons, D. W. "From Obscurity to Fame and Back Again: The Caecilii Metelli in the Roman Republic." MA thesis, Brigham Young University, 2011.

Callimachus
Cavalli, M. & G. Guidorizzi, eds. *Poeti ellenistici. Callimaco, Teocrito, Meleagro.* Milan: Mondadori, 2008.

Cato the Younger, or Cato of Utica
Bellemore, J. "Cato the Younger in the East in 66 BC." *Historia* 44, no. 3 (1995): 376–379.

Fulvia
Virlouvet, C. "Fulvia, la pasionaria." In *Roma al femminile*, edited by A. Fraschetti, 71–94. Roma-Bari: Laterza, 1994.

Caius Julius Caesar
Goldsworthy, A. K. *Caesar: Life of a Colossus.* New Haven, CT: Yale University Press, 2012.

Caius Marius
Barca, N., *Gaio Mario. Alle origini della crisi di Roma.* Rome: L'Erma di Bretshneider, 2017.

Caius Valerius Catullus
Bellandi, F. "Catullo e la politica romana." In *Letteratura e "civitas." Transizioni dalla Repubblica all'Impero*, edited by M. Citroni, 47–71. Pisa: ETS, 2012.

Cnaeus Pompeius Magnus
Fezzi, L. *Pompeo.* Roma: Salerno Editore, 2019.

Cnaeus Pompeius Strabo
Sanchez Jiménez, F. "Triumpho 'de Asculaneis Picentibus'." *Baetica* IX (1986): 255–268.

The Gracchi
Barca, N., *I Gracchi. Quando la politica finisce in tragedia*. Rome: L'Erma di Bretshneider, 2019.

Lucius Appuleius Saturninus
Cavaggioni, F. *L. Apuleio Saturnino. Tribunus plebis seditiosus*. Venezia: Istituto Veneto di Scienze Lettere ed Arti, 1998.

Lucius Calpurnius Piso Caesoninus
Cristofoli, R. "Epicuro e politico: Lucio Calpurnio Pisone Cesonino." *HSCPh* XCIV (2012): 227–250.

Lucius Cornelius Sulla
L'Età di Silla, Istituto Italiano di Storia Antica. Rome: L'Erma di Bretschneider, 2018, pp. 45–72.

Lucius Licinius Lucullus
Sherwin-White, A. N. "Lucullus, Pompey and the East. In *The Cambridge Ancient History IX: Last Age of the Roman Republic, 146–43 B.C.*, edited by J. A. Crook, A. Lintott, & E. Rawson, 229–265. Cambridge: Cambridge University Press, 1994.

Lucius Sergius Catilina
Fini, M. *Catilina, ritratto di un uomo in rivolta*. Milan: Mondadori, 1996.

Marcus Caelius Rufus
Cordier, P. "M. Caelius Rufus, le préteur recalcitrant." *Mélanges de l'Ecole Française de Rome. Antiquitè* 106 (1994): 533–577.

Marcus Licinius Crassus
Antonelli, G. *Crasso. Il banchiere di Roma*. Milan: Newton, 2000.

Marcus Porcius Cato, The Censor
Astin, A. E. *Cato the Censor*. Oxford Scholarly Classics. Oxford: Oxford University Press, 1978.

Marcus Tullius Cicero
Narducci, E. *Cicerone. La parola e la politica*. Roma-Bari: Laterza, 2010.

Meleager Of Gadara
Guidorizzi, G., ed. *Meleagro, Epigrammi*. Milan: Mondadori, 1992.

Mithridates VI Eupator
Mayor, A. *Il re Veleno. Vita e leggenda di Mitridate, acerrimo nemico dei Romani*. Milan: Einaudi, 2010.

Publius Cornelius Sulla
Syme R., "P. Sulla (cos. cand. 66 BC)," in Santangelo F. *Approaching the Roman Revolution: Papers on Republican History*. Oxford: Oxford University Press, 2016.

Publius Servilius Vatia
Adak, M. "Lokalisierung von Olympos und Korykos in Ost-Lykien." *Gephyra* 1 (2004): 27–51.

Publius Sittius
Santangelo, F. *Roma repubblicana. Una storia in quaranta vite*. Rome: Carocci, 2019, pp. 297–302.

Quintus Hortensius Hortalus
Santangelo, F. *Roma repubblicana. Una storia in quaranta vite*. Rome: Carocci, 2019, pp. 221–229.

Servilia Caepio
Treggiari, S. *Servilia and Her Family*. Oxford: Oxford University Press, 2019.

Terentia (Wife of Cicero)
Buonopane, A. "Terenzia, una matrona in domo ed in re publica agens." In *Matronae in domo et re in publica agentes. Spazi e occasioni dell'azione femminile nel mondo romano tra tarda repubblica e primo impero*, edited by F. Cenerini and F. Rohr Vio, 51–64. Trieste: EUT, 2016.

Marcus Terentius Varro Lucullus
Della Corte, F. *Varrone, il terzo gran lume romano*. Firenze: La Nuova Italia, 1970.

Tigranes II
Manandian, H. *Tigranes II & Rome: A New Interpretation Based on Primary Sources*. Costa Mesa, CA: Mazda Publishers, 2007.

Titus Pomponius Atticus
Barca, N. *Roma dopo Silla*. Gorizia: LEG, 2021, pp. 553–582.

Index

Burebista, 50, 63
Bursa, Plancus, 186
Buthrotum, 109–10
Byzantium, 18

Caelius Rufus, Marcus, 54–55, 128–31, 185–86, 201, 221–22
  and Caesar, 194, 206
Caepio Brutus, Quintus Servilius, 30, 72–73, 123, 301, 303–4
Caepio, Servilia, 3, 21, 30, 31
Caesar, Julius, 2–7, 11–16, 25, 273–75
  and Africa, 248–50, 251–57
  and Ahenobarbus, 119–20
  and Alexandria, 237–41
  and Ariovistus, 92–96
  and Belgica, 96–98, 171–76
  and Britannia, 147–48, 153–54, 155–58, 163–67
  and Caelius Rufus, 54–55
  and Catullus, 33
  and Cicero, 43, 57–58, 139–40
  and civil war, 215, 216–24
  and Clodius, 18–19, 47, 60–61, 63, 67, 102–3
  and conspiracy, 276–79, 286–88
  and consulship, 193–94
  and Crassus, 29–30
  and Dacians, 50–51
  and death, 290–96
  and the Forum, 196–97
  and Gallic War, 84, 86, 87–92, 118
  and Julian Laws, 37–39, 69
  and lex Vatinia, 34–36
  and Memmius, 106
  and Octavian, 270–71, 297–98
  and omens, 289–90
  and opponents, 19–24
  and Optimates, 189
  and Pharsalus, 227–34
  and Piso, 52
  and Pompey, 27
  and proprietorship, 9–10
  and quaestorship, 8–9
  and the Rhine, 160
  and Rubicon, 207–11
  and second consulship, 224–26
  and the Senate, 201–4, 205–6
  and Spain, 259, 260–61, 263–65
  and supplicato, 115
  and triumphs, 267–69
  and Triumvirate, 31, 120–21
  and troops, 195–96
  and Veneti, 142, 143, 144, 145
  and Vercingetorix, 176–80
  and women, 283–86
  and Zela, 242–43
Caesar, Lucius Julius, 14, 15, 37, 215
Caesar the Elder, Caius Julius, 1, 2

Calenus, Quintus Fufius, 14
Callimachus, 33, 34
Calpurnia, 52
Camillus, Marcus Furius, 2
Canidius Crassus, Publius, 333, 334, 335
Cappadocia, 242–43
Capua, 211–14
Carus, Titus Lucretius: De rerum natura, 105–6
Casca, Caius Servilius, 291
Cassius Longinus, Caius, 199, 200, 205–6, 304, 317–20
  and conspiracy, 277, 278–79, 288, 292
Cassivellaunus, 163, 166
Catilina, Lucius Sergius, 12–13
Catilinarian Conspiracy, 12–13, 16, 21–22, 43, 54–55, 71–72
Cato, Caius Porcius, 126–27, 189–90, 197, 205, 222, 245
  and elections, 131–32, 134–35
  and Gabinius, 168, 169, 170
Cato, Marcus Porcius, 4, 13, 19–22, 29, 35
  and Caesar, 50–51
  and Cicero, 43
  and Cyprus, 63–64, 65, 66, 72, 122–24
  and death, 255
Catonian faction, 19, 25, 26, 28
Catullus, Caius Valerius, 32–34, 104–5, 131, 167
Catulus Capitolinus, Quintus Lutatius, 29
Catulus Censorinus, Quintus Lutatius, 32, 36
Catuvolcus, 172, 175
censors, 59
Cicero, Marcus Tullius, 13, 41–45, 132–33, 280–81
  and Afranius, 29
  and Ahenobarbus, 119–20
  and Antony, 312
  and Atticus, 49
  Brutus, 105
  and Buthrotum, 109–10
  and Caelius Rufus, 54, 128, 129–30
  and Caesar, 4, 5, 57–58
  and Catullus, 33
  and civil war, 220
  and Clodia, 22–23
  and Clodius, 18, 19, 48, 66–69, 72, 118, 123
  and conspiracy, 300–3
  and death, 313–16
  De oratore, 161–62
  De re publica, 137
  and exile, 73–77
  and Flaccus, 53–54
  and the Forum, 197
  and friends' help, 99–102, 103–4
  and Gabinius, 136–37, 168
  and gang violence, 108
  and Metellus Celer, 32
  and Milo, 191
  and Octavian, 309, 310